229
A CONFESSION
THE GOSPEL IN BRIEF
and WHAT I BELIEVE

Oxford University Press, Ely House, London W. 1

GLASGOW NEW YORK TORONTO MELBOURNE WELLINGTON
CAPE TOWN SALISBURY IBADAN NAIROBI DAR ES SALAAM LUSAKA ADDIS ABABA
BOMBAY CALCUTTA MADRAS KARACHI LAHORE DACCA
KUALA LUMPUR SINGAPORE HONG KONG TOKYO

A CONFESSION
THE GOSPEL IN BRIEF
and WHAT I BELIEVE

By LEO TOLSTÓY

Translated
with an Introduction by
AYLMER MAUDE

LONDON
OXFORD UNIVERSITY PRESS

LEO TOLSTOY

Born, Yásnaya Polyána, Tula
28 August (old style) = 9 September, n. s. 1828

Died, Astapovo, Riazan
7 November (old style) = 20 November, n. s. 1910

A Confession was first circulated in Russia in 1882; What
I Believe *in* 1884. *They were first printed in Geneva in*
1888. The Gospel in Brief *was first published in* 1883.
In The World's Classics *Mr. Aylmer Maude's translation
was first published in* 1921, *and reprinted in* 1927 *and* 1932.
A new edition incorporating The Gospel in Brief *was first
published in* 1940 *and reprinted in* 1951, 1954, 1958,
1961, 1967, *and* 1971.

SBN 19 250229 8

PRINTED IN GREAT BRITAIN

CONTENTS

CONTENTS

INTRODUCTION

THIS volume contains three of Tolstóy's most re-markable works. Between the completion of *Anna Karénina*, early in 1877, and the resumption of his literary activity in the year 1885, with his popular Tales, Tolstóy devoted himself to religious reflec-tion and to a close study of the Gospels and of dog-matic theology, although the latter subject repelled him. Apart from the full retranslation of the Gos-pels with voluminous notes, the works contained in this volume are almost the only literary produc-tions of his that appeared between his forty-ninth and fifty-seventh year, that is to say during eight of the years when his powers were at their zenith.

An attempt was made in Russia to suppress these books, but they circulated clandestinely in large numbers, in hectographed copies and also in volumes printed abroad and smuggled into the country. No adequate reply to Tolstóy's terrific onslaughts upon Church and State was produced, and within a single generation, in Russia, the insti-tutions he attacked had crumbled to dust.

These books have been translated into all civi-lized languages and have circulated far and wide. Nowhere have the views they contain been ade-quately met. On the contrary they have now be-come part of the air we breathe, and denunciations of Church and State, Parliamentary Government, Capital, and the institution of property, as well as of law and order in general, have become common-places of democratic rhetoric, and those institutions are now in some circles regarded as offences against the people which must be swept away as a prelude to putting down the mighty from their seats, ex-alting the humble and meek, filling the hungry

with good things and sending the rich empty
away.

This is serious. Our country has not yet followed
in the footsteps of Russia; but here too an axe is
laid to the root of the tree. What is said in these
works cannot be suppressed. It is closely interwoven with some of the profoundest truths humanity has known; but it will deal a death-blow
to civilization unless it can be answered. Lowell
well exclaimed:—

> 'Oh Lord, ef folks wuz made so's't they could see
> The begnet pint there is in an idee!
> Ten times the danger in 'em th' is in steel;
> They run your soul thru an' you never feel,
> But crawl about an' seem to think you're livin',
> Poor shells o' men, nut wuth the Lord's forgivin',
> Till you come bunt ag'in a real live fect,
> An' go to pieces when you'd ough' to ect!'

If the attack here made with power, conviction,
and effect on the moral basis of our lives cannot be,
and is not, convincingly met, it will continue to
eat into the piles on which our house stands, and
the whole order of our lives will crumble into dust.

A Confession is the most important of Tolstóy's
autobiographical writings, and will bear comparison with the most famous confessions ever penned;
but it soon merges into a consideration not of his
own life alone, but of the life of us all, to whom a
brief existence ending in inevitable death has been
given here on earth.

The conclusion he reaches in A Confession and in
What I Believe is, that personal life lived for one's
own ends must be a misfortune to any one intelligent enough to realize the facts; and that the only
escape is to merge one's life with that of 'the son
of man': that light of reason manifest in all humanity, which will endure when our personal
career is ended, and which comes to us from a

source outside ourselves. Life, he says, is a blessing for him who identifies himself with the son of man in the task of establishing the kingdom of God on earth, here and now. Life is a misfortune for him who seeks his personal welfare, which is an effort death inevitably baffles.

Tolstóy's interpretation of Christ's five commandments differs very considerably from that given by the Church, but he introduces an intelligible and practical meaning which most of us had never suspected till we read his books. Together with much that is profoundly true and immensely important, Tolstóy announces and elaborates a theory of non-resistance, and expounds a doctrine of Christian anarchy which, plausibly as he states it, appears to be as gross a superstition as any of those he attacks.

If his theory be right (and he claims for it Christ's authority), nothing can, and nothing should, save our industrial, political, or national existence from destruction. If, however, Christ meant this, it is curious that he did not say more than a few words of doubtful interpretation on a matter to which Tolstóy found it necessary during the last thirty years of his life to devote many volumes. Furthermore, Christ said, 'Render unto Cæsar the things that are Cæsar's,' bidding us apparently give some recognition to government to which, Tolstóy says, we should give none. Even if Christ meant what Tolstóy says he meant, if this conflicts, as it does, with our reason, conscience, and experience of life, it is still our duty to reject it. For, as Tolstóy has said, we select Christ's teaching and prefer it to other teachings, and call it divine, because it appears to us reasonable and true. If, on the contrary, after being interpreted by Tolstóy, it turns out to be plainly false, we must reject Christ's authority rather than substitute falsehood for truth.

We here face a stupendous problem, which only those who read this book carefully are likely to realize fully.

In the second volume of my *Life of Tolstoy* I suggested that Tolstóy's interpretation of the rule of non-resistance to 'him that is evil' was faulty, and went to the length of proposing an alternative interpretation; but on one point I think Tolstóy's meaning is seldom grasped.

Strange as it seems to us English people, and slow as I myself was to grasp it, I know not only from his works but also from correspondence and conversation with him, that he interpreted the injunction to turn the other cheek to the smiter, 'and if any man would go to law with thee and take away thy coat, let him have thy cloak also', to mean that no *physical* force should be used either directly or indirectly to resist him that is evil.

Many objections may be urged against that interpretation, but at any rate Tolstóy is not open to the reproach of being illogical when he approves of resistance even in an acute form, so long as this resistance does not involve the use of *physical* force. I am aware of the intricacy of the problem, and all I want to urge here is that unless and until one grasps Tolstóy's position—that it is the use of *physical force* to restrain men against their will that is immoral—one cannot see how logical (whether sound or not) his argument is.

Another point to realize is that Tolstóy, particularly at that period of his life, looked at things very much through the eyes of the Túla peasantry. Túla was a poor agricultural district where life was primitive and hard and Government demands for taxation and army service were a burden almost too heavy to be borne. The outlook of a God-fearing Túla peasant was perhaps nearer to that of the Galilean disciples and the Evangelists than our twentieth-century English outlook is. Be that as it may, *On Life, and Essays on Religion* will show him ceasing to concern himself with the precise words of the Gospels and taking a much wider outlook on religion; but it is remarkable that even after he had ceased to attach special importance to Gospel texts he held tenaciously to the rule of Non-Resistance as being of cardinal importance, and did this not merely as a dialectical weapon against conscription, Siberian exile, capital punishment, and other evils inflicted by Government, but as an integral portion of the guidance for life that he had found while studying Christ's words.

In the years between the completion of *Anna Karénina* in 1877 and his active return to fiction and drama with the publication of *The Death of Iván Ilých* and *The Power of Darkness* in 1886, Tolstóy wrote three other large works on religion besides the two given in this edition. There is a very detailed *Harmony and Translation of the Four Gospels* in two volumes, difficult to present satisfactorily to English readers because much of it is directed against faulty renderings in the Church-Slavonic text. And there is a *Criticism of Dogmatic Theology*, which would have little appeal for English readers, since those who hold to the dogmas of the Church creeds might think it wrong to consider his arguments, while the many who are already indifferent to the creeds would think any serious discussion of them a waste of time.

To indicate Tolstóy's point of view and the difficulty of securing fair consideration for it, let me tell of an incident that occurred not long ago. Lecturing on Tolstóy, I spoke of the fact that, in the course of his search for a religion he carefully examined the Church creeds and arrived at the conclusion that the whole body of dogmatic theology was meaningless and would not bear reasonable examination. As an example I mentioned his conviction that it is harmful to a child's brain to give him a religious lesson in which he is told that someone went to the top of a hill and rose into the sky where he sat down at the right hand of his father; and then to give that boy an astronomy lesson in which he is told that the world is round and surrounded by infinite space—so that if anyone rose into the sky there would be no possibility of sitting down at anyone's right hand, and that if he stopped rising he would come back with a bump.

A dear and respected relation of my own, who is strongly attached to the Church, was in the audience, and when next I met her expressed regret that Tolstóy was so ignorant as not to know what any educated theologian could, she said, have told him, namely, that Christ did not rise in a natural body but in a 'resurrection body'.

At the moment I could only reply that that was not what Tolstóy had heard the parish priest tell the peasant children at Yásnaya, nor had I been taught it at Christ's Hospital. On reflection it now occurs to me that by making the noun 'resurrection' into an adjective and speaking of a 'resurrection body' the theologians explain nothing, nor does their restatement of the dogma supply any moral lesson. They merely evade the necessity of admitting that the dogma is meaningless, and they do this by adding further obscurity to what was already unintelligible.

Many people—notably Voltaire—have scoffed at dogmatic theology when they have attacked religion. The peculiarity of Tolstóy's case is that his rejection of the dogmas formed part of an ardent search for religious guidance, which he thought he found by disencumbering the sayings of Christ from Church dogmas which Christ evidently never taught or could have uttered.

Tolstóy's attitude, expressed in *What I Believe*, towards an after-life had altered by the time he wrote *On Life*, and in a letter to his wife dated May 6th, 1898, he wrote:

'On my way back in the evening twilight I rode through Turgénev's wood, Spásskoe: fresh grass underfoot, stars in the sky, the scent of blossoming willows and dead birch-leaves, the nightingale's notes, the sounds of cockchafers and cuckoos—cuckoos and solitude—and the brisk pleasant movement of the horse under me, and physical and spiritual health. And I thought, as I constantly do, about death. And it was so clear to me that on the other side of death it will be as good, though in a different way, and I understood why the Jews represented paradise as a garden. The enjoyment of nature is the purest form of enjoyment. It was clear to me that there it will be just as good—even better. I tried to evoke in myself doubts of that life such as I formerly felt—but I could not, just as formerly I could not feel assurance.'

In other volumes of this edition I have been careful to give the dates of first publication of each item. Here I can only give approximate dates, for Tolstóy's religious works were for the most part forbidden by the censor and first circulated clandestinely in hectographed copies, being printed some ten years later at a Russian revolutionary press in Geneva—where, curiously enough, censorship of a different kind was exercised to exclude doctrines unsympathetic to the revolutionaries. Only towards the end of the last century was the Russian text of these works printed in England, under the supervision of Tolstóy's friend V. G. Chertkóv, and not till after the 1905 revolution in Russia was the censorship sufficiently relaxed to allow of their being printed in that country.

A Confession, the first of this series of religious works, has great autobiographical as well as literary value. It is hortatory in the best sense of the word, and aims at conveying to others the experiences Tolstóy had lived through. While doing this he had no thought of sparing himself, but like Bunyan overstated his own misconduct in early life. It is also noteworthy that just when the critics were crying out that he had 'abandoned art', he was in fact, in *A Confession*, using his great artistic ability to impart his feelings and convictions to his readers. He was too great an artist to believe that it is only in the form of a novel, a poem, or a story, that a reader's feelings can be reached.

Saint Augustine's name has often been mentioned in conjunction with Tolstóy's and there are no doubt some striking resemblances between them, but an exceedingly wide gulf divides the man who believed the theological scheme of redemption to be of such vital importance that unbaptized infants would perish and who furnished the arguments on which later defenders of the persecution of heretics relied, from the author of *A Criticism of Dogmatic Theology*, who regarded that whole theory as an absurdity and detested any idea of religious persecution.

I will end this Introduction with a few more sayings uttered by Tolstóy at various periods.

Senator Andrew D. White, who was I think American Ambassador at Berlin at the time, called on Tolstóy and mentioned the Mormons, whereon Tolstóy remarked that no doubt two-thirds of their religion is deception, but that on the whole he preferred 'a religion which professed to have dug its law out of the earth engraved on plates of gold, to one which claimed that its law was let down to it from heaven on the top of a mountain engraved on tables of stone'.

When out for a walk with him one day at Yásnaya Polyána, the name of God being mentioned he turned to me and said: 'There are two Gods', and went on to explain himself: 'There is the God that people generally believe in—a God *who has to serve them* (sometimes in very refined ways, say, by merely giving them peace of mind). This God does not exist. But the God whom people forget—the God *whom we all have to serve*—exists and is the prime cause of our existence and of all that we perceive.'

He once wrote: 'God is that whole of which we acknowledge ourselves to be a part: to a materialist —matter; to an individualist—a magnified, non-natural man: to an idealist—his ideal, Love.'

When Tolstóy was very ill in the Crimea in 1901, a few months after his Excommunication, news that he was not expected to live reached the Holy Synod, which was exceedingly anxious that at least a formal submission to the Church should be secured from him before he died. Instructions were given that a priest should try to secure an interview with Tolstóy and should announce his repentance. Tolstóy, on being told by his son of the priest's repeated applications for an interview, said: 'How is it, Sergéy, that these gentlemen do not understand that even in the face of death, two and two still make four?'

Strenuously as Tolstóy expressed himself, and convinced as he generally was of the soundness of his conclusions, he never claimed to erect 'an invulnerable fortress of truth, planned and constructed once and for ever'. On the contrary, in his reply to the Synod that excommunicated him he wrote:

'I do not believe my faith to be the one indubitable truth for all time, but I see no other that is plainer, clearer, or answers better to all the demands of my reason and my heart; should I find such a one, I shall at once accept it.'

This volume and *On Life* contain the record of a very remarkable variety of religious experiences, which have never before, I think, been brought together in due sequence in any two volumes.

AYLMER MAUDE.

I WAS baptized and brought up in the Orthodox Christian faith. I was taught it in childhood and throughout my boyhood and youth. But when I abandoned the second course of the university at the age of eighteen I no longer believed any of the things I had been taught.

Judging by certain memories, I never seriously believed them, but had merely relied on what I was taught and on what was professed by the grown-up people around me, and that reliance was very unstable.

I remember that before I was eleven a grammar school pupil, Vladímir Milyútin (long since dead), visited us one Sunday and announced as the latest novelty a discovery made at his school. This discovery was that there is no God and that all we are taught about Him is a mere invention (this was in 1838). I remember how interested my elder brothers were in this information. They called me to their council and we all, I remember, became very animated, and accepted it as something very interesting and quite possible.

I remember also that when my elder brother, Dmítri, who was then at the university, suddenly, in the passionate way natural to him, devoted himself to religion and began to attend all the Church services, to fast and to lead a pure and moral life, we all—even our elders—unceasingly held him up to ridicule and for some unknown reason called him 'Noah'. I remember that Músin-Púshkin, the then Curator of Kazán University, when inviting us to a dance at his house, ironically persuaded my brother (who was declining the invitation) by the argument that even David danced before the Ark.

I sympathized with these jokes made by my elders, and drew from them the conclusion that though it is necessary to learn the catechism and go to church, one must not take such things too seriously. I remember also that I read Voltaire when I was very young, and that his raillery, far from shocking me, amused me very much.

My lapse from faith occurred as is usual among people on our level of education. In most cases, I think, it happens thus: a man lives like everybody else, on the basis of principles not merely having nothing in common with religious doctrine, but generally opposed to it; religious doctrine does not play a part in life, in intercourse with others it is never encountered, and in a man's own life he never has to reckon with it. Religious doctrine is professed far away from life and independently of it. If it is encountered, it is only as an external phenomenon disconnected from life.

Then as now, it was and is quite impossible to judge by a man's life and conduct whether he is a believer or not. If there be a difference between a man who publicly professes Orthodoxy and one who denies it, the difference is not in favour of the former. Then as now, the public profession and confession of Orthodoxy was chiefly met with among people who were dull and cruel and who considered themselves very important. Ability, honesty, reliability, good-nature and moral conduct, were more often met with among unbelievers.

The schools teach the catechism and send the pupils to church, and government officials must produce certificates of having received communion. But a man of our circle who has finished his education and is not in the government service may even now (and formerly it was still easier for him to do so) live for ten or twenty years without once remembering that he is living among Christians and is himself reckoned a member of the Orthodox Christian Church.

So that, now as formerly, religious doctrine, accepted on trust and supported by external pressure, thaws away gradually under the influence of knowledge and experience of life which conflict with it, and a man very often lives on, imagining that he still holds intact the religious doctrine imparted to him in childhood whereas in fact not a trace of it remains.

S., a clever and truthful man, once told me the story of how he ceased to believe. On a hunting expedition, when he was already twenty-six, he once, at the place where they put up for the night, knelt down in the evening to pray—a habit retained from childhood. His elder brother, who was at the hunt with him, was lying on some hay and watching him. When S. had finished and was settling down for the night, his brother said to him: 'So you still do that?'

They said nothing more to one another. But from that day S. ceased to say his prayers or go to church. And now he has not prayed, received communion, or gone to church, for thirty years. And this not because he knows his brother's convictions and has joined him in them, nor because he has decided anything in his own soul, but simply because the word spoken by his brother was like the push of a finger on a wall that was ready to fall by its own weight. The word only showed that where he thought there was faith, in reality there had long been an empty space, and that therefore the utterance of words and the making of signs of the cross and genuflections while praying were quite senseless actions. Becoming conscious of their senselessness he could not continue them.

So it has been and is, I think, with the great majority of people. I am speaking of people of our educational level who are sincere with themselves, and not of those who make the profession of faith a means of attaining worldly aims. (Such people are the most fundamental infidels, for if faith is for them a means of attaining any worldly aims, then certainly it is not faith.) These people of our education are so placed that the light of knowledge and life has caused an artificial erection to melt away, and they have either already noticed this and swept its place clear, or they have not yet noticed it.

The religious doctrine taught me from childhood disappeared in me as in others, but with this difference, that as from the age of fifteen I began to read philosophical works, my rejection of the doctrine became a conscious one at a very early age. From the time I was sixteen I ceased to say my prayers and ceased to go to church or to fast of my own volition. I did not believe what had been taught me in childhood but I believed in something. What it was I believed in I could not at all have said. I believed in a God, or rather I did not deny God—but I could not have said what sort of God. Neither did I deny Christ and his teaching, but what his teaching consisted in I again could not have said.

Looking back on that time, I now see clearly that my faith—my only real faith—that which apart from my animal instincts gave impulse to my life—was a belief in perfecting myself. But in what this perfecting consisted and what its object was, I could not have said. I tried to perfect myself mentally—I studied everything I could, anything life threw in my way; I tried to perfect my will, I drew up rules I tried to follow; I perfected myself physically, cultivating my strength and agility by all sorts of exercises, and accustoming myself to endurance and patience by all kinds of privations. And all this I considered to be the pursuit of perfection. The beginning of it all was of course moral perfection, but that was soon replaced by perfection in general: by the desire to be better not in my own eyes or those of God but in the eyes of other people. And very soon this effort again changed into a desire to be stronger than others: to be more famous, more important and richer than others.

II

Some day I will narrate the touching and instructive history of my life during those ten years of my youth. I think very many people have had a like experience. With all my soul I wished to be good, but I was young, passionate and alone, completely alone when I sought goodness. Every time I tried to express my most sincere desire, which was to be morally good, I met with contempt and ridicule, but as soon as I yielded to low passions I was praised and encouraged.

Ambition, love of power, covetousness, lasciviousness, pride, anger, and revenge—were all respected.

Yielding to those passions I became like the grown-up folk and felt that they approved of me. The kind aunt with whom I lived, herself the purest of beings, always told me that there was nothing she so desired for me as that I should have relations with a married woman: '*Rien ne forme un jeune homme, comme une liaison avec une femme comme il faut.*'[1] Another happiness she desired for me was that I should become an aide-de-camp, and if

---

[1] Nothing so forms a young man as an intimacy with a woman of good breeding.

possible aide-de-camp to the Emperor. But the greatest happiness of all would be that I should marry a very rich girl and so become possessed of as many serfs as possible.

I cannot think of those years without horror, loathing and heartache. I killed men in war and challenged men to duels in order to kill them. I lost at cards, consumed the labour of the peasants, sentenced them to punishments, lived loosely, and deceived people. Lying, robbery, adultery of all kinds, drunkenness, violence, murder—there was no crime I did not commit, and in spite of that people praised my conduct and my contemporaries considered and consider me to be a comparatively moral man.

So I lived for ten years.

During that time I began to write from vanity, covetousness, and pride. In my writings I did the same as in my life. To get fame and money, for the sake of which I wrote, it was necessary to hide the good and to display the evil. And I did so. How often in my writings I contrived to hide under the guise of indifference, or even of banter, those strivings of mine towards goodness which gave meaning to my life! And I succeeded in this and was praised.

At twenty-six years of age[1] I returned to Petersburg after the war, and met the writers. They received me as one of themselves and flattered me. And before I had time to look round I had adopted the views on life of the set of authors I had come among, and these views completely obliterated all my former strivings to improve—they furnished a theory which justified the dissoluteness of my life.

The view of life of these people, my comrades in

[1] Tolstóy makes a slip here: he was twenty-seven.—A.M.

authorship, consisted in this: that life in general goes on developing, and in this development we— men of thought—have the chief part; and among men of thought it is we—artists and poets—who have the greatest influence. Our vocation is to teach mankind. And lest the simple question should suggest itself: What do I know, and what can I teach? it was explained in this theory that this need not be known, and that the artist and poet teach unconsciously. I was considered an admirable artist and poet, and therefore it was very natural for me to adopt this theory. I, artist and poet, wrote and taught without myself knowing what. For this I was paid money; I had excellent food, lodging, women, and society; and I had fame, which showed that what I taught was very good.

This faith in the meaning of poetry and in the development of life was a religion, and I was one of its priests. To be its priest was very pleasant and profitable. And I lived a considerable time in this faith without doubting its validity. But in the second and still more in the third year of this life I began to doubt the infallibility of this religion and to examine it. My first cause of doubt was that I began to notice that the priests of this religion were not all in accord among themselves. Some said: We are the best and most useful teachers; we teach what is needed, but the others teach wrongly. Others said: No! we are the real teachers, and you teach wrongly. And they disputed, quarrelled, abused, cheated, and tricked one another. There were also many among us who did not care who was right and who was wrong, but were simply bent on attaining their covetous aims by means of this activity of ours. All this obliged me to doubt the validity of our creed.

Moreover, having begun to doubt the truth of

the authors' creed itself, I also began to observe its priests more attentively, and I became convinced that almost all the priests of that religion, the writers, were immoral, and for the most part men of bad, worthless character, much inferior to those whom I had met in my former dissipated and military life; but they were self-confident and self-satisfied as only those can be who are quite holy or who do not know what holiness is. These people revolted me, I became revolting to myself, and I realized that that faith was a fraud.

But strange to say, though I understood this fraud and renounced it, yet I did not renounce the rank these people gave me: the rank of artist, poet, and teacher. I naïvely imagined that I was a poet and artist and could teach everybody without myself knowing what I was teaching, and I acted accordingly.

From my intimacy with these men I acquired a new vice: abnormally developed pride and an insane assurance that it was my vocation to teach men, without knowing what.

To remember that time, and my own state of mind and that of those men (though there are thousands like them to-day), is sad and terrible and ludicrous, and arouses exactly the feeling one experiences in a lunatic asylum.

We were all then convinced that it was necessary for us to speak, write, and print as quickly as possible and as much as possible, and that it was all wanted for the good of humanity. And thousands of us, contradicting and abusing one another, all printed and wrote—teaching others. And without noticing that we knew nothing, and that to the simplest of life's questions: What is good and what is evil? we did not know how to reply, we all talked at the same time, not listening to one another, sometimes seconding and praising one another in order to be seconded and praised in turn, sometimes getting angry with one another—just as in a lunatic asylum.

Thousands of workmen laboured to the extreme limit of their strength day and night, setting the type and printing millions of words which the post carried all over Russia, and we still went on teaching and could in no way find time to teach enough, and were always angry that sufficient attention was not paid us.

It was terribly strange, but is now quite comprehensible. Our real innermost concern was to get as much money and praise as possible. To gain that end we could do nothing except write books and papers. So we did that. But in order to do such useless work and to feel assured that we were very important people we required a theory justifying our activity. And so among us this theory was devised: 'All that exists is reasonable. All that exists develops. And it all develops by means of Culture. And Culture is measured by the circulation of books and newspapers. And we are paid money and are respected because we write books and newspapers, and therefore we are the most useful and the best of men.' This theory would have been all very well if we had been unanimous, but as every thought expressed by one of us was always met by a diametrically opposite thought expressed by another, we ought to have been driven to reflection. But we ignored this; people paid us money and those on our side praised us, so each of us considered himself justified.

It is now clear to me that this was just as in a lunatic asylum; but then I only dimly suspected this, and like all lunatics, simply called all men lunatics except myself.

III

So I lived, abandoning myself to this insanity for another six years, till my marriage. During that time I went abroad. Life in Europe and my acquaintance with leading and learned Europeans[1] confirmed me yet more in the faith of striving after perfection in which I believed, for I found the same faith among them. That faith took with me the common form it assumes with the majority of educated people of our day. It was expressed by the word 'progress'. It then appeared to me that this word meant something. I did not as yet understand that, being tormented (like every vital man) by the question how it is best for me to live, in my answer, 'Live in conformity with progress', I was like a man in a boat who when carried along by wind and waves should reply to what for him is the chief and only question, 'whither to steer', by saying, 'We are being carried somewhere'.

I did not then notice this. Only occasionally—not by reason but by instinct—I revolted against this superstition so common in our day, by which people hide from themselves their lack of understanding of life. . . . So, for instance, during my stay in Paris, the sight of an execution revealed to me the instability of my superstitious belief in progress. When I saw the head part from the body and how they thumped separately into the box, I understood, not with my mind but with my whole being, that no theory of the reasonableness of our present progress could justify this deed; and that though everybody from the creation of the world had held it to be necessary, on whatever theory, I knew it to be unnecessary and bad; and therefore the arbiter of

[1] Russians generally make a distinction between Europeans and Russians.—A.M.

what is good and evil is not what people say and do, nor is it progress, but it is my heart and I. Another instance of a realization that the superstitious belief in progress is insufficient as a guide to life, was my brother's death. Wise, good, serious, he fell ill while still a young man, suffered for more than a year, and died painfully, not understanding why he had lived and still less why he had to die. No theories could give me, or him, any reply to these questions during his slow and painful dying. But these were only rare instances of doubt, and I actually continued to live professing a faith only in progress. 'Everything evolves and I evolve with it: and why it is that I evolve with all things will be known some day.' So I ought to have formulated my faith at that time.

On returning from abroad I settled in the country and chanced to occupy myself with peasant schools. This work was particularly to my taste because in it I had not to face the falsity which had become obvious to me and stared me in the face when I tried to teach people by literary means. Here also I acted in the name of progress, but I already regarded progress itself critically. I said to myself: 'In some of its developments progress has proceeded wrongly, and with primitive peasant children one must deal in a spirit of perfect freedom, letting them choose what path of progress they please.' In reality I was ever revolving round one and the same insoluble problem, which was: How to teach without knowing what to teach. In the higher spheres of literary activity I had realized that one could not teach without knowing what, for I saw that people all taught differently, and by quarrelling among themselves only succeeded in hiding their ignorance from one another. But here, with peasant children, I thought to evade this difficulty by letting them learn what they liked. It amuses me now when I remember how I shuffled in trying to satisfy my desire to teach, while in the depth of my soul I knew very well that I could not teach anything needful for I did not know what was needful. After spending a year at school work I went abroad a second time to discover how to teach others while myself knowing nothing.

And it seemed to me that I had learnt this abroad, and in the year of the peasants' emancipation (1861) I returned to Russia armed with all this wisdom, and having become an Arbiter[1] I began to teach, both the uneducated peasants in schools and the educated classes through a magazine I published. Things appeared to be going well, but I felt I was not quite sound mentally and that matters could not long continue in that way. And I should perhaps then have come to the state of despair I reached fifteen years later had there not been one side of life still unexplored by me which promised me happiness: that was marriage.

For a year I busied myself with arbitration work, the schools, and the magazine; and I became so worn out—as a result especially of my mental confusion—and so hard was my struggle as Arbiter, so obscure the results of my activity in the schools, so repulsive my shuffling in the magazine (which always amounted to one and the same thing: a desire to teach everybody and to hide the fact that I did not know what to teach), that I fell ill, mentally rather than physically, threw up everything, and went away to the Bashkírs in the steppes, to breathe fresh air, drink kumys,[2] and live a merely animal life.

Returning from there I married. The new condi-

[1] To keep peace between peasants and owners.—A.M.
[2] A fermented drink prepared from mare's milk.—A.M.

tions of happy family life completely diverted me from all search for the general meaning of life. My whole life was centred at that time in my family, wife and children, and therefore in care to increase our means of livelihood. My striving after self-perfection, for which I had already substituted a striving for perfection in general, i.e. progress, was now again replaced by the effort simply to secure the best possible conditions for myself and my family.

So another fifteen years passed.

In spite of the fact that I now regarded author-ship as of no importance, I still continued to write during those fifteen years. I had already tasted the temptation of authorship—the temptation of im-mense monetary rewards and applause for my insignificant work—and I devoted myself to it as a means of improving my material position and of stifling in my soul all questions as to the meaning of my own life or life in general.

I wrote: teaching what was for me the only truth, namely, that one should live so as to have the best for oneself and one's family.

So I lived; but five years ago something very strange began to happen to me. At first I ex-perienced moments of perplexity and arrest of life, as though I did not know what to do or how to live; and I felt lost and became dejected. But this passed, and I went on living as before. Then these moments of perplexity began to recur oftener and oftener, and always in the same form. They were always expressed by the questions: What is it for? What does it lead to?

At first it seemed to me that these were aimless and irrelevant questions. I thought that it was all well known, and that if I should ever wish to deal with the solution it would not cost me much effort;

just at present I had no time for it, but when I wanted to I should be able to find the answer. The questions however began to repeat themselves frequently, and to demand replies more and more insistently; and like drops of ink always falling on one place they ran together into one black blot.

Then occurred what happens to everyone sickening with a mortal internal disease. At first trivial signs of indisposition appear to which the sick man pays no attention; then these signs reappear more and more often and merge into one uninterrupted period of suffering. The suffering increases and, before the sick man can look round, what he took for a mere indisposition has already become more important to him than anything else in the world— it is death!

That was what happened to me. I understood that it was no casual indisposition but something very important, and that if these questions constantly repeated themselves they would have to be answered. And I tried to answer them. The questions seemed such stupid, simple, childish ones; but as soon as I touched them and tried to solve them I at once became convinced, first, that they are not childish and stupid but the most important and profound of life's questions; and secondly that, try as I would, I could not solve them. Before occupying myself with my Samára estate, the education of my son, or the writing of a book, I had to know *why* I was doing it. As long as I did not know why, I could do nothing and could not live. Amid the thoughts of estate management which greatly occupied me at that time, the question would suddenly occur: 'Well, you will have 6,000 *desyatínas*[1] of land in Samára Government and 300 horses, and what then?' . . . And I was quite dis-

[1] The *desyatína* is about 2¾ acres.—A.M.

concerted and did not know what to think. Or when considering plans for the education of my children, I would say to myself: 'What for?' Or when considering how the peasants might become prosperous, I would suddenly say to myself: 'But what does it matter to me?' Or when thinking of the fame my works would bring me, I would say to myself, 'Very well; you will be more famous than Gógol or Púshkin or Shakespeare or Molière, or than all the writers in the world—and what of it?' And I could find no reply at all. The questions would not wait, they had to be answered at once, and if I did not answer them it was impossible to live. But there was no answer.

I felt that what I had been standing on had collapsed and that I had nothing left under my feet. What I had lived on no longer existed, and there was nothing left.

IV

My life came to a standstill. I could breathe, eat, drink, and sleep, and I could not help doing these things; but there was no life, for there were no wishes the fulfilment of which I could consider reasonable. If I desired anything, I knew in advance that whether I satisfied my desire or not, nothing would come of it. Had a fairy come and offered to fulfil my desires I should not have known what to ask. If in moments of intoxication I felt something which, though not a wish, was a habit left by former wishes, in sober moments I knew this to be a delusion and that there was really nothing to wish for. I could not even wish to know the truth, for I guessed of what it consisted. The truth was that life is meaningless. I had as it were lived, lived, and walked, walked, till I had come to a precipice and saw clearly that there was nothing ahead of me but destruction. It was impossible to stop, impossible to go back, and impossible to close my eyes or avoid seeing that there was nothing ahead but suffering and real death—complete annihilation.

It had come to this, that I, a healthy, fortunate man, felt I could no longer live: some irresistible power impelled me to rid myself one way or other of life. I cannot say I *wished* to kill myself. The power which drew me away from life was stronger, fuller, and more widespread than any mere wish. It was a force similar to the former striving to live, only in a contrary direction. All my strength drew me away from life. The thought of self-destruction now came to me as naturally as thoughts of how to improve my life had come formerly. And it was so seductive that I had to be cunning with myself lest I should carry it out too hastily. I did not wish to hurry, because I wanted to use all efforts to disentangle the matter. 'If I cannot unravel matters, there will always be time.' And it was then that I, a man favoured by fortune, hid a cord from myself lest I should hang myself from the crosspiece of the partition in my room where I undressed alone every evening, and I ceased to go out shooting with a gun lest I should be tempted by so easy a way of ending my life. I did not myself know what I wanted: I feared life, desired to escape from it, yet still hoped something of it.

And all this befell me at a time when all around me I had what is considered complete good fortune. I was not yet fifty; I had a good wife who loved me and whom I loved, good children, and a large estate which without much effort on my part improved and increased. I was respected by my relations and acquaintances more than at any previous time. I was praised by others and without much self-deception could consider that my name was famous. And far from being insane or mentally diseased, I enjoyed on the contrary a strength of mind and body such as I have seldom met with among men of my kind; physically I could keep up with the peasants at mowing, and mentally I could work for eight and ten hours at a stretch without experiencing any ill results from such exertion. And in this situation I came to this—that I could not live, and, fearing death, had to employ cunning with myself to avoid taking my own life.

My mental condition presented itself to me in this way: my life is a stupid and spiteful joke some-one has played on me. Though I did not acknow-ledge a 'someone' who created me, yet such a presentation—that someone had played an evil and stupid joke on me by placing me in the world—was the form of expression that suggested itself most naturally to me.

Involuntarily it appeared to me that there, some-where, was someone who amused himself by watch-ing how I lived for thirty or forty years: learning, developing, maturing in body and mind, and how, having with matured mental powers reached the summit of life from which it all lay before me, I stood on that summit—like an arch-fool—seeing clearly that there is nothing in life, and that there has been and will be nothing. And *he* was amused....

But whether that 'someone' laughing at me existed or not, I was none the better off. I could give no reasonable meaning to any single action or to my whole life. I was only surprised that I could have avoided understanding this from the very beginning—it has been so long known to all. To-day or to-morrow sickness and death will come (they had come already) to those I love or to me; nothing will remain but stench and worms. Sooner or later my affairs, whatever they may be, will be forgotten, and I shall not exist. Then why go on making any effort? . . . How can man fail to see this? And how go on living? That is what is surprising! One can only live while one is intoxicated with life; as soon as one is sober it is impossible not to see that it is all a mere fraud and a stupid fraud! That is precisely what it is: there is nothing either amusing or witty about it, it is simply cruel and stupid.

There is an Eastern fable, told long ago, of a traveller overtaken on a plain by an enraged beast. Escaping from the beast he gets into a dry well, but sees at the bottom of the well a dragon that has opened its jaws to swallow him. And the unfortunate man, not daring to climb out lest he should be destroyed by the enraged beast, and not daring to leap to the bottom of the well lest he should be eaten by the dragon, seizes a twig growing in a crack in the well and clings to it. His hands are growing weaker and he feels he will soon have to resign himself to the destruction that awaits him above or below, but still he clings on. Then he sees that two mice, a black and a white one, go regularly round and round the stem of the twig to which he is clinging and gnaw at it. And soon the twig itself will snap and he will fall into the dragon's jaws. The traveller sees this and knows that he will inevitably perish; but while still hanging he looks around, sees some drops of honey on the leaves of the twig, reaches them with his tongue and licks them. So I too clung to the twig of life, knowing that the dragon of death was inevitably awaiting me, ready to tear me to pieces; and I could not understand why I had fallen into such torment. I tried to lick the honey which formerly consoled me, but the honey no longer gave me pleasure, and the white and black mice of day and night gnawed at the branch by which I hung. I saw the dragon clearly and the honey no longer tasted sweet. I only saw the unescapable dragon and the mice, and I could not tear my gaze from them. And this is not a fable but the real unanswerable truth intelligible to all.

The deception of the joys of life which formerly allayed my terror of the dragon now no longer deceived me. No matter how often I may be told, 'You cannot understand the meaning of life so do not think about it, but live', I can no longer do it: I have already done it too long. I cannot now help seeing day and night going round and bringing me to death. That is all I see, for that alone is true. All else is false.

The two drops of honey which diverted my eyes from the cruel truth longer than the rest: my love of family, and of writing—art as I called it—were no longer sweet to me.

'Family' . . . said I to myself. But my family—wife and children—are also human. They are placed just as I am: they must either live in a lie or see the terrible truth. Why should they live? Why should I love them, guard them, bring them up, or watch them? That they may come to the despair that I feel, or else be stupid? Loving them, I cannot hide the truth from them: each step in knowledge leads them to the truth. And the truth is death.

'Art, poetry?' . . . Under the influence of success and the praise of men, I had long assured myself that this was a thing one could do though death was drawing near—death which destroys all things, including my work and its remembrance; but soon I saw that that too was a fraud. It was plain to me that art is an adornment of life, an allurement to life. But life had lost its attraction for me, so how could I attract others? As long as I was not living my own life but was borne on the waves of some other life—as long as I believed that life had a meaning, though one I could not express—the reflection of life in poetry and art of all kinds afforded me pleasure: it was pleasant to look at life in the mirror of art. But when I began to seek the meaning of life and felt the necessity of living my own life, that mirror became for me unnecessary, superfluous, ridiculous, or painful. I could no longer soothe myself with what I now saw in the mirror, namely, that my position was stupid and desperate. It was all very well to enjoy the sight when in the depth of my soul I believed that my life had a meaning. Then the play of lights—comic, tragic, touching, beautiful, and terrible—in life amused me. But when I knew life to be meaningless and terrible, the play in the mirror could no longer amuse me. No sweetness of honey could be sweet to me when I saw the dragon and saw the mice gnawing away my support.

Nor was that all. Had I simply understood that life had no meaning I could have borne it quietly, knowing that that was my lot. But I could not satisfy myself with that. Had I been like a man living in a wood from which he knows there is no exit, I could have lived; but I was like one lost in a wood who, horrified at having lost his way, rushes about wishing to find the road. He knows that each step he takes confuses him more and more, but still he cannot help rushing about.

It was indeed terrible. And to rid myself of the terror I wished to kill myself. I experienced terror at what awaited me—knew that that terror was even worse than the position I was in, but still I could not patiently await the end. However convincing the argument might be that in any case some vessel in my heart would give way, or something would burst and all would be over, I could not patiently await that end. The horror of darkness was too great, and I wished to free myself from it as quickly as possible by noose or bullet. That was the feeling which drew me most strongly towards suicide.

V

'BUT perhaps I have overlooked something, or misunderstood something?' said I to myself several times. 'It cannot be that this condition of despair is natural to man!' And I sought for an explanation of these problems in all the branches of knowledge acquired by men. I sought painfully and long, not from idle curiosity or listlessly, but painfully and persistently day and night—sought as a perishing man seeks for safety—and I found nothing.

I sought in all the sciences, but far from finding what I wanted, became convinced that all who like myself had sought in knowledge for the meaning of life had found nothing. And not only had they found nothing, but they had plainly acknowledged that the very thing which made me despair—namely the senselessness of life—is the one indubitable thing man can know.

I sought everywhere; and thanks to a life spent in learning, and thanks also to my relations with the scholarly world, I had access to scientists and scholars in all branches of knowledge, and they readily showed me all their knowledge, not only in books but also in conversation, so that I had at my disposal all that science has to say on this question of life.

I was long unable to believe that it gives no other reply to life's questions than that which it actually does give. It long seemed to me, when I saw the important and serious air with which science announces its conclusions which have nothing in common with the real questions of human life, that there was something I had not understood. I long was timid before science, and it seemed to me that the lack of conformity between the answers and my questions arose not by the fault of science but from my ignorance, but the matter was for me not a game or an amusement but one of life and death, and I was involuntarily brought to the conviction that my questions were the only legitimate ones, forming the basis of all knowledge, and that I with my questions was not to blame, but science if it pretends to reply to those questions.

My question—that which at the age of fifty brought me to the verge of suicide—was the simplest of questions, lying in the soul of every man from the foolish child to the wisest elder: it was a question without an answer to which one cannot live, as I had found by experience. It was: 'What will come of what I am doing to-day or shall do to-morrow? What will come of my whole life?'

Differently expressed, the question is: 'Why should I live, why wish for anything, or do anything?' It can also be expressed thus: 'Is there any meaning in my life that the inevitable death awaiting me does not destroy?'

To this one question, variously expressed, I sought an answer in science. And I found that in relation to that question all human knowledge is divided as it were into two opposite hemispheres at the ends of which are two poles: the one a negative and the other a positive; but that neither at the one nor the other pole is there an answer to life's questions.

The one series of sciences seems not to recognize

the question, but replies clearly and exactly to its own independent questions: that is the series of experimental sciences, and at the extreme end of it stands mathematics. The other series of sciences recognizes the question, but does not answer it; that is the series of abstract sciences, and at the extreme end of it stands metaphysics.

From early youth I had been interested in the abstract sciences, but later the mathematical and natural sciences attracted me, and until I put my question definitely to myself, until that question had itself grown up within me urgently demanding a decision, I contented myself with those counterfeit answers which science gives.

Now in the experimental sphere I said to myself: 'Everything develops and differentiates itself, moving towards complexity and perfection, and there are laws directing this movement. You are a part of the whole. Having learnt as far as possible the whole, and having learnt the law of evolution, you will understand also your place in the whole and will know yourself.' Ashamed as I am to confess it, there was a time when I seemed satisfied with that. It was just the time when I was myself becoming more complex and was developing. My muscles were growing and strengthening, my memory was being enriched, my capacity to think and understand was increasing, I was growing and developing; and feeling this growth in myself it was natural for me to think that such was the universal law in which I should find the solution of the question of my life. But a time came when the growth within me ceased. I felt that I was not developing, but fading, my muscles were weakening, my teeth falling out, and I saw that the law not only did not explain anything to me, but that there never had been or could be such a law, and that I had taken for a law what I had found in myself at a certain period of my life. I regarded the definition of that law more strictly, and it became clear to me that there could be no law of endless development; it became clear that to say, 'in infinite space and time everything develops, becomes more perfect and more complex, is differentiated', is to say nothing at all. These are all words with no meaning, for in the infinite there is neither complex nor simple, neither forward nor backward, nor better or worse.

Above all, my personal question, 'What am I with my desires?' remained quite unanswered. And I understood that those sciences are very interesting and attractive, but that they are exact and clear in inverse proportion to their applicability to the question of life: the less their applicability to the question of life, the more exact and clear they are, while the more they try to reply to the question of life, the more obscure and unattractive they become. If one turns to the division of sciences which attempt to reply to the questions of life—to physiology, psychology, biology, sociology—one encounters an appalling poverty of thought, the greatest obscurity, a quite unjustifiable pretension to solve irrelevant questions, and a continual contradiction of each authority by others and even by himself. If one turns to the branches of science which are not concerned with the solution of the questions of life, but which reply to their own special scientific questions, one is enraptured by the power of man's mind, but one knows in advance that they give no reply to life's questions. Those sciences simply ignore life's questions. They say: 'To the question of what you are and why you live we have no reply, and are not occupied with that; but if you want to know the laws of light, of chemical combinations, the laws of development of organisms, if you want to know the laws of bodies and their form, and the relation of numbers and quantities, if you want to know the laws of your mind, to all that we have clear, exact, and unquestionable replies.'

In general the relation of the experimental sciences to life's question may be expressed thus: Question: 'Why do I live?' Answer: 'In infinite space, in infinite time, infinitely small particles change their forms in infinite complexity, and when you have understood the laws of those mutations of form you will understand why you live on the earth.'

Then in the sphere of abstract science I said to myself: 'All humanity lives and develops on the basis of spiritual principles and ideals which guide it. Those ideals are expressed in religions, in sciences, in arts, in forms of government. Those ideals become more and more elevated, and humanity advances to its highest welfare. I am part of humanity, and therefore my vocation is to forward the recognition and the realization of the ideals of humanity.' And at the time of my weak-mindedness I was satisfied with that; but as soon as the question of life presented itself clearly to me, those theories immediately crumbled away. Not to speak of the unscrupulous obscurity with which those sciences announce conclusions formed on the study of a small part of mankind as general conclusions; not to speak of the mutual contradictions of different adherents of this view as to what are the ideals of humanity; the strangeness, not to say stupidity, of the theory consists in the fact that in order to reply to the question facing each man: 'What am I?' or 'Why do I live?' or 'What must I do?' one has first to decide the question: 'What is the life of the whole?' (which is to him unknown and of which he is acquainted with one tiny part in one minute period of time). To understand what he is, man must first understand all this mysterious humanity, consisting of people such as himself who do not understand one another.

I have to confess that there was a time when I believed this. It was the time when I had my own favourite ideals justifying my own caprices, and I was trying to devise a theory which would allow one to consider my caprices as the law of humanity. But as soon as the question of life arose in my soul in full clearness that reply at once flew to dust. And I understood that as in the experimental sciences there are real sciences, and semi-sciences which try to give answers to questions beyond their competence, so in this sphere there is a whole series of most diffused sciences which try to reply to irrelevant questions. Semi-sciences of that kind, the juridical and the social-historical, endeavour to solve the questions of a man's life by pretending to decide, each in its own way, the question of the life of all humanity.

But as in the sphere of man's experimental knowledge one who sincerely inquires how he is to live cannot be satisfied with the reply—'Study in endless space the mutations, infinite in time and in complexity, of innumerable atoms, and then you will understand your life'—so also a sincere man cannot be satisfied with the reply: 'Study the whole life of humanity of which we cannot know either the beginning or the end, of which we do not even know a small part, and then you will understand your own life.' And like the experimental semi-sciences, so these other semi-sciences are the more filled with obscurities, inexactitudes, stupidities, and contradictions, the further they diverge from the real problems. The problem of experimental science is the sequence of cause and effect in material phenomena. It is only necessary for experimental science to introduce the question of a final cause for it to become nonsensical. The problem of abstract science is the recognition of the primordial essence of life. It is only necessary to introduce the investigation of consequential phenomena (such as social and historical phenomena) and it also becomes nonsensical.

Experimental science only then gives positive knowledge and displays the greatness of the human mind when it does not introduce into its investigations the question of an ultimate cause. And, on the contrary, abstract science is only then science and displays the greatness of the human mind when it puts quite aside questions relating to the consequential causes of phenomena and regards man solely in relation to an ultimate cause. Such in this realm of science—forming the pole of the sphere—is metaphysics or philosophy. That science states the question clearly: 'What am I, and what is the universe? And why do I exist, and why does the universe exist?' And since it has existed it has always replied in the same way. Whether the philosopher calls the essence of life existing within me, and in all that exists, by the name of 'idea', or 'substance', or 'spirit', or 'will', he says one and the same thing: that this essence exists and that I am of that same essence; but why it is he does not know, and does not say, if he is an exact thinker. I ask: 'Why should this essence exist? What results from the fact that it is and will be?' .... And philosophy not merely does not reply, but is itself only asking that question. And if it is real philosophy all its labour lies merely in trying to put that question clearly. And if it keeps firmly to its task it cannot reply to the question otherwise than thus: 'What

am I, and what is the universe?' 'All and nothing';
and to the question 'Why?' by 'I do not know'.

So that however I may turn these replies of
philosophy I can never obtain anything like an
answer—and not because, as in the clear experimental sphere, the reply does not relate to my
question, but because here, though all the mental
work is directed just to my question, there is no
answer, but instead of an answer one gets the same
question, only in a complex form.

VI

In my search for answers to life's questions I experienced just what is felt by a man lost in a forest.

He reaches a glade, climbs a tree, and clearly sees
the limitless distance, but sees that his home is not
and cannot be there; then he goes into the dark
wood and sees the darkness, but there also his home
is not.

So I wandered in that wood of human knowledge,
amid the gleams of mathematical and experimental
science which showed me clear horizons but in a
direction where there could be no home, and also
amid the darkness of the abstract sciences where I
was immersed in deeper gloom the further I went,
and where I finally convinced myself that there
was, and could be, no exit.

Yielding myself to the bright side of knowledge,
I understood that I was only diverting my gaze
from the question. However alluringly clear those
horizons which opened out before me might be,
however alluring it might be to immerse oneself in
the limitless expanse of those sciences, I already
understood that the clearer they were the less they
met my need and the less they replied to my
question.

'I know', said I to myself, 'what science so persistently tries to discover, and along that road there is no reply to the question as to the meaning of my life.' In the abstract sphere I understood that notwithstanding the fact, or just because of the fact, that the direct aim of science is to reply to my question, there is no reply but that which I have myself already given: 'What is the meaning of my life?' 'There is none.' Or: 'What will come of my life?' 'Nothing.' Or: 'Why does everything exist that exists, and why do I exist?' 'Because it exists.'

Inquiring for one region of human knowledge, I received an innumerable quantity of exact replies concerning matters about which I had not asked: about the chemical constituents of the stars, about the movement of the sun towards the constellation Hercules, about the origin of species and of man, about the forms of infinitely minute imponderable particles of ether; but in this sphere of knowledge the only answer to my question, 'What is the meaning of my life?' was: 'You are what you call your "life"; you are a transitory, casual cohesion of particles. The mutual interactions and changes of these particles produce in you what you call your "life". That cohesion will last some time; afterwards the interaction of these particles will cease and what you call "life" will cease, and so will all your questions. You are an accidentally united little lump of something. That little lump ferments. The little lump calls that fermenting its "life". The lump will disintegrate and there will be an end of the fermenting and of all the questions.' So answers the clear side of science and cannot answer otherwise if it strictly follows its principles.

From such a reply one sees that the reply does not answer the question. I want to know the meaning of my life, but that it is a fragment of the infinite, far from giving it a meaning destroys its every possible meaning. The obscure compromises which that side of experimental exact science makes with abstract science when it says that the meaning of life consists in development and in co-operation with development, owing to their inexactness and obscurity cannot be considered as replies.

The other side of science—the abstract side—when it holds strictly to its principles, replying directly to the question, always replies, and in all ages has replied, in one and the same way: 'The world is something infinite and incomprehensible. Human life is an incomprehensible part of that incomprehensible "all".' Again I exclude all those compromises between abstract and experimental sciences which supply the whole ballast of the semi-sciences called juridical, political, and historical. In those semi-sciences the conception of development and progress is again wrongly introduced, only with this difference, that there it was the development of everything while here it is the development of the life of mankind. The error is there as before: development and progress in infinity can have no aim or direction, and, as far as my question is concerned, no answer is given.

In truly abstract science, namely in genuine philosophy—not in that which Schopenhauer calls 'professorial philosophy' which serves only to classify all existing phenomena in new philosophic categories and to call them by new names—where the philosopher does not lose sight of the essential question, the reply is always one and the same—the reply given by Socrates, Schopenhauer, Solomon, and Buddha.

'We approach truth only inasmuch as we depart from life', said Socrates when preparing for death. 'For what do we, who love truth, strive after in life? To free ourselves from the body, and from all the evil that is caused by the life of the body! If so, then how can we fail to be glad when death comes to us?

'The wise man seeks death all his life and therefore death is not terrible to him.'

And Schopenhauer says:

'Having recognized the inmost essence of the world as *will*, and all its phenomena—from the unconscious working of the obscure forces of Nature up to the completely conscious action of man—as only the objectivity of that will, we shall in no way avoid the conclusion that together with the voluntary renunciation and self-destruction of the will all those phenomena also disappear, that constant striving and effort without aim or rest on all the stages of objectivity in which and through which the world exists; the diversity of successive forms will disappear, and together with the form all the manifestations of will, with its most universal forms, space and time, and finally its most fundamental form—subject and object. Without will there is no concept and no world. Before us, certainly, nothing remains. But what resists this transition into annihilation, our nature, is only that same wish to live—*Wille zum Leben*—which forms ourselves as well as our world. That we are so afraid of annihilation or, what is the same thing, that we so wish to live, merely means that we are ourselves nothing else but this desire to live, and know nothing but it. And so what remains after the complete annihilation of the will, for us who are so full of the will, is, of course, nothing; but on the other hand, for those in whom the will has turned and renounced itself, this so real world of ours with all its suns and milky way is nothing.'

'Vanity of vanities', says Solomon—'vanity of

vanities—all is vanity. What profit hath a man of all his labour which he taketh under the sun? One generation passeth away, and another generation cometh: but the earth abideth for ever. . . . The thing that hath been, is that which shall be; and that which is done is that which shall be done: and there is no new thing under the sun. Is there anything whereof it may be said, See, this is new? it hath been already of old time, which was before us. There is no remembrance of former things; neither shall there be any remembrance of things that are to come with those that shall come after. I the Preacher was King over Israel in Jerusalem. And I gave my heart to seek and search out by wisdom concerning all that is done under heaven: this sore travail hath God given to the sons of man to be exercised therewith. I have seen all the works that are done under the sun; and behold, all is vanity and vexation of spirit. . . . I communed with my own heart, saying, Lo, I am come to great estate, and have gotten more wisdom than all they that have been before me over Jerusalem: yea, my heart hath great experience of wisdom and know-ledge. And I gave my heart to know wisdom, and to know madness and folly: I perceived that this also is vexation of spirit. For in much wisdom is much grief: and he that increaseth knowledge in-creaseth sorrow.

'I said in my heart, Go to now, I will prove thee with mirth, therefore enjoy pleasure: and behold this also is vanity. I said of laughter, It is mad: and of mirth, What doeth it? I sought in my heart how to cheer my flesh with wine, and while my heart was guided by wisdom, to lay hold on folly, till I might see what it was good for the sons of men that they should do under heaven the number of the days of their life. I made me great works; I builded me houses; I planted me vineyards: I made me gardens and orchards, and I planted trees in them of all kinds of fruits: I made me pools of water, to water therefrom the forest where trees were reared: I got me servants and maidens, and had servants born in my house; also I had great possessions of herds and flocks above all that were before me in Jerusalem: I gathered me also silver and gold and the peculiar treasure from kings and from the provinces: I got me men singers and women singers; and the delights of the sons of men, as musical instruments and that of all sorts. So I was great, and increased more than all that were before me in Jerusalem: also my wisdom remained with me. And whatever mine eyes desired I kept not from them. I withheld not my heart from any joy. . . . Then I looked on all the works that my hands had wrought, and on the labour that I had laboured to do: and, behold, all was vanity and vexation of spirit, and there was no profit from them under the sun. And I turned myself to behold wisdom, and madness, and folly. . . . But I perceived that one event happeneth to them all. Then said I in my heart, As it happeneth to the fool, so it happeneth even to me, and why was I then more wise? Then I said in my heart, that this also is vanity. For there is no remembrance of the wise more than of the fool for ever; seeing that which now is in the days to come shall all be forgotten. And how dieth the wise man? as the fool. Therefore I hated life; because the work that is wrought under the sun is grievous unto me: for all is vanity and vexation of spirit. Yea, I hated all my labour which I had taken under the sun: seeing that I must leave it unto the man that shall be after me. . . . For what hath man of all his labour, and of the vexation of his heart, wherein he hath laboured under the sun?

For all his days are sorrows, and his travail grief; yea, even in the night his heart taketh no rest. This is also vanity. Man is not blessed with security that he should eat and drink and cheer his soul from his own labour. . . . All things come alike to all: there is one event to the righteous and to the wicked; to the good and to the evil: to the clean and to the unclean; to him that sacrificeth and to him that sacrificeth not; as is the good, so is the sinner; and he that sweareth, as he that feareth an oath. This is an evil in all that is done under the sun, that there is one event unto all; yea, also the heart of the sons of men is full of evil, and madness is in their heart while they live, and after that they go to the dead. For him that is among the living there is hope: for a living dog is better than a dead lion. For the living know that they shall die: but the dead know not any thing, neither have they any more a reward; for the memory of them is forgotten. Also their love, and their hatred, and their envy, is now perished; neither have they any more a portion for ever in any thing that is done under the sun.'

So said Solomon, or whoever wrote those words.[1]

And this is what the Indian wisdom tells:

Sakya Muni, a young, happy prince, from whom the existence of sickness, old age, and death had been hidden, went out to drive and saw a terrible old man, toothless and slobbering. The prince, from whom till then old age had been concealed, was amazed, and asked his driver what it was, and

[1] Tolstóy's version differs slightly in a few places from our own Authorized or Revised version. I have followed his text, for in a letter to Fet, quoted on p. 18, vol. ii, of my *Life of Tolstoy*, he says that 'The Authorized English version [of Ecclesiastes] is bad.'—A.M.

how that man had come to such a wretched and disgusting condition, and when he learnt that this was the common fate of all men, that the same thing inevitably awaited him—the young prince— he could not continue his drive, but gave orders to go home, that he might consider this fact. So he shut himself up alone and considered it. And he probably devised some consolation for himself, for he subsequently again went out to drive, feeling merry and happy. But this time he saw a sick man. He saw an emaciated, livid, trembling man with dim eyes. The prince, from whom sickness had been concealed, stopped and asked what this was. And when he learnt that this was sickness, to which all men are liable, and that he himself—a healthy and happy prince—might himself fall ill to-morrow, he again was in no mood to enjoy himself but gave orders to drive home, and again sought some solace, and probably found it, for he drove out a third time for pleasure. But this third time he saw another new sight: he saw men carrying something. 'What is that?' 'A dead man.' 'What does *dead* mean?' asked the prince. He was told that to become dead means to become like that man. The prince approached the corpse, uncovered it, and looked at it. 'What will happen to him now?' asked the prince. He was told that the corpse would be buried in the ground. 'Why?' 'Because he will certainly not return to life, and will only produce a stench and worms.' 'And is that the fate of all men? Will the same thing happen to me? Will they bury me, and shall I cause a stench and be eaten by worms?' 'Yes.' 'Home! I shall not drive out for pleasure, and never will so drive out again!'

And Sakya Muni could find no consolation in life, and decided that life is the greatest of evils; and he devoted all the strength of his soul to free himself from it, and to free others; and to do this so that, even after death, life shall not be renewed any more but be completely destroyed at its very roots. So speaks all the wisdom of India.

These then are the direct replies that human wisdom gives when it replies to life's question.

'The life of the body is an evil and a lie. Therefore the destruction of the life of the body is a blessing, and we should desire it', says Socrates.

'Life is that which should not be—an evil; and the passage into Nothingness is the only good in life', says Schopenhauer.

'All that is in the world—folly and wisdom and riches and poverty and mirth and grief—is vanity and emptiness. Man dies and nothing is left of him. And that is stupid', says Solomon.

'To live in the consciousness of the inevitability of suffering, of becoming enfeebled, of old age and of death, is impossible—we must free ourselves from life, from all possible life', says Buddha.

And what these strong minds said has been said and thought and felt by millions upon millions of people like them. And I have thought it and felt it.

So my wandering among the sciences, far from freeing me from my despair, only strengthened it. One kind of knowledge did not reply to life's question, the other kind replied directly confirming my despair, indicating not that the result at which I had arrived was the fruit of error or of a diseased state of my mind, but on the contrary that I had thought correctly, and that my thoughts coincided with the conclusions of the most powerful of human minds.

It is no good deceiving oneself. It is all—vanity! Happy is he who has not been born: death is better than life, and one must free oneself from life.

VII

NOT finding an explanation in science I began to seek for it in life, hoping to find it among the people around me. And I began to observe how the people around me—people like myself—lived, and what their attitude was to this question which had brought me to despair.

And this is what I found among people who were in the same position as myself as regards education and manner of life.

I found that for people of my circle there were four ways out of the terrible position in which we are all placed.

The first was that of ignorance. It consists in not knowing, not understanding, that life is an evil and an absurdity. People of this sort—chiefly women, or very young or very dull people—have not yet understood that question of life which presented itself to Schopenhauer, Solomon, and Buddha. They see neither the dragon that awaits them nor the mice gnawing the shrub by which they are hanging, and they lick the drops of honey. But they lick those drops of honey only for a while: something will turn their attention to the dragon and the mice, and there will be an end to their licking. From them I had nothing to learn—one cannot cease to know what one does know.

The second way out is epicureanism. It consists, while knowing the hopelessness of life, in making use meanwhile of the advantages one has, disregarding the dragon and the mice, and licking the honey in the best way, especially if there is much of it within reach. Solomon expresses this way out thus: 'Then I commended mirth, because a man hath no better thing under the sun, than to eat, and to drink, and to be merry: and that this should accompany him in his labour the days of his life, which God giveth him under the sun.

'Therefore eat thy bread with joy and drink thy wine with a merry heart. . . . Live joyfully with the wife whom thou lovest all the days of the life of thy vanity . . . for this is thy portion in life and in thy labours which thou takest under the sun. . . . What-soever thy hand findeth to do, do it with thy might, for there is no work, nor device, nor knowledge, nor wisdom, in the grave, whither thou goest.'

That is the way in which the majority of people of our circle make life possible for themselves. Their circumstances furnish them with more of welfare than of hardship, and their moral dullness makes it possible for them to forget that the advantage of their position is accidental, and that not everyone can have a thousand wives and palaces like Solomon, that for everyone who has a thousand wives there are a thousand without a wife, and that for each palace there are a thousand people who have to build it in the sweat of their brows; and that the accident that has to-day made me a Solomon may to-morrow make me a Solomon's slave. The dull-ness of these people's imagination enables them to forget the things that gave Buddha no peace—the inevitability of sickness, old age, and death, which to-day or to-morrow will destroy all these pleasures.

So think and feel the majority of people of our day and our manner of life. The fact that some of these people declare the dullness of their thoughts and imaginations to be a philosophy, which they call Positive, does not remove them, in my opinion, from the ranks of those who, to avoid seeing the question, lick the honey. I could not imitate these people; not having their dullness of imagination I could not artificially produce it in myself. I could not tear my eyes from the mice and the dragon, as no vital man can after he has once seen them.

The third escape is that of strength and energy. It consists in destroying life, when one has understood that it is an evil and an absurdity. A few exceptionally strong and consistent people act so. Having understood the stupidity of the joke that has been played on them, and having understood that it is better to be dead than to be alive, and that it is best of all not to exist, they act accordingly and promptly end this stupid joke, since there are means: a rope round one's neck, water, a knife to stick into one's heart, or the trains on the railways; and the number of those of our circle who act in this way becomes greater and greater, and for the most part they act so at the best time of their life, when the strength of their mind is in full bloom and few habits degrading to the mind have as yet been acquired.

I saw that this was the worthiest way of escape and I wished to adopt it.

The fourth way out is that of weakness. It consists in seeing the truth of the situation and yet clinging to life, knowing in advance that nothing can come of it. People of this kind know that death is better than life, but not having the strength to act rationally—to end the deception quickly and kill themselves—they seem to wait for something. This is the escape of weakness, for if I know what is best and it is within my power, why not yield to what is best? . . . I found myself in that category.

So people of my class evade the terrible contradiction in four ways. Strain my attention as I would, I saw no way except those four. One way was not to understand that life is senseless, vanity, and an evil, and that it is better not to live. I could not help knowing this, and when I once knew it could not shut my eyes to it. The second way was to use life such as it is without thinking of the future. And I could not do that. I, like Sakya Muni, could not ride out hunting when I knew that old age, suffering, and death exist. My imagination was too vivid. Nor could I rejoice in the momentary accidents that for an instant threw pleasure to my lot. The third way, having understood that life is evil and stupid, was to end it by killing oneself. I understood that, but somehow still did not kill myself. The fourth way was to live like Solomon and Schopenhauer—knowing that life is a stupid joke played upon us, and still to go on living, washing oneself, dressing, dining, talking, and even writing books. This was to me repulsive and tormenting, but I remained in that position.

I see now that if I did not kill myself it was due to some dim consciousness of the invalidity of my thoughts. However convincing and indubitable appeared to me the sequence of my thoughts and of those of the wise that have brought us to the admission of the senselessness of life, there remained in me a vague doubt of the justice of my conclusion.

It was like this: I, my reason, have acknowledged that life is senseless. If there is nothing higher than reason (and there is not: nothing can prove that there is), then reason is the creator of life for me. If reason did not exist there would be for me no life. How can reason deny life when it is the creator of life? Or to put it the other way: were there no life, my reason would not exist; therefore reason is life's son. Life is all. Reason is its fruit yet reason rejects life itself! I felt that there was something wrong here.

Life is a senseless evil, that is certain, said I to myself. Yet I have lived and am still living, and all mankind lived and lives. How is that? Why does it live, when it is possible not to live? Is it that only I and Schopenhauer are wise enough to understand the senselessness and evil of life?

The reasoning showing the vanity of life is not so difficult, and has long been familiar to the very simplest folk; yet they have lived and still live. How is it they all live and never think of doubting the reasonableness of life?

My knowledge, confirmed by the wisdom of the sages, has shown me that everything on earth—organic and inorganic—is all most cleverly arranged—only my own position is stupid. And those fools—the enormous masses of people—know nothing about how everything organic and inorganic in the world is arranged; but they live, and it seems to them that their life is very wisely arranged! . . .

And it struck me: 'But what if there is something I do not yet know? Ignorance behaves just in that way. Ignorance always says just what I am saying. When it does not know something, it says that what it does not know is stupid. Indeed, it appears that there is a whole humanity that lived and lives as if it understood the meaning of its life, for without understanding it it could not live; but I say that all this life is senseless and that I cannot live.

'Nothing prevents our denying life by suicide. Well then, kill yourself, and you won't discuss. If life displeases you, kill yourself! You live, and cannot understand the meaning of life—then finish it, and do not fool about in life, saying and writing that you do not understand it. You have come into good company where people are contented and know what they are doing; if you find it dull and repulsive—go away!'

Indeed, what are we who are convinced of the necessity of suicide yet do not decide to commit it, but the weakest, most inconsistent, and to put it

plainly, the stupidest of men, fussing about with
our own stupidity as a fool fusses about with a
painted hussy? For our wisdom, however indubitable it may be, has not given us the knowledge of
the meaning of our life. But all mankind who
sustain life—millions of them—do not doubt the
meaning of life.

Indeed, from the most distant times of which I
know anything, when life began, people have lived
knowing the argument about the vanity of life
which has shown me its senselessness, and yet they
lived attributing some meaning to it.

From the time when any life began among men
they had that meaning of life, and they led that
life which has descended to me. All that is in me
and around me, all, corporeal and incorporeal, is
the fruit of their knowledge of life. Those very
instruments of thought with which I consider this
life and condemn it were all devised not by me but
by them. I myself was born, taught, and brought
up thanks to them. They dug out the iron, taught
us to cut down the forests, tamed the cows and
horses, taught us to sow corn and to live together,
organized our life, and taught me to think and
speak. And I, their product, fed, supplied with
drink, taught by them, thinking with their thoughts
and words, have argued that they are an absurdity!
'There is something wrong', said I to myself. 'I
have blundered somewhere.' But it was a long
time before I could find out where the mistake was.

VIII

ALL these doubts, which I am now able to express
more or less systematically, I could not then have
expressed. I then only felt that however logically
inevitable were my conclusions concerning the

vanity of life, confirmed as they were by the greatest thinkers, there was something not right about them. Whether it was in the reasoning itself or in the statement of the question I did not know—I only felt that the conclusion was rationally convincing, but that that was insufficient. All these conclusions could not so convince me as to make me do what followed from my reasoning, that is to say, kill myself. And I should have told an untruth had I, without killing myself, said that reason had brought me to the point I had reached. Reason worked, but something else was also working which I can only call a consciousness of life. A force was working which compelled me to turn my attention to this and not to that; and it was this force which extricated me from my desperate situation and turned my mind in quite another direction. This force compelled me to turn my attention to the fact that I and a few hundred similar people are not the whole of mankind, and that I did not yet know the life of mankind.

Looking at the narrow circle of my equals, I saw only people who had not understood the question, or who had understood it and drowned it in life's intoxication, or had understood it and ended their lives, or had understood it and yet from weakness were living out their desperate life. And I saw no others. It seemed to me that that narrow circle of rich, learned, and leisured people to which I belonged formed the whole of humanity, and that those milliards of others who have lived and are living were cattle of some sort—not real people.

Strange, incredibly incomprehensible as it now seems to me that I could, while reasoning about life, overlook the whole life of mankind that surrounded me on all sides; that I could to such a degree blunder so absurdly as to think that my life, and Solomon's and Schopenhauer's, is the real, normal life, and that the life of the milliards is a circumstance undeserving of attention—strange as this now is to me, I see that so it was. In the delusion of my pride of intellect it seemed to me so indubitable that I and Solomon and Schopenhauer had stated the question so truly and exactly that nothing else was possible—so indubitable did it seem that all those milliards consisted of men who had not yet arrived at an apprehension of all the profundity of the question—that I sought for the meaning of my life without it once occurring to me to ask: 'But what meaning is and has been given to their lives by all the milliards of common folk who live and have lived in the world?'

I long lived in this state of lunacy, which, in fact if not in words, is particularly characteristic of us very liberal and learned people. But thanks either to the strange physical affection I have for the real labouring people, which compelled me to understand them and to see that they are not so stupid as we suppose, or thanks to the sincerity of my conviction that I could know nothing beyond the fact that the best I could do was to hang myself, at any rate I instinctively felt that if I wished to live and understand the meaning of life, I must seek this meaning not among those who have lost it and wish to kill themselves, but among those milliards of the past and the present who make life and who support the burden of their own lives and of ours also. And I considered the enormous masses of those simple, unlearned, and poor people who have lived and are living and I saw something quite different. I saw that, with rare exceptions, all those milliards who have lived and are living do not fit into my divisions, and that I could not class them as not understanding the question, for they themselves state it and reply to it with extraordinary clearness. Nor could I consider them epicureans, for their life consists more of privations and sufferings than of enjoyments. Still less could I consider them as irrationally dragging on a meaningless existence, for every act of their life, as well as death itself, is explained by them. To kill themselves they consider the greatest evil. It appeared that all mankind had a knowledge, unacknowledged and despised by me, of the meaning of life. It appeared that reasonable knowledge does not give the meaning of life, but excludes life: while the meaning attributed to life by milliards of people, by all humanity, rests on some despised pseudo-knowledge.

Rational knowledge, presented by the learned and wise, denies the meaning of life, but the enormous masses of men, the whole of mankind, receive that meaning in irrational knowledge. And that irrational knowledge is faith, that very thing which I could not but reject. It is God, One in Three; the creation in six days; the devils and angels, and all the rest that I cannot accept as long as I retain my reason.

My position was terrible. I knew I could find nothing along the path of reasonable knowledge except a denial of life; and there—in faith—was nothing but a denial of reason, which was yet more impossible for me than a denial of life. From rational knowledge it appeared that life is an evil, people know this and it is in their power to end life; yet they lived and still live, and I myself live, though I have long known that life is senseless and an evil. By faith it appears that in order to understand the meaning of life I must renounce my reason, the very thing for which alone a meaning is required.

IX

A CONTRADICTION arose from which there were two exits. Either that which I called reason was not so rational as I supposed, or that which seemed to me irrational was not so irrational as I supposed. And I began to verify the line of argument of my rational knowledge.

Verifying the line of argument of rational knowledge I found it quite correct. The conclusion that life is nothing was inevitable; but I noticed a mistake. The mistake lay in this, that my reasoning was not in accord with the question I had put. The question was: 'Why should I live, that is to say, what real, permanent result will come out of my illusory transitory life—what meaning has my finite existence in this infinite world?' And to reply to that question I had studied life.

The solution of all the possible questions of life could evidently not satisfy me, for my question, simple as it at first appeared, included a demand for an explanation of the finite in terms of the infinite, and vice versa.

I asked: 'What is the meaning of my life, beyond time, cause, and space?' And I replied to quite another question: 'What is the meaning of my life within time, cause, and space?' With the result that, after long efforts of thought, the answer I reached was: 'None.'

In my reasonings I constantly compared (nor could I do otherwise) the finite with the finite, and the infinite with the infinite; but for that reason I reached the inevitable result: force is force, matter is matter, will is will, the infinite is the infinite, nothing is nothing—and that was all that could result.

It was something like what happens in mathematics, when thinking to solve an equation, we find we are working on an identity. The line of reasoning is correct, but results in the answer that *a* equals *a*, or *x* equals *x*, or o equals o. The same thing happened with my reasoning in relation to the question of the meaning of my life. The replies given by all science to that question only result in— identity.

And really, strictly scientific knowledge—that knowledge which begins, as Descartes's did, with complete doubt about everything—rejects all knowledge admitted on faith and builds everything afresh on the laws of reason and experience, and cannot give any other reply to the question of life than that which I obtained: an indefinite reply. Only at first had it seemed to me that knowledge had given a positive reply—the reply of Schopenhauer: that life has no meaning and is an evil. But on examining the matter I understood that the reply is not positive, it was only my feeling that so expressed it. Strictly expressed, as it is by the Brahmins and by Solomon and Schopenhauer, the reply is merely indefinite, or an identity: o equals o, life is nothing. So that philosophic knowledge denies nothing, but only replies that the question cannot be solved by it—that for it the solution remains indefinite.

Having understood this, I understood that it was not possible to seek in rational knowledge for a reply to my question, and that the reply given by rational knowledge is a mere indication that a reply can only be obtained by a different statement of the question and only when the relation of the finite to the infinite is included in the question. And I understood that, however irrational and distorted might be the replies given by faith, they have this advantage, that they introduce into every answer a relation between the finite and the infinite, without which there can be no solution.

In whatever way I stated the question, that relation appeared in the answer. How am I to live?—According to the law of God. What real result will come of my life?—Eternal torment or eternal bliss. What meaning has life that death does not destroy?—Union with the eternal God: heaven.

So that besides rational knowledge, which had seemed to me the only knowledge, I was inevitably brought to acknowledge that all live humanity has another irrational knowledge—faith which makes it possible to live. Faith still remained to me as irrational as it was before, but I could not but admit that it alone gives mankind a reply to the questions of life, and that consequently it makes life possible. Reasonable knowledge had brought me to acknowledge that life is senseless—my life had come to a halt and I wished to destroy myself. Looking around on the whole of mankind I saw that people live and declare that they know the meaning of life. I looked at myself—I had lived as long as I knew a meaning of life. As to others so also to me faith had given a meaning to life and had made life possible.

Looking again at people of other lands, at my contemporaries and at their predecessors, I saw the same thing. Where there is life, there since man began faith has made life possible for him, and the chief outline of that faith is everywhere and always identical.

Whatever the faith may be, and whatever answers it may give, and to whomsoever it gives them, every such answer gives to the finite existence of man an infinite meaning, a meaning not destroyed by sufferings, deprivations, or death. This means that only in faith can we find for life a meaning and a possibility. What, then, is this faith? And I understood that faith is not merely 'the evidence of things not seen', &c., and is not a revelation (that defines only one of the indications of faith), is not the relation of man to God (one has first to define faith and then God, and not define faith through God); it is not only agreement with what has been told one (as faith is most usually supposed to be), but faith is a knowledge of the meaning of human life in consequence of which man does not destroy himself but lives. Faith is the strength of life. If a man lives he believes in something. If he did not believe that one must live for something, he would not live. If he does not see and recognize the illusory nature of the finite, he believes in the finite; if he understands the illusory nature of the finite, he must believe in the infinite. Without faith he cannot live.

And I recalled the whole course of my mental labour and was horrified. It was now clear to me that for man to be able to live he must either not see the infinite, or have such an explanation of the meaning of life as will connect the finite with the infinite. Such an explanation I had had; but as long as I believed in the finite I did not need the explanation, and I began to verify it by reason. And in the light of reason the whole of my former explanation flew to atoms. But a time came when I ceased to believe in the finite. And then I began to build up on rational foundations, out of what I knew, an explanation which would give a meaning to life; but nothing could I build. Together with the best human intellects I reached the result that o equals o, and was much astonished at that conclusion, though nothing else could have resulted.

What was I doing when I sought an answer in the experimental sciences? I wished to know why I live, and for this purpose studied all that is outside me. Evidently I might learn much, but nothing of what I needed.

What was I doing when I sought an answer in

philosophical knowledge? I was studying the
thoughts of those who had found themselves in the
same position as I, lacking a reply to the question,
'Why do I live?' Evidently I could learn nothing
but what I knew myself, namely that nothing can
be known.

What am I?—A part of the infinite. In those few
words lies the whole problem.

Is it possible that humanity has only put that
question to itself since yesterday? And can no one
before me have set himself that question—a question so simple, and one that springs to the tongue
of every wise child?

Surely that question has been asked since man
began; and naturally for the solution of that question since man began it has been equally insufficient
to compare the finite with the finite and the infinite
with the infinite, and since man began the relation
of the finite to the infinite has been sought out and
expressed.

All these conceptions in which the finite has been
adjusted to the infinite and a meaning found for
life—the conception of God, of will, of goodness—we
submit to logical examination. And all those conceptions fail to stand reason's criticism.

Were it not so terrible it would be ludicrous with
what pride and self-satisfaction we, like children, pull
the watch to pieces, take out the spring, make a toy of
it, and are then surprised that the watch does not go.

A solution of the contradiction between the finite
and the infinite, and such a reply to the question
of life as will make it possible to live, is necessary
and precious. And that is the only solution which
we find everywhere, always, and among all peoples:
a solution descending from times in which we lose
sight of the life of man, a solution so difficult that
we can compose nothing like it—and this solution

we light-heartedly destroy in order again to set the
same question, which is natural to everyone and
to which we have no answer.

The conception of an infinite God, the divinity of
the soul, the connexion of human affairs with God,
the unity and existence of the soul, man's conception of moral goodness and evil—are conceptions
formulated in the hidden infinity of human thought,
they are those conceptions without which neither
life nor I should exist; yet rejecting all that labour
of the whole of humanity, I wished to remake it
afresh myself and in my own manner.

I did not then think like that, but the germs of
these thoughts were already in me. I understood,
in the first place, that my position with Schopenhauer and Solomon, notwithstanding our wisdom,
was stupid: we see that life is an evil and yet continue to live. That is evidently stupid, for if life is
senseless and I am so fond of what is reasonable, it
should be destroyed, and then there would be no
one to challenge it. Secondly, I understood that
all one's reasonings turned in a vicious circle like
a wheel out of gear with its pinion. However much
and however well we may reason we cannot obtain
a reply to the question; and o will always equal o,
and therefore our path is probably erroneous.
Thirdly, I began to understand that in the replies
given by faith is stored up the deepest human
wisdom and that I had no right to deny them on the
ground of reason, and that those answers are the
only ones which reply to life's question.

X

I UNDERSTOOD this, but it made matters no better
for me. I was now ready to accept any faith if only
it did not demand of me a direct denial of reason—

which would be a falsehood. And I studied Buddhism and Mohammedanism from books, and most of all I studied Christianity both from books and from the people around me.

Naturally I first of all turned to the Orthodox of my circle, to people who were learned: to Church theologians, monks, to theologians of the newest shade, and even to Evangelicals who profess salvation by belief in the Redemption. And I seized on these believers and questioned them as to their beliefs and their understanding of the meaning of life.

But though I made all possible concessions, and avoided all disputes, I could not accept the faith of these people. I saw that what they gave out as their faith did not explain the meaning of life but obscured it, and that they themselves affirm their belief not to answer that question of life which brought me to faith, but for some other aims alien to me.

I remember the painful feeling of fear of being thrown back into my former state of despair, after the hope I often and often experienced in my intercourse with these people.

The more fully they explained to me their doctrines, the more clearly did I perceive their error and realized that my hope of finding in their belief an explanation of the meaning of life was vain.

It was not that in their doctrines they mixed many unnecessary and unreasonable things with the Christian truths that had always been near to me: that was not what repelled me. I was repelled by the fact that these people's lives were like my own, with only this difference—that such a life did not correspond to the principles they expounded in their teachings. I clearly felt that they deceived themselves and that they, like myself, found no other meaning in life than to live while life lasts, taking all one's hands can seize. I saw this because if they had had a meaning which destroyed the fear of loss, suffering, and death, they would not have feared these things. But they, these believers of our circle, just like myself, living in sufficiency and superfluity, tried to increase or preserve them, feared privations, suffering, and death, and just like myself and all of us unbelievers, lived to satisfy their desires, and lived just as badly, if not worse, than the unbelievers.

No arguments could convince me of the truth of their faith. Only deeds which showed that they saw a meaning in life making what was so dreadful to me—poverty, sickness, and death—not dreadful to them, could convince me. And such deeds I did not see among the various believers in our circle. On the contrary, I saw such deeds done[1] by people of our circle who were the most unbelieving, but never by our so-called believers.

And I understood that the belief of these people was not the faith I sought, and that their faith is not a real faith but an epicurean consolation in life.

I understood that that faith may perhaps serve, if not for a consolation at least for some distraction for a repentant Solomon on his death-bed, but it cannot serve for the great majority of mankind, who are called on not to amuse themselves while consuming the labour of others but to create life.

For all humanity to be able to live, and continue to live attributing a meaning to life, they, those milliards, must have a different, a real, knowledge

[1] This passage is noteworthy as being one of the few references made by Tolstoy at this period to the revolutionary or 'Back-to-the-People' movement, in which many young men and women were risking and sacrificing home, property, and life itself from motives which had much in common with his own perception that the upper layers of Society are parasitic and prey on the vitals of the people who support them.—A.M.

of faith. Indeed, it was not the fact that we, with Solomon and Schopenhauer, did not kill ourselves that convinced me of the existence of faith, but the fact that those milliards of people have lived and are living, and have borne Solomon and us on the current of their lives.

And I began to draw near to the believers among the poor, simple, unlettered folk: pilgrims, monks, sectarians, and peasants. The faith of these common people was the same Christian faith as was professed by the pseudo-believers of our circle. Among them, too, I found a great deal of superstition mixed with the Christian truths; but the difference was that the superstitions of the believers of our circle were quite unnecessary to them and were not in conformity with their lives, being merely a kind of epicurean diversion; but the superstitions of the believers among the labouring masses conformed so with their lives that it was impossible to imagine them to oneself without those superstitions, which were a necessary condition of their life. The whole life of believers in our circle was a contradiction of their faith, but the whole life of the working-folk believers was a confirmation of the meaning of life which their faith gave them. And I began to look well into the life and faith of these people, and the more I considered it the more I became convinced that they have a real faith which is a necessity to them and alone gives their life a meaning and makes it possible for them to live. In contrast with what I had seen in our circle—where life without faith is possible and where hardly one in a thousand acknowledges himself to be a believer—among them there is hardly one unbeliever in a thousand. In contrast with what I had seen in our circle, where the whole of life is passed in idleness, amusement, and dissatisfaction, I saw that the whole life of these people was passed in heavy labour, and that they were content with life. In contradistinction to the way in which people of our circle oppose fate and complain of it on account of deprivations and sufferings, these people accepted illness and sorrow without any perplexity or opposition, and with a quiet and firm conviction that all is good. In contradistinction to us, who the wiser we are the less we understand the meaning of life, and see some evil irony in the fact that we suffer and die, these folk live and suffer, and they approach death and suffering with tranquillity and in most cases gladly. In contrast to the fact that a tranquil death, a death without horror and despair, is a very rare exception in our circle, a troubled, rebellious, and unhappy death is the rarest exception among the people. And such people, lacking all that for us and for Solomon is the only good of life and yet experiencing the greatest happiness, are a great multitude. I looked more widely around me. I considered the life of the enormous mass of the people in the past and the present. And of such people, understanding the meaning of life and able to live and to die, I saw not two or three, or tens, but hundreds, thousands, and millions. And they all—endlessly different in their manners, minds, education, and position, as they were—all alike, in complete contrast to my ignorance, knew the meaning of life and death, laboured quietly, endured deprivations and sufferings, and lived and died seeing therein not vanity but good.

And I learnt to love these people. The more I came to know their life, the life of those who are living and of others who are dead of whom I read and heard, the more I loved them and the easier it became for me to live. So I went on for about two years, and a change took place in me which had long been preparing and the promise of which had always been in me. It came about that the life of our circle, the rich and learned, not merely became distasteful to me, but lost all meaning in my eyes. All our actions, discussions, science and art, presented itself to me in a new light. I understood that it is all merely self-indulgence, and that to find a meaning in it is impossible; while the life of the whole labouring people, the whole of mankind who produce life, appeared to me in its true significance. I understood that *that* is life itself, and that the meaning given to that life is true: and I accepted it.

XI

AND remembering how those very beliefs had repelled me and had seemed meaningless when professed by people whose lives conflicted with them, and how these same beliefs attracted me and seemed reasonable when I saw that people lived in accord with them, I understood why I had then rejected those beliefs and found them meaningless, yet now accepted them and found them full of meaning. I understood that I had erred, and why I erred. I had erred not so much because I thought incorrectly as because I lived badly. I understood that it was not an error in my thought that had hid truth from me so much as my life itself in the exceptional conditions of epicurean gratification of desires in which I passed it. I understood that my question as to what my life is, and the answer—an evil—was quite correct. The only mistake was that the answer referred only to my life, while I had referred it to life in general. I asked myself what my life is, and got the reply: An evil and an absurdity. And really my life—a life of indulgence of desires—was senseless and evil, and therefore the reply, 'Life is evil and an absurdity', referred only to my life, but not to human life in general. I understood the truth which I afterwards found in the Gospels, 'that men loved darkness rather than the light, for their works were evil. For everyone that doeth ill hateth the light, and cometh not to the light, lest his works should be reproved.' I perceived that to understand the meaning of life it is necessary first that life should not be meaningless and evil, then we can apply reason to explain it. I understood why I had so long wandered round so evident a truth, and that if one is to think and speak of the life of mankind, one must think and speak of that life and not of the life of some of life's parasites. That truth was always as true as that two and two are four, but I had not acknowledged it, because on admitting two and two to be four I had also to admit that I was bad; and to feel myself to be good was for me more important and necessary than for two and two to be four. I came to love good people, hated myself, and confessed the truth. Now all became clear to me.

What if an executioner passing his whole life in torturing people and cutting off their heads, or a hopeless drunkard, or a madman settled for life in a dark room which he has fouled and imagines that he would perish if he left—what if he asked himself: 'What is life?' Evidently he could get no other reply to that question than that life is the greatest evil, and the madman's answer would be perfectly correct, but only as applied to himself. What if I am such a madman? What if all we rich and leisured people are such madmen? and I understood that we really are such madmen. I at any rate was certainly such.

And indeed a bird is so made that it must fly, collect food, and build a nest, and when I see that

a bird does this I have pleasure in its joy. A goat, a
hare, and a wolf are so made that they must feed
themselves, and must breed and feed their family,
and when they do so I feel firmly assured that they
are happy and that their life is a reasonable one.
Then what should a man do? He too should produce
his living as the animals do, but with this difference,
that he will perish if he does it alone; he must obtain
it not for himself but for all. And when he does that,
I have a firm assurance that he is happy and that
his life is reasonable. But what had I done during
the whole thirty years of my responsible life? Far
from producing sustenance for all, I did not even
produce it for myself. I lived as a parasite, and on
asking myself, what is the use of my life? I got the
reply: 'No use.' If the meaning of human life lies
in supporting it, how could I—who for thirty years
had been engaged not on supporting life but on
destroying it in myself and in others—how could I
obtain any other answer than that my life was
senseless and an evil? . . . It was both senseless and
evil.

The life of the world endures by someone's will—
by the life of the whole world and by our lives someone fulfils his purpose. To hope to understand the
meaning of that will one must first perform it by
doing what is wanted of us. But if I will not do what
is wanted of me, I shall never understand what is
wanted of me, and still less what is wanted of us all
and of the whole world.

If a naked, hungry beggar has been taken from
the cross-roads, brought into a building belonging
to a beautiful establishment, fed, supplied with
drink, and obliged to move a handle up and down,
evidently, before discussing why he was taken, why
he should move the handle, and whether the whole
establishment is reasonably arranged—the beggar

should first of all move the handle. If he moves the handle he will understand that it works a pump, that the pump draws water and that the water irrigates the garden beds; then he will be taken from the pumping station to another place where he will gather fruits and will enter into the joy of his master, and, passing from lower to higher work, will understand more and more of the arrangements of the establishment, and taking part in it will never think of asking why he is there, and will certainly not reproach the master.

So those who do his will, the simple, unlearned working folk, whom we regard as cattle, do not reproach the master; but we, the wise, eat the master's food but do not do what the master wishes, and instead of doing it sit in a circle and discuss: 'Why should that handle be moved? Isn't it stupid?' So we have decided. We have decided that the master is stupid, or does not exist, and that we are wise, only we feel that we are quite useless and that we must somehow do away with ourselves.

XII

THE consciousness of the error in reasonable knowledge helped me to free myself from the temptation of idle ratiocination. The conviction that knowledge of truth can only be found by living led me to doubt the rightness of my life; but I was saved only by the fact that I was able to tear myself from my exclusiveness and to see the real life of the plain working people, and to understand that it alone is real life. I understood that if I wish to understand life and its meaning, I must not live the life of a parasite, but must live a real life, and—taking the meaning given to life by real humanity and merging myself in that life—verify it.

During that time this is what happened to me. During that whole year, when I was asking myself almost every moment whether I should not end matters with a noose or a bullet—all that time, together with the course of thought and observation about which I have spoken, my heart was oppressed with a painful feeling, which I can only describe as a search for God.

I say that that search for God was not reasoning, but a feeling, because that search proceeded not from the course of my thoughts—it was even directly contrary to them—but proceeded from the heart. It was a feeling of fear, orphanage, isolation in a strange land, and a hope of help from someone.

Though I was quite convinced of the impossibility of proving the existence of a Deity (Kant had shown, and I quite understood him, that it could not be proved), I yet sought for God, hoped that I should find Him, and from old habit addressed prayers to that which I sought but had not found. I went over in my mind the arguments of Kant and Schopenhauer showing the impossibility of proving the existence of a God, and I began to verify those arguments and to refute them. Cause, said I to myself, is not a category of thought such as are Time and Space. If I exist, there must be some cause for it, and a cause of causes. And that first cause of all is what men have called 'God'. And I paused on that thought, and tried with all my being to recognize the presence of that cause. And as soon as I acknowledged that there is a force in whose power I am, I at once felt that I could live. But I asked myself: What is that cause, that force? How am I to think of it? What are my relations to that which I call 'God'? And only the familiar replies occurred to me: 'He is the Creator and Preserver.' This reply did not satisfy me, and I felt I was losing within me what I needed for my life. I became terrified and began to pray to Him whom I sought, that He should help me. But the more I prayed the more apparent it became to me that He did not hear me, and that there was no one to whom to address myself. And with despair in my heart that there is no God at all, I said: 'Lord, have mercy, save me! Lord, teach me!' But no one had mercy on me, and I felt that my life was coming to a standstill.

But again and again, from various sides, I returned to the same conclusion that I could not have come into the world without any cause or reason or meaning; I could not be such a fledgling fallen from its nest as I felt myself to be. Or, granting that I be such, lying on my back crying in the high grass, even then I cry because I know that a mother has borne me within her, has hatched me, warmed me, fed me, and loved me. Where is she—that mother? If I have been deserted, who has deserted me? I cannot hide from myself that someone bore me, loving me. Who was that someone? Again 'God'? He knows and sees my searching, my despair, and my struggle.

'He exists', said I to myself. And I had only for an instant to admit that, and at once life rose within me, and I felt the possibility and joy of being. But again, from the admission of the existence of a God I went on to seek my relation with Him; and again I imagined *that* God—our Creator in Three Persons who sent His Son, the Saviour—and again *that* God, detached from the world and from me, melted like a block of ice, melted before my eyes, and again nothing remained, and again the spring of life dried up within me, and I despaired and felt that I had nothing to do but to kill myself. And the worst of all was, that I felt I could not do it.

Not twice or three times, but tens and hundreds

of times, I reached those conditions, first of joy and animation, and then of despair and consciousness of the impossibility of living.

I remember that it was in early spring: I was alone in the wood listening to its sounds. I listened and thought ever of the same thing, as I had constantly done during those last three years. I was again seeking God.

'Very well, there is no God', said I to myself; 'there is no one who is not my imagination but a reality like my whole life. He does not exist, and no miracles can prove His existence, because the miracles would be my imagination, besides being irrational.

'But my *perception* of God, of Him whom I seek,' I asked myself, 'where has that perception come from?' And again at this thought the glad waves of life rose within me. All that was around me came to life and received a meaning. But my joy did not last long. My mind continued its work.

'The conception of God is not God', said I to myself. 'The conception is what takes place within me. The conception of God is something I can evoke or can refrain from evoking in myself. That is not what I seek. I seek that without which there can be no life.' And again all around me and within me began to die, and again I wished to kill myself.

But then I turned my gaze upon myself, on what went on within me, and I remembered all those cessations of life and reanimations that recurred within me hundreds of times. I remembered that I only lived at those times when I believed in God. As it was before, so it was now; I need only be aware of God to live; I need only forget Him, or disbelieve Him, and I died.

What is this animation and dying? I do not live when I lose belief in the existence of God. I should long ago have killed myself had I not had a dim hope of finding Him. I live, really live, only when I feel Him and seek Him. 'What more do you seek?' exclaimed a voice within me. 'This is He. He is that without which one cannot live. To know God and to live is one and the same thing. God is life.' 'Live seeking God, and then you will not live without God.' And more than ever before, all within me and around me lit up, and the light did not again abandon me.

And I was saved from suicide. When and how this change occurred I could not say. As imperceptibly and gradually the force of life in me had been destroyed and I had reached the impossibility of living, a cessation of life and the necessity of suicide, so imperceptibly and gradually did that force of life return to me. And strange to say the strength of life which returned to me was not new, but quite old—the same that had borne me along in my earliest days.

I quite returned to what belonged to my earliest childhood and youth. I returned to the belief in that Will which produced me and desires something of me. I returned to the belief that the chief and only aim of my life is to be better, i.e. to live in accord with that Will. And I returned to the belief that I can find the expression of that Will in what humanity, in the distant past hidden from me, has produced for its guidance: that is to say, I returned to a belief in God, in moral perfection, and in a tradition transmitting the meaning of life. There was only this difference, that then all this was accepted unconsciously, while now I knew that without it I could not live.

What happened to me was something like this: I was put into a boat (I do not remember when) and pushed off from an unknown shore, shown the direction to the opposite shore, had oars put into my unpractised hands, and was left alone. I rowed as best I could and moved forward; but the further I advanced towards the middle of the stream the more rapid grew the current bearing me away from my goal and the more frequently did I encounter others, like myself, borne away by the stream. There were a few rowers who continued to row, there were others who had abandoned their oars; there were large boats and immense vessels full of people. Some struggled against the current, others yielded to it. And the further I went the more, seeing the progress down the current of all those who were adrift, I forgot the direction given me. In the very centre of the stream, amid the crowd of boats and vessels which were being borne down stream, I quite lost my direction and abandoned my oars. Around me on all sides, with mirth and rejoicing, people with sails and oars were borne down the stream, assuring me and each other that no other direction was possible. And I believed them and floated with them. And I was carried far; so far that I heard the roar of the rapids in which I must be shattered, and I saw boats shattered in them. And I recollected myself. I was long unable to understand what had happened to me. I saw before me nothing but destruction, towards which I was rushing and which I feared. I saw no safety anywhere and did not know what to do; but, looking back, I perceived innumerable boats which unceasingly and strenuously pushed across the stream, and I remembered about the shore, the oars, and the direction, and began to pull back upwards against the stream and towards the shore.

That shore was God; that direction was tradition; the oars were the freedom given me to pull for the shore and unite with God. And so the force of life was renewed in me and I again began to live.

XIII

I TURNED from the life of our circle, acknowledging that ours is not life but a simulation of life—that the conditions of superfluity in which we live deprive us of the possibility of understanding life, and that in order to understand life I must understand not an exceptional life such as ours who are parasites on life, but the life of the simple labouring folk—those who make life—and the meaning which they attribute to it. The simplest labouring people around me were the Russian people, and I turned to them and to the meaning of life which they give. That meaning, if one can put it into words, was as follows: Every man has come into this world by the will of God. And God has so made man that every man can destroy his soul or save it. The aim of man in life is to save his soul, and to save his soul he must live 'godly' and to live 'godly' he must renounce all the pleasures of life, must labour, humble himself, suffer, and be merciful. That meaning the people obtain from the whole teaching of faith transmitted to them by their pastors and by the traditions that live among the people. This meaning was clear to me and near to my heart. But together with this meaning of the popular faith of our non-sectarian folk, among whom I live, much was inseparably bound up that revolted me and seemed to me inexplicable: sacraments, Church services, fasts, and the adoration of relics and icons. The people cannot separate the one from the other, nor could I. And strange as much of what entered into the faith of these people was to me, I accepted everything, and attended the services, knelt morning and evening in prayer, fasted, and prepared to receive the Eucharist: and at first my reason did not resist anything. The very things that had formerly seemed to me impossible did not now evoke in me any opposition.

My relations to faith before and after were quite different. Formerly life itself seemed to me full of meaning and faith presented itself as the arbitrary assertion of propositions to me quite unnecessary, unreasonable, and disconnected from life. I then asked myself what meaning those propositions had and, convinced that they had none, I rejected them. Now on the contrary I knew firmly that my life otherwise has, and can have, no meaning, and the articles of faith were far from presenting themselves to me as unnecessary—on the contrary I had been led by indubitable experience to the conviction that only these propositions presented by faith give life a meaning. Formerly I looked on them as on some quite unnecessary gibberish, but now, if I did not understand them, I yet knew that they had a meaning, and I said to myself that I must learn to understand them.

I argued as follows, telling myself that the knowledge of faith flows, like all humanity with its reason, from a mysterious source. That source is God, the origin both of the human body and the human reason. As my body has descended to me from God, so also has my reason and my understanding of life, and consequently the various stages of the development of that understanding of life cannot be false. All that people sincerely believe in must be true; it may be differently expressed but it cannot be a lie, and therefore if it presents itself to me as a lie, that only means that I have not und stood it. Furthermore I said to myself, the esse ce of every faith consists in its giving life a meaning which death does not destroy. Naturally for a faith to be able to reply to the questions of a king dying in luxury, of an old slave tormented by overwork, of an unreasoning child, of a wise old man, of a half-witted old woman, of a young and happy wife, of a youth tormented by passions, of all people in the most varied conditions of life and education—if there is one reply to the one eternal question of life: 'Why do I live and what will result from my life?'—the reply, though one in its essence, must be endlessly varied in its presentation; and the more it is one, the more true and profound it is, the more strange and deformed must it naturally appear in its attempted expression, conformably to the education and position of each person. But this argument, justifying in my eyes the queerness of much on the ritual side of religion, did not suffice to allow me in the one great affair of life—religion—to do things which seemed to me questionable. With all my soul I wished to be in a position to mingle with the people, fulfilling the ritual side of their religion; but I could not do it. I felt that I should lie to myself and mock at what was sacred to me, were I to do so. At this point, however, our new Russian theological writers came to my rescue.

According to the explanation these theologians gave, the fundamental dogma of our faith is the infallibility of the Church. From the admission of that dogma follows inevitably the truth of all that is professed by the Church. The Church as an assembly of true believers united by love and therefore possessed of true knowledge became the basis of my belief. I told myself that divine truth cannot be accessible to a separate individual; it is revealed only to the whole assembly of people united by love. To attain truth one must not separate, and in order not to separate one must love and must endure things one may not agree with.

Truth reveals itself to love, and if you do not submit to the rites of the Church you transgress against love; and by transgressing against love you deprive yourself of the possibility of recognizing the truth. I did not then see the sophistry contained in this argument. I did not see that union in love may give the greatest love, but certainly cannot give us divine truth expressed in the definite words of the Nicene Creed. I also did not perceive that love cannot make a certain expression of truth an obligatory condition of union. I did not then see these mistakes in the argument and thanks to it was able to accept and perform all the rites of the Orthodox Church without understanding most of them. I then tried with all the strength of my soul to avoid all arguments and contradictions, and tried to explain as reasonably as possible the Church statements I encountered.

When fulfilling the rites of the Church I humbled my reason and submitted to the tradition possessed by all humanity. I united myself with my fore-fathers: the father, mother, and grandparents I loved. They and all my predecessors believed and lived, and they produced me. I united myself also with the millions of the common people whom I respected. Moreover, those actions had nothing bad in themselves ('bad' I considered the indulgence of one's desires). When rising early for Church services I knew I was doing well, if only because I was sacrificing my bodily ease to humble my mental pride, for the sake of union with my ancestors and contemporaries, and for the sake of finding the meaning of life. It was the same with my preparations to receive Communion, and with the daily reading of prayers with genuflections, and also with the observance of all the fasts. However insignificant these sacrifices might be I made them for the sake of something good. I fasted, prepared for Communion, and observed the fixed hours of prayer at home and in church. During Church service I attended to every word, and gave them a meaning whenever I could. In the Mass the most important words for me were: 'Let us love one another in conformity!' The further words, 'In unity we believe in the Father, the Son, and Holy Ghost', I passed by, because I could not understand them.

XIV

IT was then so necessary for me to believe in order to live that I unconsciously concealed from myself the contradictions and obscurities of theology. But this reading of meanings into the rites had its limits. If the chief words in the prayer for the Emperor became more and more clear to me, if I found some explanation for the words 'and remembering our Sovereign Most-Holy Mother of God and all the Saints, ourselves and one another, we give our whole life to Christ our God', if I explained to myself the frequent repetition of prayers for the Tsar and his relations by the fact that they are more exposed to temptations than other people and therefore are more in need of being prayed for—the prayers about subduing our enemies and evil under our feet (even if one tried to say that *sin* was the enemy prayed against), these and other prayers, such as the 'cherubic song' and the whole sacrament of the oblation, or 'the chosen warriors', &c.— quite two-thirds of all the services—either remained completely incomprehensible or, when I forced an explanation into them, made me feel that I was lying, thereby quite destroying my relation to God and depriving me of all possibility of belief.

I felt the same about the celebration of the chief holidays. To remember the Sabbath, that is to devote one day to God, was something I could understand. But the chief holiday was in commemoration of the Resurrection, the reality of which I could not picture to myself or understand. And that name of 'Resurrection' was also given to the weekly holiday.[1] And on those days the Sacrament of the Eucharist was administered, which was quite unintelligible to me. The rest of the twelve great holidays, except Christmas, commemorated miracles—the things I tried not to think about in order not to deny: the Ascension, Pentecost, Epiphany, the Feast of the Intercession of the Holy Virgin, &c. At the celebration of these holidays, feeling that importance was being attributed to the very things that to me presented a negative importance, I either devised tranquillizing explanations or shut my eyes in order not to see what tempted me.

Most of all this happened to me when taking part in the most usual Sacraments, which are considered the most important: baptism and communion. There I encountered not incomprehensible but fully comprehensible doings: doings which seemed to me to lead into temptation, and I was in a dilemma—whether to lie or to reject them.

Never shall I forget the painful feeling I experienced the day I received the Eucharist for the first time after many years. The service, confession, and prayers were quite intelligible and produced in me a glad consciousness that the meaning of life was being revealed to me. The Communion itself I explained as an act performed in remembrance of Christ, and indicating a purification from sin and the full acceptance of Christ's teaching. If that explanation was artificial I did not notice its artificiality: so happy was I at humbling and abasing myself before the priest—a simple, timid country clergyman—turning all the dirt out of my

[1] In Russia Sunday was called Resurrection-day.—A.M.

soul and confessing my vices, so glad was I to merge in thought with the humility of the fathers who wrote the prayers of the office, so glad was I of union with all who have believed and now believe, that I did not notice the artificiality of my explanation. But when I approached the altar gates, and the priest made me say that I believed that what I was about to swallow was truly flesh and blood, I felt a pain in my heart: it was not merely a false note, it was a cruel demand made by someone or other who evidently had never known what faith is.

I now permit myself to say that it was a cruel demand, but I did not then think so: only it was indescribably painful to me. I was no longer in the position in which I had been in youth when I thought all in life was clear; I had indeed come to faith because, apart from faith, I had found nothing, certainly nothing, except destruction; therefore to throw away that faith was impossible and I submitted. And I found in my soul a feeling which helped me to endure it. This was the feeling of self-abasement and humility. I humbled myself, swallowed that flesh and blood without any blasphemous feelings and with a wish to believe. But the blow had been struck and, knowing what awaited me, I could not go a second time.

I continued to fulfil the rites of the Church and still believed that the doctrine I was following contained the truth, when something happened to me which I now understand but which then seemed strange.

I was listening to the conversation of an illiterate peasant, a pilgrim, about God, faith, life, and salvation, when a knowledge of faith revealed itself to me. I drew near to the people, listening to their opinions on life and faith, and I understood the truth more and more. So also was it when I read the Lives of Holy Men, which became my favourite books. Putting aside the miracles and regarding them as fables illustrating thoughts, this reading revealed to me life's meaning. There were the lives of Makarius the Great, the story of Buddha, there were the words of St. John Chrysostom, and there were the stories of the traveller in the well, the monk who found some gold, and of Peter the publican. There were stories of the martyrs, all announcing that death does not exclude life, and there were the stories of ignorant, stupid men, who knew nothing of the teaching of the Church but who yet were saved.

But as soon as I met learned believers or took up their books, doubt of myself, dissatisfaction, and exasperated disputation were roused within me, and I felt that the more I entered into the meaning of these men's speech, the more I went astray from truth and approached an abyss.

XV

How often I envied the peasants their illiteracy and lack of learning! Those statements in the creeds which to me were evident absurdities, for them contained nothing false; they could accept them and could believe in the truth—the truth I believed in. Only to me, unhappy man, was it clear that with truth falsehood was interwoven by finest threads, and that I could not accept it in that form.

So I lived for about three years. At first, when I was only slightly associated with truth as a catechumen and was only scenting out what seemed to me clearest, these encounters struck me less. When I did not understand anything, I said, 'It is my fault,

I am sinful'; but the more I became imbued with the truths I was learning, the more they became the basis of my life, the more oppressive and the more painful became these encounters and the sharper became the line between what I do not understand because I am not able to understand it, and what cannot be understood except by lying to oneself.

In spite of my doubts and sufferings I still clung to the Orthodox Church. But questions of life arose which had to be decided; and the decision of these questions by the Church—contrary to the very bases of the belief by which I lived—obliged me at last to renounce communion with Orthodoxy as impossible. These questions were: first the relation of the Orthodox Eastern Church to other Churches—to the Catholics and to the so-called sectarians. At that time, in consequence of my interest in religion, I came into touch with believers of various faiths: Catholics, Protestants, Old-Believers, Molokáns,[1] and others. And I met among them many men of lofty morals who were truly religious. I wished to be a brother to them. And what happened? That teaching which promised to unite all in one faith and love—that very teaching, in the person of its best representatives, told me that these men were all living a lie; that what gave them their power of life was a temptation of the devil; and that we alone possess the only possible truth. And I saw that all who do not profess an identical faith with themselves are considered by the Orthodox to be heretics, just as the Catholics and others consider the Orthodox to be heretics. And I saw that the Orthodox (though they try to hide this) regard with hostility all who do not express their faith by the same external symbols and

---

[1] A sect that rejects sacraments and ritual.

words as themselves; and this is naturally so: first, because the assertion that you are in falsehood and I am in truth, is the most cruel thing one man can say to another; and secondly, because a man loving his children and brothers cannot help being hostile to those who wish to pervert his children and brothers to a false belief. And that hostility is increased in proportion to one's greater knowledge of theology. And to me who considered that truth lay in union by love, it became self-evident that theology was itself destroying what it ought to produce.

This offence is so obvious to us educated people who have lived in countries where various religions are professed and have seen the contempt, self-assurance, and invincible contradiction with which Catholics behave to the Orthodox Greeks and to the Protestants, and the Orthodox to Catholics and Protestants, and the Protestants to the two others, and the similar attitude of Old-Believers, Páshko-vites (Russian Evangelicals), Shakers, and all religions—that the very obviousness of the temptation at first perplexes us. One says to oneself: it is impossible that it is so simple and that people do not see that if two assertions are mutually contradictory, then neither of them has the sole truth which faith should possess. There is something else here, there must be some explanation. I thought there was, and sought that explanation and read all I could on the subject, and consulted all whom I could. And no one gave me any explanation, except the one which causes the Súmsky Hussars to consider the Súmsky Hussars the best regiment in the world, and the Yellow Uhlans to consider that the best regiment in the world is the Yellow Uhlans. The ecclesiastics of all the different creeds, through their best representatives, told me nothing but that they believed themselves to have the truth and the others to be in error, and that all they could do was to pray for them. I went to archimandrites, bishops, elders, monks of the strictest orders, and asked them; but none of them made any attempt to explain the matter to me except one man, who explained it all and explained it so that I never asked any one any more about it. I said that for every unbeliever turning to belief (and all our young generation are in a position to do so) the question that presents itself first is, why is truth not in Lutheranism nor in Catholicism, but in Orthodoxy? Educated in the high school he cannot help knowing—what the peasants do not know—that the Protestants and Catholics equally affirm that their faith is the only true one. Historical evidence, twisted by each religion in its own favour, is insufficient. Is it not possible, said I, to understand the teaching in a loftier way, so that from its height the differences should disappear, as they do for one who believes truly? Can we not go further along a path like the one we are following with the Old-Believers? They emphasize the fact that they have a differently shaped cross and different alleluias and a different procession round the altar. We reply: You believe in the Nicene Creed, in the seven sacraments, and so do we. Let us hold to that, and in other matters do as you please. We have united with them by placing the essentials of faith above the unessentials. Now with the Catholics can we not say: You believe in so and so and in so and so, which are the chief things, and as for the Filioque clause and the Pope—do as you please. Can we not say the same to the Protestants, uniting with them in what is most important?

My interlocutor agreed with my thoughts, but told me that such concessions would bring reproach on the spiritual authorities for deserting the faith of our forefathers, and this would produce a schism; and the vocation of the spiritual authorities is to safeguard in all its purity the Greco-Russian Orthodox faith inherited from our forefathers.

And I understood it all. I am seeking a faith, the power of life; and they are seeking the best way to fulfil in the eyes of men certain human obligations. And fulfilling these human affairs they fulfil them in a human way. However much they may talk of their pity for their erring brethren, and of addressing prayers for them to the throne of the Almighty— to carry out human purposes violence is necessary, and it has always been applied and is and will be applied. If of two religions each considers itself true and the other false, then men desiring to attract others to the truth will preach their own doctrine. And if a false teaching is preached to the inexperienced sons of their Church—which has the truth—then that Church cannot but burn the books and remove the man who is misleading its sons. What is to be done with a sectarian—burning, in the opinion of the Orthodox, with the fire of false doctrine—who in the most important affair of life, in faith, misleads the sons of the Church? What can be done with him except to cut off his head or to incarcerate him? Under the Tsar Aléxis Mikháylovich people were burned at the stake, that is to say, the severest method of punishment of the time was applied, and in our day also the severest method of punishment is applied—detention in solitary confinement.[1]

And I turned my attention to what is done in the name of religion and was horrified, and I almost entirely abjured Orthodoxy.

[1] At the time this was written capital punishment was considered to be abolished in Russia.—A.M.

The second relation of the Church to a question of life was with regard to war and executions.

At that time Russia was at war. And Russians, in the name of Christian love, began to kill their fellow men. It was impossible not to think about this, and not to see that killing is an evil repugnant to the first principles of any faith. Yet prayers were said in the churches for the success of our arms, and the teachers of the Faith acknowledged killing to be an act resulting from the Faith. And besides the murders during the war, I saw, during the disturbances which followed the war, Church dignitaries and teachers and monks of the lesser and stricter orders who approved the killing of helpless, erring youths. And I took note of all that is done by men who profess Christianity, and I was horrified.

XVI

AND I ceased to doubt, and became fully convinced that not all was true in the religion I had joined. Formerly I should have said that it was all false, but I could not say so now. The whole of the people possessed a knowledge of the truth, for otherwise they could not have lived. Moreover, that knowledge was accessible to me, for I had felt it and had lived by it. But I no longer doubted that there was also falsehood in it. And all that had previously repelled me now presented itself vividly before me. And though I saw that among the peasants there was a smaller admixture of the lies that repelled me than among the representatives of the Church, I still saw that in the people's belief also falsehood was mingled with the truth.

But where did the truth and where did the falsehood come from? Both the falsehood and the truth were contained in the so-called holy tradition and in the Scriptures. Both the falsehood and the truth had been handed down by what is called the Church.

And whether I liked or not, I was brought to the study and investigation of these writings and traditions—which till now I had been so afraid to investigate.

And I turned to the examination of that same theology which I had once rejected with such contempt as unnecessary. Formerly it seemed to me a series of unnecessary absurdities, when on all sides I was surrounded by manifestations of life which seemed to me clear and full of sense; now I should have been glad to throw away what would not enter a healthy head, but I had nowhere to turn to. On this teaching religious doctrine rests, or at least with it the only knowledge of the meaning of life that I have found is inseparably connected. However wild it may seem to my firm old mind, it was the only hope of salvation. It had to be carefully, attentively examined in order to understand it, and not even to understand it as I understand the propositions of science: I do not seek that, nor can I seek it, knowing the special character of religious knowledge. I shall not seek the explanation of everything. I know that the explanation of everything, like the commencement of everything, must be concealed in infinity. But I wish to understand in a way which will bring me to what is inevitably inexplicable. I wish to recognize anything that is inexplicable as being so not because the demands of my reason are wrong (they are right, and apart from them I can understand nothing), but because I recognize the limits of my intellect. I wish to understand in such a way that everything that is inexplicable shall present itself to me as being necessarily inexplicable, and not as being something I am under an arbitrary obligation to believe.

That there is truth in the teaching is to me indubitable, but it is also certain that there is falsehood in it, and I must find what is true and what is false, and must disentangle the one from the other. I am setting to work upon this task. What of falsehood I have found in the teaching and what I have found of truth, and to what conclusions I came, will form the following parts of this work, which if it be worth it and if anyone wants it, will probably some day be printed somewhere.

1879.

The foregoing was written by me some three years ago, and will be printed.

Now, a few days ago, when revising it and returning to the line of thought and to the feelings I had when I was living through it all, I had a dream. This dream expressed in condensed form all that I had experienced and described, and I think therefore that, for those who have understood me, a description of this dream will refresh and elucidate and unify what has been set forth at such length in the foregoing pages. The dream was this:

I saw that I was lying on a bed. I was neither comfortable nor uncomfortable: I was lying on my back. But I began to consider how, and on what, I was lying—a question which had not till then occurred to me. And observing my bed, I saw I was lying on plaited string supports attached to its sides: my feet were resting on one such support, my calves on another, and my legs felt uncomfortable. I seemed to know that those supports were movable, and with a movement of my foot I pushed away the furthest of them at my feet—it seemed to me that it would be more comfortable so. But I pushed it away too far and wished to reach it again with my foot, and that movement caused the next support under my calves to slip away also, so that my legs hung in the air. I made a movement with my whole body to adjust myself, fully convinced that I could do so at once; but the movement caused the other supports under me to slip and to become entangled, and I saw that matters were going quite wrong: the whole of the lower part of my body slipped and hung down, though my feet did not reach the ground. I was holding on only by the upper part of my back, and not only did it become uncomfortable but I was even frightened. And then only did I ask myself about something that had not before occurred to me. I asked myself: Where am I and what am I lying on? and I began to look around, and first of all to look down in the direction in which my body was hanging and whither I felt I must soon fall. I looked down and did not believe my eyes. I was not only at a height comparable to the height of the highest towers or mountains, but at a height such as I could never have imagined.

I could not even make out whether I saw anything there below, in that bottomless abyss over which I was hanging and whither I was being drawn. My heart contracted, and I experienced horror. To look thither was terrible. If I looked thither I felt that I should at once slip from the last support and perish. And I did not look. But not to look was still worse, for I thought of what would happen to me directly I fell from the last support. And I felt that from fear I was losing my last supports, and that my back was slowly slipping lower and lower. Another moment and I should drop off. And then it occurred to me that this cannot be real. It is a dream. Wake up! I try

CONCLUSION

OF *A CRITICISM OF DOGMATIC THEOLOGY*

SO this is the full disclosure of the God-revealed truth. Everything has been disclosed and there is nothing more, and it must not be otherwise understood. He who understands it otherwise is anathema, 'without doubt he shall perish ever-lastingly'.

A man asks: What is this whole world in which I find myself? He asks what sense there is in his existence and by what he is to guide himself in the freedom he is conscious of within him. He asks that, and God by the mouth of the Church He has established, gives him this reply:

You want to know what this world is? It is this: There is one God, all-knowing, all-good, and almighty. He is simply a spirit, but He has will and reason. This God is one, and at the same time three. The Father begot a Son, and the Son is in the flesh, but sits at the right hand of His Father. The Holy Spirit proceeded from the Father.[1] All three of them are God, and they are all different and are all one. This triune God had existed always, one in three, and suddenly thought of creating the world, and He made it out of nothing by His thought, wish, and word. He first created a spiritual world of angels. The angels were created good and God created them solely for their own happiness, but having been created good these beings suddenly, of themselves, became wicked. Some of them remained good, others turned wicked and became devils. God created very many angels

[1] In the Western Church from the Father and the Son.—A.M.

and divided them into nine ranks and three orders:[1] Angels, Archangels, Cherubim, Seraphim, Hosts, Rulers, Authorities, Powers, and Thrones. The devils are also divided into ranks, but the names of these ranks are not precisely known.

Then much time passed and God again began to create, and made the material world. He made it in six days. A day must be understood as the time during which the earth turns on its axis. There was a morning and an evening for the first day. If there was no sun during the first days, God Himself shook the illuminatory matter that there might be a morning and an evening. God worked at creation during six days, and on the sixth He created Adam, the first man, out of earth, and breathed a soul into him; then he made a woman. Man was created with soul and body and his destiny was to remain faithful to God's power. He was created good and quite perfect, and his whole duty was to refrain from eating a forbidden fruit. Besides having created him perfect God helped him in every way—teaching him, giving him pleasure, and visiting him in the garden. But in spite of that, Adam ate the forbidden fruit, and for that the merciful God revenged Himself on Adam, drove him out of paradise, and cursed him and all his descendants and the whole earth.

All this has to be understood not in some metaphorical sense but in its literal meaning, as having actually occurred.

After that God, this same God in three persons, all-knowing, all-good, and almighty, having created Adam and cursed him and all his progeny, still continued to provide for—that is to care for—the welfare of Adam and his progeny and all created

---

[1] This enumeration follows the classification adopted by the Eastern Church.—A.M.

beings. He preserved His creatures, co-operated with them, and ruled over them one and all.

This God directed and directs the good and bad angels and the good and bad men. The angels also assist God in ruling the world: there are angels attached to kingdoms, to nations, and to individuals. And God the all-knowing, almighty, and ever-beneficent, having created them all, cast down a multitude of bad angels for ever and cursed all men because of Adam, but did not cease to care for all men and to do so in natural and even in supernatural ways.

The supernatural way of caring for men was that when five thousand years had passed He found a method of repaying Himself for Adam's sin (He who had Himself made Adam such as he was). The method was thus: Among the persons of the Trinity was the Son. He, that person, had always been the Son. This Son was born of a virgin without infringing her virginity: the Holy Ghost entered the Virgin Mary as her husband, and the Son, Christ, emerged. This Son was called Jesus, and He was God, and a man, and a person of the Trinity. And this God-man saved mankind. This is the way He saved it: He was a prophet, a high priest, and a king. As a prophet He gave them a new law, as high priest He offered Himself up in sacrifice by dying on a cross, and as a king He performed miracles and descended into hell, released all the righteous who were there, and destroyed sin, the curse, and death in men. But this method, powerful as it was, did not save everybody. A multitude of devils still remained devils, and to avail themselves of that means of salvation men have to do it skilfully.

To avail himself of that means a man must be sanctified, and only the Church can sanctify him;

and the Church is that body of men who say about
themselves that certain men have laid their hands
on men on whom the hands of other men have been
laid, and so on till we reach those on whom were
laid the hands of the pupils of the God Jesus Himself, on whom the Saviour, God the Son Himself,
had laid His hands. And when laying on hands,
God Himself breathed on them and by that
act of breathing gave to them and to all to
whom they might transmit it the power to sanctify
men, and that same sanctification is necessary in
order to be saved. This which saves is called grace;
it sanctifies and saves a man, and it is a divine power
transmitted in certain ceremonies by the Church.
That this blessing should be efficacious it is necessary
that the man who wishes to be sanctified should
believe that he is being sanctified. He may even
not quite believe it, but must obey the Church and
above all not contradict, then grace will be transmitted. In his life the man sanctified by grace must
not think, as he had thought before, that if he does
right it is because he wished to do right; he must
think that if he does anything right it is because
grace operates in him, and so he must only be careful to have that grace in him. That grace is transmitted by the Church by various manipulations
and by pronouncing certain words which are called
sacraments. There are seven such manipulations.

1. Baptism. When a priest of the Church bathes
someone properly,[1] that person becomes cleansed
from all sin and above all from the original sin of
Adam. If an unbaptized infant dies, being full of
sins, it perishes.

2. When a man is smeared with oil the Holy
Ghost enters into him.

[1] In the Orthodox Russo-Greek Church baptism is by
immersion.—A.M.

3. When he eats bread and drinks wine under certain conditions and with the conviction that he is eating the body and drinking the blood of God, he becomes cleansed from sin and receives eternal life. (In general there is a lot of grace connected with this sacrament, and as quickly as possible after it has been received one should pray, and then, as a result of the blessing, the prayer will be heard according to the grace.)

4. When a priest has heard a man's sins and says certain words, the sins are gone.

5. When seven priests smear a man with oil his bodily and spiritual maladies are cured.[1]

6. When wreaths are put on a bridal couple, grace enters into them.

7. When hands are laid on, the gift of the Holy Ghost enters a man.

Baptism, anointing, confession, and receiving the eucharist sanctify a man, and do so always independently of the spiritual condition of the priest or the recipient of the sacrament, if only it is all done duly and there is no ground for its cassation.

In these manipulations lie the means of redemption which God has devised. He who believes that he is sanctified and cleansed and will receive eternal life, is actually sanctified and cleansed and will have eternal life. All those who believe in this receive a reward, first a personal one immediately after death, and later a general one after the end of the world. The believers' personal reward is that they will be glorified on earth and in heaven. On earth their relics and icons will be honoured with incense and candles, and in heaven they will be with Christ in His glory. But before attaining this they will pass through aerial spaces where they will be

[1] This again refers to a rite practised in the Orthodox Russo-Greek Church.—A.M.

stopped and questioned by angels and devils who will contend for them. Those for whom the angels' defence is stronger than the accusations of the devils, will reach paradise, but those whom the devils win will go into eternal torments in hell. The righteous, those who go to paradise, will there occupy various positions and those who are nearer to the Trinity will be able there in paradise to pray for us to God, and so here we must worship their relics, their garments, and their icons. These objects work miracles and we should say our prayers to God near them, and then the righteous up there will plead for us. Sinners—all heretics, the un-baptized people, the unbelievers, and those who do not receive the eucharist—will go to hell, to the devils, but they will occupy different places there according to the degree of their guilt, and they will be there till the end of the world. The prayers of priests, especially if uttered immediately after the eucharist, may mitigate their condition in hell.

But there is also to be an end of the world and a general judgement. The end of the world will be like this: One of the persons of the Trinity, the God Jesus who is sitting in fleshly form on the clouds at the right hand of the Father, will come down to earth in the human form in which He lived here. Angels will blow trumpets and all the dead will rise in their own bodies, but those bodies will be slightly changed. Then all the angels and devils, and all men, will be gathered together and Christ will judge them. The righteous will be set apart on the right hand: they and the angels will go to paradise. The sinners will be put on the left hand: they and the devils will go to hell and will there be tormented for ever with torments worse than burning. These torments will be everlasting. But the righteous will for ever glorify God's mercy.

In reply to my question, what meaning has my life in this world?—the answer is:

God, for a whim, created a strange sort of world. An absurd God—half man, half monster—created the world as He wished it, and such a man as He pleased, and kept saying that it was good, that it was all good, and that man was good. But it all turned out very bad. The man and all his progeny fell under a curse, but the good God continued to create men in the wombs of their mothers knowing that they all, or many of them, would perish. And after He had devised a means of saving them, things remained the same, or even worse: for previously, as the Church tells us, men could, like Abraham and Jacob, save themselves by their good lives, while now, if I am born a Jew or a Buddhist and do not happen to come under the sanctifying action of the Church, I shall certainly perish and be eternally tormented by the devils. More than that, even if I am one of the lucky ones, but have the misfortune to consider the demands of my reason legitimate and do not renounce them in order to believe the Church teaching, I too must perish. And besides, even if I believe it all but have had no time to receive the last eucharist, and my relations absent-mindedly omit to have prayers said for me, I may still go to hell and remain there.

The meaning of my life according to this teaching is an utter absurdity, incomparably worse than what presented itself to me by the light of my unaided reason. Then I saw that I am alive and as long as I live I enjoy life, and that when I die I shall no longer feel anything. Then I was frightened by the senselessness of my personal life and the insolubility of the question: What are my efforts and my life for, since it will all end? But now it is still worse: it will not all end—all this senselessness, this caprice of someone's, will continue for ever.

To the question as to how I should live, the reply given by this teaching also contradicts all that my moral feelings require, and demands what has always seemed to me most immoral—namely, hypocrisy. From all the moral applications of the dogmas only this emerges: save yourself by faith. If you cannot understand what you are told to believe, say that you believe it. With all the strength of your soul suppress the demand for light and truth: say that you believe, and do what results from that belief. The matter is plain. In spite of all provisos that for some reason it is necessary to do good works and to follow Christ's teaching about love, meekness, humility, and self-sacrifice, it is evident that those deeds are not necessary, and the life of believers confirms this. Logic is inexorable. What is the use of works when I am redeemed by the death of a God, when even my future sins are all redeemed, and when it is only necessary to believe? And how can I struggle and strive towards goodness—which I formerly understood to consist in good deeds alone—when the chief dogma of the faith is that man can of himself do nothing, but all is done of itself by grace? It is only necessary to seek for grace; but grace is not obtained by me alone, it is imparted to me by others. Even if I have not time to become sanctified by grace during my lifetime there is a way to avail myself of it after death. I can leave money to the Church and I shall be prayed for. All that is asked of me is that I should seek for grace. But grace is given by the sacraments and the prayers of the Church, so I must fly to it and place myself so as never to be deprived of them. I must have priests around me, or live in a monastery, and leave as much money as possible for prayers for my soul. More than that, having insured myself for the future life I may calmly enjoy this one, and for this life make use of those instruments which the Church offers me, praying to the providence of God for aid in my worldly affairs in the ways indicated to me to make these prayers most efficacious. Prayers are more efficacious when uttered near to icons and relics and during a religious service.

And the answer to my question as to what I should do follows clearly from the teaching, and that answer is very well known to everyone and very coarsely contradicts one's conscience; but it is inescapable.

I remember that when I did not yet doubt the Church teaching and read in the Gospel that 'Blasphemy against the son of man shall be forgiven, but blasphemy against the Holy Spirit shall not be forgiven either in this world or in the world to come', I could not at all understand those words.

But now they are only too terribly clear to me. This is it—that blasphemy against the Holy Spirit, which will not be forgiven either in this world or in the world to come.

That blasphemy is this terrible doctrine, the basis of which is the teaching about the Church.

INTRODUCTION TO AN EXAMINATION OF THE GOSPELS

HAVING by reason been brought to despair and a negation of life, I looked around on living people and became convinced that such despair is not the common lot of mankind, but that men have lived, and do live, by faith.

I saw around me men who had that faith and drew a meaning of life from it which gave them strength to live and die peacefully and joyfully, but my reason could not explain that meaning to me. I tried to arrange my life as those believers did, tried to unite with them, doing all that they did in life and in the external worship of God, thinking that in that way the meaning of life would disclose itself to me. The more I came together with the peasants and lived like them, practising all the external rites of divine worship, the more I became conscious of two contradictory forces acting upon me. On the one hand I became conscious of a meaning of life that satisfied me and was not destroyed by the approach of death; while on the other hand I saw much that was false in that external profession of faith and that worship of God. I understood that the masses, from their ignorance, lack of leisure, and disinclination to think, might not see that falsehood; but I could not help seeing it, and having once seen it could not close my eyes to it, as educated believers advised me to do. The longer I continued to fulfil the obligations of a believer the more did that falsity startle me and demand an investigation of where falsity ended and truth began; for I no longer doubted that the very truth of life was contained in the Christian teaching. My inner discord finally reached such a pitch that I could no longer intentionally close my eyes, as I had done before, but was inevitably compelled to investigate the religious doctrine I wished to make my own.

At first I asked priests, monks, bishops, metropolitans, and learned theologians, for explanations. Explanations of all the obscure passages were given, but these were often unscrupulous and still oftener contradictory, and they were all based on the holy fathers, the catechisms, and theology. So I took the theological books and began to study them, and that study led me to the conviction that the faith our hierarchy professes and teaches to the people is not only false but is an immoral deception.

In the Orthodox doctrine I found no teaching at all about life or its meaning, but found instead the exposition of most incomprehensible, blasphemous, and shocking propositions, not merely incompatible with reason, but quite incomprehensible and contrary to morality. And I could not help seeing that this theological exposition was evidently directed not towards explaining the meaning of life and teaching how it should be lived, but merely to asserting very incomprehensible and to me unnecessary propositions, and to the repudiation of all who do not accept those propositions. This exposition, directed to the denial of other doctrines, involuntarily caused me to direct my attention to those other creeds, and these other disputed creeds turned out to be of the same character as the Orthodox teaching which refuted them. Some are more absurd, others less so, but all alike affirm incomprehensible propositions which are useless for life, and in their name deny one another and infringe the unity of men, *the chief basis of Christian teaching*.

I was brought to the conviction that there is no

Church at all. Christians of all denominations call themselves true Christians and repudiate the others, and each of these separate collections of Christians calls itself alone the Church, and assures us that it is the true one from which the others have separated and fallen away, and that it alone remains erect. All the believers of the different sects quite fail to see that their creed is not the true one because their faith has remained such and such, but that they call it true because they were born into it or have adopted it, and that the others say just the same about their creeds. So it is evident that there never has been some one Church, that the Church is not one, or two, but two thousand, and that each denies all the others and asserts that it alone is the true and only Church. Each of them says one and the same thing: 'Ours is the True, Holy, Catholic, Apostolic, and Universal Church. Our Scripture is sacred and our traditions are sacred. Jesus Christ is the Head of our Church and the Holy Ghost guides it, and it alone comes by direct succession from Christ—that is from God.'

If one takes any twig of a spreading bush it will be quite correct to say that from twig to branch, and from branch to limb, and from limb to trunk, every part is derived from the root, but none of them is exclusively so derived. To say of any particular twig that it is the only true twig would be absurd. Yet that is just what is said by the Churches.

Indeed there are a thousand traditions and each denies and curses the others and regards its own as the true one: Catholics, Lutherans, Protestants, Calvinists, Shakers, Mormons, Orthodox-Greeks, Old-Believers, the Popóvtsi, the Priestless, the Molokáni, the Menonites, the Baptists, the Mutilators, the Dukhobórs, and the rest—and they all alike declare that their own faith is the only true one, that in it alone is the Holy Spirit present, that its head is Christ, and that all the others are in error. There are a thousand faiths, and each calmly considers itself alone holy. And they all know this, and each man who declares his faith to be the only true one knows that another faith quite similarly regards itself as true and all the others as heresies. And for nearly eighteen hundred years this self-delusion has been and still is going on.

In worldly matters men know how to detect and avoid most ingenious pitfalls, but millions of men have lived for eighteen hundred years in this deception, shutting their eyes to it, and in our European world and in America (where everything is done in a new way) everybody as if by agreement repeats one and the same stupid deception: each professing his own faith, considering it to be the only true one, and not noticing that people of all the other creeds are doing exactly the same.

Yet free-thinkers ridiculed this stupidity acutely and cleverly long long ago, and clearly showed how inane it is. They clearly showed that this whole Christian teaching with all its ramifications has long since outlived its day and that the time has come for a new faith, and some of them have even invented new faiths, but nobody listens to them or follows them, and people all continue each to believe in his own special Christian faith as before: the Catholics theirs, the Lutherans theirs, our sectarian-Popóvtsi theirs, the Priestless theirs, the Mormons theirs, the Molokáns theirs, and the Orthodox Russo-Greeks (whom I wished to join) theirs.

What does this mean? Why do men not abandon that teaching? The one answer—in which the free-thinkers who reject religion and all men of other religions agree—is that Christ's teaching is good, and therefore so precious to people that they cannot live without it. But why have these men who believe in Christ's teaching all divided into different sects, and why do they still continue to divide up more and more, denying and condemning one another, and why are they unable to unite in one faith? Again the answer is simple and obvious.

The cause of the division among Christians is simply this teaching about the Church, a teaching which asserts that Christ established a single true Church which is in its essence holy and infallible and can and must teach others. Were it not for this conception of 'the Church', such division among Christians could not exist.

Each Christian Church, that is, each of the religious doctrines, indubitably derives from the teaching of Jesus himself but is not the only one that derives from it: all the other doctrines derive from it too. They have all grown from one seed, and what unites them and is common to them all is that from which they grew—the seed. And therefore to understand the teaching of Jesus rightly we should not examine it from branch to trunk, as each separate sect does, nor need we examine it from its foundation, proceeding from trunk to branches, as is equally uselessly done by science—the history of religion. Neither the one nor the other gives us the meaning of the teaching. Its meaning is only to be found by knowing the seed of the fruit from which they have all come and for the sake of which they all exist. They have all come from the life and works of Jesus, and they all exist to perform the works of Jesus, that is, to do good. And only in these works can they unite.

It was search for the meaning of life, that is, search for a path of life—to know how to live—that brought me to belief, and when I had seen the life of men who adopted Christ's teaching I clung to them. Such men, who professed Christ's teaching by their works, I encountered equally and indiscriminately among the Orthodox Russo-Greeks, the different sects of dissenters, and the Catholics and Lutherans, so that evidently the general sense of life given by Christ's teaching was drawn not from the creeds but from something else that is common to all the communities. I watched good people of more than one faith, and observed in them all the same understanding based on the teaching of Jesus. In all these different sects of Christians I saw full agreement in the conception of what is good and evil and as to how one ought to live. And all these people explained this conception of theirs by the teaching of Jesus. The doctrines had divided them, but the basis was one and the same; therefore it is what lies at the basis of all the faiths that alone is true. And just this truth is what I now seek to learn. The truth of the faith must lie not in separate interpretations of Christ's revelation—those interpretations which have divided Christians into a thousand sects—but in the primary revelation of Christ himself. That revelation—the words of Christ himself—is in the Gospels. And so I turned to the study of the Gospels.

I know that according to Church doctrine the meaning of this teaching is not to be found in the Gospels alone, but in the whole of the Scriptures and Traditions guarded by the Church. I assume that after what has already been said,[1] this sophistry —to the effect that the scriptures which I am taking as the basis of my commentary are not subject to

---

[1] This refers to the *Criticism of Dogmatic Theology* which Tolstóy had written.

investigation because the right to interpret them belongs exclusively to the Church—cannot be repeated, especially as each interpretation is cancelled by the contrary interpretation of another Church; all the holy churches reject one another. This prohibition to read and understand the scriptures for oneself is merely an indication of the Church's consciousness of its own errors of interpretation.

God revealed truth to men. I am a man and so am not only entitled but am under obligation to make use of it and face it directly without intermediaries. If God speaks in these books He also knows the weakness of my mind, and will speak so as not to lead me into deception. The argument of the Church that it cannot allow individuals to interpret the Scriptures lest they should err and separate into many sects, can have no importance for me. It might have significance if the Church's interpretation were intelligible and there were but one Church and one interpretation; but now since the Church's interpretation—of the son of God, of a God in three persons, of a virgin who bore a child without infringing her virginity, of the body and blood of God which is eaten in the form of bread, and so on—cannot find place in a sane head, and since it is not one interpretation but a thousand, that argument, however often repeated, has no validity. On the contrary, an interpretation is needed, and one that all may agree to. But for this the interpretation must be reasonable. Despite our differences we all agree only on what is reasonable. If this revelation of the Scriptures is the truth, it should not and must not fear the light of reason— to be convincing it should welcome it. If the whole revelation turns out to be an absurdity, so much the better—and God be with it! 'All is possible to God'

—that is true, but He cannot talk nonsense. And to write a revelation which cannot be understood would be stupid.

I call revelation that which opens out to us, when reason has reached its utmost limits, the contemplation of what is divine, that is, of truth that is superior to our reason. I call revelation that which gives an answer to the question, insoluble by reason, which brought me to despair and almost to suicide —the question: What meaning has my life? That answer must be intelligible and must not contradict the laws of reason as would, for instance, the assertion that an infinite number is odd or even. It must not contradict reason, for I shall not believe an answer that does so, and it must be intelligible and not arbitrarily assumed, but inevitable to one's reason as, for instance, a recognition of infinity is to any man who is able to count. The answer must reply to the question: What meaning has my life? A reply that does not answer that question is useless to me. The answer must be such that though its essence may be incomprehensible in itself (as is the essence of God) all the deductions derived from its consequences should correspond to every demand of reason, and the meaning it ascribes to my life should solve all my questions as to how to live. The answer must be not merely reasonable and clear but also true, that is, such as I can believe in with my whole soul inevitably, as I believe in the existence of infinity.

Revelation cannot be based on faith as the Church understands it—that is, as trust in something that will be told me later. Real faith results from the inevitability and truth of a revelation that fully satisfies reason. In the Church's conception, faith is an obligation imposed on man's soul by threats and enticements. In my conception it is simply this: that the foundation from which every action of my reason springs is true. Faith is a knowledge of the revelation without which it is impossible to live or think. Revelation is a knowledge of that to which man cannot attain by reason, but which is produced by all humanity from the source of all things hidden in infinity. Such in my opinion must be the nature of a revelation that produces faith, and such I seek in the tradition about Christ, and so I address myself to it in the strictest and most rational terms.

I do not consider the Old Testament, for the question is not what was the faith of the Jews, but in what does the faith of Christ consist, in which men find the meaning that makes it possible for them to live? The Hebrew books may be interesting as explaining the forms in which Christianity has been expressed, but we cannot recognize a continuity of faith from Adam to our times, for the faith of the Jews, before Christ, was local. The faith of the Jews, foreign to us, is interesting to us as is, for instance, the faith of the Brahmins. But the faith of Christ is the one by which we live. To study the faith of the Jews in order to understand the Christian faith is like studying a candle before it is lit, in order to understand the significance of the light which comes from a burning candle. The one thing that can be said is that the nature and quality of the light may depend on the candle, just as the form of expression in the New Testament may depend on its relation to Judaism, but the light cannot be explained by the fact that it proceeds from this and not from that candle.

And so the mistake the Church makes in regarding the Old Testament as a scripture equally divinely inspired with the New Testament, is reflected in the most obvious way by the fact that, having recognized this in words, the Church does not actually so regard it, but has lapsed into contradictions from which she could never extract herself if she considered sound sense in any way obligatory on her.

And so I leave the books of the Old Testament and treat of the written revelation (as the Church calls it) in the twenty-seven books of the New Testament. But in reality the tradition is not expressed in twenty-seven books, or in five, or in a hundred and thirty-eight, for God's revelation cannot be expressed in a number of pages and letters. To say that the revelation of God is expressed by a hundred and eighty-five sheets of writing on paper, is the same as to say that the soul of such and such a man weighs five hundredweight or that the light from a lamp measures seven bushels. The revelation was expressed in men's souls, and they transmitted it to one another and wrote some of it down. Of all that was written, it is known that there were more than a hundred Gospels and Epistles not accepted by the Church, which selected twenty-seven books only and called them canonical. But evidently some books expressed the tradition better and some worse, and there was no definite line dividing the one from the other. The Church had to draw a line somewhere herself, to separate what she should acknowledge as divinely inspired, and obviously it could nowhere sharply divide complete truth from complete falsehood. The tradition was like a shade between white and black or between true and false, and no matter where the line might be drawn it was impossible to get pure white. So the Church drew that line, sorting out the various traditions and calling some books canonical and others apochryphal; and it is remarkable how well she did it. She chose so well that the most recent investigations have shown nothing that should be added, and have made it clear that all that was known and was best was included by the Church in the canonical books. More than that, as if to correct the inevitable error made in drawing that line, the Church has accepted some traditions from the Apochryphal books.

All that could be done was done excellently. But in drawing that line the Church made one grave error. To reject more emphatically the books she did not accept, and to give more weight to those she did accept, she put one general seal of infallibility on all that she approved: it all proceeded from the Holy Ghost and every word was true. By this she ruined and harmed all that she accepted, for having accepted in that stripe of tradition the white, the less white, and the grey—that is, the more or less pure teaching—and having stamped it all with a seal of infallibility, she deprived herself of the right to combine, exclude, and elucidate what was accepted, which it was her duty to do but which she has not done and is not doing. It is all holy: the miracles, the Acts of the Apostles, Paul's advice about wine, the ravings of the Apocalypse, and all the rest. So that though these books have existed for eighteen hundred years they still lie before us in the same rough, awkward, contradictory form, full of absurdities, in which they have ever been. Assuming that every word of the Scriptures was true and holy, the Church tried to combine, elucidate, disentangle, and understand the contradictions; and she did all that could be done in that direction, that is, she gave as much sense as possible to what was absurd. But the first mistake was fatal. Having acknowledged it all as sacred truth it was necessary to justify everything, to shut one's eyes, to hide, to manipulate, to fall into contradictions and, alas, often to say what was not true. Having in words accepted everything, the Church has had in fact to reject certain books—such as the Apocalypse in its entirety, and parts of the Acts of the Apostles—for these often contain nothing instructive and are simply scandalous.

Evidently the miracles were written by Luke to confirm men's faith, and no doubt there were then some people who were strengthened in their faith by such reading. But now one cannot find a more blasphemous book than the Acts of the Apostles, nor one that more undermines faith. A candle may be needed in the dark, but where there is light there is no need to illuminate it with a candle, for it is seen of itself. Christ's miracles are candles brought to the light to illuminate it. If there is light it is seen of itself, and if there is no light then only the candle is seen.

And so it is neither necessary nor possible to read the twenty-seven books one after another acknowledging every word to be true, as the Church does; for by doing this you would arrive at what the Church has arrived at, namely, self-contradiction. To understand the contents of the Scriptures belonging to the Christian faith it is first of all necessary to decide which of the twenty-seven books offered us as the Holy Scriptures are more, and which are less, essential and important, and then begin with the most important ones. These undoubtedly are the four Gospels. All that preceded them can for the most part only be historical material for their understanding, and all that follows is but an elucidation of them. And so it is not necessary to insist on harmonizing all the books as the Churches do. I am convinced that that, more than anything else, has led the Church to preach unintelligible things. But it is necessary to seek the chief basis of the teaching in those four books, which according to the teaching of the Church itself set forth the most essential revelation, and not to conform them to any other books. And this is not because I do not wish so to conform them, but because I fear the mistakes of the other books, of which there are such striking and evident examples.

In these books I shall seek for the following:

1. What I can understand, for no one can believe what is unintelligible;
2. What answers the question as to what I am and what God is; and
3. What is the chief and sole basis of the whole revelation.

And so I shall read incomprehensible, obscure, and semi-intelligible passages, not capriciously, but so that as far as possible they should agree with the parts that are quite clear and should lead to one basis.

Reading both the Scriptures themselves and what has been written about them not once or twice but many times, I came to the conclusion that the whole Christian tradition is contained in the four Gospels, that the books of the Old Testament can serve only as an explanation of the form Christ's teaching took, and that this can only obscure and in no way elucidate the meaning of Christ's teaching; that the Epistles of John and James are private interpretations of the teaching evoked by special occasions, and that it is sometimes possible to find Christ's teaching expressed in them from a new side, but nothing more. Unfortunately we can often find, especially in the Epistles of Paul, an expression of the teaching which is liable to involve readers in perplexity, obscuring the teaching itself. The Acts of the Apostles (like many of the Epistles of Paul) have often nothing in common with the Gospels and the Epistles of John, Peter, and James, but even contradict them. The Book of Revelation reveals absolutely nothing. But the chief thing is that the Gospels, at whatever different times written, give the exposition of the whole teaching and everything else is only an interpretation of it.

I read the Gospels in Greek, the language in which they have been handed down to us, and I translated them as the sense and the dictionaries demanded, digressing occasionally from the translations existing in modern languages and made after the Church had comprehended and defined the meaning of the tradition in its own way. Besides translating, I was inevitably led to the necessity of harmonizing the four Gospels, as they all give an account, though variously, of the same incidents and the same teaching.

The new exegetical proposition that John's Gospel, being exclusively theological, should be considered separately, had no importance for me as my aim is not historical, philosophical, or theological criticism, but to find the meaning of the teaching. The meaning of the teaching is expressed in all four Gospels, and so if they all four express one and the same revelation of truth they should confirm and elucidate one another. So I examined them, uniting all the Gospels into one without excluding the Gospel of John.

Many attempts have been made to unite the Gospels into one; but those known to me, by Arnolde de Vence, Farrar, Reuss, and Grechulévich, take an historical basis for their harmonizations and are all unsuccessful. Not one of them is better than another in an historical sense, and they are all equally satisfactory as regards the teaching. I leave the historical significance entirely aside and unite them only according to the meaning of the teaching. A harmonization of the Gospels on this basis has this advantage, that the true teaching represents as it were a circle, all parts of which equally determine their mutual significance, and the examination of which can begin indifferently at one or other point.

Studying the Gospel in this way, in which the historical events of Christ's life are so closely connected with the teachings, the historic sequence appeared quite indifferent and for the sequence of events it did not matter which harmonization of the Gospels I took as basis. I took the two latest harmonies, by authors who have utilized the labours of all their predecessors—Grechulévich and Reuss. But as Reuss separated John from the Synoptics, Grechulévich's harmony suited me better and I took him for the basis of my work, compared him with Reuss, and diverged from them both when the sense demanded it.

of the enlightenment I experienced while
LEO TOLSTÓY

PREFACE

TO FIRST EDITION OF *A HARMONY, TRANSLATION,*
AND EXAMINATION OF THE FOUR GOSPELS

(The book was not allowed to be printed in Russia, but after a lapse of ten years arrangements were made to have it printed in Russian in Switzerland, and it was for that edition that this Preface was written.)

FRIENDS of mine have offered to print this harmony and translation of the Gospels which I composed ten years ago, and I have agreed to this though the work is far from being completed and contains many defects. I do not now feel able to correct and finish it, as the concentrated and sustained intensity of spiritual enthusiasm I experienced during the whole time I was writing it cannot now be renewed.

But I think that such as it is the work may be of use to people if it conveys to them even a small portion of the enlightenment I experienced while at work on it, and the firm conviction of the truth of the path that was opening out to me, which I still follow with the more joy the further I proceed.

LEO TOLSTÓY.

YÁSNAYA POLYÁNA,
    29th August 1891 o.s.

PREFACE

TO A LATER AND MORE CAREFULLY EDITED
EDITION PRINTED IN ENGLAND, IN THE RUSSIAN
LANGUAGE, AFTER ANOTHER INTERVAL OF TEN
YEARS

THIS book was written by me during an unforgettable period of rapturous realization of the fact that the Christian teaching expressed in the Gospels is not the strange doctrine that had tormented me by its contradictions and that is preached by the Church—but a clear, profound and simple explanation of life, which corresponds to the highest needs of the human soul.

Under the influence of that delight and enthusiasm I unfortunately did not confine myself to setting out the comprehensible parts of the Gospels which give this teaching; nor did I omit what does not harmonize with the fundamental and main meaning and neither confirms nor contradicts it, but I tried to give to those obscure passages a sense in conformity with the general meaning. These efforts involved me in artificial and probably inaccurate philological explanations which instead of strengthening the conviction of the general meaning tend rather to weaken it; and now, though I have realized this mistake, yet being fully absorbed in other work of a similar nature, I have decided not to rearrange the book in an endeavour to separate the superfluous from the essential—for I know that comment on this marvellous book, the Four Gospels, can never be ended, and I leave my work in its present form and consent to its now being reprinted in that shape.

Those to whom truth is precious and who are free from prejudice and sincerely seek the truth, will be able themselves to separate the superfluous from the essential parts without infringing what is essential in it. For those who are prejudiced and have decided in advance that truth is only to be found in the Church interpretations, no exactitude or clarity of exposition could be convincing.

LEO TOLSTÓY.

KOREIZ,
    26th March 1902.

THE GOSPEL IN
BRIEF

CHAPTER CONTENTS

CHAPTER CONTENTS

PREFACE BY TOLSTÓY

THIS short exposition of the Gospel is a summary of a large work which exists in manuscript and cannot be published in Russia.[1]

That work consists of four parts:

1. An account (*Confession*) of the course of my own life and of the thoughts which led me to the conviction that the Christian teaching contains the truth.

2. An examination of the Christian teaching: first according to its interpretation by the Orthodox Russo-Greek Church, then according to its interpretation by the Church in general—by the Apostles, the Councils, the so-called Fathers of the Church—and an exposure of what is false in those interpretations.

3. An examination of Christian teaching not according to those interpretations but solely according to what has come down to us of Christ's teaching, as ascribed to him in the Gospels.

4. An exposition of the real meaning of Christ's teaching, the reasons why it has been perverted, and the consequences to which it should lead.

From the third of those parts the present account has been compiled.

The harmonization of the four Gospels has been made in accord with the sense of the teaching. In making it I hardly had to digress from the order in which it is set down in the Gospels, so that there are not more but fewer transpositions of the verses than in most of the concordances known to me, or than

---

[1] Long after this Preface was written the two volumes of the 'large work' referred to—*A Harmony, Translation, and Examination of the Gospels*—were published in Russian, first in Switzerland and afterwards in England.

in Grechulévich's arrangement of the Four Gospels. In my treatment of the Gospel of John there are no transpositions, but everything follows the order of the original.

The division of the Gospel into twelve chapters (or six if each two be united) came about of itself from the sense of the teaching. This is the meaning of those chapters:

1. Man is the son of an infinite source: a son of that Father not by the flesh but by the spirit.

2. Therefore man should serve that source in spirit.

3. The life of all men has a divine origin. It alone is holy.

4. Therefore man should serve that source in the life of all men. Such is the will of the Father.

5. The service of the will of that Father of life gives life.

6. Therefore the gratification of one's own will is not necessary for life.

7. Temporal life is food for the true life.

8. Therefore the true life is independent of time: it is in the present.

9. Time is an illusion of life; life in the past and in the future conceals from men the true life of the present.

10. Therefore man should strive to destroy the illusion of the temporal life of the past and future.

11. True life is life in the present, common to all men and manifesting itself in love.

12. Therefore he who lives by love in the present, through the common life of all men, unites with the Father, the source and foundation of life.

So each two chapters are related as cause and effect.

In addition to these twelve chapters an introduction from the first chapter of the Gospel of John is added, in which the writer of that Gospel speaks, in his own name, as to the meaning of the whole teaching, and a conclusion from the same writer's Epistle (written probably before the Gospel) containing a general deduction from all that precedes.

These two parts do not form an essential part of the teaching, but though they both might be omitted without losing the sense of the teaching (the more so as they come in the name of John and not of Jesus)—I have retained them because in a straightforward understanding of Christ's teaching these parts, confirming one another an the whole, furnish, in contradiction to the queer interpretation of the Churches, the plainest indication of the meaning that should be ascribed to the teaching.

At the beginning of each chapter, besides a brief indication of its subject, I have given the words which correspond to that chapter from the prayer Jesus taught his disciples.

When I had finished my work I found to my surprise and joy that the Lord's Prayer is nothing but a very concise expression of the whole teaching of Jesus in the very order in which I had arranged the chapters, and that each phrase of the prayer corresponds to the meaning and sequence of the chapters:

1. *Our Father,*	Man is a son of God.
2. *Which art in Heaven,*	God is the infinite spiritual source of life.
3. *Hallowed be Thy Name,*	May this source of life be held holy.
4. *Thy Kingdom come,*	May his power be realized in all men.
5. *Thy will be done, as in heaven,*	May the will of this infinite source be fulfilled as it is in himself,
6. *so on earth.*	so also in the bodily life.
7. *Give us our daily bread*	Temporal life is the food of the true life.

8. *each day.*	True life is in the present.
9. *And forgive us our debts as we forgive our debtors.*	And let not the mistakes and errors of the past hide that true life from us.
10. *And lead us not into temptation,*	And may they not lead us into delusion,
11. *But deliver us from evil,*	And so there shall be no evil.
12. *For thine is the kingdom, the power, and the glory.*	And may thy power, and strength, and wisdom, prevail.

In the full exposition, in the third part, everything in the Gospels is set down without any omissions. But in the present rendering the following are omitted: the conception and birth of John the Baptist, his imprisonment and death, the birth of Jesus, his genealogy, his mother's flight with him to Egypt; his miracles at Cana and Capernaum; the casting out of the devils; the walking on the sea; the blasting of the fig-tree; the healing of the sick; the raising of the dead; the resurrection of Christ himself, and the references to prophecies fulfilled by his life.

Those passages are omitted in the present short exposition because, containing nothing of the teaching but only describing events that took place before, during, or after the period in which Jesus taught, they complicate the exposition. Those verses, however they may be understood, do not contain either contradiction or confirmation of the teaching. Their sole significance for Christianity was to prove the divinity of Jesus to those who did not believe in it. But for one who understands that a story of miracles is unconvincing, and who also doubts that the divinity of Jesus is asserted in his teaching, those verses drop away of themselves as superfluous.

In the larger work every deviation from the ordinary version, as well as every inserted comment and every omission, is explained and justified by comparison of the different variants of the Gospels, by examination of contexts, and by philological and other considerations. In the present brief rendering all such proofs and refutations of the false understanding of the Churches, as well as the detailed notes and references, are omitted, on the ground that however exact and correct the discussions of each separate passage may be, they cannot carry conviction as to the true understanding of the teaching. The justness of the understanding of the teaching is better proved not by the discussion of particular passages but by its own unity, clarity, simplicity and completeness, and by its accordance with the inner feeling of all who seek the truth.

In respect of all the divergences of my rendering from the Church's authorized text, the reader should not forget that the customary conception that the four Gospels with all their verses and syllables are sacred books is a very gross error.

The reader should remember that Jesus never wrote any book himself, as Plato, Philo, or Marcus Aurelius did; nor even, like Socrates, transmitted his teaching to educated men, but that he spoke to many uneducated men and only long after his death did people begin to write down what they had heard about him.

The reader should remember that there were very many such accounts from among which the Churches selected first three Gospels and then one more, and that in selecting those best Gospels— as the proverb, 'There is no stick without knots' says—they had to take in many knots with what they selected from the whole mass of writings about Christ, and that there are many passages in the canonical Gospels just as poor as in the rejected apocryphal ones.

The reader should remember that it is the teaching of Christ which may be sacred, but certainly not any definite number of verses and syllables, and that certain verses picked out from here to there cannot become sacred merely because people say they are.

Moreover the reader should remember that these selected Gospels are also the work of thousands of different human brains and hands, that they have been selected, added to, and commented on, for centuries, that all the copies that have come down to us from the fourth century are written in continuous script without punctuation, so that even after the fourth and fifth centuries they have been subject to very diverse readings, and that there are not less than fifty thousand such variations of the Gospels.

This should all be borne in mind by the reader, that he may not be misled by the customary view that the Gospels in their present form have come to us direct from the Holy Ghost.

The reader should remember that far from it being blameworthy to discard useless passages from the Gospels and elucidate some passages by others, it is on the contrary irrational not to do so and to hold a certain number of verses and syllables as sacred.

On the other hand I beg readers to remember that if I do not regard the Gospels as sacred books that have come down to us from the Holy Ghost, even less do I regard them as mere historical monuments of religious literature. I understand the theological as well as the historical view of the Gospels, but regard them myself differently, and so I beg the reader not to be confused either by the Church view or by the historical view customary in our day among educated people, neither of which do I hold.

I regard Christianity neither as an exclusive divine revelation nor as an historical phenomenon, but as a teaching which gives us the meaning of life. I was led to Christianity neither by theological nor historical investigations but by this—that when I was fifty years old, having asked myself and all the learned men around me what I am and what is the meaning of my life, and received the answer that I am a fortuitous concatenation of atoms and that life has no meaning but is itself an evil, I fell into despair and wanted to put an end to my life; but I remembered that formerly in childhood when I believed, life had a meaning for me, and that for the great mass of men about me who believe and are not corrupted by riches life has a meaning; and I doubted the validity of the reply given me by the learned men of my circle and I tried to understand the reply Christianity gives to those who live a real life. And I began to seek Christianity in the Christian teaching that guides such men's lives. I began to study the Christianity which I saw applied in life and to compare that applied Christianity with its source.

The source of Christian teaching is the Gospels, and in them I found the explanation of the spirit which guides the life of all who really live.

But together with this source of the pure water of life I found, wrongfully united with it, mud and slime which had hidden its purity from me: by the side of and bound up with the lofty Christian teaching I found a Hebrew and a Church teaching alien to it. I was in the position of a man who receives a bag of stinking dirt, and only after long struggle and much labour finds that amid that dirt lie priceless pearls; and he understands that he was not to blame for disliking the stinking dirt, and that those who have collected and preserved these pearls together with the dirt are also not to blame but deserve love and respect.

I did not know the light and had thought there was no light of truth to be found in life, but having convinced myself that men live by that light alone, I began to look for its source and found it in the Gospels, despite the false Church interpretations. And on reaching that source of light I was dazzled by it, and found full replies to my questions as to the meaning of my own life and that of others— answers in full agreement with those I knew of from other nations, but which in my opinion were superior to them all.

I was looking for an answer to the question of life and not to theological or historical questions, and so for me the chief question was not whether Jesus was or was not God, or from whom the Holy Ghost proceeded and so forth, and equally unimportant and unnecessary was it for me to know when and by whom each Gospel was written and whether such and such a parable may, or may not, be ascribed to Christ. What was important to me was this light which has enlightened mankind for eighteen hundred years and which enlightened and still enlightens me; but how to name the source of that light, and what materials he or someone else had kindled, did not concern me.

On that this preface might end were the Gospels recently discovered books and had Christ's teaching not suffered eighteen hundred years of false inter-pretation. But now to understand the teaching of Jesus it is necessary to know clearly the chief methods used in these false interpretations. The most customary method of false interpretation, and one which we have grown up with, consists of preaching under the name of Christianity not what Christ taught but a Church teaching composed of explanations of very contradictory writings into which Christ's teaching enters only to a small degree, and even then distorted and twisted to fit together with other writings. According to this false interpretation Christ's teaching is only one link in a chain of revelations beginning with the commencement of the world and continuing in the Church until now. These false interpreters call Jesus God; but the fact that they recognize him as God does not make them attribute more importance to his words and teaching than to the words of the Pentateuch, the Psalms, the Acts of the Apostles, the Epistles, the Apocalypse, or even to the decisions of the Councils and the writings of the Fathers of the Church.

These false interpreters do not admit any understanding of the teaching of Jesus which does not conform to the previous and subsequent revelations; so that their aim is not to explain the meaning of Christ's teaching, but as far as possible to harmonize various extremely contradictory writings, such as the Pentateuch, the Psalms, the Gospels, the Epistles, and the Acts—that is, all that is supposed to constitute the Holy Scriptures.

Such explanations aiming not at truth but at reconciling the irreconcilable, namely, the writings of the Old and the New Testament, can obviously be innumerable, as indeed they are. Among them are the Epistles of Paul and the decisions of the Councils (which begin with the formulary: 'It has pleased Us and the Holy Ghost'), and such enactments as those of the Popes, the Synods, the pseudo-Christs, and all the false interpreters who affirm that the Holy Ghost speaks through their lips. They all employ one and the same gross method of affirming the truth of their interpretations by the assertion that their interpretations are not human utterances but revelations from the Holy Ghost. Without entering on an examination of these beliefs, each of which calls itself the true one, one cannot help seeing that by the method common to them all of acknowledging the whole immense quantity of so-called scriptures of the Old and New Testament as equally sacred, they themselves impose an insuperable obstacle to an understanding of Christ's teaching; and that from this mistake arises the possibility and inevitability of endlessly divergent interpretations of the teaching. The reconcilement of a number of revelations can be infinitely varied, but the interpretation of the teaching of one person (and one looked upon as God) should not occasion discord.

If God descended to earth to teach people, his teaching, by the very purpose of his coming, cannot be understood in more than one way. If God came down to earth to reveal truth to men, at least he would have revealed it so that all might understand: if he did not do that he was not God; and if the divine truths are such that even God could not make them intelligible to mankind, men certainly cannot do so.

If Jesus is not God, but a great man, then still less can his teaching produce discord. For the teaching of a great man is only great because it expresses intelligibly and clearly what others have expressed unintelligibly and obscurely. What is incomprehensible in a great man's teaching is not great, and therefore a great man's teaching does not engender sects. Only an exposition which affirms that it is a revelation from the Holy Ghost and is the sole truth, and that all other expositions are lies, gives birth to discord and to the mutual animosities among the Churches that result therefrom. However much the various Churches affirm that

they do not condemn other communities, that they
have no hatred of them but pray for union, it is
untrue. Never, since the time of Arius, has the
affirmation of any dogma arisen from any other
cause than the desire to condemn a contrary belief
as false. It is a supreme degree of pride and ill will
to others to assert that a particular dogma is a
divine revelation proceeding from the Holy Ghost:
the highest presumption because nothing more
arrogant can be said than that the words spoken
by me are uttered through me by God; and the
greatest ill will because the avowal of oneself as in
possession of the sole indubitable truth implies an
assertion of the falsity of all who disagree. Yet that
is just what all the Churches say, and from this
alone flows and has flowed all the evil which has
been committed and still is committed in the world
in the name of religion.

But besides the temporary evil which such an
interpretation by the Churches and the sects produces, it has another important inner defect which
gives an obscure, indefinite, and insincere character
to their assertions. This defect consists in the fact
that all the Churches—having acknowledged the
latest revelation of the Holy Ghost, who descended
on the apostles and has passed and still passes to the
supposedly elect—nowhere define directly, definitely, and finally, in what that revelation consists;
and yet they base their belief on that supposedly
continuing revelation and call it Christian. All the
churchmen who acknowledge the revelation from
the Holy Ghost recognize (like the Mohammedans)
three revelations: that of Moses, of Jesus, and of the
Holy Ghost. But in the Mohammedan religion it
is believed that after Moses and Jesus, Mahomet is
the last of the prophets and that he explained the
revelations of Moses and Jesus, and this revelation

of Mahomet every True Believer has before
him.

But it is not so with the Church faith. That also,
like the Mohammedan, acknowledges three revelations: that of Moses, of Jesus, and of the Holy Ghost,
but it does not call itself Holy Ghostism after the
name of the last revealer, but affirms that the basis
of its faith is the teaching of Christ. So that while
preaching its own doctrines it attributes their
authority to Christ. Churchmen acknowledging
the last revelation explaining all previous ones,
should say so and call their religion by the name
of whoever received the last revelation—acknowledging it to be that of Paul, or of this or that
Council of the Church, or of the Pope, or of the
Patriarch. And if the last revelation was that of the
Fathers, a decree of the Eastern Patriarchs, a Papal
encyclical, or the syllabus or catechism of Luther
or of Philaret—they should say so and call their
religion accordingly, because the last revelation
which explains all the preceding is always the most
important one. But they do not do so, but while
preaching doctrines quite alien to Christ's teaching,
affirm that their doctrine was taught by Christ.
So that according to their teaching Jesus declared
that by his blood he had redeemed the human race
ruined by Adam's sins; that God is three persons;
that the Holy Ghost descended upon the apostles
and was transmitted to the priesthood by the laying
on of hands; that seven sacraments are necessary
for salvation; that communion should be received
in two kinds, and so on. They would have us
believe that all this is the teaching of Jesus, whereas
in reality there is not a word about any of it in his
teaching. Those false teachers should call their
teaching and religion the teaching and religion of
the Holy Ghost but not of Christ; for only that

faith can be called Christian which recognizes the
revelation of Christ reaching us in the Gospels as
the final revelation.

It would seem that the matter is plain and not
worth speaking about, but, strange to say, up to
now the teaching of Christ is not separated on the
one side from an artificial and quite unjustifiable
amalgamation with the Old Testament, and on the
other from the arbitrary additions and perversions
made in the name of the Holy Ghost.

To this day there are some who, calling Jesus the
second person of the Trinity, do not conceive of his
teaching otherwise than in conjunction with those
pseudo revelations of the third Person which they
find in the Old Testament, the Epistles, the decrees
of the Councils and the decisions of the Fathers, and
they preach the strangest beliefs, affirming them
to be the religion of Christ.

Others not acknowledging Jesus as God, similarly conceive of his teaching not as he could have
taught it but as understood by Paul and other
commentators. While regarding Jesus not as God
but as a man, these commentators deny him a most
legitimate human right, that of answering only
for his own words and not for false interpretations
of them. Trying to explain his teaching, these
learned commentators attribute to Jesus things he
never thought of saying. The representatives of
this school of interpreters—beginning with the most
popular of them, Renan—without troubling to
separate what Jesus himself taught from what the
slanders of his commentators have laid upon him,
and without troubling to understand his teaching
more profoundly, try to understand the meaning of
his appearance and the spread of his teaching by
the events of his life and the circumstances of his
time.

The problem that confronts them is this: eighteen hundred years ago a certain pauper appeared and said certain things. He was flogged and executed. And ever since that time (though there have been numbers of just men who died for their faith), milliards of people, wise and foolish, learned and ignorant, have clung to the belief that this man alone among men was God. How is this amazing fact to be explained? The churchmen say that it occurred because Jesus was God. In that case it is all understandable. But if he was not God how are we to explain that everyone looked upon just this common man as God? And the learned men of that school assiduously explore every detail of the life of Jesus, without noticing that however much they explore those details (in reality they have gathered none), even if they were able to reconstruct his whole life in the minutest detail, the question why he, just he, had such an influence on people would still remain unanswered. The answer is not to be found in knowledge of the society Jesus was born into, or how he was educated, and so on, still less is it to be found in knowledge of what was being done in Rome, or in the fact that the people of that time were inclined to superstition, but only by knowing what this man preached that has caused people, from that time to this, to distinguish him from all others and to acknowledge him as God. It would seem that the first thing to do is to try to understand that man's teaching, and naturally his own teaching and not coarse interpretations of it that have been spread since his time. But this is not done. These learned historians of Christianity are so pleased to have understood that Jesus was not God and are so anxious to prove that his teaching is not divine and is therefore not obligatory, that— forgetting that the more they prove him to have been an ordinary man and his teaching not to be divine the further they are from solving the problem before them—they strain all their strength to do so. To see this surprising error clearly, it is worth recalling an article by Havet, a follower of Renan's, who affirms that *Jésus Christ n'avait rien de chrétien*, or Souris, who enthusiastically argues that Jesus Christ was a very coarse and stupid man.

The essential thing is, not to prove that Jesus was not God and that therefore his doctrine is not divine, or to prove that he was a Catholic, but to know in all its purity what constituted that teaching which was so lofty and so precious to men that they have acknowledged and still acknowledge its preacher to have been God.

And so if the reader belongs to the great majority of educated people brought up in the Church belief but who have abandoned its incompatibilities with common sense and conscience—whether he has retained a love and respect for the spirit of the Christian teaching or (as the proverb puts it 'has thrown his fur coat into the fire because he is angry with the bugs') considers all Christianity a harmful superstition—I ask him to remember that what repels him and seems to him a superstition is not the teaching of Christ; that Christ cannot be held responsible for the monstrous tradition that has been interwoven with his teaching and presented as Christianity: that to judge of Christianity, only the teaching of Christ as it has come down to us must be learned—that is, the words and actions attributed to Christ and that have an instructive meaning.

Studying the teaching of Christ in that way the reader will convince himself that Christianity, far from being a mixture of the lofty and the low, or a superstition, is a very strict, pure, and complete metaphysical and ethical doctrine, higher than which the reason of man has not yet reached, and in the orbit of which (without recognizing the fact) human activity—political, learned, poetic, and philosophic—is moving.

If the reader belongs to that small minority of educated people who hold to the Church religion and profess it not for outward purposes but for inward tranquillity, I ask him to remember that the teaching of Christ as set forth in this book (despite the identity of name) is quite a different teaching from that which he professes, and that therefore the question for him is not whether the doctrine here offered agrees or disagrees with his belief, but is simply, which best accords with his reason and conscience—the Church teaching composed of adjustments of many scriptures, or the teaching of Christ alone? The question for him is merely whether he wishes to accept the new teaching or to retain his own belief.

But if the reader is one of those who outwardly profess the Church creed and values it not because he believes it to be true but because he considers that to profess and preach it is profitable to him, then let him remember that however many adherents he may have, however powerful they may be, on whatever thrones they may sit, and by whatever great names they may call themselves, he is not one of the accusers but of the accused. Let such readers remember that there is nothing for them to prove, that they have long ago said what they had to say and that even if they could prove what they wish to, they would only prove, each for himself, what is proved by all the hundreds of opposing Churches; and that it is not for them to demonstrate, but to excuse themselves: to excuse themselves for the blasphemy of adjusting the teaching of the God-Christ to suit the teaching of Ezras, of the Councils, and Theophilacts, and allowing themselves to interpret and alter the words of God in conformity with the words of men; to excuse themselves for their libels on God by which they have thrown all the fanaticism they had in their hearts onto the God-Jesus and given it out as his teaching; to excuse themselves for the fraud by which, having hidden the teaching of God who came to bestow blessing on the world, they have replaced it by their own blasphemous creed, and by that substitution have deprived and still deprive milliards of people of the blessing Christ brought to men, and instead of the peace and love he brought have introduced into the world sects, condemnations, murders, and all manner of crimes.

For such readers there are only two ways out: humble confession and renunciation of their lies, or a persecution of those who expose them for what they have done and are still doing.

If they will not disavow their lies, only one thing remains for them: to persecute me—for which I, completing what I have written, prepare myself with joy and with fear of my own weakness.

LEO TOLSTÓY.

YÁSNAYA POLYÁNA, 1883.[1]

[1] Some corrections in this preface were made by Tolstóy as late as January 19th, 1904.

THE GOSPEL IN BRIEF

Announcement of welfare by Jesus Christ
the Son of God

A PROLOGUE

THE UNDERSTANDING OF LIFE

Jesus Christ's announcement replaced the belief in an
external God by an understanding of life.

THE announcement of welfare by Jesus
Christ, the son of God. Mark I. i

The announcement of welfare consists
in this, that all men who believe that they
are the sons of God obtain true life. The John XX.
understanding of life is at the basis and the xxxi
beginning of all. The understanding of life
is God. And by the announcement of Jesus I. i.
it has become the basis and beginning of
all things. ii.

All things have come to life by understanding, and without it nothing can live. iii.
Understanding gives true life. Under- iv.
standing is the light of truth, and the light
shines in the darkness and the darkness
cannot extinguish it. v.

The true light has always existed in the
world and enlightens every man who is
born in the world. It was in the world, ix.
and the world only lived because it had
that light of understanding.

But the world did not retain it. He x.
came unto his own, and his own retained
him not. xi.

Only those who understood the enlightenment were able to become like

him because they believed in his reality. John I. xii.
Those who believed that life lies in the
understanding became no longer sons of xiii.
the flesh, but sons of understanding.

And the understanding of life, in the
person of Jesus Christ, manifested itself
in the flesh, and we understood his meaning to be that the son of understanding,
man in the flesh, of one nature with the
Father the source of life, is such as the
Father, the source of life. xiv.

The teaching of Jesus is the full and true
faith, for by fulfilling the teaching of Jesus xv.
we understand a new faith instead of the
former. Moses gave us a law, but we re- xvi.
ceived the true faith through Jesus Christ. xvii.

No one has seen God or will ever see
God, only his son, who is in the Father,
has shown us the path of life. xviii.

I

THE SON OF GOD

*Man, the son of God, is weak in the flesh but
free in the spirit.*

'OUR FATHER'

THE birth of Jesus Christ was thus:

His mother Mary was engaged to
Joseph. But before they began to live as
man and wife it appeared that Mary was
pregnant. Joseph however was a good Matt. I.
xviii.
man and did not wish to shame her: he
took her as his wife and had no relations
with her till she had given birth to her xix, xxiv,
first son and had named him Jesus. xxv.

And the boy grew and matured and was intelligent beyond his years. Luke II. xl.

When Jesus was twelve years old Mary went once with Joseph for the holiday at Jerusalem and took the boy with her. xli. xlii. When the holiday was over they started homeward and forgot about the boy. xliii. Then they remembered, but thought he had gone with other lads, and on the way they inquired about him but he was nowhere to be found, so they went back for him to Jerusalem. And not till the xliv. xlv. third day did they find the boy in the church, where he was sitting with the teachers and asking questions. And every- xlvi. one was surprised at his intelligence. His xlvii. mother saw him and said: 'What have you done to us? Your father and I have been looking for you and grieving.' And xlviii. he said to them: 'But where did you look for me? Surely you knew that a son should be looked for in his Father's house?' And xlix. they did not understand him, nor did they understand whom he called his Father. l.

And after this Jesus lived with his mother and obeyed her in everything. And he li. advanced in stature and in intelligence. lii. And everyone thought that Jesus was the son of Joseph. And so he lived to the age of thirty. III. xxiii.

At that time a prophet John announced himself in Judea. He lived in the open Matt. III. i. country of Judea near the Jordan. His Mark I. iv.
Luke III. dress was of camelhair belted with a strap, iii. and he fed on bark and on herbs.

John said: Bethink yourselves, for the Matt. III.
iv. Kingdom of Heaven is at hand.

He called on the people to change
their lives and get rid of wickedness, and
as a sign of that change of life he bathed
them in the Jordan. He said: A voice
calls to you; Open a way for God through   Matt. III. ii;
the wilderness, level a path for him. Make   Mark I. iv.
it so that all may be level, that there may   Luke III. iv.
be neither hollows nor hills, neither high
nor low. Then God will be among you   v.
and all will find salvation.   vi.

And the people asked him: What must
we do? He replied: Let him that has two   x.
suits of clothes give one to him that has
none, and let him that has food give to
him that has none. And tax-gatherers   xi.
came to him and asked: What are we to
do? He said to them: Extort nothing   xii.
beyond what is due. And soldiers asked: xiii.
How are we to live? He said: Do no one
any harm, nor defraud any man, and be
content with what is served out to you.   xiv.

And inhabitants of Jerusalem came to
him, and the Jews in the neighbourhood
of Judea near the Jordan. And they   Matt. III. v.
acknowledged their wrong-doings to him,
and as a sign of a changed life he bathed
them in the Jordan.   vi.

And many of the Orthodox and con-
ventional religionists came to John, but
secretly. He recognized them and said:
You are a race of vipers: or have you also
seen that you cannot escape the will of
God? Then bethink yourselves and change
your faith! And if you wish to change your   vii.
faith let it be seen by your fruits that you
have bethought yourselves. The axe is   viii.
already laid to the tree. If the tree pro-

duces bad fruit it will be cut down and
cast into the fire.   Matt. III. x.

As a sign of a changed life I cleanse you
in water, but as well as that bathing you   xi.
must also be cleansed with the spirit.
The spirit will cleanse you as a master
cleanses his threshing-floor when he
gathers the wheat and burns the chaff.   xii.

Jesus, too, came from Galilee to the
Jordan to be bathed by John, and was
bathed and heard John's preaching.   xiii.

And from the Jordan he went into the
wild places and there felt the power of the
spirit.   IV. i.

Jesus remained in the desert forty days
and forty nights without food or drink.   ii.

And the voice of the flesh said to him: iii.
If you were the son of Almighty God you
could make bread out of stones, but you
cannot do so, therefore you are not a son   Luke IV. iii;
of God.   Matt. IV.
    iii.

But Jesus said to himself: If I cannot
make bread out of stones, it means that
I am not a son of God in the flesh but in
the spirit. I am alive not by bread but by
the spirit. And my spirit is able to dis-   Luke IV. iv;
regard the flesh.   Matt. IV. iv.

But still hunger tormented him, and the
voice of the flesh again said to him: If you
live only by the spirit and can disregard
the flesh, you can throw off the flesh and
your spirit will remain alive.

And it seemed to him that he was standing on the roof of the temple and the voice
of the flesh said to him: If you are a son of
God in the spirit, throw yourself from
the temple, you will not hurt yourself, but   Luke IV. ix.

an unseen force will keep you, support
you, and save you from all harm. But
Jesus said to himself: I can disregard the
flesh, but I may not throw it off, for I was
born by the spirit into the flesh. That was
the will of the Father of my spirit, and I
cannot oppose him.

Luke IV. x,
xi.

xii;
Matt. IV.
vii.

Then the voice of the flesh said to him:
If you cannot oppose your Father by
throwing yourself from the temple and
discarding life, then you cannot oppose
your Father by hungering when you need
to eat. You must not make light of the
desires of the flesh; they are placed in you,
and you must serve them. Then Jesus
seemed to see all the kingdoms of the
earth and all the peoples, just as they live
and labour for the flesh, expecting gain
therefrom. And the voice of the flesh said
to him: There, you see, these people work
for me and I give them what they wish
for. If you will work for me you will have
the same. But Jesus said to himself: My
Father is not flesh but spirit. I live by
him. I am always aware of his presence
in me. Him alone I honour and for him
alone I work, expecting reward from him
alone.

Luke IV. v;
Matt. IV.
viii.

Luke IV. vi.
vii.

viii;
Matt. IV. x.

Then the temptations ceased and Jesus
knew the power of the spirit.

Luke IV.
xiii.

And when he had experienced the
power of the spirit, Jesus went out of the
wild places and came again to John and
stayed with him.

And when Jesus was leaving John, John
said of him: That is the saviour of men.

John I.
xxxvi.

On hearing those words of John two

of his pupils left their former teacher and
went after Jesus. He, seeing them following him, stopped and said: What do you
want? They replied: Teacher, we wish
to be with you and to know your teaching.
He said: Come with me and I will tell
you everything. They went with him and
stayed with him, listening to him till ten
o'clock.

One of these pupils was called Andrew.
He had a brother Simon. Having heard
Jesus, Andrew went to his brother Simon
and said to him: We have found him of
whom the prophets wrote—the Messiah—
he has told us of our salvation. Andrew
took Simon and brought him also to Jesus.
Jesus called this brother of Andrew's,
Peter, which means a stone. And both
these brothers became pupils of Jesus.

Afterwards, before entering Galilee,
Jesus met Philip and called him to go with
him. Philip was from Bethsaida and a
fellow-villager of Peter and Andrew.
When Philip had got to know Jesus he
went and found his brother Nathanael
and said to him: We have found the
chosen of God of whom Moses and the
prophets wrote. This is Jesus, the son of
Joseph of Nazareth. Nathanael was surprised that he of whom the prophets wrote
should be from a neighbouring village,
and he said: It is most unlikely that the
messenger of God should be from Nazareth.
Philip said: Come with me, you shall
see and hear for yourself. Nathanael agreed
and went with his brother and met Jesus,
and when he had heard him he said to

John I.
xxxvii.

xxxviii.

xxxix.

xl.

xli.

xlii.

xliii.
xliv.

xlv.

jesus: Yes, now I see that it is true that you are a son of God and the King of Israel. Jesus said to him: Learn something more important than that: henceforth the heavens are opened and men may be in communion with the heavenly powers. Henceforth God will no longer be separate from men.

John I.
xlvi–xlix.

li.

And Jesus came home to Nazareth and on a holiday went as usual into the Assembly and began to read. They gave him the book of the prophet Isaiah; and unrolling it he read. In the book was written: The spirit of the Lord is in me. He has chosen me to announce happiness to the unfortunate and the broken-hearted, to announce freedom to those who are bound, light to the blind, and salvation and rest to the tormented, to announce to all men the day of God's mercy.

Luke IV.
xvi.

xvii.

xviii, xix.

He folded the book, returned it to the attendant, and sat down. And all waited to hear what he would say. And he said to them: That writing has now been fulfilled before your eyes.

xx.

xxi.

II
THE SERVICE OF GOD

*Therefore man should work not for the flesh,
but for the spirit.*

'WHICH ART IN HEAVEN'

IT happened that Jesus was walking across a field with his pupils one Saturday. The pupils were hungry, and on the way they plucked ears of corn and rubbed them in their hands and ate the grain. But according to the teaching of the Orthodox, God had given Moses a law that everyone should observe Saturday and do nothing that day. According to the teaching of the Orthodox, God had ordered that anyone who worked on Saturday should be stoned.

Matt. XII. i.
Mark II.
xxiii;
Luke VI. i.

The Orthodox noticed that the pupils rubbed ears of corn on a Saturday and said to them: It is wrong to do that on a Saturday. One must not work on Saturday, and you are rubbing ears of corn. God made Saturday holy, and commanded that the breaking of it should be punished by death.

Matt. XII.
ii.

Jesus heard this, and said: If you understood what is meant by the words of God: 'I desire love and not sacrifice'—you would not condemn what is harmless. Man is more important than Saturday.

vii, viii.

It happened another time on a Saturday that when Jesus was teaching in the Assembly a sick woman came to him and asked him to help her. And Jesus began to cure her.

Luke XIII.
x, xi, xii.

The Orthodox church-elder was angry with Jesus, and said to the people: In the law of God it is said: 'There are six days in the week on which to work.' But Jesus then asked the Orthodox professors of the law: Do you think it is wrong to help a man on Saturday? And they did not know what to answer.

xiv.

Then Jesus said: Deceivers! Does not each of you untie his ox from its manger

XIV. iii, vi.

and take it to water on Saturday? And if
his sheep fell into a well would not any
one of you pull it out even on Saturday?
A man is much better than a sheep: yet
you say that it is wrong to help a man.
What then do you think we should do on
Saturday—good or evil? Save life or
destroy it? Good should be done always,
even on Saturday.

Luke XIV.
v.
Matt. XII.
ii.

xii.

Jesus one day saw a tax-gatherer receiving taxes. The tax-gatherer's name was
Matthew. Jesus talked to him and
Matthew understood him, liked his teaching, and invited him to his house and
showed him hospitality.

IX. ix.

When Jesus came to Matthew's house
some of Matthew's friends were also there
—tax-gatherers and unbelievers. Jesus did
not disdain them, but he and his pupils
sat down with them. And when the
Orthodox saw him, they said to his pupils:
How is it that your teacher eats with tax-
gatherers and unbelievers? For according
to the teaching of the Orthodox, God forbids any intercourse with unbelievers.

x.

xi.

Jesus heard this, and said: He who
boasts of good health needs no doctor, but
a sick man does. Understand what the
words of God mean: 'I desire love and not
sacrifice.' I cannot teach a change of faith
to those who consider themselves Orthodox, but to those who consider themselves
unbelievers.

xii.

xiii.

Some Orthodox professors of the law
came to Jesus from Jerusalem. And they
saw that his pupils, and Jesus himself, ate
bread without having washed their hands,

XV. i.
Mark VII. i.

and these Orthodox began to blame him
for that, for they themselves strictly ob-   Matt. XV.
served the Church tradition as to how the   ii.
dishes should be washed, and would not   Mark VII.
eat unless they had been so washed. And   iii.
they would also not eat anything from the
market until they had washed their hands.   iv.

And the Orthodox professors of the law
asked him: Why do you not follow the
Church traditions, but take bread with
unwashed hands and eat it? And he   v.
answered them: How is it that you with
your Church traditions break God's com-   Matt. XV.
mandment? God said to you: 'Honour   iii.
your father and mother'. But you have   Mark VII.
arranged that anyone may say: 'I give   x.
to God what I used to give to my parents',   xi.
and then he is not bound to feed his father
and mother. So by the Church tradition   xii.
you break the law of God. Deceivers!   xiii.
Well did the prophet Isaiah say of you: Matt. XV.
'Because these people fall down before me   vii.
only in words, and honour me only with
their tongue, while their heart is far from
me; and because their fear of me is only   viii.
a human law which they have learnt by
rote, I will do a wonderful, an extraordinary thing among them: the wisdom
of their wise men shall be lost, and the
understanding of their thinkers shall be
dimmed. Woe to those who seek to hide
their desires from the Highest, and who
do their deeds in darkness.'   ix.

So it is with you: You neglect what is
important in the law—the commandment
of God—but observe your own traditions   Mark VII.
as to the washing of cups!   viii.

And Jesus called the people to him and said: Hear all of you and understand: there is nothing in the world that entering a man can defile him; but what goes forth from him, that can defile a man. Let love and mercy be in your soul, then all will be clean. Try to understand this.

Mark VII. xiv.

xv; Luke XI. xli; Mark VII. xvi.

And when he returned home his pupils asked him what those words meant. And he said: Do you also not understand? Do you not understand that what is external, bodily, cannot defile a man? For it does not enter his soul but his belly. It enters his belly and passes out again. Only that which goes out of him from his soul can defile a man. For out of a man's soul proceed evil, adulteries, obscenity, murders, thefts, covetousness, wrath, deceit, insolence, envy, calumny, pride, and every kind of folly. And this evil is out of man's soul and it alone can defile him.

xvii.

xviii.

xix.

xx.

xxi, xxii. xxiii.

After this came the Passover, and Jesus went to Jerusalem and entered the temple. In the courts of the temple were cattle: cows, bulls, and sheep; and there were cotes for pigeons; and money-changers behind their counters. All this was wanted for offerings to God. The animals were killed and offered up in the Temple. That was how the Jews prayed, as they had been taught by the Orthodox professors of the law. Jesus went into the Temple, plaited a whip, drove all the cattle out of the porch, turned out all the doves, and scattered all the money, and bade them not bring such things into the Temple.

John II. xiii.

xiv.

xv.

xvi.

He said: The prophet Isaiah said to

you: 'The house of God is not the Temple in Jerusalem, but the whole world of God's people.' And the prophet Jeremiah also told you: 'Do not believe the falsehood that the house of God is here; do not believe this, but change your lives: do not judge falsely, do not oppress a stranger, a widow, or an orphan, do not shed innocent blood, and do not come into the house of God and say: Now we can quietly do evil. Do not make my house a den of thieves.'

Matt. XXI. xiii.

And the Jews objected and said: You say that our way of serving God is wrong. How can you prove that? And Jesus turned to them and said: Destroy this temple and in three days I will raise a new, living temple. And the Jews said: How can you suddenly build a new temple, when this one took forty years to build? And Jesus said to them: I speak to you of what is more important than the temple. You would not speak as you do if you understood the meaning of the prophet's words: 'I, God, do not rejoice in your sacrifices, but in your love of one another.' The living temple is the whole world of men when they love one another.

John II. xviii.
xix.
xx.
Matt. XII. vi.
vii.

And many people in Jerusalem believed in what he said. But he himself believed in nothing external for he knew that everything is within man. He had no need that anyone should give witness of man, for he knew that the spirit is in man.

John II. xxiii.
xxiv.
xxv.

And Jesus had once to pass through Samaria. He came to the Samaritan village of Sychar, near the place that

IV. iv.

Jacob gave to his son Joseph. Jacob's well John IV. v. was there, and Jesus, being tired by his journey, sat down by it while his pupils vi. went into the town to fetch bread. viii.

And a woman came from Sychar to draw water, and Jesus asked her to give him to drink. She said to him: How is it vii. that you ask me to give you water? For you Jews have no dealings with us Samaritans. ix.

But he said to her: If you knew me and knew what I teach you would not say that, but would give me to drink and I would give you the water of life. Whoever x. drinks of the water from this well will thirst again, but whoever drinks of the xiii. water of life shall always be satisfied, and it will bring him to everlasting life. xiv.

The woman understood that he was speaking of divine things, and said to him: I see that you are a prophet and wish to teach me. But how can you teach me xix. divine things when you are a Jew and I am a Samaritan? Our people pray to God upon this mountain, but you Jews say that the house of God is only in Jerusalem. You cannot teach me divine things, for you have one religion and we have an-other. xx.

Then Jesus said to her: Believe me, woman, the time has arrived when people will come neither to this mountain nor to Jerusalem to pray to the Father. The xxi. time has come when the real worshippers of God will honour the heavenly Father in spirit and by their works. The Father has need of such worshippers. The woman xxiii.

did not understand what he meant by saying that God is a spirit, and she said: I have heard that a messenger of God will come, he whom they call the anointed. He will tell us everything. *John IV. xxv.*

Jesus said to her: It is I who am speaking to you. Do not expect anything more. *xxvi.*

After this Jesus came to the country of the Jews and lived there with his pupils and taught. At that time John was teaching near Salim, and bathing people in the river Enon, for he had not yet been imprisoned. *III. xxii. xxiii. xxiv.*

And a dispute arose between John's pupils and those of Jesus as to which was better—John's cleansing by water, or the teaching of Jesus. And they came to John and said to him: You cleanse with water, but Jesus only teaches, and all go to him. What do you say about him? *xxv. xxvi.*

John said: A man can of himself teach nothing unless God teach him. He who speaks of the earth is of the earth, but he who speaks of God is from God. It cannot be proved whether spoken words are from God or not from God. God is a spirit; He cannot be measured and cannot be proved. He who understands the words of the spirit proves thereby that he is of the spirit. The Father, loving his son, has entrusted everything to him. He who believes in the son has life, but he who does not believe in the son has no life. God is the spirit in man. *xxvii. xxxi. xxxii–xxxiv. xxxv. xxxvi.*

After this one of the Orthodox came to Jesus and invited him to dinner. Jesus went in and sat down to table. The *Luke XI. xxxvii.*

Orthodox man noticed that Jesus did not wash before the meal and was surprised. Jesus said to him: You Orthodox people wash everything outside, but is everything clean within you? Be kind to all men, and everything will be clean. Luke XI. xxxviii.

xxxix, xli.

And while he was in the house of the Orthodox man, a woman of the town who was a wrong-doer came there. She had learnt that Jesus was in that house and came there and brought a bottle of perfume. And she knelt at his feet and wept, and wetting his feet with her tears wiped them with her hair, and poured the perfume over them. Luke VII. xxxvii.

xxxviii.

The Orthodox man saw this and thought to himself: He can hardly be a prophet. If he were really a prophet he would know what sort of a woman it is that is washing his feet: he would know that she is a wrong-doer and would not let her touch him. xxxix.

Jesus, guessing his thought, turned to him and said: Shall I tell you what I think? Yes, do so, replied his host. Then Jesus said: There were two men who held themselves debtors to one master, one for five hundred pieces of money and the other for fifty. And neither of them had anything to pay with. And the creditor forgave them both. Which of them do you think would love the creditor and care for him most? The host replied: He of course that owed most. xl.

xli.

xlii.

xliii.

Then Jesus pointed to the woman and said: So it is with you and this woman. You consider yourself Orthodox, and therefore a small debtor; she considers herself a wrong-doer and therefore a great debtor. I came into your house and you did not give me water to wash my feet; she washes them with her tears and wipes them with her hair. You did not kiss me, but she kisses my feet. You gave me no oil for my head, but she anoints my feet with precious perfume. He who considers himself Orthodox will not do works of love; only he who considers himself a wrong-doer will do them. And for works of love everything is forgiven. And he said to her: Your wickedness is forgiven you. And Jesus said: Everything depends on what a man considers himself to be. He who considers himself good will not be good, but he who considers himself bad is good.

Luke VII.
xliv.

xlv.

xlvi.

xlvii.

And he added: Two men came into the Temple to pray. One was Orthodox, and the other was a tax-farmer.

xlviii.

XVIII. x.

The Orthodox man prayed: I thank thee, O God, that I am not as other men, not miserly, nor a libertine, nor a deceiver, nor such a wretch as that tax-farmer. I fast twice a week, and give away a tenth of my property.

xi.

xii.

But the tax-farmer stood far away, and dared not look up to heaven but only beat his breast, saying: God, look upon me, sinner that I am.

xiii.

This was a better prayer than that of the Orthodox man, for he who exalts himself abases himself, and he who humbles himself raises himself.

xiv.

Then some pupils of John came to

Jesus and said: Why do your pupils not fast, while we and the Orthodox fast a great deal? The law of God orders fasting.

Luke V.
xxxiii.

And Jesus said to them: While the bridegroom is at the wedding no one grieves. Only when the bridegroom has gone do they grieve.

xxxiv.
xxxv.

Having life, one should not grieve. The external service of God cannot be combined with the activity of love. The old teaching of external service of God cannot be combined with my teaching of active love of one's neighbour. To unite my teaching with the old is like tearing a piece from a new garment and sewing it onto an old one. The new one will be torn and the old one will not be mended. Either all my teaching must be accepted or all the old, and having accepted my teaching it is impossible to keep the old teaching of purification, fasting, and keeping Saturday—just as new wine must not be poured into old wine-skins, or the old skins will burst and the wine will be spilt. New wine must be put into new wine-skins and then they will both be preserved.

xxxvi.
xxxvii.
xxxviii.

III

THE SOURCE OF LIFE

The life of all men proceeds from the spirit of the Father.

'HALLOWED BE THY NAME'

LATER on, some of John's pupils came to ask Jesus whether it was he of whom John spoke: Did he reveal the Kingdom of God and renew men by the spirit?

Matt. XI.
ii–iii.

Jesus answered and said: Look for yourselves, and listen to the teaching—and tell John whether the Kingdom of God has begun and whether people are being renewed by the spirit. Tell him what Kingdom of God I am preaching. It is said in the prophecies that when the Kingdom of God comes all men will be blessed. Tell him that my Kingdom of God is such that the poor are blessed, and so is everyone who understands the teaching.

Matt. XI.
iv.

v.

vi.

And having let John's pupils go, Jesus began to speak to the people about the Kingdom of God that John announced. He said: When you went to John in the wilderness to be baptized, what did you go to see? Orthodox teachers of the law went to see John too, but they did not understand what he was talking about, and considered him of no account. Those Orthodox teachers of the law only consider true what they themselves invent and hear from one another, or the law they have themselves devised; but what John says and what I say, they do not listen to and do not understand. Of what John says they have only understood that he fasts in the wilderness, and they say: 'There is a devil in him.' Of what I say they have understood only that I do not fast, and they say: 'He eats and drinks with tax-gatherers and sinners—he is a friend of theirs.' They are like children in the street who chatter to one another and wonder that no one listens to them. And you may judge of their wisdom by

vii.
xvi.

xviii.

xix.
xvii.
xix.

what they do. If you went to John to see
a man dressed in rich clothes—why, such
men live here in the palaces. What then
is it you went to see in the wilderness? Did
you go because you think John is like
other prophets? Do not think so! John is
not a prophet like the others. He is more
than all the prophets. The others foretold
what might happen. He announces what
is: namely, that the Kingdom of God was,
and is, here on earth. I tell you truly: no
one greater than John has ever been born.
He has declared the Kingdom of God on
earth and is therefore above all the others.
The law and the prophets were necessary
till John came, but now he has announced
that the Kingdom of God is on earth, and
that he who makes an effort can enter
into it.

And some of the Orthodox came to
Jesus and asked him: How and when
will the Kingdom of God come? And he
answered them: The Kingdom of God
which I preach is not what the former
prophets preached. They said that God
would come with divers visible signs, but
I speak of a Kingdom of God the coming
of which cannot be seen with the eyes.
And if anyone tells you: See, it has come,
or is coming; or, See, it is here, or there;
do not believe them. The Kingdom of
God is not in any definite time or place.
It is like lightning—here, there and everywhere. And it has neither time nor place,
for the Kingdom of God that I preach is
within you.

After that, one of the Orthodox, a

Margin references:

Matt. XI.
viii.

ix.

x.

Luke XVI.
xvi.

XVII. xx.

xxiii.

xxiv.

xxi.

Jewish ruler named Nicodemus, came to Jesus at night and said: You do not bid men keep Saturday, or tell them to observe cleanliness, or to offer sacrifices, or to fast, and you would abolish the temple, and say that God is a spirit and that the Kingdom of God is within us. What is this Kingdom of God? John III. i, ii.

And Jesus answered him: Understand that if man is conceived from heaven there must be something heavenly in him. You must be born again. iii.

Nicodemus did not understand this, and said: How can a man, born of the flesh and grown up, return to his mother's womb and be conceived afresh? v.

And Jesus answered him: Understand what I say: I say that man is born not from the flesh alone but also from the spirit, and so every man is conceived of flesh and of spirit, and therefore the kingdom of heaven is within him. Of the flesh he is flesh. From flesh spirit cannot be born; spirit can come only from spirit. v. The spirit is the living thing within you which lives in freedom and reason; it is that of which you know neither the beginning nor the end and which every man feels within him. So why do you wonder that I said that we must be born from heaven? vi. vii, viii.

Nicodemus said: Still I do not believe that this can be so. ix.

Then Jesus said to him: What kind of a teacher are you if you do not understand this? Understand that I am not talking any kind of mystery; I speak of what we x.

all know, and assure you of what we all see. How will you believe in what is in heaven if you do not believe in what is on earth and within yourself? John III. xi.

xii.

No one has ever gone up to heaven, and we have only man on earth who has come from heaven and is himself of heaven. It is this heavenly son of man that must be exalted, that all may believe in him and not perish but have heavenly life. Not for man's destruction, but for their good, did God implant in man this son of his, like unto Himself. He gave him that everyone should believe in him and not perish but have eternal life. He did not bring this son of his (this inner life) into the world of men to destroy it, but brought forth his son (this inner life) that the world of men should live by him. xiii. xv. xvi. xvii.

He who commits his life to this son of man does not die, but he who does not commit his life to him destroys himself by not trusting to what is life itself. Division (death) consists in this, that life came into the world, but men go away from that life. xviii.

Light is the life of men; light came into the world, but men prefer darkness to light, and do not go to the light. He who does wrong avoids the light that his deeds may not be seen, and so deprives himself of life. But he who lives in the truth goes to the light that his deeds may be seen, and he has life and is united to God. xix. xx. xxi.

The Kingdom of God must be understood not as you imagine—that the Kingdom of God will come for all men at a certain time and in a certain place—but thus: in the whole world there are always some people who rely on the heavenly son of man, and these become sons of the Kingdom; the others who do not rely on him perish. The Father of the spirit in man is the Father of those only who acknowledge themselves as his sons. And therefore only those exist to him who have preserved within them what he gave them.

After this Jesus began to explain to the people what the Kingdom of God is, and he taught it them by parables.

He said: The Father—who is the spirit—sows the life of understanding in the world as a husbandman sows grain in his field. He sows over the whole field without remarking which seeds fall in what place. And some seeds fall on the path and the birds come and eat it. Other seeds fall among stones and though they come up they wither, because there is no room for their roots. Others again fall among wormwood and the wormwood chokes them, and though ears form they do not fill. But other seeds fall on good ground and grow and make up for the lost seed, and bear ears which fill, and which yield thirtyfold, or sixtyfold, or a hundredfold. So God also has sown the spirit broadcast in man: in some it is lost but in others it yields a hundredfold. It is these last that form the Kingdom of God.

So the Kingdom of God is not what you imagine—that God will come to reign over you. God has sown the spirit, and the

Matt. XIII iii.

iv.

v.

vii.

viii.

Kingdom of God will be only in those who preserve it. Mark IV. xxvi.

God does not force men but, like a sower, casts seed on the ground and thinks no more of it. The seed itself swells, xxvii. sprouts, puts forth leaf, stalk, and ears that fill with grain. Only when it has xxviii. ripened does the husbandman send reapers to gather in the harvest. In the same way God gave His Son—the spirit—to the world; and the spirit grows in the world of itself, and the sons of the spirit make up the Kingdom of God. xxix.

A woman puts yeast into a kneading trough and mixes it with flour. She then mixes it no more but lets the yeast and the bread rise. As long as people live God does not interfere with their life. He gave the spirit to the world and the spirit lives in men, and those who live by the spirit constitute the Kingdom of God. For the spirit there is neither death nor evil. Death and evil exist for the flesh but not for the spirit. Matt. XIII. xxxiii.

The Kingdom of God may be compared to this: a farmer sowed good seed in his field. The farmer is the spirit, the Father; the field is the world; the good seed xxiv. are the sons of the Kingdom of God. Then the farmer lay down to sleep and an enemy came and sowed darnel in the field. The enemy is temptation, and the xxv. darnel represents those who yield to temptation. Then the labourers came to the farmer and said: Can you have sown bad seed? Much darnel has come up on your field. Send us to weed it out. And

the farmer said: No, do not do that, or in Matt. XIII. xxvii, xxviii, xxix.
weeding out the darnel you will trample
the wheat. Let them grow together.
When the harvest comes I will tell the
reapers to gather the darnel and burn it,
but the wheat I will store in the barn.
The harvest is the end of human life,
the harvesters are the powers of heaven.
They will burn the darnel, but the wheat
will be winnowed and gathered. So also
at life's end all that was temporary illusion
will perish, and the true life of the spirit
will alone be left. Evil does not exist for
the Father, the spirit. The spirit keeps
what it needs and what is not of it does
not exist for it.

The kingdom of heaven is like a net. xxx. xlvii.
When spread out in the sea it catches all
kinds of fish, and when it is drawn in, the
worthless fish are set aside and thrown
back into the sea. So will it be at the end
of the age: the powers of heaven will take
the good and the evil will be cast away. xlviii, xlix.

And when he had finished speaking,
his pupils asked him what these parables
meant. And he said to them: These x.
parables must be understood in two ways.
I speak all these parables because there
are some like you, my pupils, who understand what the Kingdom of God consists
of, and understand that it is within each
man, and understand how to enter it; but
others do not understand this. They look
but do not see, they hear but do not
understand, for their hearts have become
gross. So I speak these parables with two xi, xiv
meanings, for these people and for those.

To the others I speak of God, of what His Kingdom is for Him, and they may understand that. But for you I speak of what the Kingdom of God is for you—the kingdom that is within you. *Matt. XIII. xv.*

And see that you understand the parable of the sower rightly. For you that parable means this: To everyone who has understood the meaning of the Kingdom of God, but has not accepted it in his heart, evil comes and robs him of what was sown; this is the seed by the wayside. *xviii.* That which was sown on stony ground represents the man who receives the teaching readily and gladly, but has no root and *xix.* only accepts it for a time, and as soon as *xx.* pressure and persecution comes because *xxi.* of the meaning of the kingdom, he at once denies it. That which is sown among the wormwood is he who understands the meaning of the kingdom, but worldly *xxii.* cares and eagerness for riches strangle the meaning in him and he does not bear fruit. And that which was sown on good ground is he who understands the meaning of the kingdom and takes it into his heart; *xxiii.* he bears fruit a hundredfold, or sixtyfold, or thirtyfold. For to him that keeps the spirit much is given; but from him who does not keep it everything will be taken away. *xii.*

So see how you understand these parables. Understand them so as not to yield to deceptions, wrong-doings, and cares, but so as to yield thirtyfold, sixtyfold, or a hundredfold. *Luke VIII. xviii.*

The kingdom of heaven in the soul

grows up from nothing but gives everything. It is like a birch-seed, which is a very small seed, but when it grows up becomes a very big tree, and the birds of heaven build their nests in it.

Matt. XIII.
xxxi, xxxii.

IV

THE KINGDOM OF GOD

Therefore the will of the Father is the life and welfare of all men.

'THY KINGDOM COME'

JESUS went about in the towns and villages and taught all men the happiness of doing the Father's will. And he was sorry for people because they perish without knowing what true life consists of, and trouble and torment themselves without knowing why, like scattered sheep that have no shepherd.

Matt. IX.
xxxv.

xxxvi.

Once many people came to Jesus to hear his teaching and he went up on a hill and sat down. His pupils surrounded him. And he began to teach the people what the Father's will is. He said:

V. i.

Blessed are the poor and the homeless, for they live in the will of the Father. If they are hungry they shall be satisfied, and if they sorrow and weep they shall be comforted. If people despise them, thrust them aside, and drive them away, let them be glad of it, for so God's people have always been treated and they receive a heavenly reward.

Luke VI.
xx, xxi.

xxii.

xxiii.

But woe to the rich, for they have

G

already got what they wanted, and will get nothing more.

Now they are satisfied, but they too will be hungry. Now they rejoice, but they too will be sad. Woe to those whom everyone praises, for only deceivers are praised by everybody.

Blessed are the poor and homeless; but blessed only if they are poor not merely outwardly but also in spirit—just as salt is good only when it has saltness in it and is not salt merely in appearance.

So you also, the poor and homeless, are the teachers of the world; you are blessed if you know that true happiness is in being homeless and poor. But if you are poor only outwardly then, like salt that has no savour, you are good for nothing. You are the light of the world, therefore do not hide your light but let men see it. When a man lights a candle he does not put it under the bench but on the table that it should give light to everyone in the room. So you, too, should not hide your light but show it by your actions, that men may see that you have the truth, and seeing your good deeds may understand your heavenly Father.

And do not think that I free you from the law. I teach not release from the law but fulfilment of the eternal law. As long as there are men under heaven the eternal law remains. There will be no release from law till men of themselves fulfil the eternal law completely. And now I give you the commandments of that eternal law. If anyone releases himself

Luke VI.
xxiv.

xxv, xxvi.

xx.

Matt. V.
xiii.

xiv.

xv.

Matt. V. xvi.

xvii.

xviii.

from any of these short commandments
and teaches others that they may do so,
he shall be least in the kingdom of heaven,
but he who fulfils them and thereby
teaches others to fulfil them shall be great
in the kingdom of heaven. For if your
virtue is no more than the virtue of the
Orthodox legalists you will never reach
the kingdom of heaven.

These are the commandments:

In the former law it was said: Do not
kill, and if anyone kills another he must be
judged.

But I tell you that everyone who grows
angry with his brother-man deserves
judgement, and still more to blame is he
who speaks abusively to his brother-
man.

So if you wish to pray to God, first think
whether there is anyone who has something against you. If you remember even
one man who considers that you have
offended him, leave your prayers and go
first to make peace with your brother-
man, and then you may pray. Know that
God requires neither sacrifice nor prayer,
but only peace, concord, and love among
men; and that you can neither pray nor
think of God if there is a single man
towards whom you do not feel love.

So this is the first commandment: Do
not be angry, and do not rail; and if you
have spoken harshly to anyone make peace
with him and do it so that no one should
have a grudge against you.

In the former law it was said: Do not
commit adultery, and if you wish to put

Matt. V.

xix.

xx.

xxi.

xxii.

xxiii.

xxiv.

away your wife, give her a letter of divorcement.

But I tell you that if you look lustfully at a woman's beauty you are already committing adultery. All sensuality destroys the soul, and so it is better for you to renounce the pleasures of the flesh than to destroy your life.

Matt. V. xxvii, xxviii, xxix, xxxi.

And if you put away your wife, then besides being vicious yourself you drive her to wantonness too, as well as him with whom she may unite.

So that is the second commandment: Do not think that love of a woman is good, do not desire women, but live with her with whom you have become united, and do not leave her.

xxxii.

In the former law it was said: Do not utter the name of the Lord God in vain, do not call upon God when lying, and do not dishonour the name of your God. Do not swear to any untruth and so profane your God.

xxxiii.

But I tell you that every oath is a profanation of God. Therefore do not swear at all. Man cannot promise anything, for he is wholly in the power of the Father. He cannot make one grey hair black. How then can he swear beforehand that he will do this or that, and swear to it by God? Every oath is a profanation of God, for if a man is compelled to fulfil under an oath that which is against the will of God it shows that he had promised to act contrary to God's will, and so every oath is an evil. But when men ask you about anything, say Yes if it is yes, or

xxxiv, xxxv, xxxvi.

No if it is no; anything added to that is evil.

So the third commandment is: Never swear anything for anyone. Say Yes when it is yes, No when it is no, and understand that every oath is evil.

Matt. V.
xxxvii.

In the former law it was said that if a man killed another he must give a life for a life, an eye for an eye, a tooth for a tooth, an arm for an arm, an ox for an ox, a slave for a slave, and much else.

xxxviii.

But I say to you: Do not fight evil by evil, and not only do not exact at law an ox for an ox, a slave for a slave, a life for a life, but do not resist evil at all. If anyone wishes to take an ox from you, give him another; if he wants to take your coat by law, give him your shirt as well; if anyone knocks out a tooth on one side, turn the other side to him. If he would make you do one piece of work for him, do two. If men wish to take your property, let them have it. If they owe you money and do not return it, do not demand it.

xxxix.

xl.

And therefore: Do not judge or go to law, do not punish, and you yourself will not be judged or punished. Forgive everyone and you will be forgiven; but if you judge others they will judge you also.

Luke VI.
xxx.

xxxvii.

You cannot judge, for men are all blind and do not see the truth. How can you see a speck in your brother's eye when there is dust in your own? You must first get your own eye clear—but whose eyes are perfectly clear? Can a blind man lead the blind? They will both fall into the

Matt. VII. i.

iii.

pit. And those who judge and punish are
like blind men leading the blind.

Luke VI.
xxxix.

Those who judge, and condemn others
to violent treatment, wounds, mutilation,
or death, wish to correct them, but what
can come of their teaching except that the
pupils will learn to become just like their
teacher? What then will they do when
they have learnt the lesson? Only what
their teacher does: violence and murder.

xl.

And do not expect to find justice in the
courts. To entrust one's love of justice to
men's courts is like throwing precious
pearls to swine: they will trample on
them and will tear you to pieces.

Matt. VII.
vi;
V. xxxix.

And therefore the fourth commandment is: However men may wrong you,
do not return evil, do not judge or go to
law, do not sue, and do not punish.

In the former law it was said: Do good
to men of your own nation and do harm to
foreigners.

xliii.

But I tell you: Love not only your own
countrymen, but people of other nations
also. Let others hate you, attack you, and
wrong you, but speak well of them and do
good to them. If you are attached only
to your own countrymen, remember that
all men are attached to their own
countrymen, and wars result from that.
But behave equally well to men of all
nations, and you will be sons of the Father.
All men are His children, so they are all
brothers to you.

xliv.

xlv, xlvi.

And so this is the fifth commandment:
Treat foreigners as I have told you to treat
one another. To the Father of all men

there are no separate nations or separate kingdoms: all are brothers, all sons of one Father. Make no distinctions among people as to nations and kingdoms.

And so: (1) Do not be angry, but live at peace with all men. (2) Do not indulge yourself in sexual gratification. (3) Do not promise anything on oath to anyone. (4) Do not resist evil, do not judge and do not go to law. (5) Make no distinction of nationality, but love foreigners as your own people.

All these commandments are contained in one: All that you wish men to do to you, do you to them.

Matt. VII. xii.

Do not fulfil these commandments for praise from men. If you do it for men, then from men you have your reward. But if you do it not for men, your reward is from your heavenly Father. So if you do good to others do not boast about it before men. That is what the hypocrites do, to obtain praise. And they get what they seek. But if you do good to men, do it so that no one sees it, and that your left hand should not know what your right hand does. And your Father will see it and will give you what you need.

VI i.

ii.

iii.

iv.

And if you wish to pray, do not do it as the hypocrites do. They love to pray in the churches and in the sight of men. They do it for men's praise, and from men receive what they aim at.

v.

But if you wish to pray, go where no one will see you, and pray to the Father of your spirit, and He will see what is in your soul and will give you what your soul desires.

vi.

When you pray, do not wag your tongue as the hypocrites do. Your Father knows what you need before you open your lips. Matt. VI. vii.

Pray only thus:

Our Father, without beginning and without end, like the heavens!

May Thy being alone be holy.

May power be Thine alone, so that Thy will may be done, without beginning and without end, on earth.

Give me the food of life this present day.

Efface my former mistakes and wipe them out, as I efface and wipe out all the mistakes my brothers have made; that I may not fall into temptation, but be saved from evil.

For the power and strength are Thine, and the decision is Thine. ix–xiii.

If you pray, free yourself above all from malice against anyone. For if you do not forgive others their faults, your Father will not forgive you yours. Mark XI. xxv.

xxvi.

If you fast, do so without any parade of it before others. The hypocrites fast that people should see it and praise them—and people do praise them, so they get what they wanted. But you should not do so; if you suffer want, go about with a cheerful face that men may not see, but that your Father may see and give you what you need. Matt. VI. xvi.

xvii, xviii.

Do not lay up store for yourself on earth. On earth maggots consume, and rust eats, and thieves steal: but lay up for yourselves heavenly riches. Heavenly riches are not consumed by maggots, nor eaten away by rust, nor do thieves steal them. Where your riches are, there will your heart be also. xix.

xx.

xxi.

The light of the body is the eye, and the Matt. VI. xxii. light of the soul is the heart. If your eye is dim your whole body will be in darkness. xxiii. And if the light of your heart is dim your whole soul will be in darkness. You cannot serve two masters at the same time. If you please the one you will offend the other. You cannot serve both God and the flesh. xxiv. Either you will work for the earthly life or for God. Therefore do not be anxious about what you will eat or drink, or how you will be dressed. For the life is more wonderful than food and clothing and God has given you this. xxv.

Look on God's creatures, the birds. They do not sow or reap or gather in the harvest, yet God feeds them. In God's sight man is not less than a bird. If God xxvi. gave man life, He will be able to feed him too. And you yourselves know that you can do nothing of yourselves, however xxvii. you may strive. You cannot lengthen your life by an hour. And why do you trouble about clothing? The flowers of the field xxviii. do no work and do not spin, but they are adorned as Solomon in all his luxury never was. xxix.

And if God has so adorned the grass which grows to-day, and to-morrow is cut down, will He not clothe you? xxx.

Do not be afraid and do not worry; do not say that you must think of what you will eat and how you will be clothed. All men need these things and God knows that you need them. So do not trouble xxxi. about the future. Live in the present day. xxxii. Take care to be in the Father's will. Desire xxxiii.

that which alone is important, and the rest will come of itself. Seek only to be in the will of the Father, and do not trouble about the future, for when it comes its trouble will come too. There is enough evil in the present.

Matt. VI. xxxiv.

Ask and it shall be given you; seek and ye shall find; knock and it will be opened to you. Where is there a father who would give his son a stone instead of bread, or a snake instead of a fish? Then why do you think if we wicked men can give our children what they need, that your Father in heaven will not give you what you truly need, if you ask Him? Ask, and the heavenly Father will give the spirit of life to them that ask Him.

Luke XI. ix.

Matt. VII. ix, x.

xi.

Narrow is the path to life, but enter by that narrow way. There is only one entry to life—a strait and narrow one. Great and wide is the field around, but it leads to destruction. The narrow way alone leads to life, and few find it. But do not be afraid, little flock! The Father has prepared the Kingdom for you.

xiii.

xiv.

Luke XII. xxxii.

Only, beware of false prophets and teachers; they come to you in sheep's clothing, but inwardly are ravening wolves. By their fruits—by what comes from them—you will know them. From the burdock you do not gather grapes, nor apples from an aspen. A good tree bears good fruit and a bad tree bad fruit. So you will know these men by the fruits of their teaching.

Matt. VII. xv. xvi.

xvii–xx.

A good man out of his good heart brings forth all that is good. But an evil man out of his evil heart brings forth all that is evil. For from the overflow of the heart the lips speak. And therefore if teachers tell you to do to others what would be bad for yourselves, if they teach violence, executions, and wars—then you may know that they are false teachers. Luke VI. xlv.

For it is not those who say: 'Lord, Lord!' who will enter the kingdom of heaven, but those who fulfil the will of the heavenly Father. The false teachers will say: 'Lord, Lord! We taught your doctrine, and by your teaching drove out evil.' But I will disown them and say: 'No, I never recognized you and do not recognize you now, Go away from me; you do what is unlawful.' Matt. VII. xxi. xxii. xxiii.

He who hears these words of mine and acts on them is like a reasonable man who builds his house on a rock. And his house will stand against all storms. But he who hears these words of mine and does not act on them is like a foolish man who builds his house on the sand. When a storm comes his house will fall and all in it will perish. xxiv, xxv. xxvi. xxvii.

And the people were all astonished at this teaching, for the teaching of Jesus was quite different from that of the Orthodox professors of the law. They taught a law that had to be obeyed, but Jesus taught that all men are free. And in Jesus Christ were fulfilled the prophecies of Isaiah: that a people living in darkness, in the shadow of death, saw the light of life. That he who brought this light of truth did no violence or harm to men, Luke IV. xxxii. Matt. IV. xiv.

but was meek and gentle. To bring truth into the world he neither disputes nor shouts, nor is his voice raised, and he will not break a straw or put out the smallest light, and all the hope of men is in his teaching. Matt. IV. xvi. XXII. xix. xx.

V

THE TRUE LIFE

The satisfaction of the personal will leads to death; the satisfaction of the Father's will gives true life.

'THY WILL BE DONE'

AND Jesus rejoiced in the power of the spirit and said:

I acknowledge the spirit of the Father, the source of everything in heaven and earth, who has revealed what was hidden from the wise and learned to the simple, because they acknowledge themselves sons of the Father. Matt. XI. xxv.

All who are concerned for the happiness of the body have put on a yoke not made for them, and have harnessed themselves to a load they cannot draw.

Understand my teaching and follow it and you shall have peace and joy in life. I give you another yoke and another load —the spiritual life. Yoke yourselves to this, and you shall learn from me peace and happiness. xxviii.

Be tranquil and meek-hearted and you will find blessedness in your life. For my teaching is a yoke made for you, and to obey my teaching is to have a light load with a yoke suited to you. xxix. xxx.

Once when he was asked whether he John IV.
xxxi.
wished to eat, he replied: I have food you
do not know of. They thought someone xxxii.
had brought him food, but he said: xxxiii.

My food is to do the will of Him who
gave me life and to accomplish what he
has entrusted to me. Do not say: There is xxxiv.
still time, as a farmer says while waiting
for the harvest. He who fulfils the will of
the Father is always satisfied and knows
neither hunger nor thirst. The fulfilment
of the will of God always satisfies and is
always a reward in itself. You must not
say: 'I will do the will of God later.'
While you have life you always can and
should do the will of the Father. Our life
is a field God has sown, and our business xxxv, xxxvi.
is to gather its fruits. If we gather its
fruits we receive the reward of a life beyond time. We do not give ourselves xxxvii.
life, someone else gives it us. And if we
labour to gather in life, then like harvest-
men, we receive a reward. I teach you to
gather in this life which the Father gives
you. xxxviii.

Once Jesus went to Jerusalem. There V. i.
was then a bathing-place in the city, of ii.
which people said that an angel came
down into it, and that his coming stirred
the water and he who first plunged in after
that would be cured of whatever illness he
had. There were shelters set up around iv.
the pool, and under those shelters sick ii.
people lay, waiting for the water in the
pool to bubble, in order to plunge into it. iii.

And there was a man who had been
there thirty-eight years, and was weak.

Jesus asked him what ailed him. And the man told him that he had been ill for thirty-eight years and was waiting to get into the pool first after the water bubbled, in order to be healed, but all these thirty-eight years he had not been able to get in first for someone always got into the pool before him.

John V. v.

And Jesus saw that the man was old, and said to him: Do you wish to get well?

vi.

The man replied: Yes, I do wish to, but I have no one to help me into the pool in time. Someone always gets in before me.

vii.

And Jesus said to him: Arouse yourself, take up your bedding and go.

viii.

And the sick man took up his bedding and walked away.

And it was on a Saturday. And the Orthodox said: You must not carry your bedding for to-day is Saturday.

ix, x.

He replied: He who raised me told me to take up my bedding.

xi.

And the infirm man went away and told the Orthodox that it was Jesus who had cured him. And they were angry, and accused Jesus because he did such things on Saturday.

xv.

xvi.

And Jesus said: What the Father always does, I also do. I tell you truly: the son can do nothing for himself; he does only what he has understood from the Father. What the Father does, he also does. The Father loves the son, and has taught him all the things the son needs to know.

xvii.

xix.

xx.

As the Father gives life to the dead so the son gives life to him who desires it,

because as the business of the Father is John V. xxi.
life so the business of the son must be life.
The Father has not condemned men to
death, but has given them power to die
or live at will. And if they honour the son   xxii.
as the Father they will live.   xxiii.

I tell you truly that he who has understood my teaching and believed in the
common Father of all men, has life
already and is delivered from death. They   xxiv.
who have understood the meaning of hu-
man life have already escaped from death
and will always live. For as the Father   xxv.
has life in Himself so He has given the son
to have life in himself also, and has given   xxvi.
him freedom. It is in this way that he is
the son of man.   xxvii.

Henceforth mortals are divided into two
kinds: those who do good and thereby   xxviii.
find life, and those who do evil and are
thereby destroyed. And this is not my   xxix.
decision, but is what I have understood
from the Father. And my decision is just,
for I decide so not in order to do what
I wish, but in order that all may do the
will of the Father of all men.   xxx.

If I assure you that my teaching is true,
that does not confirm my teaching; what   xxxi.
confirms it is the conduct I teach. That
shows that I do not teach from myself but
from the Father of all men. And my   xxxvi.
Father, He who has taught me, confirms
the truth of my commandments in the
souls of all.

But you do not wish to understand or to   xxxvii.
know His voice. And you do not accept
the meaning that voice declares. You do

not wish to believe in that voice in yourselves which is the spirit that has descended from heaven.

John V. xxxviii.

Enter into the meaning of your scriptures. You will find in them the same as in my teaching: commands to live not for yourselves alone but to do good to men. Why then do you not wish to believe my commandments—which are those that give life to all men? I teach you in the name of the common Father of all men, and you do not accept my teaching, but if someone teaches you in his own name, him you believe.

xxxix.

xl.

xliii.

You should not believe all that people say to one another, but must believe only that there is in every man a son like the Father.

xliv.

And that men should not think that the kingdom of heaven is something visible—but should understand that it consists in fulfilment of the Father's will and that that fulfilment depends on each man's efforts—and that people might understand that life is given not for oneself personally but only for the fulfilment of the Father's will, which alone saves us from death and gives life, Jesus spoke a parable, and said:

There was a rich man who had to leave home. Before he set out he called his slaves and gave them ten pounds, one to each, and said: While I am away, work each of you, at what I have set you. And it happened that when he had gone, some of the people of that town said: We do not wish to serve him any more.

Luke XIX. xi, xii.

xiii.

xiv.

When the rich man returned, he called

the slaves to whom he had given the money, and asked what each of them had done with it.

Luke XIX. xv.

The first one came and said: See, master, with your one pound I have earned ten. And the master said to him: Well done, good slave, you have been faithful in a small matter and I will set you over much: be one with me in all my estate.

xvi.

xvii.

A second slave came and said: See master, with your pound I have earned five. And the master said to him: Well done, good slave, be one with me in all my estate.

xviii.

xix.

Another one came and said: See, here is your pound. I put it in a cloth and buried it because I was afraid of you. You are a hard man, you take where you did not store and gather where you did not sow.

xx.

xxi.

And the master said to him: Foolish slave! I will judge you by your own words. You say that from fear of me you hid the pound in the earth and did not make use of it. If you knew that I am severe and take where I have not given, then why did you not do as I bade you? If you had used my pound the estate would have been added to and you would have fulfilled what I bade you. But now you have not done what the pound was given you for, and so you must not have it.

xxii.

xxiii.

Matt.XXV. xxvi, xxvii.

And the master had the pound taken from him who had not used it and given to him who had done most. But the slaves remonstrated, and said to him: Master, he has a great deal already. But the master said: Give to him who worked

xxviii. Luke XIX. xxiv.

xxv.

much, for to him who looks after what he Luke XIX.
xxvi.
has, more shall be given. Drive out those
who did not wish to be in my power, and
let none of them remain. Matt. XXV.
xxx.

The master is the source of life, the
spirit, the Father. His slaves are men.
The pounds are the life of the spirit. As
the master did not work on his estate
himself but told the slaves each to work
by himself, so also the spirit of life in men
has told them to work for the life of all
men, and has then left them alone. Those
who sent to say that they did not acknowledge the master's power are those who do
not acknowledge the spirit of life. The
return of the master and his call for an
account is the destruction of the bodily
life and the decision of the people's fate:
whether they have increased the life that
was given them. Some, those slaves who
fulfil the master's will, use what is given
them and greatly increase it. These are
they who, having received life, understand
that life is the will of the Father and is
given them to serve the life of others. The
foolish and wicked slave who hid his
pound and did not use it, represents those
who only follow their own desires and
not the will of the Father, and do not serve
the life of others. The slaves who fulfil
the Master's will and work to increase his
estate become sharers in the master's whole
estate, but the slaves who do not fulfil the
master's will and do not work for him are
bereft of what was given them. Men who
fulfil the Father's will and serve life become sharers in the life of the Father and

receive more life notwithstanding the
destruction of the flesh. Those who do not
fulfil the will and do not serve life are bereft
of what life they had, and are destroyed.
Those who do not wish to acknowledge
the master's authority do not exist for
him: he drives them forth. Those who do
not acknowledge the life of the spirit
within themselves—the life of the son of
man—do not exist for the Father.

After this Jesus went into a desert place John VI. i.
and many people followed him. He went   ii.
up a hill and sat down there with his
pupils. And he saw many people coming   iii.
and said: Where can we get bread for all   v.
these people? Philip said: Even two
hundred pennyworth would not be   vii.
enough to give each of them something.
We have only a little bread and fish. And   Matt. XIV.
another pupil said: Some of them have   xvii;
bread: there is a boy who has five loaves   John VI.
and two small fishes. And Jesus said: Tell   x.
them all to lie down on the grass.

And Jesus took the bread he had, and
gave it to his pupils and bade them give it
to the other people. And so they all began
to give to one another what they had, and
they all had enough to eat and much was
left over.   xi.

Next day the people again came to
Jesus, and he said to them: You come to
me not because you have seen wonders,
but because you ate bread and were
satisfied. Do not work for food which   xxvi.
perishes, but for food which will last for
ever, such as only the spirit of the son of
man, sealed by the Father, gives you.   xxvii.

The Jews said: What must we do to fulfil the will of God?

And Jesus said: The work of God consists in believing in the life He has given
you.

They said: Give us proofs that we may
believe. What do you do? Our fathers ate
manna in the wilderness. God gave them
food to eat, so it is written.

Jesus answered them: The true heavenly
bread is the spirit of the son of man, which
the Father gives. For the food of man is
the spirit that descends from heaven. It
is that which gives life to the world.

My teaching gives true nourishment.
He who follows me will not hunger, and
he who believes in my teaching will never
know thirst. But I have already told you
that you have seen this and yet do not
believe.

All that life which the Father has given
to the son will be realized by my teaching,
and everyone who believes in it will share
that life. For I came down from heaven
not to do my own will but the will of the
Father who gave me life. And the will of
the Father who sent me is that I should
keep all the life He gave and not lose any
of it. So it is the will of the Father who
sent me, that everyone who sees the son
and believes in him should have everlasting life. And my teaching gives life at the
last day (of the flesh).

The Jews were disturbed at his saying
that his teaching had come down from
heaven. They said: Why, this is Jesus the
son of Joseph: we know his father and

John VI. xlii.

mother. How is it that he says his teaching has come down from heaven?

xliii.

And Jesus said: Do not discuss who I am and where I came from. My teaching is true, not because, like Moses, I declare that God spoke to me on Sinai, but because it exists in you too. Everyone who believes my commandments does so not because it is *I* who speak, but because our common Father draws him to Himself; and my teaching will give him life at the last day. It is written in the prophets that all men shall be taught of God. Everyone who understands the Father, and learns to know His will, yields himself to my teaching.

xliv.

No one has ever seen the Father, but he that is of God has seen and sees Him.

xlv.

xlvi.

He who believes in me (in my teaching) has everlasting life. My teaching is the food of life. Your fathers ate manna, food sent from heaven, and yet died. But the true food of life which descends from heaven is such that he who feeds on it will not die. And my teaching is this food of life that has descended from heaven. He who feeds on it lives for ever. And this food which I teach is my body which I give for the life of mankind.

xlvii.

xlviii.

xlix.

li.

The Jews did not at all understand what he said, and began to dispute as to how it was possible to give one's body for the life of men, and why.

lii.

And Jesus said to them: If you do not give your body for the life of the spirit there will be no life in you. He who does not give his body for the life of the spirit

liii.

has no real life. Only that in me which John VI. liv. gives up the body for the spirit has real life. And therefore our bodies are truly lv. food for the real life. Only that in me which consumes my body, that which gives up the bodily life for the true life—is really I—it is in me, and I am in it. And lvi. as I live in the body by the will of the Father, so that which lives in me lives by my will. lvii.

And some of his pupils when they heard this, said: These are hard words, and it is difficult to understand them. lx.

And Jesus said to them: Your minds are so confused, that my saying about what man was, is, and always will be, seems to you difficult. Man is a spirit in the flesh, lxi. and the spirit alone gives life—the flesh does not give life. In the words that seem to you so difficult I said no more than that the spirit is life. lxii, lxiii.

Afterwards Jesus chose seventy men from among those near him, and sent Luke X. i. them to places he himself wished to go to. He said to them: Many men do not know the blessing of real life. I am sorry for them all, and wish to teach them. ii.

But as a husbandman cannot himself reap his whole harvest, so I, too, cannot do all that is needed. Go you to different towns and proclaim everywhere the fulfilment of the will of the Father.

Say: The will of the Father is this: not to be angry, not to lust, not to take oaths, not to resist evil, and not to make any distinction between people. And accordingly fulfil these laws yourselves in everything. iii–v.

I send you like sheep among wolves. Be wise as serpents and pure as doves. Above all, have nothing of your own; take nothing with you, neither wallet, nor bread, nor money, only the clothes you wear and shoes. Make no distinction between people; do not choose out the people with whom you will stay. But stay in whatever house you first come to. When you enter a house, greet the master. If he take you in, stay there; if not, go to another house.

Matt. X.
xvi.

Luke X. iv.

Mark VI. x.

xi.

For what you will say they will hate you and fall upon you and drive you away. But when you are driven out go to another village, and if you are driven from there, go to yet another. You will be pursued as wolves pursue sheep, but do not be afraid, endure to the last hour. They will take you to the Courts and try you, and will flog you and take you before the authorities for you to justify yourselves before them. But do not be afraid when you are taken to the Courts, and do not prepare what you will say: the spirit of the Father in you will tell you what to say. Before you have passed through all the towns some people will understand your teaching and turn to it.

Matt. X.
xxii.

xxiii.

xix

xxiii.

So be not afraid. What is hidden in men's souls will come forth. What you will say to two or three will spread among thousands. Above all, do not be afraid of those who can kill your body. They can do nothing to your souls, so fear them not. Fear rather that which can destroy both body and soul by the non-fulfilment of

xxvi.

xxvii.

xxviii.

the Father's will—fear that. Five spar-
rows are sold for a farthing, but even they
do not die without the Father's will. And
no hair falls from the head without the
Father's will. So what have you to fear
if you live in that will?

Matt. X.
xxix.

xxx.
xxxi.

Not everyone will believe in my teaching. And those who do not believe will
hate it because it deprives them of what
they love. So dissensions will come from
my teaching. It will kindle the world like
a fire, and from it strife must arise. There
will be dissension in every house, father
against son, mother against daughter.
Families will hate those members who
understand my teaching, and will kill
them. For to him who understands my
teaching there will be no meaning in
'father', or 'mother', or 'wife', or 'children',
or 'property'.

xxxiv.

Luke XII.
xlix, li, lii.

liii.

Then the learned Orthodox gathered at
Jerusalem and went to Jesus who was in
a village near by. A crowd of people had
thronged into the house where he was and
stood around it.

XIV. xxvi.

Matt. XII.
xv.

The Orthodox began to speak to the
people, telling them not to listen to the
teaching of Jesus. They said that he was
possessed of a devil, and that if men lived
by his commandments there would be
still more evil in the world than now.
They said that he drove out evil by evil
means.

xxiv.

Jesus called them to him and said: You
say that I drive out evil by evil. But no
power destroys itself. If it destroyed itself
it would cease to exist. You try to drive

xxvi.

out evil by threats, executions, and murders, but evil still exists precisely because it cannot fight against itself. I do not drive out evil by evil as you try to.

Matt. XII. xxvii.

I drive out evil by calling on men to fulfil the will of the Father's spirit which gives life to all men. Five commandments express the will of that spirit, which gives happiness and life. And they therefore destroy evil. That is a proof that they are true.

xxviii.

If men were not sons of one spirit it would not be possible to overcome evil, just as it is not possible to enter a strong man's house and rob it. To rob his house it is necessary first to bind the strong man. And men are bound by their unity in the spirit of life.

xxix.

And so I say to you that all mistakes of men and every false opinion shall escape punishment, but false interpretations of the holy spirit, which gives life to all, will not be forgiven.

xxxi.

If anyone speaks ill of a man it may not be counted against him, but if anyone speaks against the holy spirit in man, that cannot pass without harm to him. Abuse me as much as you like, but do not decry the commandments of life I have disclosed to you. It cannot pass harmlessly for a man if he calls what is good—evil.

xxxii.

Man must be at one with the spirit of life. He who is not at one with it is against it. Man must serve the spirit of life and goodness in all men, and not in himself alone.

Either you believe life and happiness

to be good for the whole world, and should
then love life and happiness for all men,
or you believe life and happiness to be evil,
and should then not love them even for
yourself. Either you consider a tree good
and its fruit good, or else you consider
the tree bad and its fruit bad. For a tree
is valued by its fruit.

Matt. XII.
xxxiii.

VI

THE FALSE LIFE

*To obtain true life, man must on earth resign the false life
of the flesh and live by the spirit.*

'AS IN HEAVEN SO ON EARTH'

ONCE his mother and brothers came to
Jesus, and could not get to him because
there were so many around him. A man
seeing them went to Jesus and said: Your
family, your mother and brothers, are
standing outside wanting to see you.

Luke VIII.
xix.
Matt. XII.
xlvi.
Luke VIII.
xx.

But Jesus said: My mother and my
brothers are those who have understood
the will of the Father, and do it.

xxi.

And a woman exclaimed: Blessed is the
womb that bore you and the breasts that
you have sucked!

XI. xxvii.

And Jesus replied: Only they are blessed
who have understood the spirit of the
Father and keep it.

xxviii.

And a man said to Jesus: I will follow
you wherever you may go.

IX. lvii.

Jesus answered him: There is nowhere
for you to follow me to: I have neither
house nor any place to live in. The beasts

have their dens and their lairs, but man is at home everywhere if he lives by the spirit.

Luke IX. lviii.

It happened once that Jesus was sailing with his pupils in a boat. He said: Let us cross to the other side. A storm arose on the lake and the boat began to fill so that it nearly sank. But Jesus lay in the stern and slept. They woke him and said: Master, is it nothing to you if we are drowned? And when the storm subsided he said: Why are you so timid? You have no faith in the life of the spirit.

Mark IV. xxxv.

xxxvii.
xxxviii.

xl.

To one man Jesus said: Follow me.

But the man replied: I have a father who is old; let me first bury him and then I will follow you.

Luke IX. lix.

And Jesus said to him: Let the dead bury the dead, but if you wish really to live fulfil the Father's will and publish it.

lx.

Another man said: I wish to be your pupil and will fulfil the Father's will as you command, but let me first arrange my family affairs.

lxi.

And Jesus said to him: If a ploughman looks back he cannot plough. As long as you look back you cannot plough. You must forget everything except the furrow you are driving and only then can you plough. If you consider what may befall your bodily life you cannot live, because you have not understood the real life.

lxii.

After this it happened that Jesus went with his pupils into a village, and a woman named Martha asked him into her house. She had a sister, Mary, who sat at Jesus' feet and listened to his teaching, while

X. xxxviii.

Martha was busy preparing a good meal for them.　　　　Luke X. xxxix.

And Martha went up to Jesus and said: Do you not see that my sister leaves me to do all the work? Tell her to help me with it.　　　　xl.

In reply Jesus said to her: Martha, Martha! You busy yourself and are anxious about many things, but only one thing is needful; Mary has chosen that one necessary thing which no one shall take from her. The one thing needful for life is food for the soul.　　　　xli. xlii.

And Jesus said to them all:

He who wishes to follow me, let him put aside his own will and be ready to endure all hardships and sufferings of the flesh throughout his life; only then can he follow me. He who wishes to take heed for his bodily life will destroy his true life, but he who obeys the will of the Father, even though he may destroy his bodily life, will save his true life. And what profit is it to a man if he gains the whole world but destroys or harms his true life?　　　　IX. xiii. xxiv. xxv.

And he said: Beware of riches, for your life does not depend on possessing more than others.　　　　XII. xv.

There was once a rich man who had a large harvest. And he thought to himself: I will rebuild my barns and put up larger ones and gather all my wealth into them, and I will say to my soul: There, my soul, you have all you desire; rest, eat, drink, and live for your pleasure. But God said to him: Foolish man, to-night your soul will be taken and all that you have stored up will go to others.　　　　xvii. xviii. xix. xx.

So it is with everyone who provides for his bodily life and does not live in God.

Luke XII. xxi.

And Jesus said to them: You tell me that Pilate slew the Galileans. Were those Galileans any worse than others, that this happened to them? Not at all. We are all such, and we also shall all perish unless we find salvation from death. Or were those eighteen men who were crushed by a falling tower, worse than all the other people of Jerusalem? Not at all. If we do not save ourselves from death, to-day or to-morrow we too shall perish.

XIII. ii.

iii.

iv.

v.

If we have not yet perished as they did, we must think of our position thus:

A man had an apple-tree in his garden and he came and looked at the tree and saw there was no fruit on it. And he said to the gardener: This is the third year I have been here and found that apple-tree always barren. It must be cut down, for it only takes up space uselessly. But the gardener said: Let us wait awhile, master. I will dig round it, manure it, and we will see next summer. Perhaps it will bear fruit, but if not, then cut it down.

vi.

vii.

viii.

So we, too, while we live in the flesh and do not bear fruit of the life of the spirit, are barren apple-trees. Only by someone's mercy are we left for another year. But if we do not bear fruit we too shall perish—like him who rebuilt his barns, like the Galileans, like the eighteen men crushed by the falling tower, and like all who do not bear fruit—perishing and dying for ever.

To understand this no wisdom is neces-

sary; everyone can see it for himself. Not
only in domestic affairs but in all that
goes on in the world we can reason and
guess what is coming. If the wind is from
the west, we say: It will rain—and so it
happens. But if there is wind from the Luke XII
liv.
south, we say: It will be fine—and so it
happens. How is it that we can tell the lv
weather, but cannot foresee that we shall
all die and perish, and that the only
salvation for us is in the life of the spirit—
in the fulfilment of its will? lvi.

And many people followed Jesus, and
he again said to them all: XIV. xxv.

He who would be my follower, let him
put out of mind his father, mother, wife,
children, brothers, sisters, and all his
property, and let him at all times be ready
for anything. Only he who does what I do xxvi.
and follows my teaching can save himself
from death. xxvii.

For every man before beginning anything considers whether what he would do
is profitable; if it seems profitable he does
it, but if it seems unprofitable he will
abandon it. Every man who builds a
house first sits down and reckons how
much it will cost, how much he has, and
whether he can finish it; that it may not xxviii.
happen that having begun to build he
should be unable to finish, and so be
laughed at. xxix.

So also he who wishes to live the life of
the flesh should first consider how he can
finish what he is engaged on. xxx.

Every king who wishes to go to war will
first consider whether he can go against

twenty thousand men with only ten thousand. If he sees that he cannot, he will
send an ambassador to make peace, and
will not go to war.

So let every man, before giving himself
to the life of the flesh, bethink himself
whether he can resist death or whether
death is stronger than he, and whether he
had not better make peace at once.

Each of you should first reckon all that
he considers his own: family, money, and
property. When he has considered what
all this avails him, and understands that
it avails him nothing, only then can he be
my follower.

And hearing this, a man said: That is
well if there be a life of the spirit. But
what if we give up everything and there is
no such life?

To that Jesus replied: Not so. Everyone
knows the life of the spirit. You all know
it. You do not practice what you know,
not because you doubt, but because you
are diverted from the true life by false
cares and excuse yourself from it.

This is like what you do: A master
prepared a dinner and sent to invite
guests, but they began to decline. One
said: I have bought some land and must
go to see it. Another said: I have bought
some oxen and must try them. A third
said: I have married and must give a
wedding feast. And the servants came and
told the master that no one would come.
Then the master sent his servants to call
in the poor, and they did not refuse but
came. And when they had come there

was still room to spare, so the master sent Luke XIV.
xxii. to call in others, saying: Go and persuade everyone you meet to come to my dinner, that there may be still more guests. But those who refused because they were busy missed the dinner. xxiii, xxiv.

All men know that the fulfilment of the will of the Father gives life, but they do not accept his invitation because they are drawn away by the guile of riches.

He who gives up false transitory riches for true life in accord with the Father's will, acts as a clever steward did.

There was a steward to a rich master. This steward saw that his master would soon dismiss him and he would be left without food or shelter. And he thought XVI. i, iii. to himself: This is what I will do. I will secretly give away some of my master's goods to the peasants and reduce their debts, and then if my master sends me away the peasants will remember my kindness and will help me. And he did so. iv. He called the peasants who were in debt to his master, and re-wrote their quittances. For him who owed a hundred he v. made it fifty; instead of sixty he put down twenty, and for the others in the same way. vi, vii. When the master heard of this he said to himself: My steward has acted cleverly, for he saw he would have been left with nothing. He has caused me loss, but he has acted cleverly for himself.

For in the bodily life we all understand what is advantageous, but in regard to the life of the spirit we do not wish to understand. We should give away the transitory viii.

and false riches of this life in order to Luke XVI. ix. obtain the life of the spirit. If we grudge such trifles as riches for the life of the spirit, we shall not receive it. If we do not give up the false life our true life will not be given us.

It is not possible to serve two masters at once—God and riches: the will of the Father and your own will. You must serve xiii. either the one or the other.

The Orthodox heard this, and as they loved wealth they ridiculed him. xiv.

But he said to them: You think that because you are honoured by men for your wealth you are really honourable. It is not so. God does not look at the exterior, but at the heart. That which is esteemed among men is despicable in God's sight. Even now the Kingdom of xv. God is attainable on earth, and they who enter it are great. And it is not the rich who enter that kingdom, but those who have nothing. This always was so, and is so by your law and by Moses and the prophets. Listen how the rich the and poor stand, even in your belief: xvi, xvii.

There was a rich man, who dressed in fine clothes and went to amuse himself xix. and to make merry every day. And there xx. was a beggar named Lazarus, covered with sores, who came to the rich man's yard to see if some scraps might not be left over from the rich man's feast; but Lazarus did not get even these, the rich man's dogs ate them all up and even licked Lazarus's sores. And both Lazarus and the rich man died. And when in hell xxi.

the rich man saw Abraham afar off, and Luke XVI.
the beggar Lazarus sitting with him. And xxii.
the rich man cried: Father Abraham, xxiii.
Lazarus the beggar is sitting with you,
who used to lie outside my fence. I dare
not trouble you; but send Lazarus the
beggar to me: let him but dip his finger
in water and cool my tongue, for I am
burning in the fire. But Abraham said: xxiv.
Why should I send Lazarus into the fire
to you? In the world you had what you
wished, but Lazarus only had sorrow, so
now he must be comforted. And even xxv.
though I might like to do it, I cannot send
him to you, for there is a great gulf
between us and you which cannot be
crossed. We are living and you are dead. xxvi.
Then the rich man said: Well, Father
Abraham, at least send Lazarus to my
house. I have five brothers and am sorry xxvii.
for them. Let him tell them everything,
and show them how harmful riches are,
or they too may fall into this torment. xxviii.
But Abraham said: They know already
that it is harmful. Moses and all the
prophets have told them so. But the rich xxix.
man said: Still, it would be better if someone were to rise from the dead and go to
them, they would then bethink themselves. xxx.
But Abraham said: If they do not listen
to Moses and the prophets, they would
not listen even to one who rose from the
dead. xxxi.

That a man ought to share with his
brother and do good to all men, is known
to everyone. The whole law of Moses and
the prophets only says that. You know it,

but because you love riches you cannot obey it.

And a rich Orthodox official came to Jesus and said to him: You are a good teacher. What must I do to obtain everlasting life?

Mark X. xvii.

Jesus said to him: Why do you call me good? Only the Father is good. If you wish to have life, fulfil the commandments.

The official said: There are many commandments—which must I fulfil?

xviii.

And Jesus said: Do not kill, do not lust, do not lie, do not steal. Also, honour your Father and fulfil his will, and love your neighbour as yourself.

xix.

And the Orthodox official said: I have kept all those commandments since I was a child; but I ask what else must I do according to your teaching?

Jesus looked at him and at his rich clothes, smiled, and said: One little thing you have not yet done. You have not fulfilled everything, as you say. If you wish to fulfil the commandments: not to kill, not to lust, not to steal, not to lie, and the chief command, to love your neighbour as yourself—then sell all your possessions at once and give to the poor. Then you will fulfil the Father's will.

xx.

xxi.

Hearing this, the official frowned and went away, for he was loth to part with his possessions.

xxii.

And Jesus said to his pupils: As you see, it is quite impossible to be rich and to fulfil the Father's will.

xxiii.

The pupils were horrified at these words,

but Jesus repeated them again, and said: Yes, children, it is impossible for him who has riches to be in the Father's will. A camel can pass through the eye of a needle sooner than he who trusts in riches fulfil the will of the Father.

And they were still more horrified and said: How then can one preserve one's life?

But he said: To a man it seems that he cannot support his life without property, but God preserves a man's life without property.

Jesus was once passing through the town of Jericho. And a prominent tax-farmer was there, a rich man named Zacchaeus, who had heard of Jesus' teaching and believed in it, and when he learnt that Jesus was in Jericho he wished to see him. But there was such a crowd round Jesus that it was impossible to push through to him. Zacchaeus was a small man, so he ran ahead and climbed a tree that he might see Jesus as he went past. When passing the tree Jesus saw him, and knowing that he believed in his teaching said: Come down from the tree and go home. I will come to you. Zacchaeus climbed down, ran home, made ready to welcome Jesus, and received him joyfully.

The people disapproved of this and said of Jesus: Why, he has gone to a tax-farmer's—to a scoundrel's house!

At that very time Zacchaeus was saying to Jesus: See, Master, what I will do: I will give half my property to the poor, and out of what is left I will repay fourfold to all whom I have wronged.

And Jesus said: You have saved your-self. You were dead but have come to life; you were lost, but have found yourself; for you have done as Abraham did when by being ready to kill his own son he showed his faith. For herein is the whole life of man; to find and save that which is perishing in his soul. A sacrifice cannot be measured by its size. Luke XIX. ix.

x.

It happened once that Jesus was sitting with his pupils near a collecting-box. People were placing contributions in the box for God's service. Rich men went up to the box and put in much, and a poor widow came and put in two farthings. Mark XII. xli, xlii.

And Jesus pointed to her and said: See, this poor widow, a beggar-woman, has given two farthings, and she has given more than all the others. For they gave what they did not need, while she has given all she had; she has put in her whole substance. xliii.

xliv.

It happened that Jesus was at the house of Simon the leper. Matt. XXVI. vi.

And a woman came into the house and she had a jar of precious oil, worth thirty pounds. Jesus was saying to his pupils that his death was near, and the woman heard this and was sorry for him, and to show him her love poured oil on his head. And she forgot everything, and broke her jar, and anointed both his head and his feet, and poured out all the oil.

And the pupils began to discuss it, and said she had acted badly. And Judas, who afterwards betrayed Jesus, said: See how much she has wasted. That oil might vii.

viii.

have been sold for thirty pounds, with which many poor people could have been clothed. And the pupils began blaming the woman, who was abashed and did not know whether she had done well or ill.

Matt. XXVI. ix.

Then Jesus said: You are wrong to trouble the woman; she has indeed done a good deed, and you are wrong to speak about the poor. If you want to do good to them, do so—they are always there. But why speak of them now? If you pity the poor, go with your pity and do them good. But this woman has pitied me and done good truly, for she has given away all that she had. Which of you can tell what is needful and what is not? How do you know that there was no need to anoint me with the oil? She has poured it on me to prepare my body for burial, and for that it was wanted. She has truly done the will of the Father by forgetting herself and pitying another. She forgot her worldly reckonings and gave away all that she had.

x.

xi, xii.

xiii.

And Jesus said: My teaching is to do the Father's will, and His will can only be fulfilled by deeds, and not by words only. If a man's son keeps saying, 'I will, I will', to his father's bidding, but does not do what his father says, then he does not fulfil his father's will. But if another son says: 'I do not wish to obey', but then goes and does his father's bidding—he indeed fulfils his father's will. So also with men: not he is in the Father's will who says: 'I am in the Father's will', but he who does what the Father wishes.

XXI. xxviii, xxx.

xxix, xxxi.

VII

I AND THE FATHER ARE ONE

The true food of everlasting life is the fulfilment of the Father's will.

'GIVE US OUR DAILY BREAD'

AFTER that the Jews wished to condemn Jesus to death, and he went away into Galilee and lived with his relations.   John VII. i.

The Jewish feast of tabernacles was come, and the brothers of Jesus prepared to go to the feast, and called him to go with them. They did not believe in his teaching and said to him: ii.

iii.

v.

You say that the Jewish service of God is wrong and that you know the real way to serve God by deeds. If you really think that no one but you knows how to serve God come with us to the feast. Many people will be there and you can declare before them all that the teaching of Moses is wrong. If they all believe you, then your pupils also will see that you are right. Why hide yourself? You say that our service is wrong, and that you know the true service of God: well then, show it to everybody.   iii.

iv.

And Jesus said: You have a special time and place in which to serve God, but for me there is none. I work for God everywhere and always. That is just what I show to people. I show them that their service of God is wrong and that is why they hate me. Go you to the feast, and I will go when I am ready.   vi.

vii.

viii.

And his brothers went, but he remained behind, and only went up at the middle of the feast.

John VII.
ix, x.

The Jews were shocked that he did not honour their feast and delayed coming to it, and they disputed about his teaching. xi. Some said that he was right, while others said that he only disturbed the people. xii.

In the middle of the feast Jesus went into the Temple and began to teach the people that their service of God was wrong, and that God should be served not in a temple and by sacrifices, but in the spirit and by deeds. xiv.

They all listened to him and wondered that he, an unlearned man, should have such wisdom. And Jesus, knowing that xv. all wondered at his wisdom, said to them:

My teaching is not my own, but His that sent me. If any man wishes to do the will of the spirit that sent us into life, he xvi. will know that I have not invented this teaching but that it is of God. For a man xvii. who invents from himself follows his own imagination, but he who seeks to know the mind of Him that sent him is true and there is no falsehood in him. xviii.

Your law of Moses is not the Father's law, and so those who follow it do not fulfil the Father's law, but do evil and tell falsehoods. I teach you the fulfilment of xix. the will of the Father alone. In my teaching there can be no contradictions, but your written Mosaic law is full of contradictions. Do not judge by externals, but by the spirit. xxi, xxii, xxiii, xxiv.

And some said: They said he was a false

prophet, but he condemns the law and no one says anything to him. Perhaps he is really a true prophet and even the rulers have recognized him. But there is one reason for not believing him: it is written that when God's messenger shall come no one will know whence he came, but we know where this man was born and we know his whole family.

The people still did not understand his teaching, and still sought proofs.

Then Jesus said to them: You know me, and where I came from in the body, but you do not know where I come from in the spirit. You do not know Him from whom I come in spirit, and that is the one thing it is necessary to know. If I had said: 'I am the Christ', you would have believed me, the man, but you would not have believed the Father who is in me and in you. You should believe in the Father only.

For the short space of my life I point out to you the path to that source of life from which I have come. But you ask of me proofs, and wish to condemn me. If you do not know that path, then when I am no longer here you will not be able to find it. You should not judge me but should follow me. He who does what I say will know whether what I say is true. He for whom the life of the flesh has not become merely food for the spirit, he who does not seek truth as a thirsty man seeks for water, cannot understand me. He who thirsts for truth, let him come to me and drink. And he who believes my teaching

John VII.
xxv.

xxvi.

xxvii.

xxviii.

xxix.

xxxiii.

xxxiv.

xxxvii.
xxxviii.

will obtain true life. He will receive the
life of the spirit.

John VII.
xxxix.

And many believed his teaching and
said: What he says is true, and is of God.
Others did not understand him, and were
always seeking in the prophecies for proofs
that he was sent from God. And many
disputed with him but no one was able to
controvert him. The Orthodox teachers
of the law sent their assistants to contend
with him, but these assistants returned to
them and said: We can do nothing with
him.

xl.

xli, xlii.

xliii.

And the chief priest said: How is it you
have not convicted him?

xliv.

They replied: No one ever spoke as he
does.

xlv.

xlvi.

Then the Orthodox said: It signifies
nothing that you cannot refute him and
that the people believe his teaching. We
do not believe it and none of the rulers
believe it. The people are accursed, they
always were stupid and ignorant, and will
believe anyone.

xlvii.

xlviii.

xlix.

But Nicodemus, to whom Jesus had
explained his teaching, said to the chief
priests: A man should not be condemned
without being heard, and without understanding what he teaches.

l.

li.

But they said to him: There is nothing
to hear or to understand. We know that
no prophet can come from Galilee.

lii.

Another time Jesus spoke to the Orthodox and said: There can be no proof of
the truth of my teaching, just as you cannot have an illumination of light. My
teaching is the real light by which people

see what is good and what is bad, and so
it is impossible to prove my teaching;
everything else is proved by it. He who
follows me will not be in darkness but will
have life. Life and enlightenment are one
and the same.

John VIII.
xii.

But the Orthodox said: It is only you
who say this.

xiii.

And he replied: If I alone say it, still I
am right, for I know whence I come and
whither I go. In my teaching life has a
meaning, but according to yours it has
none. Besides, not I alone teach this, but
my Father, the spirit, teaches it too.

xiv.

xviii.

They said: Where is your Father?

He replied: You do not understand my
teaching or you would know my Father.
You do not know whence you are nor
whither you go.

xix.

I show you the way, but instead of
following me you discuss who I am; and
so you cannot reach that salvation and
life to which I wish to lead you. And you
will perish if you remain in this error and
do not follow me.

xxi.

xxiv.

The Jews asked: Who are you?

He said: I told you when I first began
to teach: I am the son of man, acknowledging the spirit as my Father, and what
I have understood from him I tell to the
world. When you exalt the son of man in
yourselves you will know what I am,
because I do and speak not of myself as
a man, but what the Father has taught me.
He who sent me is always in me and will
not leave me, for I do His will. He who
keeps to my understanding of life and

xxv.

xxvi.

xxviii.

xxix.

fulfils the will of the Father will be truly
taught by me. To know the truth you
must do good to men. He who does harm
to men loves the darkness and goes towards it; he who does good to men goes
to the light. So to understand my teaching you must do good. He who does good
will know the truth; he will be free from
evil, from death. For everyone who errs
becomes the slave of his error.

John VIII.
xxxi.

xxxii.

xxxiv.

And as a slave does not always live in
his master's house while the master's son
does, so a man if he errs in life and becomes
the slave of his errors does not live always,
but dies. Only he who is in the truth
remains always living. To know truth is
to be a son and not a slave. If you err, you
will be slaves and will die: but if you are in
the truth you will be free sons and will live.

xxxv.
xxxvi.

You say of yourselves that you are sons
of Abraham, and that you know the truth.
Yet you wish to kill me because you do
not understand my teaching. And it
comes to this, that I speak what I have
understood from my Father while you
wish to do what you have understood
from your father.

xxxvii.

xxxviii.

They said: Our father is Abraham.

Jesus said to them: If you were the sons
of Abraham you would do his deeds. But
you wish to kill me because I have told
you what I have learnt from God. Abraham did not act like that. You do not
serve God, but serve another father.

xxxix.

xl.

They said to him: We are not bastards,
we are all sons of one Father, we are all
God's children.

xli.

And Jesus said to them: If your father were one with me you would love me, for I came forth from the Father; I was not born of myself. You are not children of one Father with me, so you do not understand my words and my understanding of life finds no place in you. If I am of the Father and you are of the same Father, then you cannot wish to kill me. If you wish to kill me, we are not of the same Father.

John VIII. xlii.

xliii.

I am from the Father of goodness, God: but you are from the father of evil, the devil. You wish to do the lusts of your father who always was a murderer and a liar with no truth in him. If he, the devil, says anything, he says not what is common to all, but what is his own, and he is the father of lies. So you are servants of the devil and are his children.

You see how plainly you are convicted of error. If I err, convict me; but if there is no error in me why do you not believe me?

xliv.

xlvi.

And the Jews began to revile him and to say that he was possessed.

xlviii.

He said: I am not possessed. I honour the Father, and you wish to kill me, which shows that you are not my brothers but sons of another father.

It is not I who affirm that I am right, but the truth that speaks for me. And so I repeat to you: he who comprehends my teaching and performs it shall not see death.

l.

li.

And the Jews said: Now, were we not right in saying that you are a Samaritan and have a devil? You convict yourself!

The prophets died, so did Abraham, yet you say that he who fulfils your teaching shall not see death. Abraham died, and will you not die? Or are you greater than Abraham? John VIII. lii.

liii.

The Jews discussed what he—Jesus of Galilee—was, whether he was an important or an unimportant prophet, and forgot that he had told them that he said nothing of himself as a man but spoke of the spirit that was within him.

And Jesus said: I do not make myself out to be anything. If I spoke of myself, of what I imagine, then all I might say would be of no importance. But there is that source of all things which you call God. It is of that I speak. You have not known, and do not know, the true God. But I know Him and if I said I do not know Him I should be a liar like you. I know Him and know and fulfil His will. liv.

lv.

Your father Abraham saw and rejoiced at what I understand. lvi.

The Jews said: You are not yet thirty: how could you be alive in Abraham's day? lvii.

He replied: Before Abraham existed there was the understanding of good that I tell you of. lviii.

Then the Jews picked up stones to throw at him, but he escaped. lix.

And on the road Jesus saw a man who had no understanding from the time of his birth. IX. i.

And his pupils asked him: Who is at fault that this man is without understanding since his birth? He, or his parents for not having taught him? ii.

And Jesus replied: Neither his parents nor he are at fault. It is God's doing, that there may be light where there was darkness. If I have a teaching, it is the light of the world.

John IX.
iii.
v.

And Jesus explained to the ignorant man that he was a son of God in the spirit, and on receiving this teaching the ignorant man was conscious of light. Those who had known him previously did not recognize him. Though resembling what he had been, he had now become another man. But he said: I am he, and Jesus has shown me that I am a son of God, and the light has reached me, so that now I see what I used not to see.

vi, vii.

viii, ix.

xi.

This man was taken to the Orthodox teachers; and it was on a Saturday.

xiii, xiv.

The Orthodox asked him how he had come to understand what he had not seen before.

He said: I do not know how; I only know that now I understand everything.

xv.

They said: You do not understand in a godly way, for Jesus did this on a Saturday, and besides, a layman cannot enlighten people.

And they began to dispute, and asked the man who had been enlightened: What do you think of Jesus?

xvi.

He said: I think he is a prophet.

xvii.

But the Jews did not believe that he had been ignorant and was now enlightened, so they called his parents and asked them: Is this your son, who has been ignorant since his birth? How is it he has now become enlightened?

xviii.

xix.

His parents said: We know that he is our son and that he was ignorant from his birth, but how he has become enlightened we do not know. He is of age, you should ask him.

John IX.
xx.

xxi.

The Orthodox called the man a second time, and said: Pray to our God, the real God. The man who enlightened you is a layman, and is not sent by God. We are sure of that.

xxiv.

And the man who had been enlightened said: Whether he is from God or not I do not know. But I know that I used not to see the light and that I see it now.

xxv.

The Orthodox again asked: What did he do to you when he enlightened you?

xxvi.

He replied: I have told you already, but you do not believe. If you wish to be his pupils I will tell you again.

xxvii.

They began to revile him and said: You are his pupil, but we are the pupils of Moses. God Himself spoke to Moses, but we do not even know whence this man is.

xxviii.

xxix.

And the man answered: It is strange that he has enlightened me and yet you do not know whence he is. God does not hear sinners but hears those who honour Him and do His will. It can never be that one who is not from God could enlighten an ignorant man. If he were not from God he could do nothing.

xxx.

xxxi.

xxxiii.

The Orthodox were angry at this, and said: You are altogether sunk in delusions and yet you want to teach us. And they drove him away.

xxxiv.

And Jesus said: My teaching is an

awakening to life. He who believes in my teaching, though he die in the flesh, remains living, and everyone who lives and believes in me will not die.

John XI. xxv.

And yet a third time Jesus taught the people. He said:

Men accept my teaching not because I myself prove it. It is impossible to prove the truth. The truth itself proves all else. But men accept my teaching because there is no other that is native to them and promises life.

X. ii.

My teaching is to men like the familiar voice of the shepherd to the sheep, when he comes to them through the door and gathers them to lead them to pasture. No one believes your teaching, for it is foreign to them, and they see your own lusts in it. Men feel with you as sheep do at the sight of someone who does not enter by the door but climbs over the fence: the sheep do not know him, and feel that he is a robber. My teaching is the one true teaching, like the one door for the sheep. All your teachings of the law of Moses are false, as thieves and robbers are to the sheep. He who yields to my teaching will find true life, just as the sheep go forth and find food if they follow the shepherd. A thief only comes to steal, rob, and destroy, but the shepherd comes to give life. And my teaching alone promises to give true life.

iii, iv.

v.

vii.

viii.

ix.

x.

There are shepherds for whom the sheep are their life and who are ready to give their life for the sheep. These are the true shepherds. But there are hirelings who

xi.

care nothing for the sheep, because they are hirelings and the sheep are not theirs. If a wolf comes they abandon the sheep and run away, and the wolf devours them. They are false shepherds. So also there are false teachers who care nothing for the life of people, but true teachers give up their lives for the life of men. John X. xii.

xiii, xv.

I am such a teacher. My teaching is this—to give up one's life for the life of men. No one will take my life from me, but I myself freely give it up for men to receive true life. That commandment I have received from my Father. As my Father knows me so also I know Him, and therefore I lay down my life for men. And my Father loves me because I fulfil His commandment. xiv.

xi.

xviii.

xv.

xvii.

And all men, not only those here and now, but all men, shall understand my voice; and they will all come together in me and all men shall be one and their teaching one. xvi.

And the Jews surrounded him and said: What you say is hard to understand and does not agree with our scriptures. Do not torment us, but tell us simply and plainly whether you are the Messiah, who according to our scriptures should come into the world. xxiv.

Jesus answered them: I have already told you who I am, but you do not believe. If you do not believe my words then believe my works; by them you can understand who I am and for what I have come. xxv.

You do not believe because you do not follow me. He who follows me and does xxvi.

what I say will understand me. And those John X.
who understand my teaching and fulfil it, xxvii.
receive true life. My Father has united xxviii.
them with me, and no one can disunite us.
I and the Father are one. xxix, xxx.

And the Jews were offended at this and
took up stones to kill him. xxxi.

But he said to them: I have shown you
many good works and have disclosed the
teaching of my Father. For which of these
good works do you wish to stone me? xxxii.

They said: Not for your good works do
we wish to stone you, but because you, a
man, make yourself God. xxxiii.

And Jesus replied to them: The same is
written in your scriptures where it is said
that God Himself said to the wicked
rulers: 'Ye are Gods.' If He called even xxxiv.
wicked men Gods, why do you consider
it blasphemous to call what God in his
love has sent into the world, 'the son of
God'? Every man in the spirit is a son of xxxv, xxxvi.
God. If I do not live in God's way, then
do not believe that I am a son of God. But xxxvii.
if I live after God's way then believe by
my life that I am with the Father, and
understand that the Father is in me and I
in Him. xxxviii.

And the Jews began to dispute. Some
said that he was possessed and others said: xix, xx.
A man who is possessed cannot enlighten
men. xxi.

And they did not know what to do with
him and could not condemn him. And he xxxix.
again went beyond the Jordan and stayed
there. xl.

And many believed in his teaching and

said that it was true as the teaching of John was. Therefore many believed in it. *John X. xli. xlii.*

And Jesus once asked his pupils: Tell me, how do people understand my teaching about the son of God and the son of man? *Matt. XVI. xiii.*

They said: Some understand it like the teaching of John: others like the prophecies of Isaiah: others again say it is like the teaching of Jeremiah. They understand that you are a prophet. *xiv.*

And he asked them: But how do you understand my teaching? *xv.*

And Simon Peter said to him: I think your teaching is that you are the chosen son of the God of life. You teach that God is the life within man. *xvi.*

And Jesus said to him: Happy are you, Simon, that you have understood this. No man could disclose it to you: you have understood it because the divine spirit in you has disclosed it to you. Not human understanding and not I by my words have disclosed it to you, but God, my Father, has disclosed it to you directly. *xvii.* And on this is founded the society of men for whom there is no death. *xviii.*

VIII

LIFE IS NOT TEMPORAL

Therefore true life must be lived in the present.

'EACH DAY'

JESUS said: He who is not prepared to suffer all bodily sufferings and deprivations has not understood me. He who *Matt. X. xxxviii.*

obtains all that is best for his bodily life destroys the true life. But he who sacrifices his bodily life in fulfilling my teaching will receive the true life.

Matt. X. xxxix.

And at those words, Peter said to him: See, we have obeyed you, have thrown off all ties and property, and have followed you. What reward shall we receive for this?

XIX. xxvii.

Jesus said to him: Everyone who has given up home, sisters, brothers, father, mother, wife, children, or lands, for my teaching, shall receive a hundredfold more than sisters, brothers, and fields, and all that is needful in this life, and besides that obtains also life beyond the bounds of time. There are no rewards in the kingdom of heaven, the kingdom of heaven is its own aim and reward. In the kingdom of heaven all are equal, there is neither first nor last.

Mark X. xxix, xxx.

xxxi.

For the kingdom of heaven is like this: The master of a house went in the morning to hire labourers for his garden. He hired them at a penny a day, and set them to work. At midday he went again and hired more labourers and sent them to work in his garden; towards evening he hired some more, and sent them to work. And he agreed with them all at a penny. When the time came for payment, the master had them all paid alike: first those who were hired last, and afterwards those who had been hired first. When those who had been hired first saw that those hired last received a penny each, they thought they would receive more, but

Matt. XX. i.

ii.

iii, vii.

viii

ix

they also were paid a penny. They took it and said: How is it that the others who worked only one shift and we who worked all four shifts receive the same? That is not fair. But the master came and said: Why are you dissatisfied? Have I wronged you? I have given you what we agreed on. Our agreement was for a penny. Take your pay and go. If I give to these last the same as to you, have I not the right to do what I will with my own? Or are you envious because you see that I am good? Matt. XX. x. xi. xii. xiii. xiv. xv. xvi.

In the kingdom of heaven there is no first or last—it is the same for all.

After this, two of his pupils, James and John, came to Jesus and said: Teacher, promise us that you will give us what we ask. Mark X. xxxv.

He said: What do you want?

They said: That we may be equal with you. xxxvi. xxxvii.

Jesus said to them: You do not know what you are asking. You can live as I do and can cleanse yourselves from the fleshly life like me, but it is not in my power to make you like myself. Each man can by his own efforts enter the kingdom of the Father by submitting to His power and fulfilling His will. xxxviii, xl. Matt. XX. xxiii.

On hearing this the other pupils grew angry with the two brothers for having wished to be equal to their teacher, and chiefs among the pupils. Mark X. xlі.

But Jesus called them, and said: If you brothers, John and James, have asked me to make you such as I am in order to be chief among my pupils, you made a mistake; and if you, my other pupils, were angry with them for wishing to be above you, then you also made a mistake. In the world, kings and governors reckon by seniority, that they may rule the people: but among you there can be neither senior nor junior.

Mark X. xlii.
Matt. XX. xxv.

Among you, to be more than another you must be the servant of all. Among you, let him who wishes to be first consider himself last. For the will of the Father is that the son of man should live not to be served but to serve all and give up his bodily life as a ransom for the life of the spirit.

xxvi.
xxvii.
Mark X. xlv.

Jesus said to the people: The Father seeks to save that which is perishing. He rejoices over it as a shepherd rejoices when he finds a lost sheep. If one sheep is lost, the shepherd will leave ninety-nine and go to save the lost one. And if a woman loses a penny, she will sweep out the whole hut and seek till she finds it. The Father loves the son and calls him to himself.

Matt. XVIII. xi, xii.
Luke XV. viii. ix.

And he told them another parable showing that they who live according to God's will must not exalt themselves. He said: If you are invited to a dinner, do not seat yourself in a front place, or someone of more importance than you will come and the host will say to you: 'Leave your place and let someone better than yourself have it', and you will be put to shame. Take the lowest place: the host will then find you and call you to a higher one, and you will be honoured.

XIV. viii. ix.
x.

So also in the kingdom of God there is no room for pride. He who exalts himself, by so doing lowers himself; but he who humbles himself and considers himself unworthy, raises himself in the kingdom of God.

Luke XIV. xi.

A man had two sons. The younger son said to his father: Father, give me my share of the property.

XV. xi.

And the father gave him his share. The younger son took it, went to a far country, squandered it all, and fell into want. In that far country he became a swineherd, and he was so hungry that he ate acorns with the pigs. And he bethought himself of his life, and said: Why did I take my share and leave my father? He had plenty of everything, even his labourers were well fed. But here am I eating the same food as the pigs. I will go to my father, fall at his feet, and say: I have done wrong, father, and am unworthy to be your son. Take me back as a labourer. So he thought, and he went to his father. And as he drew near, his father recognized him at a distance, and ran to meet him and embraced him and began to kiss him. And the son said: Father, I am to blame before you, and am unworthy to be your son. But the father did not even listen, and said to the servants: Bring the best clothes and the best boots, quickly, and put them on him. And go and catch a fatted calf and kill it, and we will rejoice because this son of mine was dead and is now alive, was lost and is now found.

xii.

xiii, xiv, xv.

xvi.

xvii.

xviii, xix.

xx.

xxi.

xxii.
xxiii.

xxiv.

Then the elder brother came from the

field, and as he drew near he heard sounds of music in the house and called a boy and said: Why are they making merry? And the boy said: Have you not heard that your brother has returned? Your father is glad, and has had the fatted calf killed for joy that his son has come home. But the elder brother was vexed and did not go into the house. His father came out and called him, but he said to his father: Father, I have worked for you for many years, and have never disobeyed your orders, but you never killed a fatted calf for me. My younger brother left home and has squandered all his property with drunkards, and for him you have had a calf killed. And his father said: You are always with me and all that is mine is yours; you should not be vexed but rejoice that your brother who was dead has become alive again—was lost and is found.

Luke XV. xxv. xxvi. xxvii. xxviii. xxix. xxx. xxxi. xxxii.

A master planted a garden, cultivated it, and did everything to make it yield as much fruit as possible. And he sent labourers into the garden to work there, pay him for it according to agreement, and gather the fruit.

Mark XII. i.

ii.

(The master is the Father; the garden the world; the labourers men. The Father has sent His son—the son of man—into the world only that men should make return of that—the understanding of life—which He implanted in them.) The time came when the master sent a servant to receive payment. (The Father has always told men that they must fulfil His will.)

The labourers drove away the master's servant empty-handed and remained in the garden imagining that it was their own, and that they were settled in it of their own will. (Men reject reminders of the will of God, and continue to live each one for himself, imagining that the purpose of life is to serve the flesh.) Then the master sent, one after another, his chosen ones and finally his son, to remind the labourers of their debt. But they quite lost their reason and imagined that if they killed the master's son, who reminded them that the garden was not theirs, they would be left alone. So they killed him.

Mark XII.
iii.

iv-vi.

vii.
viii.

(People do not like even a reminder of the spirit that lives in them and shows them that it is eternal and that they are not so; and as far as they can they have killed their consciousness of the spirit: they have wrapped the talent in a cloth and buried it.)

What then was the master to do? Simply to drive out those labourers and send others.

Matt. XXI.
xl.

What is the Father to do? Sow until there is fruit. And this He does.

xli.

Men have not understood and do not understand that the consciousness of the spirit that is in them, and which they hide because it troubles them, brings life to them. They reject the stone on which everything rests. And they who do not take the life of the spirit as their foundation do not enter the kingdom of heaven and do not receive life. To have faith and to

xlii.

receive life it is necessary to understand
your position and not expect rewards.

Matt. XXI.
xliii.

Then the pupils said to Jesus: Increase
our faith in us; tell us what will make us
believe more firmly in the life of the spirit,
that we may not regret the life of the flesh.
See how much has to be sacrificed, and
continually sacrificed, for the life of the
spirit. Yet you yourself say that there is
no reward.

Luke XVII.
v.

To this Jesus replied: You can readily
believe that a great tree grows from a
birch seed—if you had as much faith in
the seed of the spirit which is within you
and whence true life springs, you would
not ask me to increase your faith.

Faith does not consist in believing something wonderful, but it consists in understanding your position and where salvation lies. If you understand your position
you will not expect rewards but will
believe in that which has been entrusted
to you.

When a master returns from the field
with his labourers, he does not seat them
at table but bids them see to the cattle,
and get his supper ready, and only afterwards says to them: Sit down and eat and
drink. The master does not thank the
labourer for having done what he ought
to do. And the labourer, if he understands
that he is a labourer, is not offended but
does his work believing that he will receive
his due.

vi.

vii.

viii.

ix.

So you too should fulfil the will of the
Father and remember that we are unprofitable servants who have only done

what we ought to, and not expect rewards but be satisfied that you will receive your due. Luke XVII. x.

You should not be anxious to believe that there will be a reward and life, that cannot be otherwise, but be careful not to destroy this life and do not forget that it is given us that we may bring forth its fruits and fulfil the will of the Father.

So be always ready, like servants awaiting a master, to answer him immediately he comes. The servants do not know whether he will come early or late, but they should always be ready. And if they meet their master they have fulfilled his will and it will be well for them. XII. xxxv, xxxvi.

So it is in life. Always, at every minute of the present, you should live the life of the spirit, not thinking of the past or the future and not saying to yourself: then or there I will do this or that. xxxvii, xxxviii.

If a master knew when a thief would come, he would not sleep, so you too should never sleep; because for the life of the son of man time is nothing; he lives only in the present and does not know when his life begins or ends. xxxix, xl.

Our life is like the life of a slave whom his master left to manage his household. It is well for that slave if he always does his master's will. But if he says: The master will not return just yet, and neglects his business, his master will come unexpectedly and drive him out. Matt. XXIV. xlv, xlvi.

xlviii, l, li.

Do not be downcast, but live always in the present, by the spirit. For the life of the spirit there is no time. Look to it that Mark XIII. xxxiii.

you do not weigh yourself down with
cares, and do not befog yourself with
drunkenness or gluttony, and do not let
the time for salvation pass. The time for
salvation is thrown like a net over all—
it is always there. Live therefore always
the life of the son of man.

Luke XXI.
xxxiv–
xxxvi.

We may compare the kingdom of
heaven to this: Ten maidens went with
lamps to meet a bridegroom. Five of
them were wise and five were foolish.
The foolish ones took lamps without any
extra oil, but the wise ones took lamps
and a supply of oil. While they waited
for the bridegroom they went to sleep.
When the bridegroom was approaching
the foolish maidens saw that they had
too little oil and went to buy some, but
while they were gone the bridegroom
came. And the wise maidens who had
oil went in with him and the doors were
shut. Their business was only this: to
meet the bridegroom with lights. But the
foolish ones had forgotten that it was
important not only that the lights should
burn, but that they should burn at the
proper time. And in order that they
should be alight when the bridegroom
came, it was necessary that they should
burn all the time.

Matt. XXV.
i.
ii.
iii.
iv.
v, vi.
vii.
viii.
x.

Life is only for this: to exalt the son of
man, and the son of man is always here,
he does not belong to some particular
time, and so to serve him one must live
without time—in the present alone.

xiii.

Therefore strive to enter into the life of
the spirit now. If you do not make efforts

you will not enter it. You will say: We
said so and so. But there will be no good
works to show, and there will be no life.
For the son of man—the one true spirit of
life—will appear in each man according to
his deeds.

Luke XIII.
xxiv.
xxv, xxvii.

Matt. XVI.
xxvii.

Mankind is divided according to the
way men serve the son of man. And by
their works men will be separated into
two groups, as sheep from goats in a flock.
The one will live, the other will perish.

XXV. xxxii,
xxxiii.

They who have served the son of man
will receive what has been theirs from the
beginning of the world—the life which
they have preserved. They have preserved
life by serving the son of man. They have
fed the hungry, clothed the naked, wel-
comed strangers, visited those in prison.
They have lived by the son of man, felt
that he is the same in all men, and have
therefore loved their neighbours.

Those who have not lived by the son of
man, have not served him, have not understood that he is the same in all men and
have therefore not united with him, have
lost the life they had in him and have
perished.

xxxiv, xlvi.

IX

TEMPTATIONS

*The deceptions of temporal life hide from men the
true life in the present.*

'AND FORGIVE US OUR DEBTS AS WE FORGIVE OUR DEBTORS'

SOME children were brought to Jesus, and
he saw that his pupils were sending them
away. He was grieved at this, and said:

Matt. XIX.
xiii.

It is wrong to send children away. They are better than anyone, for they live according to the will of the Father: they are indeed in the kingdom of heaven. Matt. XIX. xiv. Instead of sending them away you should learn from them, for to live in the Father's will you must live as children do. They do not abuse people, do not bear ill-will, do not lust, do not bind themselves by oaths, do not resist evil, do not go to law with anyone, acknowledge no difference between their own and other nations; and so they are better than grown-up people and are in the kingdom of heaven. If you Luke XVIII. xvii. do not become as children and refrain from all the snares of the flesh, you will not be in the kingdom of heaven. Matt. XVIII. iii.

Only he understands my teaching who recognizes that children are better than we, because they do not infringe the Father's will. v.

Only he who understands my teaching understands the will of the Father. We Luke IX. xlviii. must not despise children. They are better than we, and their hearts are always with the Father and are pure in his sight. Matt. XVIII. x.

Not one child perishes by the Father's will. They perish only because men entice them and draw them away from the truth. xiv. Be careful therefore not to lead a child away from the Father and from true life; for he who leads a child away from purity does evil. To lead a child away from goodness, to tempt him, is as bad as to hang a millstone about his neck and throw him into the water. It is hard for him to get out, and he is more likely to drown. Equally hard is it for a child to escape from the temptations into which a grown-up man leads him.

Matt. XVIII. vi.

The world of men is unhappy only because of temptations. Temptations are everywhere in the world; they always were and always will be, and man perishes on account of them.

vii.

So give up everything, sacrifice everything, in order to avoid falling into temptation. If a fox is caught in a trap it will wrench off its paw to escape, and the paw will heal and the fox remain alive. You too should be ready to give up everything in order not to sink into temptation.

viii, ix.

Beware of the temptation to break the first commandment: not to be angry with people when they injure you and you wish for revenge.

Luke XVII. iii.

If a man has injured you do not forget that he is a son of the same Father and is your brother. If he has offended you go and appeal to his conscience face to face. If he listens to you, you are a gainer and have found a new brother. If he does not listen to you, take two or three others with you to persuade him, and if he repents forgive him. Forgive him always, even if he offends you seven times and seven times asks for forgiveness. If he will not listen to you then tell the congregation of those who believe in my teaching, and if he will not listen to them, still forgive him, and have nothing more to do with him.

Matt. XVIII. xv, xvi.

Luke XVII. iv.

Matt. XVIII. xvii.

For the Kingdom of God may be compared to this: A king began to settle with his vassals. And they brought to him a man who owed him a million and had nothing to pay with. And the king would have had to sell the vassal's land, his wife, his children, and the man himself. But the vassal begged mercy of the king, and the king had mercy on him and forgave him all his debt. Now this same man went home and saw a peasant who owed him fifty pence. And he seized the peasant and began to throttle him, and said: Pay what you owe me. And the peasant fell at his feet and said: Have patience with me and I will pay you all. But the other showed him no mercy and put him in prison, to stay there till he paid everything. Other peasants saw this and went to the king and told what the vassal had done. Then the king called the vassal and said to him: Wretched man, I forgave you all your debt because you begged me to, and you should have forgiven your debtor as I forgave you. And the king was angry and handed the vassal over to be tortured till his whole debt should be paid.

And the Father will deal with you in like manner if you do not with your whole heart forgive all those who are to blame in your sight.

You know that if you have a quarrel with a man, it is better to make it up with him without going to law. You know that, and act accordingly, because you know that if you go to law you will lose more. So it is with all anger. If you know that

Matt.
XVIII.
xxiii.
xxiv.
xxv.
xxvi.
xxvii.
xxviii.
xxix.
xxx.
xxxi.
xxxii.
xxxiii.
xxxiv.
xxxv.

anger is an evil thing and separates you from the Father, then get rid of the anger as quickly as possible and make peace.

Matt. V. xxv.

You know that as you become bound on earth, so will you be bound before the Father. And as you free yourselves on earth so you will also be free before the Father.

XVIII. xviii.

Understand that if two or three are united on earth in my teaching, all that they desire they already have from my Father. Because where two or three are joined together in the name of the spirit in man, that spirit of man already lives in them.

xix.

xx.

Beware also of temptation under the second commandment: about men changing their wives.

Some Orthodox teachers once came to Jesus, and trying him, said: May a man put away his wife?

Mark X. ii.

He answered: From the very beginning man was created male and female: that was the Father's will.

Matt. XIX. iii, iv.

Therefore a man leaves father and mother and cleaves to his wife, and the husband and wife unite in one body. So that his wife is for a man the same as his own flesh. Therefore a man must not break the natural law of God and divide what is united. In your law of Moses it is said that you may put away your wife and take another, but that is wrong. According to the Father's will it is not so. And I tell you that he who casts off his wife drives both her and him who unites with her into depravity. And by casting

v, vi.

viii.

off his wife a man spreads dissoluteness abroad.

And his pupils said to Jesus: It is too hard to be always bound to one wife. If that must be, it would be better not to marry at all.

He said to them: You may refrain from marriage but you must understand what that means. If a man wishes to live without a wife, let him be quite pure and not approach women: but let him who loves women unite with one wife and not cast her off or look at other women.

Beware of temptation against the third commandment: about being forced to fulfil obligations as a result of taking oaths.

The tax-collectors once came to Peter and asked him: What about your teacher —does he pay the tax? Peter said: No, he does not. And he went and told Jesus that the tax-collectors had stopped him and had said that everyone was bound to pay the taxes.

Then Jesus said to him: A king does not take taxes from his sons, nor do they have to pay them to anyone else. Is that not so? So it is with us. If we are sons of God we are bound to no one but God, and are free from all obligations. But if they demand the tax from you, then pay: not that you are under obligation to do so but because you must not resist evil. Otherwise resistance to evil will produce worse evil.

Another time the Orthodox together with Caesar's officials went to Jesus to entrap him in his words. They said to him: You teach everyone according to the

Matt. XIX.
ix.

x.

xi.

xii.

XVII.
xxiv.

xxv, xxvi.

xxvii.

truth. Tell us, then, are we bound to pay Matt.
taxes to Caesar or not? Jesus understood XXII. xvi.
xvii.
that they wished to convict him of not
acknowledging the duty to Caesar. And xviii.
he said to them: Show me what the taxes
to Caesar are paid with. They handed
him a coin. He looked at it and said: xix.
What is this on it? Whose is this image
and inscription? They said: Caesar's. xx.
And he said: Then give back to Caesar
what is Caesar's, but that which is God's
—your soul—give to no one but God.
Money, property, your labour, give to
him who asks them of you. But give your
soul to no one but God. xxi.

Your Orthodox teachers go about
everywhere making people swear and vow
that they will fulfil the law. But by this
they only pervert people and make them
worse than before. It is impossible to let
the body put the soul under obligation. XXIII. xv.
In your soul, God is; and you cannot make
promises on God's behalf to other men. xvi-xxii.

Beware of the temptation to break the
fourth commandment—about judging and
executing people and calling on others to
take part in these judgements and executions.

The pupils of Jesus once went into a
village and asked for a night's lodging but
were not admitted. Then they went to Luke IX.lii.
Jesus to complain, and said: Let lightning
destroy these people! liii, liv.

Jesus answered: You still do not understand of what spirit you are. I do not lv.
teach to destroy people but to save
them. lvi.

Once a man came to Jesus and said: Luke XII.
Bid my brother give me my inheritance. xiii.

Jesus said to him: No one has made me
a judge over you, and I judge no one.
Neither may you sentence anyone. xiv.

The Orthodox once brought a woman
to Jesus and said: See, this woman was John VIII.
taken in adultery. Now by the law she iii.
should be stoned to death, but what do iv, v.
you say about it?

Jesus answered nothing, and waited for
them to bethink themselves. But they
pressed him, and asked him what he vi.
would adjudge to this woman? Then he
said: Let him among you who has no
fault cast the first stone at her. And he
said nothing more. vii, viii.

Then the Orthodox looked within themselves and their conscience smote them,
and those in front drew behind the others
and they all went away.

Jesus remained alone with the woman.
He looked round, saw that there was no ix.
one else, and said to her: Has no one
condemned you? x.

She said: No one!

Then he said: Neither do I condemn
you. Go, and in future do not sin. xi.

Beware! The temptation against the
fifth commandment is for men to consider it their duty to do good to their
fellow-countrymen only and to regard
other nations as enemies.

A teacher of the law wished to try Jesus
and said to him: What must I do to
obtain life? Luke X.

Jesus replied: You yourself know what xxv.

to do: love your Father, God, and your
brothers, His sons, whether they are your
fellow-countrymen or not.

Luke X.
xxvii.

And the teacher of the law said: That
would be well if there were not different
nations, but how am I to love an enemy of
my own people?

xxix.

And Jesus said: There was a Jew who
fell into misfortune. He was beaten,
robbed, and left on the road. A Jewish
priest passed by, looked at the injured
man and went on. Then a Jewish Levite
passed, looked at the injured man and
also passed by. Then there came a man of
another, a hostile, nation—a Samaritan.
This Samaritan saw the Jew and pitied
him, not thinking of the Jews' contempt
for the Samaritans. He washed and
bound up his wounds, took him on his
own ass to an inn, paid money for him
to the innkeeper and promised to call
again and pay for him.

xxx.
xxxi.
xxxii.
xxxiii.
xxxiv.
xxxv.

See that you too behave like that to
foreigners and to those who despise and
ruin you. Then you will obtain true life.

Jesus said: The world loves its own but
hates God's people. Therefore men of the
world—priests, preachers, officials—will
harass those who fulfil the Father's will.
I am going to Jerusalem and they will
torture and kill me, but my spirit cannot
be killed and will remain alive.

Matt. XVI
xxi

Having heard that Jesus would be tortured and killed in Jerusalem, Peter was
sad and took Jesus by the hand and said
to him: If that is so, you had better not go
to Jerusalem.

Mark VIII
xxxi

Then Jesus said to Peter: Do not say that. What you say is a temptation. If you fear tortures and death for me it means that you are not thinking of what is godly—of the spirit—but are thinking of what is human.

Mark VIII. xxxiii.

And having called the people and his pupils to him Jesus said: He that wishes to live according to my teaching let him forsake his fleshly life and be ready for all physical sufferings: he who fears for his physical life will ruin his true life, but he who disregards his fleshly life will save his true life.

xxxiv, xxxv.

But they did not understand this, and then some materialists came, and he explained to all what true life and the awakening from death means.

These materialists believed that after the death of the body there is no other life. They said: How can anybody rise from the dead? If everybody rose, they could not live together. For instance, there were seven brothers among us. The first married and died. His wife married the second brother, and he died; and she then married the third, who also died, and so on to the seventh. Now how can those seven brothers all live with one wife if they all rise from the dead?

Matt. XXII. xxiii.

xxiv.

xxv, xxvi.

xxviii.

Jesus answered them: Either you purposely confuse things or you do not understand what the awakening to life is. In this life people marry. But those who earn everlasting life and awaken from death do not marry and cannot die, for they are united to the Father. In your scriptures

Luke XX. xxxiv, xxxv, xxxvi.

it is written that God said: I am the God of Abraham and Jacob. And this was said when Abraham and Jacob had died from among men. So those who are dead from among men are alive to God. If God is, and God does not die, then they who are with God live always. The awakening from death is to live in the will of the Father. For the Father there is no time, and therefore by fulfilling the Father's will and uniting with him man departs from time and death.

Matt. XXII. xxxi, xxxii.

When they heard this the Orthodox did not know what to devise to silence Jesus, and together they began to question him. And one of them said:

Teacher, which in your opinion is the chief commandment of the whole law?

xxxiv, xxxv.

They thought that Jesus would get confused in answering about the law.

xxxvi.

But Jesus said: The chief commandment is that you should love with all your soul the Lord your God in whose power you are. And the other commandment to love your neighbour follows from it, for the same Lord God is in him also. In this is the substance of all that is written in your scriptures.

xxxvii.
xxxix.
xl.

And he said further: What in your opinion is Christ? Is he someone's son?

They said: In our opinion Christ is the son of David.

xlii.

He replied: How then is it that David calls Christ his Lord? Christ is neither David's son, nor anyone's son after the flesh, but Christ is that same Lord, our Ruler, whom we know in ourselves as our life. Christ is that consciousness which is within us.

Matt. XXII. xliii.

And Jesus said: Beware of the leaven of the Orthodox teachers. Beware also of the leaven of the materialists and of the rulers. But most of all, beware of the leaven of the self-styled 'Orthodox', for in them is the chief stumbling-block.

Luke XII. i. Mark VIII. xv.

Matt. XVI. xi, xii.

And when the people understood what he was speaking about, he repeated:

Most of all, beware of the teaching of the scholars, the self-styled Orthodox. Beware of them, because they occupy the place of the prophets who declared the will of God to the people. They have of themselves assumed the authority to preach the will of God to the people. They preach words, but do nothing. They only say: Do this and do that. But there is nothing to do, because they do nothing good, but only talk. They tell people to do what cannot be done, and they themselves do nothing. They only try to keep the teaching in their own hands, and for that purpose strive to appear imposing; they dress themselves up and exalt themselves. Know therefore that no one should call himself a teacher and leader. The self-appointed Orthodox call themselves teachers, and by so doing hinder you from entering into the kingdom of heaven, and do not enter it themselves. These Orthodox think that people can be brought to God by external ceremonies and pledges. Like blind men they do not see that the outside show is of no importance and that every-

Luke XX. xlvi.

Matt. XXIII. ii.

iii.

iv.

v.

vi, vii, viii.

xiii.

xv.

thing depends on the soul. They them- Matt.
XXIII. xvi.
selves do what is easy and external, but
what is needful and difficult—love, mercy,
and truth—they neglect. They only wish xxiii.
to appear to be within the law and to
bring others outwardly to the law. There- xxviii.
fore they are like painted tombs, which
seem clean externally but are loathsome
within. They outwardly honour the holy xxvii.
martyrs, but in fact they are just the xxix, xxx.
people who torture and kill the saints.
They were, and are, the enemies of all
that is good. All the evil in the world
comes of them, because they hide the
good and put forward evil in its stead.
Most of all to be feared, therefore, are the
self-appointed teachers. You yourselves
know that every other mistake may be xxxi.
corrected, but if people are mistaken as to Mark III.
xxviii.
what is good it cannot be corrected, and xxix.
that is the case with the self-appointed
leaders.

And Jesus said: I wished here in Jerusalem to unite all men in one understanding
of true happiness, but the people here are
only capable of putting the teachers of
goodness to death. Therefore they will Matt.
XXIII.
remain as godless as they were, and will xxxvii.
not know the true God till they lovingly
accept the understanding of Him. And xxxviii.
Jesus went away from the temple. xxxix.

Then his pupils said to him: But what
will happen to the temple of God, with all
the embellishments people have brought
to it to give to God? XXIV. i.

And Jesus said: I tell you truly that this
whole temple with all its embellishments

will be destroyed, and nothing will be left
of it. There is only one true temple of Matt.
XXIV. ii.
God—the hearts of men when they love
one another.

And they asked him: When will that
temple be? iii.

And Jesus said to them: It will not be
yet. People will for a long time be deceived in the name of my teaching, and
this will cause wars and rebellions. There iv-vii.
will be much wrong-doing and little love. xii.
But when the true teaching spreads
abroad among all men, then there will be
an end of evil and temptations. xiv.

X

THE STRUGGLE WITH TEMPTATION

*So, not to fall into temptation, we must at every moment of
our life be at one with the Father.*

'AND LEAD US NOT INTO TEMPTATION'

AFTER this, the Orthodox chief priests
tried to do all they could to ensnare Jesus,
so as in one way or other to destroy him.
They assembled in council and began to
consider. Luke XI.
liii, liv.

They said: We must somehow finish
with this man. He so proves his teaching John XI.
xlvii.
that if we let him alone everyone will believe in him and cast off our belief. Now
already half the people believe in him.
But if the Jews come to believe his teaching that all men are sons of one Father and
are brothers, and that our Hebrew people
are not different from others, then the

Romans will overwhelm us completely and we shall no longer have a Hebrew kingdom. John XI. xlviii.

And the Orthodox chief priests and scholars long consulted together and could not decide what to do with him, for they could not make up their minds to kill him. Luke XIX. xlvii, xlviii.

Then one of them, Caiaphas, who was the high priest that year, said to them: You must remember that it is expedient to kill one man rather than let the whole people perish, and if we leave this man alone the people will perish. I warn you of that, so it is better to kill Jesus. Even if the people did not perish, still they will be scattered and will go astray from the one faith unless we kill this man. So it is better to kill him. John XI. xlix.

l.

lii.

And when Caiaphas said this they all agreed not to hesitate, but that it was necessary to kill Jesus without fail. liii.

They would at once have taken him and killed him, but he withdrew from them into the desert. But just then the feast of the Passover occurred, when many people assembled in Jerusalem for the holiday; and the Orthodox chief priests counted on Jesus coming with the people to the feast. So they made known to the people that if anyone saw Jesus he should bring him to them. liv.

lv.

lvi.

lvii.

And it so happened that six days before the Passover Jesus said to his pupils: Let us go to Jerusalem. vii.

But the pupils said to him: Do not go. The chief priests have resolved to stone

you to death. If you go there they will
kill you.

John XI.
viii.

Jesus said to them: I cannot fear anything because I live in the light of understanding. And as every man, that he may
not stumble, walks by day and not by
night, so every man, that he may not
doubt or fear, must live by this understanding. Only that man doubts and
fears who lives by the flesh; he who lives
by understanding neither doubts nor fears
anything.

ix.

x.

And Jesus came to the village of Bethany
near Jerusalem, to the house of Martha
and Mary. And when he sat at supper
Martha waited on him. But Mary took
a pound of fresh scented oil, poured it over
his feet and wiped them with her hair.

XII. ii.

When the scent of the oil had filled the
whole room, Judas Iscariot said: Mary
was wrong to waste this expensive oil;
it would have been better to sell it for three
hundred pence and give it to the poor.

iii.

iv.

v.

But Jesus said: You will have the poor
always with you, but I shall soon have
gone away. She has done well! She has
prepared my body for its burial.

viii.

vii.

In the morning Jesus went to Jerusalem
where many people had come for the
feast, and when they recognized Jesus they
surrounded him, tore branches from the
trees, and threw down their clothes on the
road before him, and all shouted: He is
our true King, he has taught us to know
the true God.

xii.

xiii.

Jesus rode on an ass's foal, and the
people ran before him and shouted. So he

xiv.

entered Jerusalem. And when he had ridden thus into the town all the people were excited and asked: Who is he? And those who knew him answered: Jesus, the prophet of Nazareth in Galilee.

Matt. XXI.
x.

xi.

And Jesus went into the temple and again drove out thence all the buyers and sellers.

Mark XI.
xv.

When the Orthodox chief priests saw all this they said to each other: See what this man is doing. All the people follow him.

John XII.
xix.

And they dared not take him straight from among the people, because they saw that the people were on his side, and they considered how to take him by cunning.

Mark XI.
xviii.

Meanwhile Jesus was in the temple and taught the people, among whom besides the Jews there were Greeks who were heathen. The Greeks had heard of Jesus's teaching and understood that he taught the truth not only to Hebrews but to all men; so they also wished to be his pupils and spoke about this to Philip. And Philip told it to Andrew.

John XII.
xx.

xxi.

These two feared to bring Jesus and the Greeks together. They feared that the people would be angry with Jesus for not making any difference between the Hebrews and other nations, and they long hesitated about telling him. Afterwards they told him both together, and hearing that the Greeks wished to be his pupils Jesus was troubled. He knew that the people would hate him for making no difference between Hebrews and heathen, and yet he acknowledged himself to be one with the heathen.

xxii.

He said: The time is come to explain what I understand by the son of man. And though I perish in explaining this, because I destroy the distinction between Jews and heathen, I will still speak the truth. A grain of wheat only fructifies when it itself perishes. He who loves his fleshly life loses the true life, but he who disregards the life of the flesh preserves the life everlasting. Let him who wishes to follow my teaching do as I do. And he who does as I do shall be rewarded by my Father. My soul is now troubled: shall I yield to consideration for my temporal life, or fulfil the will of the Father now at this hour? Can it be that now, when the hour in which I live has come, I shall say: Father, deliver me from that which I ought to do? I cannot say that, for I now live. Therefore I say: Father, show Thyself in me.

And Jesus said: Henceforth the present society of men is doomed to destruction. From this time that which rules this world shall be destroyed. And when the son of man is exalted above the earthly life he will unite all in one.

Then the Jews said to him: We understand from the scriptures that there is an eternal Christ. How then do you say that the son of man shall be exalted? What does it mean—to exalt the son of man?

To this Jesus replied: To exalt the son of man means to live by the light of understanding that is in you. To exalt the son of man above the earthly life means to

John XII.
xxiii.
xxiv.

xxv.

xxvi.

xxvii.
xxviii.

xxxi.

xxxii.

xxxiv.

xxxv.

believe in the light while there is light, in
order to be a son of understanding.   John XII.
xxxvi.

He who believes in my teaching believes not in me but in that spirit which
gave life to the world. And he who under-   xliv.
stands my teaching understands that
spirit which gave life to the world. If   xlv.
anyone hears my words and does not
fulfil them, it is not I who blame him, for I
came not to accuse but to save. He who   xlvii.
does not accept my teaching is accused,
not by my teaching but by the understanding which is in himself. It is that   xlviii.
which accuses him. I do not speak of
myself, but say what my Father—the
living spirit within me—suggests to me.   xlix.
That which I say has been told me by the
spirit of understanding, and that which I
teach is the true life.   l.

Having said this, Jesus went away and
again hid from the chief priests.   xxxvi.

And among those who heard these
words of Jesus were many powerful and
wealthy people who believed his teaching
but were afraid to acknowledge it to the
chief priests. Not one of the chief priests
acknowledged that he believed the teaching, for they were accustomed to judge by   xlii.
human standards and not by God's.   xliii.

After Jesus had hidden himself, the chief
priests and elders again gathered together
at the palace of Caiaphas. And they   Matt.
began to plan how to take Jesus unknown   XXVI. iii,
to the people, for they were afraid to take   iv, v.
him openly.

And one of the first twelve pupils of
Jesus, Judas Iscariot, came to their council

and said: If you want to take Jesus Matt.
XXVI. xiv.
secretly so that the people may not see it,
I will find a time when there will be few
people with him, and will show you where
he is and then you can take him. But
what will you give me for that? They
promised him thirty pieces of silver. He xv.
agreed; and from that time began to seek
opportunity to lead the chief priests upon
Jesus to take him. xvi.

Meanwhile Jesus withdrew from the
people and only his pupils were with him.
When the first feast of unleavened bread
was at hand the pupils said to Jesus:
Where shall we keep the Passover? And xvii.
Jesus said: Go into the village, enter a
house, say that you have not had time
to prepare for the feast, and ask the man
who lives there to admit us to celebrate
the Passover. xviii.

The pupils did this: they asked a man in
the village and he invited them in. xix.

So they came and sat down to table—
Jesus and twelve pupils, Judas among them. xx.

Jesus knew that Judas Iscariot had
already promised to betray him to death:
but he did not accuse him and did not
revenge himself, but as all his life he had
taught his pupils love, so now he only
reproved Judas lovingly. When they all John XIII.
xi.
twelve had sat down to table, he looked at
them and said: Among you sits one who
has betrayed me. Yes, he who eats and Matt.
XXVI. xxi;
drinks with me will destroy me. And he Mark XIV.
xviii.
said nothing more, so that they did not Matt.
know of whom he spoke, and began to eat. XXVI.
xxiii.

When they began to eat, Jesus took

bread, broke it into twelve pieces, gave
each of the pupils a piece, and said: Take
and eat this—it is my body. And then he
filled a cup with wine, handed it to the
pupils and said: Drink all of you of this
cup. And when they had all drunk he
said: This is my blood. I shed it that
people may know my will that they
should forgive one another their sins. For
I shall soon die and shall not be with you
any more in this world, but shall join you
only in the kingdom of heaven.

After that Jesus rose from table, girt
himself with a towel, took a ewer of
water, and began to wash the feet of all
the pupils. When he came to Peter, Peter
protested and said: Why should you wash
my feet? Jesus said to him: It seems
strange to you that I should wash your
feet, but you will soon know why I do this.
Though you are clean, not all of you are
so: among you is my betrayer, to whom
I gave bread and wine with my own hands
and whose feet I wish to wash.

And when Jesus had washed the feet of
all his pupils, he sat down again and said:
Do you understand why I did this? I have
done it that you may always do the same
to one another. I, your teacher, do this
that you may know how to behave with
those who do you harm. If you have
understood this and will do it, then you
will be happy. When I said that one of
you would betray me I did not speak of
you all, for only one of you, whose feet I
washed and who ate bread with me, will
destroy me.

Matt.
XXVI.
xxvi.

xxvii.

xxviii.

Luke XXII.
xviii.

John XIII.
iv.

v.

vi.

vii.

x.

xii.

xiv.

xvii.

xviii.

And having said this Jesus was troubled in spirit and again said: Yes, yes, one of you will betray me. John XIII. xxi.

And again the pupils began to look at one another, not knowing of whom he spoke. One of them sat near Jesus, and Simon Peter made a sign to him that he should ask Jesus who the betrayer was. And he did so. xxii, xxiii, xxiv. xxv.

Jesus said: I will soak a bit of bread and will give it to him and he to whom I give it is my betrayer. And he gave the bread to Judas Iscariot and said to him: What you wish to do, do quickly. xxvi. xxvii.

And Judas understood that he must go away, and as soon as he had taken the sop he at once went out. And he could not be followed as it was night. xxx.

When Judas had gone, Jesus said: It is now clear to you what the son of man is— that in him is God, to make him as blessed as God Himself. xxxi.

Children! I shall not be with you long. Do not argue over my teaching, as I said to the Orthodox, but do what I do. I give you a new commandment: as I have always and to the end loved you; do you always and to the end love one another. By that alone will you be distinguished. Seek only thus to be distinguished from other men—love one another. xxxiii. xxxiv. xxxv.

And after that they went to the Mount of Olives. Matt. XXVI. xxx.

On the way there Jesus said to them: Now the time is coming when what was said in the scriptures will happen: the shepherd will be killed and the sheep will

all be scattered. It will happen to-night.
I shall be taken and you will all abandon
me and scatter.

Matt.
XXVI.
xxxi.

And Peter said to him: Though all
others may be frightened and scatter, I
will not deny you. I am ready to go with
you to prison and to death.

xxxiii.

And Jesus said to him: I tell you that
to-night, after I have been taken, before
cock-crow, you will deny me not once but
thrice.

xxxiv.

Peter answered that he would never
deny him; and all the other pupils said
the same.

xxxv.

Then Jesus said to them: Formerly
neither I nor you lacked anything. You
went without a wallet and without change
of shoes, as I bade you. But now that I
am considered an outlaw we can no
longer do this, but must procure supplies
and get knives that we may not perish
uselessly.

Luke XXII.
xxxv.

xxxvi.

The pupils said: See, we have two knives
—and Jesus replied: It is well.

xxxviii.

Having said this, Jesus went with the
pupils to the garden of Gethsemane. And
on reaching the garden he said: Wait you
here, I wish to pray.

Matt.
XXVI.
xxxvi.

And coming up to Peter and the two
sons of Zebedee he was sorrowful and distressed and he said to them: It is very
hard for me—I am sad before my death.
Wait here, and do not be cast down as I am.

John
XVIII. i.
Matt.
XXVI.
xxxvii.

xxxviii.

And he went off a little way, lay prone
on the ground, and began to pray, saying:
My Father, the spirit! Let it be not as I
wish, which is that I should not die, but

as you wish. Let me die. But for you, as
a spirit, all is possible—grant that I may
not fear death and may not be tempted by
the flesh. Matt.
XXVI.
xxxix.

Then he arose, went to the pupils, and
saw that they were cast down. And he
said to them: How is it that you are not
able for one hour to live in the spirit as I
do? Exalt your spirit, so as not to yield
to the temptation of the flesh. The spirit
is strong, but the flesh is weak. xl.

xli.

And again Jesus went apart from them,
and again began to pray, saying: Father!
If I must suffer and die, then let me die,
and let Thy will be done! xlii.

Having said this, he again came to the
pupils and saw that they were still more
cast down and were ready to weep. xliii.

And he again went apart from them
and for the third time said: Father, let
Thy will be done. xliv.

Then he returned to his pupils and said
to them: Now calm yourselves and be at
ease, for it is now decided that I shall give
myself up into the hands of worldly men. xlv.

XI

THE FAREWELL DISCOURSE

The personal life is an illusion of the flesh, an evil.
The true life is a life common to all men.

'BUT DELIVER US FROM EVIL'

AND Peter said to Jesus: Where are you
going? Jesus replied: You cannot go
where I am going now, but later on you
will go there too. John XIII.
xxxvi.

And Peter said: Why do you think I have not the strength now to go where you are going? I would give my life for you.

John XIII.
xxxvii.

Jesus said: You say you would give your life for me: see that you do not deny me thrice before cock-crow.

xxxviii.

And he turned to the pupils and said: Do not be troubled or afraid, but believe in the true God of life, and in my teaching.

XIV. i.

The life of the Father is not only the life here on earth, there is another life also. If the life of the Father were only such a life as this, I would promise you that when I die I would go to Abraham's bosom and prepare a place for you there and that I would come and take you and that we should be happy together in Abraham's bosom. But I point out to you the path to another life.

i.

iii.
iv.

Thomas said: But we do not know where you are going and so we cannot know the way. We want to know what there is after death.

v.

Jesus said: I cannot show you what will be there; my teaching is the way and the truth and the life. It is impossible to be joined with the Father of life except through my teaching. If you fulfil my teaching you will know the Father.

vi, vii, viii.

Philip said: But who is the Father?

Jesus replied: The Father is He who gives life. I have fulfilled the Father's will and therefore by my life you can recognize the will of the Father.

ix.

I live in the Father and the Father lives in me. All that I say and do, I do by the

will of the Father. My teaching is that I
am in the Father and the Father in me.
If you do not understand my teaching, yet
you see me and what I do: and by this
you may understand what the Father is.
You know that he who follows my teaching
may do the same as I, and even more, for
I shall die, while he will still be alive. He
who lives according to my teaching shall
have all that he desires, for the son will be
one with the Father. Whatever wish you
may have that accords with my teaching
will be fulfilled. But for that, you must
love my teaching. My teaching will give
you an intercessor and a comforter in my
place. That comforter will be the consciousness of truth which worldly men do
not understand, but you will know it in
yourselves. You will never be alone, for the
spirit of my teaching will be in you. I
shall die and worldly men will not see me,
but you will see me because my teaching
lives and you will live by it. And then if
my teaching is in you, you will understand that I am in the Father and the
Father in me. He who fulfils my teaching
will feel the Father in him and my
spirit will live in him.

Then Judas (not Iscariot) said to him:
But why cannot all men live by the spirit
of truth?

And Jesus replied: The Father loves only
him who fulfils my teaching and only in
him can my spirit abide. My Father cannot love him who does not fulfil my
teaching, for that teaching is not mine
but the Father's. This is all I can tell you

now. But my spirit, the spirit of truth John XIV.
which will take up its abode in you after xxv.
I am gone, will reveal all things to you
and you will remember and will understand much of what I have told you: xxvi.
so that you may always have a peaceful
spirit, not the peace that worldly people
seek, but such peace of mind that you will
not fear anything. If you fulfil my teach- xxvii.
ing you need not regret my death. I, as
the spirit of truth, will come to you and
settle in your hearts together with a
knowledge of the Father. If you fulfil my
teaching you should rejoice, for instead of
having me with you in the flesh, you will
have the Father with you in your heart,
and that is better for you. xxviii.

My teaching is a tree of life. The
Father is He who tends the tree. He xv. i.
prunes and cherishes those branches on
which there is fruit, that they may yield
more. Hold to my teaching of life and you ii.
will have more life. As a shoot lives not of
itself but by being part of the tree, so you
should live by my teaching. My teaching iv.
is the tree, you are the shoots. He who
lives by my teaching of life will bring
forth much fruit, for without my teaching
there is no life. He who does not live by v.
my teaching withers and perishes, just as
dead branches are cut off and burnt. vi.

If you live by my teaching and fulfil it
you will have all you desire. For it is the vii.
will of the Father that you may live the
true life and have what you desire. As my viii.
Father has given me what is good, so I
give you the same. Hold on to this good. ix, x.

I have life because the Father loves me
and I love the Father. You too should live
by that same love, and if you live by it
you will be blessed.   John XV. xi.

My commandment is that you love one
another as I have loved you. There is no   xii.
greater love than to sacrifice one's life
for others as I have done.   xiii.

You are my equals if you do what I have
taught you. I do not consider you as   xiv.
slaves to whom orders are given, but as
equals, for I have explained to you all that
I have understood from the Father. You   xv.
do not choose my teaching of your own
will, you choose it because I have shown
you the one truth by which you can live,
and from which you will have all that you
wish.

The whole teaching is—to love one   xvi.
another.   xvii.

If the world hates you, do not be surprised: it hates my teaching. If you were   xviii.
at one with the world it would love you.
But I have taken you out of the world,
and for that it will hate you.   xix.

If they have persecuted me, they will
persecute you also, and they will do all   xx.
this because they do not know the true
God. I explained to them, but they did   xxi.
not wish to hear me. They did not under-   xxii.
stand my teaching because they did not
understand the Father. They saw my life   xxiii.
and my life showed them their error, and   xxiv.
they hated me yet more on that account.   xxv.

The spirit of truth which will come to
you will confirm this to you. But confirm   xxvi.
it yourselves. I tell you this beforehand,   xxvii.

that you may not be deceived when they persecute you. They will cast you out; they will think that by killing you they are doing what pleases God. And they will do all this because they do not understand either my teaching or the true God. I tell you this beforehand that you may not be surprised when it comes about.

John XVI.
i.
ii.
iii.
iv.

So I go now to that spirit which sent me, and now that you understand, you need not ask me where I am going to. Before this you were grieved that I did not tell you whither I go.

v.
vi.

But I tell you truly that it is well for you that I am going. If I do not die the spirit of truth will not come to you, but if I die it will abide in you. That spirit will dwell in you, and it will be clear to you what is false, what is true, and how to make decision. The falsity is, that men do not believe in the life of the spirit: the truth is, that I am one with the Father: and the decision is, to destroy the power of bodily life.

vii.
viii, ix.
x.
xi.

I would say much more to you, but it is hard for you to understand. But when the spirit of truth dwells in you it will show you the whole truth because it will not tell you a new thing of its own, but what is from God; and it will show you the way in all circumstances of life. It too will be from the Father as I am from the Father, and therefore it will tell you the same that I do.

xii.
xiii.
xv.

But when I, as the spirit of truth, shall be in you, you will not always know that

I am there. Sometimes you will, and sometimes you will not, hear me.

And the pupils said to one another: What does this mean? He says: Sometimes you will, and sometimes you will not, hear me. What does it mean—Sometimes you will and sometimes you will not?

Jesus said to them: Do you not understand what it means—Sometimes you will, and sometimes you will not, hear me? You know how it is in the world: some are sad and grieved while others rejoice. You too will grieve, but your sorrow will be turned into joy. A woman in labour suffers torment, but when it is over she does not remember the suffering, for joy that she has brought a child into the world. So you will grieve, and will then suddenly realize my presence: the spirit of truth will enter into you and your grief will be turned into joy. Then you will ask nothing of me, because you will have all you desire. Then all that any one of you desires in the spirit he will have from his Father.

You formerly asked nothing of the spirit, but then you shall ask what you will and it will all be yours, so that your joy will be full. Now, as a man, I cannot tell you this clearly in words, but then—when as the spirit of truth I shall live in you—I will proclaim to you clearly about the Father. Then all that you ask of the Father in the name of the spirit will be given you not by me but by the Father, for He loves you for having received my teaching and understood that the spirit John XVI. xxvii. comes into the world from the Father and returns from the world to the Father. xxviii.

Then the pupils said to Jesus: Now we understand everything and have nothing more to ask. We believe that you are xxix. from God. xxx.

And Jesus said: All that I have told you is to give you peace and confidence in my teaching. Whatever ills may befall you xxxi. in the world, fear nothing: my teaching will overcome the world. xxxiii.

After that Jesus raised his eyes to heaven, and said:

My Father! You have given your son the freedom of life in order that he should John XVII. i. receive the true life. Life is the knowledge of the true God of the understanding revealed by me. I have revealed you to men iii. on earth. I have done what you bade me. iv. I have shown men on earth that you exist. They were yours before, but by your will I have revealed the truth to them and they have recognized you. vi. They have understood that all they have, their very life, is from you alone and that vii. I have taught them not of myself, but that I as well as they have come from you. I viii. pray to you for those who acknowledge you. They have understood that all I ix. have is yours and that what is yours is mine. I am no longer of this world, for I x. am returning to you; but they are in the world, and therefore, Father, I pray you, preserve in them your understanding. I xi. do not ask that you should take them from the world, but that you should deliver

them from the evil of the world and con- John XVII.
firm them in your truth. An under- xv.
standing of you is the truth. My Father! xvii.
I wish them to be as I am, to understand
as I do that the true life began before the
commencement of the world: that they xviii.
should all be one, as you, Father, are in
me and I in you, and that they should be xxi.
one with us—I in them and you in me,
so that all should be one: and that men
should understand that they were not
self-created, but that you have sent them
into the world in love, as you sent me. xxiii.
Father of truth! The world did not know
you, but I knew you and men have
known you through me. I have made
plain to them what you are. You are in xxv.
me that the love with which you have
loved me may be in them also. You have
given them life, which is proof that you
love them. I have taught them to know
this and to love you, so that your love may
return to you from them. xxvi.

XII

THE VICTORY OF SPIRIT OVER MATTER

*And so for a man who lives not the personal life but the
common life in the will of the Father, there is no
death. Physical death is union with the Father.*

'FOR THINE IS THE KINGDOM, THE POWER, AND THE GLORY'

AFTER this Jesus said: Come now, let us
go: he who will betray me is near. Matt.
XXVI.
xlvi.

Hardly had he said this before Judas,
one of the twelve pupils, appeared, and

with him a large throng carrying sticks and swords. Judas said to them: I will show you where he is with his pupils, and that you may know him among them all, he whom I shall first kiss, is he. And he at once went up to Jesus and said: Hail, master! and kissed him.

Matt. XXVI. xlvii. xlviii.

And Jesus said to him: Why are you here, friend?

xlix.

Then the guard surrounded Jesus and were about to take him.

l.

And Peter snatched a sword from a servant of the high priest and slashed the man's ear.

li.

But Jesus rebuked him and said: You must not resist evil. Do not do so. Give back the sword to him from whom you took it, for he who takes the sword shall perish with the sword.

lii.

Then he turned to the crowd and said: Why have you come out against me with weapons as if I were a robber? I was among you every day teaching in the temple and you did not take me. But now is your hour and the power of darkness.

lv.
Luke XXII. liii.

And seeing that he was taken, the pupils all fled.

Matt. XXVI. lvi.

Then the officer told the soldiers to take Jesus and bind him. They did so and took him first to Annas. This was the father-in-law of Caiaphas, who was high priest that year and lived in the same palace with Annas. He was the same Caiaphas who had planned how to destroy Jesus, saying that it was good for the people that Jesus should be killed, and that if this was not done it would be worse for the whole

John XVIII. xii.

xiii.

people. So Jesus was taken to the palace where this high priest lived.

John XVIII. xiv.
Mark XIV. liii.

When Jesus came there one of his pupils, Peter, followed him from afar to see where they would take him, and when Jesus was led into the court of the high priest, Peter went in also to see how the matter would end. And a girl in the yard saw Peter and said to him: You also were with Jesus of Galilee! But Peter was afraid that he might be accused, and said aloud before all the people: I do not know what you are talking about! Afterwards, when Jesus had been taken into the house, Peter also went into the passage with the people. A woman was warming herself there at the fire, and Peter went up to it. She looked at Peter and said to the others: See, this man is like one who was with Jesus of Nazareth. Peter was still more frightened, and swore that he had never been with Jesus and did not know him at all. A little later people went up to Peter and said: It is easy to see that you also were one of these disturbers. We can tell by your speech that you are from Galilee. Then Peter began to affirm and swear that he had never known or seen Jesus.

Matt. XXVI. lviii.

lxix.

lxx.

lxxi.

lxxii.

lxxiii.

And he had hardly said this before the cock crew. And he remembered the words Jesus had said to him when he had assured Jesus that though all should abandon him he would not deny him: 'Before the cock crows this night you will deny me thrice.' And Peter went out into the yard and wept bitterly. He wept because he had fallen into temptation: he had

lxxiv.

fallen into one temptation, that of strife, when he tried to defend Jesus, and into another temptation, the fear of death, when he denied Jesus.

Matt.
XXVI.
lxxv.

And the Orthodox chief priests, the scribes, and the officers, came together to the high priest. And when they were all assembled, they brought in Jesus, and the high priest asked him what his teaching was and who were his pupils.

Mark XIV.
liii.

John
XVIII. xix.

And Jesus answered: I always spoke openly before all men and hid nothing, and I hide nothing from anyone. Why do you ask me? Ask those who heard and understood my teaching. They will tell you.

xx.

xxi.

When Jesus said this, a servant of the high priest struck him in the face and said: To whom are you speaking? Is that the way to answer the High Priest?

Jesus said: If I have spoken ill, tell me what I have said that is wrong. But if I said nothing ill, why strike me?

xxii.

xxiii.

The Orthodox chief priests tried to accuse Jesus, but at first found no proof on which he could be condemned. Then they found two witnesses who said of him: We ourselves heard this man say: 'I will destroy this temple of yours made with hands and in three days will build up another temple to God, not made with hands.' But this evidence also was not enough to convict him. And so the high priest called Jesus up and said: Why do you not answer their evidence?

Matt.
XXVI. lix.

lx.

Mark XIV.
lviii, lix.

Jesus remained silent.

Then the high priest said to him: Tell me, are you the Christ, a son of God?

Matt.
XXVI. lxii.

lxiii.

Jesus answered him and said: Yes, I am the Christ, a son of God. And you will yourself now see that the son of man is equal to God.

Then the high priest cried out: You blasphemer! Now we need no more evidence. We have all heard that you are a blasphemer! And the high priest turned to the assembly and said: You have yourselves heard that he blasphemes God. What do you condemn him to for that?

And they answered: We condemn him to death.

Then all the people and the guards fell upon Jesus and spat in his face and struck him and mishandled him. They bound his eyes, and hit him on the cheek and asked: Now, prophet, who was it that struck you?

Jesus held his peace.

Having reviled him, they led him bound to Pontius Pilate and took him to the hall of judgement.

Pilate the governor came out to them and asked: Of what do you accuse this man?

They said: He is an evil doer, so we have brought him to you.

Pilate said to them: But if he does you harm, judge him yourselves according to your law.

But they replied: We have brought him to you that you may execute him, for the law does not allow us to kill anyone.

And so what Jesus had expected came to pass. He had said that he must be ready to die on the cross at the hands of the

Matt. XXVI. lxiv.

lxv.

lxvi.

lxviii.

XXVII. ii; John XVIII. xxviii.

xxix.

xxx.

xxxi.

Romans instead of dying a natural death or perishing at the hands of the Jews.

John XVIII. xxxii.

And when Pilate asked what they accused him of, they said he was guilty of stirring up the people, forbidding them to pay tribute to Caesar, and made himself out to be the Christ and a king.

Luke XXIII. ii.

Pilate listened to what they had to say, and then ordered Jesus to be brought to him to the judgement seat. When he came in, Pilate said: So you are king of the Jews?

John XVIII. xxxiii.

Jesus replied: Do you really think I am a king, or are you only repeating what has been told you?

xxxiv.

Pilate said: I am not a Jew so you cannot be my king, but your own people have brought you to me. What kind of a man are you?

xxxv.

Jesus replied: I am a king, but my kingdom is not an earthly one. If I were an earthly king my subjects would fight for me and would not have given me up to the chief priests. But, as you see, my kingdom is not an earthly one.

xxxvi.

Pilate replied: Yet you consider yourself a king? Jesus said: Not only I, but you also, cannot but account me a king. I only teach in order to reveal to all men the truth of the kingdom of heaven. And everyone who lives by the truth is a king.

xxxvii.

Pilate said: You speak of 'the truth'— but what is truth?

And having said this he turned away and went out to the chief priests and said to them: I do not find that this man has done anything wrong.

xxxviii.

But the chief priests insisted, and said that he did much evil and stirred up the people and had raised all Judaea, right from Galilee. Luke XXIII. v; Mark XV. iii.

Then Pilate again began to question Jesus in the presence of the chief priests, but Jesus did not answer. Pilate then said to him: Do you not hear how they accuse you? Why do you not defend yourself? iv.

But Jesus was still silent and said not another word, so that Pilate wondered at him. v.

Then Pilate remembered that Galilee was under the jurisdiction of King Herod, and asked: Is he not from Galilee?

They told him: Yes. Luke XXIII. vi.

Then he said: If he is from Galilee he is under Herod's authority and I will send him to him.

Herod was then in Jerusalem, and Pilate, to rid himself of Jesus, sent him to Herod. vii.

Herod was very glad to see Jesus when they brought him. He had heard much about him and wished to know what kind of a man he was. So he called him up before him and began to question him about all he wished to know. But Jesus gave him no answer. And the chief priests and scribes accused him vehemently, as they had done before Pilate, and said that he was a rioter. And Herod regarded Jesus as an empty fellow, and to mock him had him dressed in a crimson robe, and sent him back to Pilate. Herod was pleased that Pilate had treated him with respect by sending Jesus to him to be viii. ix. x. xi.

judged, and so they were reconciled after ^{Luke} having previously been at variance. _{XXIII. xii.}

Now when Jesus was brought back to Pilate, Pilate again called the chief priests _{xiii.} and rulers of the Jews and said to them. You brought this man to me for stirring up the people, and I examined him in your presence and do not find him to be a rioter. I sent him with you to Herod, and _{xiv.} you see that again he is not convicted of any wrong-doing. I do not see any reason for condemning him to death: would it not be better to chastise him and let him go? _{xv.}

But when the chief priests heard this, they all cried out: No, punish him in the _{Matt.} Roman way! Crucify him! _{XXVII. xxiii.}

Pilate listened to the chief priests and said to them: Very well! But you have a custom at the feast of the Passover to pardon one prisoner. Well, here I have in prison Barabbas, a murderer and robber. Which of the two shall be released: Jesus or Barabbas?

Pilate wished thus to save Jesus, but the chief priests had so influenced the people that they all cried out: Barabbas! Barabbas! _{xxi.}

And Pilate said: But what shall be done with Jesus?

They again cried: Crucify him in the Roman way, crucify him! _{xxii.}

And Pilate tried to persuade them, and said: Why are you so hard on him? He has done nothing to deserve death and has _{xxiii.} done you no harm. I will let him go, for I ^{John XIX.} find no fault in him. _{iv.}

The chief priests and their servants cried: Crucify him! Crucify him!

And Pilate said to them: Then take him and crucify him yourselves, for I see no fault in him.

The chief priests answered: We ask only what our law demands. By our law he ought to die for making himself out to be a son of God.

When Pilate heard these words he was troubled, for he did not know what the term 'son of God' meant. And returning to the judgement hall he again called up Jesus and asked him: Who are you and where are you from?

But Jesus did not answer him.

Then Pilate said to him: Why do you not answer me? Do you not see that you are in my power and that I can crucify you or set you free?

Jesus answered him: You have no power. All power is above.

Still Pilate wished to release Jesus, and he said to the Jews: How is it that you wish to crucify your king?

But they said to him: If you release Jesus you will show yourself a disloyal servant to Caesar, for he who sets himself up as a king is Caesar's enemy. Our king is Caesar; but let this man be crucified!

When Pilate heard these words he understood that he could not refuse to execute Jesus. And he went out to the Jews, took some water, washed his hands, and said: I am not guilty of the blood of this just man.

John XIX.
vi.

vii.

viii.

ix.

x.

xi.

xii.

xv.

xii.

xv.

xiii.

Matt.
XXVII.
xxiv.

And the people all cried: Let his blood be upon us and on our children! Matt. XXVII. xxv.

So the chief priests prevailed. And Pilate sat on his judgement seat and ordered Jesus first to be scourged. Luke XXIII. xxiii; John XIX. xiii;

After the soldiers had scourged him they put a wreath on his head and a rod in his hand and threw a red cloak on him and began to mock him, bowing down before him mocking and saying: Hail, King of the Jews! And they struck him on the cheek and on the head, and spat in his face. Matt. XXVII. xxvi.

xxviii.

But the chief priests cried: Crucify him! Our king is Caesar! Crucify him!

So Pilate gave orders that he should be crucified. John XIX. xv, xvi.

They stripped Jesus of the red cloak and put on him his own clothing, and bade him carry the cross to a place called Golgotha, there to be crucified. And he carried his cross and so came to Golgotha. And there they stretched him on a cross between two other men. Matt. XXVII. xxxi.

John XIX. xviii.

When they were nailing him to the cross, Jesus said: Father, forgive them: they know not what they do. Luke XXIII. xxiv.

And when Jesus was hanging on the cross the people thronged round him and railed at him. They went up, wagged their heads at him, and said: So you wished to destroy the temple of Jerusalem and rebuild it in three days! Well now, save yourself and come down from the cross! And the chief priests and leaders stood there also and mocked him, saying: He saved others, but cannot save himself. xxxv.

Mark XV. xxix.

xxx.

xxxi.

Show us now that you are the Christ. Come down from the cross and we will believe you. He said he was the son of God and that God would not forsake him! Has not God forsaken him? And the people and the chief priests and the soldiers railed at him, and even one of the robbers crucified with him railed at him.

Mark XV. xxxii.

This robber, railing at him, said: If you are the Christ, save yourself and us!

Luke XXIII. xxxix.

But the other robber heard this and said: Do you not fear God? You are yourself on the cross and yet rail at an innocent man. You and I are executed for our deserts, but this man has done no harm.

xl.

xli.

And turning to Jesus he said: Lord, remember me in your kingdom!

xlii.

And Jesus said to him: Even now you are blessed with me!

xliii.

And at the ninth hour Jesus, worn out, cried aloud: *Eli, Eli, lama sabachthani!* which means: My God, my God! Why hast thou forsaken me?

Matt. XXVII. xlvi.

And when the people heard this, they began to jeer and said: He is calling the prophet Elias! Let us see whether Elias will come!

xlvii, xlix.

Then Jesus said: I thirst! And a man took a sponge, dipped it in vinegar that stood by, and gave it to Jesus on a reed.

John XIX. xxviii, xxix.

And when Jesus had sucked the sponge he cried out in a loud voice: It is finished! Father, into Thy hands I resign my spirit! And letting his head droop he gave up the ghost.

xxx.

Luke XXIII. xlvi.

A SUMMARY OF THE CHAPTERS

I

JESUS in his childhood spoke of God as his 'Father'.

There was in Judaea at that time a prophet named John, who preached the coming of God on earth. He said that if people changed their way of life, considered all men equal, and instead of injuring helped one another, God would appear and His Kingdom would be established on earth.

Having heard this preaching, Jesus withdrew into the desert to consider the meaning of man's life and his relation to the infinite origin of all, called God. Jesus recognized as his Father that infinite source of being whom John called God.

Having stayed in the desert for some days without food, Jesus suffered hunger and thought within himself:

As a son of God Almighty I ought to be all-powerful as He is, but now that I want to eat and cannot create bread to satisfy my hunger, I see that I am not all-powerful. But to this reflection he made answer: I cannot make bread out of stones, but I can refrain from eating, and so, though I am not all-powerful in the body, I am all-powerful in spirit and can quell the body. Therefore I am a son of God not through the flesh but through the spirit.

Then he said to himself: I am a son of the spirit. Let me therefore renounce the body and do away with it. But to this he replied: I am born as spirit embodied in flesh. Such is the will of my Father and I must not resist His will.

But—he went on thinking—if I can neither satisfy the needs of my body nor free myself from it, then I ought to devote myself to the body and enjoy all the pleasures it can afford me. But to this he replied: I cannot satisfy the needs of my body, and cannot rid myself of it; but my life is all-powerful in that it is the spirit of my Father. Therefore in my body I should serve the spirit, my Father, and work for Him alone.

And becoming convinced that man's true life lies only in the spirit of the Father, Jesus left the desert and began to declare this teaching to men. He said that the spirit dwelt in him, that henceforth the heavens were open and the powers of heaven brought to man, and a free and boundless life had begun for man, and that all men, however unfortunate in the body, might be happy.

II

THE Jews who considered themselves Orthodox worshipped an external God, whom they regarded as creator and ruler of the universe. According to their teaching this external God had made an agreement with them by which He had promised to help them if they would worship Him. A chief condition of this alliance was the keeping of Saturday, the Sabbath.

But Jesus said: The Sabbath is a human institution. That man should live in the spirit is more than all external ceremonies. Like all external forms of religion the keeping of the Sabbath involves a delusion. You are forbidden to do anything on the Sabbath, but good actions should always be done and if keeping the Sabbath hinders the doing of a good action then the keeping of the Sabbath is an error.

According to the Orthodox Jews another condition of the agreement with God was avoidance of intercourse with unbelievers.

Of this Jesus said that God desires not sacrifice to Himself, but that men should love one another.

Yet another condition of the agreement related to rules for washing and purifying, as to which Jesus said that what God demands is not external cleanliness, but pity and love towards man. He also said that external rules are harmful, and that the church tradition is itself an evil. Their church tradition set aside the most important things, such as love for one's mother and father—and justified this by its traditional rulings.

Of all the external regulations of the old law defining the cases in which a man was considered to have defiled himself, Jesus said: Know all of you, that nothing from outside can defile a man, only what he thinks and does can defile him.

After this Jesus went to Jerusalem, the city considered holy, and entered into the temple where the Orthodox considered that God Himself dwelt, and there he said that it was useless to offer God sacrifices, that man is more important than a temple, and that our only duty is to love our neighbour and help him.

Furthermore Jesus taught that it is not necessary to worship God in any particular place, but to serve the Father in spirit and in deed. The spirit cannot be seen or shown. The spirit is man's consciousness of his sonship to the Infinite Spirit. No temple is necessary. The true temple is the society of men united in love. He said that all external worship of God is not only false and injurious when it conduces to wrong-doing—like the Jew's worship which prescribed killing as a punishment, and allowed the neglect of parents—but also because a man performing external rites accounts himself righteous and free from the need of doing what love demands. He said that only he seeks what is good and does good deeds, who feels his own imperfections. To do good deeds a man must be conscious of his own faults, but external worship leads to a false self-satisfaction. All external worship is unnecessary, and should be thrown aside. Deeds of love are incompatible with ceremonial performances, and good cannot be done in that way. Man is a spiritual son of God and should therefore serve the Father in spirit.

III

JOHN's pupils asked Jesus what he meant by his 'kingdom of heaven', and he answered them: The kingdom of heaven I preach is the same as that preached by John—that all men, however poor, may be happy.

And Jesus said to the people: John is the first prophet to preach to men a Kingdom of God which is not of the external world, but in the soul of man. The Orthodox went to hear John, but understood nothing because they know only what they have themselves invented about an external God; they teach their inventions and are astonished that no one pays heed to them. But John preached the truth of the Kingdom of God within us, and therefore he did more than anybody before him. By his teaching the law and the prophets, and all external forms of worship, are superseded. Since he taught, it has been made clear that the Kingdom of God is in man's soul.

The beginning and the end of everything is the soul of man. Every man, though he realizes that he was conceived by a bodily father in his mother's womb, is conscious also that he has within him a spirit that is free, intelligent, and independent of the body.

That eternal spirit proceeding from the infinite, is the origin of all and is what we call God. We know Him only as we recognize Him within ourselves. That spirit is the source of our life; we must rank it above everything and by it we must live. By making it the basis of our life we obtain true and everlasting life. The Father-spirit who has given that spirit to man cannot have sent it to deceive men—that while conscious of everlasting life in themselves they should lose it. This infinite spirit in man must have been given that through him men should have an infinite life. Therefore the man who conceives of this spirit as his life has infinite life, while a man who does not so conceive it has no true life. Men can themselves choose life or death: life in the spirit, or death in the flesh. The life of the spirit is goodness and light: the life of the flesh is evil and darkness. To believe in the spirit, means to do good deeds; to disbelieve means to do evil. Goodness is life, evil is death. God—an external creator, the beginning of all beginnings—we do not know. Our conception of Him can only be this: that He has sown the spirit in men as a sower sows his seed, everywhere, not discriminating as to what part of the field; and the seed that falls on good ground grows, but what falls on sterile ground perishes. The spirit alone gives life to men, and it depends on them to preserve it or lose it. For the spirit, evil does not exist. Evil is an illusion of life There is only that which lives and that which does not live.

Thus the world presents itself to all men, and each man has a consciousness of the kingdom of heaven in his soul. Each one can of his own free will enter that kingdom or not. To enter it he must believe in the life of the spirit, for he who believes in that life has everlasting life.

IV

JESUS was sorry for people because they did not know true happiness, therefore he taught them. He said:

Blessed are they who have no property or fame and do not care for them, and unhappy are they who seek riches and fame; for the destitute and the oppressed are in the Father's will, but the rich and famous seek only rewards from men in this temporary life.

To fulfil the will of the Father do not fear to be poor and despised, but rejoice that you can show men what true happiness is.

To carry out the will of the Father which gives life and welfare to all men, five commandments must be obeyed:

The first commandment is to do no ill to anyone so as not to arouse anger, for evil begets evil.

The second commandment is not to go after women and not to desert the wife with whom you have once been joined; for desertion and change of wives causes all the world's dissoluteness.

The third commandment is to take no oath of any kind. A man can promise nothing, for he is altogether in the Father's power; and oaths are taken for bad purposes.

The fourth commandment is not to resist evil, not to condemn, and not to go to law; but to endure wrong and to do even more than people demand, for every man is full of faults and incapable of guiding others. By taking revenge, we only teach others to do the same.

The fifth commandment is not to discriminate between fellow-countrymen and foreigners, for all are children of one Father.

These five commandments should be observed not

to win praise from men, but for your own welfare; therefore do not pray, or fast, in the sight of men.

The Father knows all that people need, and there is no need to pray for anything; all that is necessary is to seek to be in the Father's will. And His will is that we should not feel enmity towards anyone. It is unnecessary to fast, for men fast merely to win praise from men and their praise should be avoided. It is necessary only to take care to live in the Father's will, and the rest will all be added of itself. A man concerned with the things of the body cannot be concerned with the kingdom of heaven. Even though a man does not trouble about food and clothing, he can live: the Father will give life. All that is needful is to be in the will of the Father at the present moment, for the Father gives his children what they need. Desire only the power of the spirit, which the Father gives. The five commandments show the path to the kingdom of heaven, and this narrow path alone leads to everlasting life.

False teachers—wolves pretending to be sheep— always try to lead people astray from this path. Beware of them! False teachers can always be detected by the fact that they teach evil in the name of good. If they teach violence and executions they are false teachers. By what they teach they may be known.

Not he fulfils the Father's will who calls on the name of God, but he who does what is good. He who fulfils these five commandments will have a secure and true life, of which nothing can deprive him: but he who does not fulfil them will have an insecure life which will soon be taken from him, leaving him nothing.

The teaching of Jesus surprised and attracted the

people by the fact that it recognized all men as free. It was the fulfilment of Isaiah's prophecy, that God's chosen one would bring light to men, would overcome evil and re-establish truth, not by violence but by gentleness, meekness, and kindness.

V

WISDOM lies in recognizing life as the offspring of the Father's spirit. People set themselves the aims of the bodily life, and in seeking these aims torment themselves and others. But they will find full satisfaction in the life meant for them—the life of the spirit—if they accept the doctrine of the spiritual life and of subduing and controlling the body.

It happened once that Jesus asked a woman of another religion to give him some water to drink. She refused on the plea that she was of a different faith. Jesus then said to her: If you understood that he who is asking for water is a living man in whom the spirit of the Father lives, you would not refuse him, but by doing a kindness would try to unite yourself in spirit with the Father, and that spirit would give you not such water as this—after drinking which a man thirsts again—but water that gives everlasting life. One need not pray to God in any special place, but should serve Him by deeds of love—by ministering to those in whom His spirit dwells.

And Jesus said to his pupils: The true food of man is to fulfil the will of the Father-spirit, and this fulfilment is always possible. Our whole life is a gathering up of the fruits of the spirit sown within us by the Father. Those fruits are the good we do to men. We should do good to men unceasingly and expect no reward.

After this Jesus happened to be in Jerusalem and

came to a bathing-place beside which lay a sick man, waiting for a miracle to cure him. Jesus said to him: Do not expect to be cured by a miracle, but live according to your strength and do not mistake the meaning of life. The invalid obeyed Jesus, got up, and went away. Seeing this, the Orthodox began to reproach Jesus for having cured an invalid on the Sabbath. Jesus said to them: I have done nothing new. I have only done what our common Father-spirit does. He lives and gives life to men, and I have done likewise. To do this is every man's business. Everyone has freedom to choose life or reject it. To choose life is to fulfil the will of the Father by doing good to others; to reject it is to do one's own will and not do good to others. It is in each one's power to do the one or the other: to receive life or destroy it.

The true life of man can be compared to this: A master apportioned to his slaves a valuable property and told them each to work on what was given him. Some of them worked, others simply put away what had been given them. Then the master demanded an account of what they had done, and to those who had worked he gave still more of his property, while from those who had not worked he took away all that they had.

The portion of the master's valuable property is the spirit of life in man, who is the son of the Father-spirit. He who in this life works for the sake of the spirit-life receives infinite life, he who does not work loses what was given him.

The only true life is the life common to all, and not the life of the individual. Each should work for the life of others.

After that Jesus went to a desert place and many people followed him. Towards evening his pupils came and said: How can we feed all these people?

Among the gathering were some who had no food, and some who had bread and fish. Jesus said to his pupils: Give me what bread you have. And he took the loaves and gave the bread to his pupils, and they gave it away to others, who began to do the same. So everyone ate what was distributed in this way, and they all had enough without eating all the food that was there. And Jesus said: That is how you should always act. It is not necessary for each man to obtain food for himself but it is needful to do what the spirit in man demands, namely to share what there is with others.

The true food of man is the spirit of the Father. Man lives only by the spirit.

We must serve all that has life, for life lies not in doing one's own will but the will of the Father of life. And that will is that the life of the spirit, which each one has, should remain in him and that all should cherish the life of the spirit in them until the hour of death. The Father, the source of all life, is the spirit. Life consists only in carrying out the will of the Father, and to carry out that will of the spirit one must surrender the body. The body is food for the life of the spirit. Only by sacrificing the body does the spirit live.

After this Jesus chose certain pupils and sent them about to preach the doctrine of the life of the spirit. When sending them he said: You are going to preach the life of the spirit, therefore renounce in advance all fleshly desires and have nothing of your own. Be prepared for persecution, privation, and suffering. Those who love the life of the body will hate you, torment you, and kill you; but do not be afraid. If you fulfil the will of the Father you possess the life of the spirit, of which no one can deprive you.

The pupils set out and when they returned they

announced that they had everywhere overcome the teaching of evil.

Then the Orthodox said to Jesus that his teaching, even if it overcame evil, was itself an evil, for those who carry it out must endure sufferings. To this Jesus said: Evil cannot overcome evil. Evil can only be mastered by goodness, and that goodness is the will of the Father-spirit, common to all men. Every man knows what is good for himself, and if he does that for others—if he does that which is the will of the Father—he will do good. And so the carrying out of the will of the Father-spirit is good even if it be accompanied by the suffering and death of those who fulfil that will.

VI

JESUS said that his mother and his brothers had no prior claim on him as such, only those were near to him who fulfilled the will of their common Father.

A man's life and blessedness depend not on family relationships, but on the life of the spirit. Jesus said: Blessed are those who retain their understanding of the Father. A man living in the spirit has no home—the spirit cannot own a house. He said that he himself had no fixed abode. To fulfil the Father's will no special place is needed, for it is always and everywhere possible.

The death of the body cannot be dreadful to a man who resigns himself to the will of the Father, for the life of the spirit does not depend on that of the body. Jesus says that he who believes in the life of the spirit can fear nothing.

No cares make it impossible for a man to live in the spirit. To one who said that he would obey the teaching of Jesus later, but must first bury his father, Jesus replied: Only the dead trouble about the burial of the dead, the living live always by fulfilling the will of the Father.

Family and household cares must not hinder the life of the spirit. He who is troubled about what results to his bodily life from the fulfilment of the Father's will, acts like a ploughman who looks back while ploughing, instead of in front of him.

Cares for the pleasure of the bodily life, which seem so important to men, are delusions. The only real business of life is the announcement of the Father's will, attention to it, and fulfilment of it. When Martha complained that she alone busied herself about the supper, while her sister Mary listened to his teaching instead of helping, Jesus replied: You blame her unjustly. If you need the results of your work, busy yourself with it, but let those who do not need physical pleasures attend to the one thing essential for life.

Jesus said: He who desires to obtain true life, consisting in the fulfilment of the Father's will, must first of all give up his own personal desires. He must not only not plan his life according to his own wishes, but must be ready to endure privation and suffering at any moment.

He who desires to arrange his bodily life according to his own desires, will wreck the true life of fulfilment of the Father's will. And there is no advantage in gain for the physical life if that gain wrecks the life of the spirit.

Most ruinous of all for the life of the spirit is the love of gain, of getting rich. Men forget that whatever riches or goods they obtain they may die at any moment, and that property is not essential for life. Death hangs over each of us. Sickness, murder, or accident, may at any moment end our life. Bodily death is an inescapable condition of every second of our life. While a man lives he should regard every hour of life as a postponement of death granted by someone's kindness. We should remember this, and not say we do not know it. We know and foresee all that happens on earth and in the sky, but forget death, which we know awaits us at any moment. Unless we forget death we cannot yield ourselves to the life of the body; for we cannot reckon on it. To follow the teaching of Christ we must count up the advantages of following our own will and serving the bodily life, and the advantages of fulfilling the Father's will. Only he who has clearly taken account of this can be a disciple of Christ. But he who makes the calculation will not regret having to forgo this unreal happiness and unreal life in order to obtain the true good and the true life. True life is given to men and they know it and hear its call, but constantly distracted by the cares of the moment they deprive themselves of it. True life is like a feast a rich man gave, and to which he invited guests. He called them—just as the voice of the Father-spirit calls all men to Himself. But some of those invited were busy with trading, others with their farms, others again with family affairs, and they did not go to the feast. Only the poor who had no worldly cares went to the feast and gained happiness. So men distracted by cares for the bodily life deprive themselves of true life. He who does not wholly reject the cares and gains of the bodily life cannot fulfil the Father's will, for no man can serve himself a little and the Father a little: he has to consider whether it is better to serve his body and whether it is possible to arrange his life according to his own will. He must do as a man does who wishes to build a house, or to prepare for war. That man first considers whether he has means to finish his house, or to conquer his enemy. And if he sees that he has not, he will not waste his labour or his army uselessly, and make himself a laughing-stock to his neighbours. If a man could arrange his bodily life to his own will, then it might be well to serve the body, but as that is impossible, it is better to reject bodily things and serve the spirit. Otherwise you will gain neither the one thing nor the other. You will not arrange the bodily life satisfactorily, and will lose the life of the spirit. Therefore to fulfil the Father's will it is necessary to sacrifice the bodily life.

The bodily life is wealth entrusted to us by another, which we should use so as to gain our own true riches.

If a rich man has a manager who knows that however well he may serve his master, that master will dismiss him leaving him with nothing, the manager will be wise if while managing his master's affairs he does favours to other people. Then when the master dismisses him, those whom he has benefited will receive him and sustain him. That is how men deal in their bodily life. The bodily life is that wealth, not our own, which is entrusted to us for a time. If we make good use of that wealth which is not our own, then we shall receive true wealth which will be our own.

If we do not give up wealth that is not our own, we shall not receive our true wealth. We cannot serve both the illusory life of the body and the life of the spirit; we must serve the one or the other. A man cannot serve property and God. What is honourable among men is an abomination before God. In God's sight riches are evil. A rich man is guilty in that he eats much and luxuriously, while at his door the poor are hungry. And everyone knows that property not shared with others is held in non-fulfilment of the Father's will.

A rich, Orthodox ruler came once to Jesus and

began to boast that he fulfilled all the commandments of the law. Jesus reminded him that there is a commandment to love others as oneself and that that is the Father's will. The ruler said he kept that also. Then Jesus said to him: That is not true; if you really wished to fulfil the Father's will you would not possess property. You cannot fulfil the Father's will if you have property of your own which you do not give to others. And Jesus said to his pupils: Men think it impossible to live without property, but I tell you that true life consists in giving what you have to others.

A certain man named Zaccheus heard the teaching of Jesus and believed it, and having invited Jesus to his house said to him: I am giving half my fortune to the poor and will restore fourfold to those I have wronged. And Jesus said: Here is a man who fulfils the Father's will, for a man's whole life must be passed in fulfilment of that will, and there is no condition in which a man can say: 'I have fulfilled the will of God.'

Good cannot be measured; it is impossible to say who has done more or less. A widow who gives away her last farthing gives more than a rich man who gives thousands. Nor can goodness be measured by its usefulness.

Let the case of the woman who felt pity for Jesus and recklessly poured over his feet many pounds' worth of costly oil serve as an example. Judas said she had acted foolishly because the cost of the oil would have sufficed to feed many people. But Judas was a thief and a liar, and when he spoke of the material advantage he was not thinking of the poor. The essential thing lies not in the utility of an action or the largeness of a gift, but what is necessary is always, every moment, to love others and give them what one has.

VII

ANSWERING the Jews' demand for proofs of the
truth of his teaching, Jesus said: The truth of my
teaching lies in the fact that I teach not something
of my own but what comes from the common
Father of us all. I teach what is good for the Father
of all and is therefore good for all men.

Do what I say, fulfil the five commandments, and
you will see that what I say is true. Fulfilment of
these five commandments will drive away all evil
from the world, and therefore they are certainly
true. It is clear that he who teaches the will of
Him who sent him, and not his own will, teaches
the truth. The law of Moses teaches the fulfilment
of human desires and so it is full of contradictions;
my teaching is to fulfil the will of the Father and so
it is harmonious.

The Jews did not understand him and looked for
external proofs of whether he was the Christ mentioned in the prophecies. On this he said to them:
Do not question who I am and whether it is of me
that your prophecies speak, but attend to my
teaching and to what I say about our common
Father.

You need not believe in me as a man, but you
should believe what I tell you in the name of the
common Father of us all.

It is not necessary to inquire about external
matters as to where I come from, but it is necessary to follow my teaching. He who follows it
will receive true life. There can be no proofs of
the truth of my teaching. It is the light itself,
and as light cannot be illuminated, so truth cannot be proven true. My teaching is the light.
He who sees it has light and life and needs no

proofs, but he who is in darkness must come to the light.

But the Jews again asked him who he was as to his bodily personality. He said to them: I am, as I told you from the first, a man, the son of the Father of life. Only he who so regards himself (this is the truth I teach) will fulfil the will of the common Father; only he will cease to be a slave and become a free man. We are enslaved only by the error of taking the life of the body to be the true life. He who understands the truth—that life consists only in the fulfilment of the Father's will—becomes free and immortal. As a slave does not always remain in the house of his master, but the son does; so a man who lives as a slave to the flesh does not remain alive for ever, but he who fulfils in his soul the Father's will has eternal life. To understand me you must understand that my Father is not the same as your father whom you call God. Your father is a god of the flesh, but my Father is the spirit of life. Your father, your god, is a jealous god, a man-slayer, one who executes men. My Father gives life, and so we are the children of different fathers. I seek the truth, and you wish to kill me for that, to please your god. Your god is the devil, the source of evil, and in serving him you serve the devil. My teaching is that we are sons of the Father of life, and he who believes in my teaching shall not see death. The Jews asked: How can it be that a man will not die, when all those who pleased God most—even Abraham—have died? How then can you say that you, and those who believe in your teaching, will not die?

To this Jesus replied: I speak not by my own authority. I speak of that same source of life that you call God, and that dwells in men. That source I know and cannot help knowing, and I know His will and fulfil it, and of that source of life I say that it has been, is, and will be, and that for it there is no death.

Demands for proofs of the truth of my teaching are as if one demanded from a man who had been born blind, proofs of why and how he sees the light when his sight has been restored.

The blind man whose sight has been restored, remaining the same man he was, can only say that he was blind but now sees. And one who formerly did not understand the meaning of life but now does understand it, can only say the same, and nothing else.

Such a man can only say that formerly he did not know the true good in life but now he knows it. A blind man whose sight has been restored, if told that he has not been cured in a proper manner and that he who restored his sight is an evil-doer, and that he should be cured differently, can only reply: I know nothing about the correctness of my cure or the sinfulness of him who cured me, or of a better way of being cured; I only know that whereas I was blind, now I see. And in the same way one who has understood the meaning of the teaching of true welfare and of the fulfilment of the Father's will, can say nothing as to the regularity of that teaching or whether he who disclosed it to him was a sinner, or of the possibility of a still greater blessedness, but can only say: Formerly I did not see the meaning of life, but now I see it and that is all I know.

And Jesus said: My teaching is the awakening of a life till then asleep: he who believes my teaching awakens to eternal life and lives after death.

My teaching is not proven in any way: men yield to it because it alone has the promise of life for all men.

As sheep follow the shepherd who gives them food and guards their life, so men accept my teaching because it gives life to all. And as the sheep do not follow a thief who climbs over into the fold, but shy away from him, so men cannot believe these doctrines which teach violence and executions. My teaching is as a door for the sheep, and all who follow me shall find true life. As only those shepherds are good who own and love the sheep and devote their lives to them, while hirelings who do not love the sheep are bad shepherds, so also only that teacher is true who does not spare himself, and he is worthless who cares only for himself. My teaching is that a man should not spare himself, but should sacrifice the life of the body for the life of the spirit. This I teach and fulfil.

The Jews still did not understand and still wanted proofs of whether or not Jesus was the Christ, and whether, therefore, they should believe him or not. They said: Do not torment us, but tell us plainly, are you the Christ or not? And to this Jesus replied: Belief must be given not to words but to deeds. By the example I set, you may know whether I teach the truth or not. Do what I do, and do not discuss words. Fulfil the will of the Father, and then you will all be united with me and with the Father; for I, the son of man, am the same as the Father and the same that you call God and that I call the Father. I and the Father are one. Even in your own scriptures it is said that God said to men: 'You are Gods.' Every man by his spirit is a son of this Father. And if a man lives fulfilling the Father's will he becomes one with the Father. If I fulfil His will, the Father is in me and I am in the Father.

After this Jesus asked his pupils how they understood his teaching about the son of man. Simon

Peter answered him: Your teaching is that you are
the son of the God of life, and God is the life of the
spirit in man. And Jesus said to him: You are
happy, Simon, to have understood that. Man
could not have disclosed it to you, but you have
understood it because the God in you has revealed
it to you. On this understanding the true life of
men is founded. For that life there is no death.

VIII

IN reply to doubts expressed by his pupils as to
the reward resulting for renouncing the life of the
flesh, Jesus said: For him who understands the
meaning of my teaching there can be no question
of a reward, first because a man who for its sake
gives up family, friends, and possessions, gains a
hundredfold more friends and more possessions, and
secondly, because a man who seeks a reward seeks
to have more than others have, and that is quite
contrary to the fulfilment of the Father's will. In
the kingdom of heaven there is neither greater nor
less, all are equal. Those who seek a reward for
goodness are like labourers who, because in their
opinion they were more deserving than others,
demanded larger pay than they had agreed upon
with their employer. According to the teaching of
Jesus no one can be either higher or more important than another.

All can fulfil the Father's will, but in doing so no
one becomes superior or more important or better
than another. Only kings and those who serve
them reckon in that way. According to my teaching, said Jesus, there can be no superior rank; he
who wishes to be better should be the servant of all.
My teaching is, that life is given to man not that
others may serve him, but that he should give his

whole life to the service of others. He who exalts himself instead of doing this, will fall lower than he was.

The meaning and purpose of life must be understood before a man can be rid of thoughts of his own elevation. The meaning of life lies in fulfilling the will of the Father, and His will is that what He has given us shall be returned to Him. As a shepherd leaves his whole flock and goes to seek a lost sheep, and as a woman will search everywhere to find a lost penny, so the Father's continual work is manifested to us by the fact that He draws to Himself that which pertains to Him.

We must understand wherein true life consists. True life always appears in the lost being restored to where it belongs, and in the awakening of those that sleep. People who have the true life and have returned to the source of their being, cannot, like worldly men, account others as being better or worse, but being sharers of the Father's life can only rejoice at the return of the lost to the Father. If a son who has gone astray repents and returns to the father he had left, how can other sons of the same father be envious of his joy, or fail to rejoice at their brother's return?

To believe in the teaching and to change our way of life and fulfil that teaching, what is needed is not external proofs or promises of rewards, but a clear understanding of what true life is. If men think themselves completely masters of their own lives, and believe that life is given them for bodily enjoyment, then clearly any sacrifice they make for others will seem to them an act worthy of reward, and without such reward they will give nothing. If tenants forgot that a garden was let to them on condition that they returned the fruits to the owner, and that rent was demanded of them again and again, they would seek to kill the collector. So it is with those who think themselves masters of their own lives and do not understand that life is granted them by an understanding which demands the fulfilment of its will. To believe and to act, it is necessary to understand that man can do nothing of himself, and that if he gives up his bodily life to serve goodness he does nothing that deserves either thanks or reward. We must understand that in doing good a man only does his duty and what he necessarily must do. Only when he understands life in that way can a man have faith enabling him to do truly good deeds.

The kingdom of heaven consists in that understanding of life. It is not a visible kingdom that can be pointed out in this or that place. The kingdom of heaven is in man's understanding. The whole world lives as of old: men eat and drink, marry, trade, and die, and along with this in the souls of men lives the kingdom of heaven—an understanding of life growing as a tree that in spring puts out leaves of itself.

True life is the fulfilment of the will of the Father, not in the past or in the future, but now; it is what each of us must do at the present moment. And therefore to live the true life we must never relax. Men are set to guard life, not in the past or in the future, but the life now being lived, and in it to fulfil the will of the Father of all men. If they let this life escape them by not fulfilling the Father's will, they will not receive it back again. A watchman set to watch all night does not perform his duty if he falls asleep even for a moment, for a thief may come at that moment. So man should direct his whole strength to the present hour, for only then can he fulfil the Father's will; and that will is the life and blessing of all men. Only those live who are

doing good. Good done to men now in the present,
is the life that unites us with the common Father.

IX

MAN is born with a knowledge of the true life
which lies in the fulfilment of the Father's will.
Children live by that knowledge: in them the will
of the Father is seen. To understand the teaching
of Jesus one must understand the life of children
and be like them.

Children live in the Father's will, not infringing
the five commandments, and they would never
infringe them were they not misled by adults. Men
ruin children by leading them to break these commandments. And by so doing they act as if they
tied a millstone to a man's neck and threw him into
the river. The world is unhappy only because
people yield to temptations, but for that the world
would be happy. Temptations lure men to do evil
for the sake of imaginary advantages in their
temporal life. Yielding to temptation ruins men,
and therefore everything should be sacrificed rather
than fall into temptation.

The temptation to infringe the first commandment comes from men considering themselves in the
right towards others, and others in the wrong towards themselves. To avoid falling into that temptation we must remember that all men are always
infinitely in debt to the Father and can only acquit
themselves of that debt by forgiving their brother
men.

Therefore men must forgive injuries, and not be
deterred though the offender injures them again
and again. However often a man may be wronged
he must forgive, not remembering the wrong; for
only by forgiveness can the kingdom of heaven be
attained. If we do not forgive others, we act as a

certain debtor did when, heavily in debt, he went to his creditor and begged for mercy. His creditor forgave him everything, but the debtor went away and meeting a man who owed him only a small sum, began to throttle him. To have life we must fulfil the Father's will. We ask forgiveness of Him for failing to fulfil His will, and hope to be forgiven. What then are we doing if we do not ourselves forgive others? We are doing to them what we dread for ourselves.

The will of the Father is well-being; and evil is that which separates us from the Father. How then can we fail to seek to quench evil as quickly as possible, since it is that which ruins us and robs us of life? Evil entangles us in bodily destruction. In so far as we escape from that entanglement we obtain life and have all that we can desire. We are not separated from one another by evil but are united by love.

Men are tempted to infringe the second commandment by thinking of woman as created for bodily pleasure, and by supposing that by leaving one wife and taking another they will obtain more pleasure. To avoid falling into this temptation we must remember that the Father's will is, not that man should delight himself with woman's charms but that each man having chosen a wife should be one with her. The Father's will is for each man to have one wife and each wife one husband. If each man keeps to one wife, each man will have a wife and each woman a husband. He who changes his wife deprives her of a husband and gives occasion for some other man to leave his wife and take the deserted one. A man need not marry at all, but must not have more than one wife, for if he does he goes against the will of the Father which is that one man should unite with one woman.

Men are tempted to infringe the third commandment by creating, for the advantage of their temporal life, established authorities, and demanding from one another oaths by which they bind themselves to do what those authorities demand. To avoid falling into this temptation men must remember that they are indebted for their life to no power but God. The demands of authorities should be regarded as violence but, following the command of non-resistance to evil, men should yield what goods and labour the authorities may demand. But they must not pledge their conduct by taking oaths, for the oaths that are imposed lead to evil. He who recognizes his life as being in the will of the Father cannot bind his actions by pledges, for such a man holds his life most sacred.

Men are tempted to infringe the fourth commandment by thinking that they can reform others by themselves yielding to anger and revenge. If a man wrongs another, people think he should be punished and that justice lies in human judgement.

To avoid falling into this temptation we must remember that men are called not to judge but to save one another, and that they cannot judge one another's faults because they are themselves full of wickedness. The one thing they can do is to teach others by an example of purity, forgiveness, and love.

Men are tempted to infringe the fifth commandment by thinking that there is a difference between their own countrymen and those of other nations, and that it is therefore necessary to defend themselves against other nations and do them harm. To avoid falling into this temptation it is necessary to know that all the commandments may be summed up in this: to do good to all men without distinction, and thus fulfil the will of the Father who has given life and well-being to all. Even if others make such distinctions, and though nations, considering themselves alien to one another, go to war, yet each man, to fulfil the will of the Father, should do good to all—even to those belonging to a nation with which his country is at war.

To avoid falling into human illusions we must think not of the physical but the spiritual life. If a man understands that life consists solely in now being in the Father's will, neither privations, nor sufferings, nor death, can seem dreadful to him. Only that man receives true life who is ready at every moment to give up his physical life in order to fulfil the Father's will.

And that everyone may understand that true life is that in which there is no death, Jesus said: Eternal life should not be understood as being like the present life. For true life in the will of the Father there is neither space nor time.

Those who are awake to the true life live in the Father's will for which there is neither space nor time. They live with the Father. If they have died for us, they live for God. Therefore one commandment includes in itself all: to love all men, each of whom has the source of life within him.

And Jesus said: That source of life is the Christ you are awaiting. The comprehension of that source of life, for whom there is no distinction of persons and no time or place, is the son of man whom I teach. All that hides that source of life from men is temptation. There is the temptation of the scribes, of the bookmen, and of the materialists —do not yield to it. There is the temptation of authority, do not yield to that: and there is also the most terrible temptation, from the religious teachers who call themselves Orthodox. Beware of this last temptation more than of all the others, because these self-ordained teachers, just they, by devising the worship of a false God decoy you from the true God. Instead of serving the Father of life by deeds, they substitute words, and teach words while they themselves do nothing. You can learn nothing from them but words, and the Father requires deeds. They can teach nothing because they themselves know nothing, and only for their own advantage wish to set themselves up as teachers. But you know that no man can be the teacher of another. There is one teacher for all men—the Lord of life— the understanding. But these self-styled teachers, thinking to teach others, deprive themselves of true life and hinder others from understanding it. They teach men that their God will be pleased by external rites, and think they can bring men to religion by vows. They are only concerned about externals. An outward assumption of religion satisfies them, but they do not think of what goes on in men's hearts. And so they are like showy sepulchres, handsome outside but loathsome within. In words they honour the saints and the martyrs, but they are just the people who formerly killed and tortured and who now kill and torture the saints. From them come all the world's temptations, for under the guise of good they teach evil.

The evil they create is the root of all others, for they defile the most holy thing in the world. They will continue their deceptions and increase evil in the world, and it will be long before they are changed. But a time will come when all their churches and all external worship of God will be destroyed, and men will understand, and unite in love, to serve the one God of life and to fulfil His will.

X

THE Jews saw that the teaching of Jesus would destroy their State religion and their nationality, and at the same time saw that they could not refute it, so they decided to kill him. His innocence and rectitude hindered them, but the high priest Caiaphas devised a pretext for killing him even though Jesus was not guilty in any way. Caiaphas said: We need not discuss whether this man is innocent or guilty; we have to consider whether we wish our people to remain a separate Jewish nation or whether we wish it to be broken up and dispersed. The nation will perish and the people be scattered if we let this man alone and do not put him to death. This argument decided the matter, and the Orthodox agreed that Jesus must be put to death; and they instructed the people to seize him as soon as he appeared in Jerusalem.

Though he knew of this, Jesus nevertheless went to Jerusalem for the feast of the Passover. His pupils entreated him not to go, but he said: What the Orthodox wish to do to me, and all that any man may do, cannot alter the truth for me. If I see the light I know where I am and where I am going. Only he who does not know the truth can fear anything or doubt anything. Only he who does not see, stumbles. And he went to Jerusalem, stopping on the way at Bethany. There Mary emptied a jar of precious oil on him, and when the pupils reproached her for wasting so much precious oil, Jesus, knowing that his bodily death was near at hand, said that what she had done was a preparation for his burial. When he left Bethany and went to Jerusalem crowds met and followed him, and this convinced the Orthodox still more of the need to kill him. They only wanted an opportunity to seize him. He knew that the least indiscreet word from him now, contrary to the law, would be used as a reason for his execution; but notwithstanding this he went into the temple and again declared that the Jewish worship of God with sacrifices and libations was false, and he again announced his teaching. But his teaching, based on the prophets, was such that the Orthodox could still find no palpable breach of the law for which they could condemn him to death, especially as most of the common people were on his side. But at the feast there were certain heathen who having heard of Jesus's teaching, wished to discuss it with him. The pupils hearing of this were alarmed. They feared lest Jesus by talking with the heathen might betray himself and excite the people. At first they did not want to put the heathen in touch with Jesus, but afterwards they decided to tell him that these men wished to speak with him. On hearing this, Jesus was troubled. He understood that his talk with the heathen would make clear his rejection of the whole Jewish law, would turn the crowd from him, and would give occasion to the Orthodox to accuse him of having intercourse with the hated heathen; and knowing this he was troubled. But he also knew that his mission was to make clear to men, the sons of one Father, their unity without distinction of faith. He knew that to do this would cost him his bodily life but that its loss would give men a true understanding of life, and therefore he said: As a grain of wheat perishes to bear fruit, so I, a man, must give up my bodily life in order to bear spiritual fruit. He who holds fast to his bodily life loses his true life, but he who does not grudge his bodily life obtains the true life. I am troubled at what awaits me, but I have lived till now only in preparation for this hour, how then can I fail to act as I ought? So let the Father's will be manifested through me now.

And turning to the people, heathen and Jews, Jesus declared openly what he had only said privately to Nicodemus. He said: Men's lives, with their different creeds and governments, must all be changed. All human authorities must disappear. It is only necessary to understand the nature of man as a son of the Father of life, and this understanding destroys all divisions of men and of authorities and makes all men one. The Jews said: You are destroying our whole creed. Our law tells of a Christ, but you speak only of a Son of Man and say that he should be exalted! What does that mean? He replied: To exalt the son of man means living by the light of understanding that exists in man, and while there is light, living by that light. I teach no new faith but only what each man may know within himself. Each man knows the life in himself, and each man knows that life is given to him and to all men by the Father of life. My teaching is only that man should love the life that the Father gives to us all.

Many of the unofficial folk believed Jesus; but the notables and official classes did not believe him, because they did not wish to consider the universal purport of what he said, and thought only of its temporal bearings. They saw that he turned the people from them and they wished to kill him; but they feared to take him openly, and wanted to do so secretly—not in Jerusalem and in the daytime. And one of his twelve pupils, Judas Iscariot, came to them, and they bribed him to take their emissaries to Jesus when he should be away from the people. Judas promised to do this, and went back to Jesus, awaiting a suitable opportunity to betray him. On the first day of the feast Jesus kept the

Passover with his pupils, and Judas, thinking that Jesus was not aware of his treachery, was with them. But Jesus knew that Judas had sold him, and as they all sat at table he took bread, broke it into twelve pieces, and gave one to each of the pupils, to Judas as well as to the others, and without naming anyone, said: Take, eat my body. Then he took a cup with wine, gave it to them all, including Judas, to drink, and said: One of you will shed my blood. Drink my blood. Then he rose and washed all the pupils' feet, and when he had done so said: I know that one of you will betray me to death and will shed my blood, but I have fed him and given him drink and washed his feet. I have done this to show you how to behave to those who harm you. If you act so, you will be blessed. And the pupils all asked which of them was the betrayer. But Jesus did not name him, that they might not turn on him. When it grew dark, however, Jesus indicated Judas and at the same time told him to go away, and Judas got up from the table and went off and no one hindered him. Then Jesus said: This is what it means to exalt the son of man. To exalt the son of man is to be as kind as the Father not only to those who love us but to all men, even to those who do us harm. Therefore do not argue about my teaching, do not pick it to pieces as the Orthodox do, but do as I do and as I have now done before your eyes. This one commandment I give you: love men. My whole teaching is to love men always and to the end. After this, fear came over Jesus, and he went in the dark with his pupils to a garden to be out of the way. And on the road he said to them: You are all of you wavering and timid; if they come to take me you will all run away. To this Peter replied: No, I will never desert you and will defend you even to the death. And the other pupils all said the same.

Then Jesus said: If that is so, then prepare for defence, get weapons to defend yourselves and collect your provisions, for we shall have to hide. The pupils replied that they had two knives. When Jesus heard the mention of knives, anguish came over him. And going to a lonely spot he began to pray and urged the pupils to do the same, but they did not understand him. Jesus said: My Father—the spirit! End in me this struggle with temptation. Confirm me in the fulfilment of Thy will. I want to overcome my own wish to defend my bodily life, and to do Thy will—not resisting evil. The pupils still did not understand. And he said to them: Do not consider the body, but try to exalt the spirit in yourselves; strength is in the spirit, but the flesh is weak. And again he said: My Father! If suffering must be, then let it come: but in the suffering I want one thing only, that not my will, but Thine, may be fulfilled in me. The pupils did not understand. And again he strove with temptation and at last overcame it; and coming to his pupils he said: Now it is decided, you can be at rest. I shall not fight, but shall give myself up into the hands of the men of this world.

XI

AND Jesus, feeling himself prepared for death, went to give himself up, but Peter stopped him and asked where he was going. Jesus replied: I am going where you cannot go. I am ready for death, but you are not yet ready for it. Peter said: I am ready to give my life for you now. Jesus replied: A man cannot pledge himself to anything. And he said to all his pupils: I know that death awaits me, but I believe in the life of the Father and therefore do not fear it. Do not be disturbed at my death, but believe in the true God and Father of life, and then my death will not seem dreadful to you. If I am united to the Father of life, then I cannot be deprived of life. It is true that I do not tell you what or where my life after death will be, but I point out to you the way to true life. My teaching does not tell you what that life is to be, but it reveals the only true path to that life, which is to be in unity with the Father. The Father is the source of life. My teaching is that man should live in the will of the Father and fulfil His will for the life and welfare of all men. Your teacher when I am gone will be your knowledge of the truth. In fulfilling my teaching you will always feel that you are in the truth and that the Father is in you and you in the Father. And knowing the Father of life in yourselves, you will experience a peace nothing can deprive you of. And therefore if you know the truth and live in it, neither my death nor your own can alarm you.

Men think of themselves as separate beings each with his own separate will to live, but that is only an illusion. The only true life is that which recognizes the Father's will as the source of life. My teaching reveals this oneness of life, and presents life not as separate growths but as one tree on which all the branches grow. Only he lives who lives in the Father's will like a branch on its parent tree: he who wishes to live by his own will dies like a branch that has been torn away. The Father gave me life to do good, and I have taught you to live to do good. If you fulfil my commandments you will be blessed, and the commandment which sums up my whole teaching is simply that all men should love one another. And love is to sacrifice the bodily life for the sake of another: there is no other definition. And in fulfilling my law of love you will not fulfil it like slaves who obey their master's orders without understanding them; but you will live as free men like myself, for I have made clear to you the purpose of life flowing from a knowledge of the Father of life. You have received my teaching not because you accidentally chose it, but because it is the only truth by which men are made free.

The teaching of the world is that men should do evil to one another, but my teaching is that they should love one another. Therefore the world will hate you as it has hated me. The world does not understand my teaching and therefore will persecute you and do you harm, thinking to serve God by so doing. Do not be surprised at this, but understand that it must be so. The world, not understanding the true God, must persecute you, but you must affirm the truth.

You are distressed at their killing me, but they kill me for declaring the truth, and my death is necessary for the confirmation of the truth. My death, at which I do not recede from the truth, will strengthen you, and you will understand what is false and what is true and what results from a knowledge of falsehood and of truth. You will understand that it is falsehood for men to believe in the bodily life and not in the life of the spirit, and that truth consists in unity with the Father from which results the victory of the spirit over the flesh.

When I am no longer with you in the bodily life, my spirit will be with you; but like all men you will not always feel within you the strength of the spirit. Sometimes you will weaken and lose the strength of the spirit and fall into temptation, and sometimes you will again awaken to the true life. Hours of bondage to the flesh will come upon you, but only for a time; you will suffer and be again restored to the spirit, as a woman suffers in childbirth and then feels joy that she has brought a human being into the world. You will experience the same when after being enslaved by the body you again rise in spirit, and feel such joy that there will be nothing more for you to desire. Know this in advance: in despite of persecution, of inward struggle and depression of spirit, the spirit lives within you and the one true God is the knowledge of the Father's will that I have revealed.

And addressing the Father, the spirit, Jesus said: I have done what Thou commandedst me, and have revealed to men that Thou art the source of all things, and they have understood me. I have taught them that they all come from one source of infinite life and that therefore they are all one, and that as the Father is in me and I am in the Father, so they, too, are one with me and the Father. I have revealed to them also that as Thou in love hast sent them into the world, they too should serve the world by love.

XII

WHEN Jesus had finished speaking to his pupils, he rose and, instead of running away or defending himself, went to meet Judas who was bringing soldiers to take him. Jesus went to him and asked him why he had come. But Judas did not answer and a crowd of soldiers came round Jesus. Peter rushed to defend him and, drawing a knife, began to fight. But Jesus stopped him and told him to give up the knife, saying that he who fights with a knife himself perishes by a knife. Then he said to those who had come to take him: I have till now gone about among you alone without fear, and I feel no fear now, I give myself up to you to do with me as you please. And all his pupils ran away and deserted him. Then the officer of the soldiers ordered Jesus to be bound and taken to Annas, a former high priest who lived in the same house as

Caiaphas, who was high priest that year and who had devised the pretext upon which it was decided to kill Jesus: namely, that if he were not killed the whole nation would perish. Jesus, feeling himself in the will of the Father, was ready for death and did not resist when they took him, and was not afraid when they led him away; but that very Peter who had just assured Jesus that he would rather die than renounce him, the same Peter who had tried to defend Jesus, now when he saw Jesus being led to execution was afraid they would execute him too, and when the door-keeper asked whether he had not been with Jesus, denied him and deserted him. Only later, when the cock crowed, did Peter understand all that Jesus had said to him. He understood that there are two temptations of the flesh—fear and strife—and that Jesus had resisted these when he prayed in the garden and asked the pupils to pray. And now he, Peter, had yielded to both these temptations against which Jesus had warned him: he had tried to resist evil, and to defend the truth had been ready to fight and do evil himself; and now in fear of bodily suffering he had renounced his master. Jesus had not yielded either to the temptation to fight when the pupils had two knives ready for his defence, or to the temptation of fear—first before the people in Jerusalem when the heathen wished to speak to him, and now before the soldiers when they bound him and led him to trial.

Jesus was brought before Caiaphas, who began to question him about his teaching. But knowing that Caiaphas asked not to find out about his teaching but only to convict him, Jesus did not reply, but said: I have concealed nothing and conceal nothing now: if you wish to know what my teaching is, ask those who heard it and understood it. For this answer the high priest's servant struck Jesus on the cheek. Jesus asked why he struck him, but the man did not answer him and the high priest continued the trial. Witnesses were brought and gave evidence that Jesus had boasted that he would destroy the Jewish faith. And the high priest questioned Jesus, but seeing that they did not ask in order to learn anything, but only to pretend that it was a just trial, he answered nothing.

Then the high priest asked him: Tell me, are you Christ, a son of God? Jesus said: Yes, I am Christ, a son of God; and now in torturing me you will see how the son of man resembles God.

The high priest was glad to hear these words and said to the other judges: Are not these words enough to condemn him? And the judges said: They are enough: we sentence him to death. And when they said this, the people threw themselves upon Jesus and began to strike him, to spit in his face, and to insult him. He remained silent.

The Jews had not the right to put anyone to death: to do this permission was needed from the Roman governor. So having condemned Jesus in their court, and having subjected him to ignominy, they took him to the Roman governor Pilate that he might order his execution. Pilate asked why they wished to put Jesus to death, and they answered that he was a criminal. Pilate said that if that was so, they should judge him by their own law. They answered: We want you to put him to death, because he is guilty before the Roman Caesar: he is a rebel, he agitates the people, forbids them to pay taxes to Caesar, and calls himself the King of the Jews. Pilate called Jesus before him, and said: What is the meaning of this—are you King of the Jews? Jesus said: Do you really wish to know what my kingdom is, or are you only asking me for form's sake? Pilate answered: I am not a Jew, and it is the same to me whether you call yourself King of the Jews or not, but I ask you who you are and why do they call you a king? Jesus replied: They say truly that I call myself a king. I am indeed a king, but my kingdom is not an earthly one, it is a heavenly one. Earthly kings have armies and go to war and fight, but as you see they have bound and beaten me and I did not resist. I am a heavenly king and my power is in the spirit.

Pilate said: So it is true that you consider yourself a king? Jesus replied: You know it yourself. Everyone who lives by the spirit is free. I live by this alone, and teach only to show men the truth—that they are free if they live by the spirit. Pilate said: You teach the truth, but nobody knows what truth is. Everyone has his own truth. And having said this he turned away from Jesus and went back again to the Jews, and said: I find nothing criminal in this man. Why do you wish me to put him to death? The chief priests said: He ought to be executed because he stirs up the people. Then Pilate began to examine Jesus before the chief priests, but Jesus, seeing that this was only for form's sake, answered nothing. Then Pilate said: I alone cannot condemn him. Take him to Herod.

At the trial before Herod, Jesus again did not answer the chief priests' accusations, and Herod, taking Jesus to be an empty fellow, mockingly ordered him to be dressed in a red cloak and sent back to Pilate. Pilate pitied Jesus and began to try to persuade the chief priests to forgive him, if only on account of the feast; but they held to their demand, and they all, and the people with them, cried out to have Jesus crucified. Pilate again tried to persuade them to let Jesus go, but the priests and the people cried out that he must be executed. They said: He is guilty of calling himself a son of

God. Pilate again called Jesus to him, and asked.
What does it mean that you call yourself a son of
God? Who are you? Jesus answered nothing.
Then Pilate said: How is it that you do not answer
me, when I have the power to execute you or to set
you free? Jesus replied: You have no power over me.
All power is from above. And Pilate for the third
time tried to persuade the Jews to set Jesus free, but
they said to him: If you will not execute this man
whom we have denounced as a rebel against Caesar,
then you yourself are not a friend to Caesar, but a
foe. And on hearing these words Pilate gave way and
ordered the execution of Jesus. But they first stripped
Jesus and flogged him, and then dressed him again
in the red cloak. And they beat him and insulted him
and mocked him. Then they gave him a cross to carry
and led him to the place of execution, and there
they nailed him to the cross, and as he hung on the
cross the people all mocked at him. And to this
mockery Jesus answered: Father, do not punish
them for this, they do not know what they are doing.
And later, when he was already near to death, he
said: My Father! Into Thy care I yield my spirit.
And bowing his head he breathed his last.

WHAT I BELIEVE

WHAT I BELIEVE

CONTENTS OF 'WHAT I BELIEVE'

INTRODUCTION

I LIVED in the world for fifty-five years, and after the first fourteen or fifteen of childhood I was for thirty-five years a nihilist in the real meaning of that word, that is to say, not a Socialist or revolutionary, as those words are generally understood, but a nihilist in the sense of an absence of any belief.

Five years ago I came to believe in Christ's teaching, and my life suddenly changed; I ceased to desire what I had previously desired, and began to desire what I formerly did not want. What had previously seemed to me good seemed evil, and what had seemed evil seemed good. It happened to me as it happens to a man who goes out on some business and on the way suddenly decides that the business is unnecessary and returns home. All that was on his right is now on his left, and all that was on his left is now on his right; his former wish to get as far as possible from home has changed into a wish to be as near as possible to it. The direction of my life and my desires became different, and good and evil changed places. This all occurred because I understood Christ's teaching otherwise than as I had formerly understood it.

I am not seeking to interpret Christ's teaching, but only to tell how I understood what is simple, plain, clear intelligible, indubitable, and addressed to all men in it, and how what I understood changed my soul and gave me tranquillity and happiness.

I do not wish to interpret Christ's teaching, but should only wish to prevent artificial interpretations of it.

All the Christian Churches have always admitted that all men—unequal in their knowledge and minds, wise or foolish—are equals before God, and that

God's truth is accessible to them all. Christ even said that it was the will of God that to the foolish should be revealed what was hidden from the wise.

Not all can be initiated into the deepest mysteries of dogmatics, homiletics, patristics, liturgics, hermeneutics, apologetics, &c., but all may and should understand what Christ said to all the millions of simple, unlearned people who have lived and are living. And it is just this which Christ said to all these simple people who had as yet no possibility of turning for explanations of his teaching to Paul, Clement, St. John Chrysostom, and others—it is just this that I want to tell to all men. The thief on the cross believed Jesus and was saved. Would it really have been evil or have harmed anyone had the thief not died on the cross but come down from it and told men how he learned to believe in Christ?

I, like that thief on the cross, have believed Christ's teaching and been saved. And this is no far-fetched comparison but the closest expression of the condition of spiritual despair and horror at the problem of life and death in which I lived formerly, and of the condition of peace and happiness in which I am now.

I, like the thief, knew that I had lived and was living badly, and saw that the majority of people around me lived as I did. I, like the thief, knew that I was unhappy and suffering, and that around me people suffered and were unhappy, and I saw no way of escape from that position except by death. I was nailed by some force to that life of suffering and evil, like the thief to the cross. And as, after the meaningless sufferings and evils of life, the thief awaited the terrible darkness of death, so did I await the same thing.

In all this I was exactly like the thief, but the difference was that the thief was already dying, while I was still living. The thief might believe that his salvation lay there beyond the grave, but I could not be satisfied with that, because besides a life beyond the grave life still awaited me here. But I did not understand that life. It seemed to me terrible. And suddenly I heard the words of Christ and understood them, and life and death ceased to seem to me evil, and instead of despair I experienced happiness and the joy of life undisturbed by death.

Surely it can harm no one if I tell how this befell me?

MOSCOW,
  22 *January* 1884.

I

A KEY TO THE GOSPEL TEACHING

I HAVE told why I formerly did not understand Christ's teaching and how and why I have now understood it, in two large works: *A Criticism of Dogmatic Theology* and *A New Translation and Harmony of the Four Gospels, with Explanations*. In those works I try methodically and step by step to examine all that hides the truth from men, and verse by verse retranslate, compare, and synthesize the four Gospels.

For six years this has been my work. Every year, every month, I discover fresh and fresh elucidations and confirmations of my fundamental thought, correct errors that from haste or over-eagerness have crept into my work, and add to what has been done. My life, not much of which remains, will probably end before this work is completed.[1] But I am convinced that the work is needed, and therefore while I still have life I do what I can.

Such is my prolonged external work on theology and the Gospels. But my internal work, of which I wish to tell here, was different. It was not a methodical investigation of theology and of the texts of the Gospels, but an instantaneous discarding of all that hid the real meaning of the teaching and an instantaneous illumination by the light of truth. It was an occurrence such as might befall a man who, by the guidance of a wrong drawing, was vainly seeking to reconstruct something from a confused heap of small bits of marble, if he suddenly guessed from the largest piece that it was quite a different statue from what he had supposed, and having

[1] This book was completed in January 1884, Tolstóy continued to live and work till November 1910.—A.M.

begun to reconstruct it, instead of the former incoherence of the pieces, saw a confirmation of his belief in every piece which with all the curves of its fracture fitted into other pieces and formed one whole. That was what happened to me, and it is this that I wish to relate.

I wish to relate how I found the key to the understanding of Christ's teaching, which revealed to me the truth with a clearness and assurance that excluded all doubt.

This discovery was made by me thus. Since I first read the Gospels for myself when almost a child, what touched and affected me most of all was Christ's teaching of love, meekness, humility, self-sacrifice, and repayment of good for evil. Such always was for me the essence of Christianity—that in it which my heart loved, and for the sake of which, after passing through despair and unbelief, I accepted as true the meaning the labouring Christian folk attribute to life, and submitted myself to the faith professed by them, namely the faith of the Orthodox Church. But, having submitted to the Church, I soon noticed that I did not find in her teaching confirmation or explanation of those principles of Christianity which seemed to me most important. I noticed that that aspect of Christianity which was dear to me is not the chief thing in Church teaching. I saw that what seemed to me most important in Christ's teaching is not so recognized by the Church; she treats something else as most important. At first I did not attach importance to this peculiarity of Church teaching. 'Well, what of it?' thought I—'The Church, besides ideas of love, humility, and self-sacrifice, admits also this dogmatic, external meaning. This is foreign to me and even repels me, but there is nothing harmful in it.'

But the longer I lived in submission to the Church the more noticeable it became that this characteristic of her teaching was not so harmless as it at first seemed to me to be. The Church repelled me by the strangeness of her dogmas and her acceptance and approval of persecutions, executions, and wars. The mutual denunciation by one another of various congregations also repelled me. But what shattered my trust in the Church was just her indifference to what seemed to me the essence of Christ's teaching, and her partiality for what seemed to me unessential.

I felt that something was wrongly put, but what was wrong I could not at all make out. I could not make it out because the teaching of the Church not only did not deny what seemed to me the chief thing in Christ's teaching, but fully acknowledged it, acknowledging it somehow so that what was chief in Christ's teaching no longer occupied the first place. I could not reproach the Church for denying what was essential, but the Church acknowledged the essential matter in a way that did not satisfy me; she did not give me what I expected of her.

I went over from nihilism to the Church only because I was conscious of the impossibility of life without faith, without a knowledge of what is good and what is evil apart from my animal instincts. This knowledge I thought I should find in Christianity, but Christianity as it then appeared to me was only a certain frame of mind, very indefinite, from which clear and obligatory rules of conduct were not deducible, and for such rules I turned to the Church. But the Church gave me rules that did not bring me any nearer to the state of mind dear to me, but rather removed me further from it, and I could not follow her. What was necessary and dear to me was life based on the Christian truths;

the Church, however, gave me rules of life which were quite foreign to the truths I prized. The rules given by the Church about faith in dogmas, observance of the Sacraments, fasts, and prayers, were to me unnecessary; and rules based upon the Christian truths were absent. Nor was that all. The Church rules weakened and sometimes plainly destroyed that Christian frame of mind which alone gave meaning to my life. What disturbed me most of all was that all human evils—the condemnation of individuals, of whole peoples, of other religions, and the executions and wars which resulted from such condemnations—were all justified by the Church. The teaching of Christ about humility, not judging, forgiveness of injuries, self-sacrifice, and love, was extolled in words, but at the same time in practice the Church approved of what was incompatible with this teaching.

Was it possible that the teaching of Christ was such that these contradictions were inevitable? I could not believe it. Moreover, what always seemed to me surprising was that, as far as my knowledge of the Gospels went, those passages on which the definite Church dogmas were based were the most obscure, while those from which one derived the practical teaching were the clearest and most definite. Yet the dogmas and those Christian obligations which result from them were defined by the Church in the clearest and most precise manner, while of the practical fulfilment of the teaching mention was made in the most indefinite, foggy, mystical way. Could Christ possibly have wished this when delivering his teaching? A solution of my doubts could only be found in the Gospels. So I read and re-read them. Out of them all, the Sermon on the Mount always stood out for me as something special, and I read it more often than anything else. No-

where else did Christ speak with such authority—
nowhere else does he give so many clear, intelligible,
moral rules directly appealing to the heart of every
man. Nowhere did he speak to a larger crowd of
the common people. If there were any clear, definite
Christian rules, they ought to be expressed here.
In these three chapters of Matthew I sought a solution of my perplexity. Often and often did I re-read
the Sermon on the Mount and experienced the same
feeling every time: a thrill of exaltation at the verses
about turning the other cheek, surrendering one's
cloak, reconciliation with all men, love of one's
enemies, but also a dissatisfied feeling. The words
of God addressed to all lacked clearness. A too impossible renunciation of everything was demanded,
destroying all life as I understood it, and therefore
it seemed to me that such renunciation could not be
the obligatory condition of salvation; but if that
were not so, then there was nothing definite and
clear. I read not the Sermon on the Mount alone,
but all the Gospels, as well as all the theological
commentaries on them. The theological explanation that the precepts of the Sermon on the Mount
are indications of the perfection towards which men
should strive, but that fallen man, immersed in sin,
cannot by his own strength attain this perfection,
and that his safety lies in faith, prayer, and the
Sacraments—such explanations did not satisfy me.

I did not agree with this because it always seemed
strange to me why Christ, knowing in advance that
the fulfilment of his teaching was unattainable by
man's individual strength, gave such clear and admirable rules relating directly to each individual
man. In reading these rules it always seemed to
me that they related directly to me and demanded
my personal fulfilment. Reading them, I always
experienced a joyous confidence that I could

immediately, from that very hour, fulfil them all, and I wished and endeavoured to do this. But as soon as I experienced difficulty in doing this, I involuntarily remembered the Church's teaching that man is weak and cannot do these things by his own strength, and I weakened.

They told me we must believe and pray.

But I felt I had little faith, and therefore could not pray. They told me one must pray God to give faith—the very faith that gives the prayer that gives the faith that gives the prayer—and so on to infinity.

But both reason and experience showed me that only *my* efforts to fulfil Christ's teaching could be effective.

And so, after many, many vain seekings and studyings of what was written in proof and disproof of the Divinity of this teaching, and after many doubts and much suffering, I was again left alone with my heart and the mysterious book. I could not give it the meaning others gave it, could not find any other meaning for it, and could not reject it. And only after disbelieving equally all the explanations of the learned critics and all the explanations of the learned theologians, and after rejecting them all (in accord with Christ's words, 'Except ye turn and become as little children, ye shall in no wise enter into the kingdom of heaven'), I suddenly understood what I had not formerly understood. I understood it not as a result of some artificial, recondite transposition, harmonization, or reinterpretation; on the contrary, everything revealed itself to me because I forgot all the interpretations. The passage which served me as key to the whole was Matt. v. 38, 39: 'Ye have heard that it was said, An eye for an eye and a tooth for a tooth: But I say unto you, Resist not him that is evil.' And suddenly, for the first time, I understood this verse simply and directly. I understood that Christ says just what he says, and what immediately happened was not that something new revealed itself, but that everything that obscured the truth fell away, and the truth arose before me in its full meaning. 'Ye have heard that it was said, An eye for an eye and a tooth for a tooth: But I say unto you, Resist not him that is evil.' These words suddenly appeared to me as something quite new, as if I had never read them before. Previously when reading that passage I had always, by some strange blindness, omitted the words, '*But I say unto you, Resist not him that is evil*', just as if those words had not been there, or as if they had no definite meaning.

Subsequently, in my talks with many and many Christians familiar with the Gospels, I often had occasion to note the same blindness as to those words. No one remembered them, and often when speaking about that passage Christians referred to the Gospels to verify the fact that the words were really there. In the same way I had missed those words and had begun understanding the passage only from the words which follow, 'But whosoever smiteth thee on thy right cheek, turn to him the other also . . .' and so forth; and these words always appeared to me to be a demand to endure sufferings and deprivations that are unnatural to man. The words touched me, and I felt that it would be admirable to act up to them; but I also felt that I should never be strong enough to fulfil them merely in order to suffer. I said to myself, 'Very well, I will turn the other cheek, and I shall again be struck. I will give what is demanded and everything will be taken from me. I shall have no life—but life was given me, so why should I be deprived of it? It cannot be that Christ demands it.' That was what I formerly said to myself, imagining that in these words Christ extolled sufferings and deprivations, and extolling them, spoke with exaggeration and therefore inexactly and obscurely. But now, when I had understood the words about not resisting him that is evil, it became plain to me that Christ was not exaggerating nor demanding any suffering for the sake of suffering, but was only very definitely and clearly saying what he said. He says: 'Do not resist him that is evil, and while doing this know in advance that you may meet people who, having struck you on one cheek and not met with resistance, will strike you on the other, and having taken away your coat will take your cloak also; who, having availed themselves of your work, will oblige you to do more work, and will not repay what they borrow . . . should this be so, continue nevertheless to abstain from resisting the evil man. Continue, in spite of all this, to do good to those who will beat you and insult you.' And when I understood these words as they are said, at once all that was obscure became clear, and what had seemed exaggerated became quite exact. I understood for the first time that the centre of gravity of the whole thought lies in the words, 'Resist not him that is evil', and that what follows is only an explanation of that first proposition. I understood that Christ does not command us to present the cheek and to give up the cloak in order to suffer, but commands us not to resist him that is evil, and adds that this may involve having to suffer. It is just like a father sending his son off on a distant voyage, who does not order the son not to sleep at night and not to eat enough, and to be drenched and to freeze, but says to him, 'Go your road, and if you have to be drenched and to freeze, continue

your journey nevertheless'. Christ does not say,
'Offer your cloak and suffer', but he says, 'Resist
not him that is evil, and no matter what befalls you
do not resist him'. These words, 'Resist not evil',
or 'Resist not him that is evil', understood in their
direct meaning, were for me truly a key opening
everything else, and it became surprising to me that
I could so radically have misunderstood the clear
and definite words: 'It was said, An eye for an eye
and a tooth for a tooth: But I say unto you, Resist
not him that is evil, and no matter what he does
to you, suffer and surrender, but resist him not.'
What can be clearer, more intelligible, and more indubitable than that? And I only needed to understand these words simply and directly as they were
said and at once Christ's whole teaching, not only
in the Sermon on the Mount but in the whole of
the Gospels, everything that had been confused,
became intelligible; what had been contradictory
became harmonious, and, above all, what had appeared superfluous became essential. All merged
into one whole, and one thing indubitably confirmed another like the pieces of a broken statue
when they are replaced in their true position. In
this Sermon and in the whole of the Gospels everything confirmed the same teaching of non-resistance
to evil. In this Sermon, as everywhere else, Christ
never represents his disciples—that is to say, the
people who fulfil the law of non-resistance to evil—
otherwise than as turning the cheek to the smiter,
giving up the cloak, persecuted, beaten, and destitute. Everywhere Christ repeatedly says that only
he can be his disciple who takes up his cross and
abandons everything; that is to say, only he who is
ready to endure all consequences that result from
the fulfilment of the law of non-resistance to evil.
To his disciples Christ says: 'Be beggars; be ready

without resisting evil to accept persecution, suffering, and death.' He himself prepares for suffering and death without resisting evil, and sends Peter away because he complains of this. He himself dies forbidding resistance to evil, and without deviating from his teaching. All his first disciples fulfilled this commandment of non-resistance, and passed their lives in poverty and persecutions, never returning evil for evil.

So Christ says what he says. It is possible to affirm that it is very difficult always to obey this rule. It is possible not to agree with the statement that every man will be happy if he obeys this rule. It may be said that it is stupid, as unbelievers say that Christ was a dreamer and an idealist who enunciated impracticable rules which his disciples followed from stupidity. But it is quite impossible not to admit that Christ said very clearly and definitely just what he meant to say, namely that according to his teaching man should not resist evil, and that therefore whoever accepts his teaching must not resist evil. And yet neither believers nor unbelievers understand this simple, clear meaning of Christ's words.

II

THE COMMAND OF NON-RESISTANCE

When I understood that the words 'resist not him that is evil' meant 'resist not him that is evil', my former conception of the meaning of Christ's teaching was suddenly changed, and I was horrified, not at the fact that I had not understood it, but at the strange way in which I had understood the teaching up to that time. I knew, we all know, that the meaning of Christ's teaching is in love to men. To say 'turn your cheek, love your enemies' is to express the essence of Christianity. I knew this from childhood. But why did I not understand these simple words simply, but sought in them some allegorical meaning? 'Resist not him that is evil' means 'never resist him that is evil', that is, never do violence, never do an act that cannot but be contrary to love, and if they then insult you, bear the insult and still do not inflict violence on anyone else. He said it so clearly and simply that it is impossible to say it more clearly. How was it that I, believing or trying to believe that he who said it was God, declared that to fulfil this by my own strength was impossible? The Master says to me, 'Go and chop wood', and I reply, 'I cannot do that by my own strength'. Replying so, I say one of two things, either that I do not believe what the Master says, or that I do not wish to do what he commands. Of the commandment of God which he gave us to perform, and of which he said, 'Whoso doeth this and teacheth men so shall be called great', &c.—of which he said that only those who do it shall receive life; the command which he himself fulfilled and which he expressed so clearly and simply that there can be no doubt about its meaning: it was of this command that I who had never even tried to fulfil it said, 'It is impossible to perform it by my own strength; I need supernatural aid'. God came down on earth to give salvation to men. That salvation consists in this. The Second Person of the Trinity, God the Son, suffered for people and redeemed their sins before his Father, and gave men the Church in which is preserved the grace which is administered to believers. But besides all this that same Son of God also gave people a teaching and an example of life for their salvation. How was it that I said that the rules of life expressed by him simply and clearly for all men were so difficult of accomplishment as to be even impossible without miraculous aid? He not only did not say that, but he said, 'Do it. He that does not do it will not enter into the kingdom of heaven'. And he never said that the performance was difficult. On the contrary he said, 'My yoke is easy and my burden is light'. John the Evangelist said, 'His law is not hard'. How was it that I said that what God had told us to do, that act the performance of which he had so exactly defined and of which he had said that to do it was easy, that which he himself performed as a man and which was performed by his first followers—how was it that I said that to do it was so difficult as to be even impossible without miraculous aid? If a man applied the whole strength of his mind to destroy some law that had been given, what more effective for the destruction of such a law could that man say than that the law itself was impracticable, and that the intention of the lawgiver himself concerning his law was that it was impracticable and that to fulfil it needed miraculous aid? And that is just what I thought concerning the law of non-resistance to evil; and I began to remember how this strange thought entered my head—that the law of Christ was divine but that its fulfilment was impossible—and re-considering my past I understood that that thought was never conveyed to me in its complete naked-ness (it would have repelled me), but that I, with-out noticing it, had sucked it in with my mother's milk from my very first childhood, and the whole of my subsequent life had only confirmed in me this strange delusion.

From childhood I was taught that Christ was God and that his teaching was divine, but at the same time I was taught to respect those institutions which secured by violence my safety from evil men. I was taught to respect these institutions by the priests. I was taught to resist the evil man, and it was inculcated that it is degrading and shameful to submit to the evil man and to endure him. They taught me to judge and to execute; afterwards they taught me to go to war—that is to say to resist the evil man by murder, and the army of which I was a member was called the 'Christ-loving Army', and its activities were sanctified by the blessings of the Church. Moreover, from childhood and until I was a man I was taught to respect what directly contradicted the law of Christ; to resist an injurer, to revenge myself by violence for a personal, family, or national insult. All this was not merely not condemned, but it was instilled into me that all this was excellent and not contrary to the law of Christ.

All my circumstances, my tranquillity, the safety of myself and my family and my property were all based on the law repudiated by Christ, on the law of a tooth for a tooth. The doctors of the Church taught that Christ's teaching was divine, but its performance impossible on account of human frailty, and only Christ's blessing can assist its performance. The worldly teachers and the whole construction of our life plainly admitted the impracticability and fantastic nature of Christ's teaching, and by words and deeds taught what was opposed to it. The admission of the impracticability of God's teaching had gradually to such a degree impregnated me and had become so familiar, and it coincided to such a degree with my desires, that I had never before noticed the contradiction with which I was faced. I did not see that it is impossible at one and the same time to confess Christ as God, the basis of whose teaching is non-resistance to him that is evil, and consciously and calmly to work for the establishment of property, law-courts, government, and military forces, to establish a life contrary to the teaching of Christ, and to pray to the same Christ that the law of non-resistance to him that is evil and of forgiveness should be fulfilled among us. That which is so clear had not yet occurred to me: that it would be much simpler to arrange and organize life according to the law of Christ, and then to pray that there should be law-courts, executions, and wars if they are so necessary for our welfare.[1]

And I understood how my mistake had arisen. It had arisen from obedience to Christ in words and denial of him in deeds.

The command of non-resistance to him that is evil is one that makes a complete whole of all the teaching, but this only if it is not a mere saying, but an obligatory rule—a law to be fulfilled.

It is really a key which opens everything, but only when it is pushed into the lock. The treatment of this statement as a mere saying impossible of fulfilment without supernatural aid is the destruction of the whole teaching, and what but an impossibility

[1] Once accept the thesis that Jesus, by saying 'resist not him that is evil', intended to forbid any use of physical force to prevent anyone from doing whatever evil he likes, and that he was divinely and absolutely right in laying down that principle, and there is no logical escape from the ultimate conclusion that any Government using force, all compulsory law, all police, and all protection of life or property is immoral.

In the *Life of Tolstóy* in this series, an argument is adduced —and one that has nowhere been refuted—to show that Christ's injunction admits of a different understanding from that which Tolstóy attributes to it. But be that as it may, Christ's injunction has till now been so little regarded, and reliance on it has been so generally the signal for scornful repudiation, that what Tolstóy has to say in its support should not be overlooked or carelessly thrust aside. The governments of the world systematically reject both Christ's injunction and Tolstóy's Non-Resistant theory, but while they have been doing so wars have become more and more terrible, till at last we are faced by the prospect, perhaps in the near future, of defenceless men, women, and children, being massacred in millions while our whole world crashes to destruction.—A.M.

can any teaching appear to men from which the
unifying, fundamental thesis has been removed?
To an unbeliever it even appears simply stupid and
cannot appear otherwise.

To put an engine in position, to heat the boiler, to
set it in motion, but not to attach the connecting
belt, was what was done with the teaching of Christ
when people began to teach that you can be a
Christian without fulfilling the law of non-resistance
to him that is evil.

I was recently reading the Fifth Chapter of
Matthew with a Jewish Rabbi. At almost every
sentence the Rabbi said, 'That is in the Jewish
Canon. That is in the Talmud', and he pointed out
to me in the Old Testament and the Talmud *dicta*
very similar to the *dicta* of the Sermon on the Mount.
But when we came to the verse about non-resistance
to him that is evil he did not say, 'And that is in the
Talmud', but only ironically asked me: 'Do the
Christians fulfil that? Do they turn the other cheek?'
I had no reply, especially as I knew that at that very
time Christians were not only not turning the other
cheek, but were striking cheeks the Jews had turned.
But I was interested to know whether there was
anything similar in the Old Testament or in the
Talmud, and I asked him about this. He replied:
'No, it is not there. But tell me whether the
Christians fulfil this law.' By this question he
showed me that the presence of this rule in the
Christian law, which not only is not performed by
anyone, but which Christians themselves admit to
be impracticable, is an admission of the irrationality
and superfluity of the Christian law. And I had no
reply to give him.

Now having understood the meaning of this
teaching, I see clearly the strange internal contradiction with which I was faced. Having admitted

Christ to be God and his law to be divine, and having at the same time arranged my life in contradiction to the teaching, what was left me but to admit that the teaching was impracticable? In words I admitted the teaching of Christ to be holy, in practice I professed a quite unchristian teaching and admitted and submitted to unchristian institutions which surrounded me on all sides.

The whole of the Old Testament says that the misfortunes of the Jewish people were the effect of their believing in false gods and not in the true God. Samuel, in his First Book, chapters viii and xii, told the people that to all their former disobedience they had added a new one. Instead of God who had been their King they had chosen a man-king, whom they thought would save them. Do not believe in 'vain things', says Samuel to the people (xii. 21). It cannot help you or save you because it is 'vain'— empty. That you may not perish together with your king, cling to the one God.

And it was faith in that 'vain thing', in empty idols, that hid the truth from me. On the path to it, hiding its light from me, stood those 'vain things' which I had not strength to reject.

I was walking the other day towards the Borovítski Gates of the Moscow Kremlin. At the gates sat an old crippled beggar, wrapped round the ears with some rag. I took out my purse to give him something.[1] Just then, coming down from the Kremlin, ran a manly, ruddy young fellow, a grena-

---

[1] Tolstóy always gave away small change to beggars he met, in accord with the usual practice of religious folk in a country which had no State poor-relief organization, and also in accord with the injunction 'Give to him that asketh of thee!' He sometimes admitted that his gift might do harm and that the man might go and drink it; but he argued that the goodwill on the giver's part indicated by the gift was more important than the possible ill-effects to the recipient.—A.M.

dier in his regimental sheepskin coat. The beggar, on seeing the soldier, jumped up in dismay, and ran limping down towards the Alexándrov Gardens. The grenadier started to catch him, but, without overtaking him, stopped and began abusing the beggar for sitting at the gateway though it was prohibited. I awaited the grenadier at the gate. When he came up to me I asked him if he could read.

'I can, what about it?' 'Have you read the Gospels?' 'I have.' 'And have you read, "For I was an hungered, and ye gave me no meat"?' And I quoted that passage. He knew it and listened to it, and I saw that he was uneasy. Two passers-by stopped to listen. It was plain that the grenadier was hurt to feel that he, fulfilling his duty excellently and driving beggars away from the place they had to be driven from, suddenly appeared to be in the wrong. He was agitated, and was evidently seeking a rejoinder. Suddenly in his clever black eyes a light gleamed, and he turned sideways to me as though to walk away. 'And have you read the Military Code?' asked he. I said I had not read it. 'Then don't talk', said the grenadier tossing his head triumphantly, and adjusting his coat he proceeded confidently to his post. This was the only man I ever met in all my life who quite logically decided the eternal question with which our social state, being what it is, faced me and faces every man who calls himself a Christian.

III

THE LAW OF GOD AND THE LAW OF MAN

It is wrongly said that the Christian teaching relates only to personal salvation and not to public, political questions. That is merely an audacious and barefaced assertion which is most obviously false and collapses as soon as it is seriously considered. 'Very well, I will not resist the evil doer, I will turn my cheek as a private individual', say I to myself; but if an enemy comes, or the people are oppressed, and I am called on to take part in the struggle against the evil men and to go and kill them, then it is imperative ror me to decide wherein lies the service of God, and wherein the service of 'the vain thing'. Am I to go to the war or not? I am a peasant, and am chosen to serve as a village elder, a judge, or a juryman, and I am told to take an oath to judge and to inflict punishment. What am I to do? Again I have to choose between the law of God and the law of man. Or I am a monk living in a monastery, and some peasants have taken our hay and I am sent to participate in the struggle against the evil men and to take legal proceedings against the peasants. Again I have to choose. No one can escape from the question. I speak not merely of our class whose activity consists almost entirely in resisting evil men: in the army, in the courts of justice, or in civil offices, there is not a single private person, however humble, who has not to choose between serving God by obeying His command, or serving the 'vain thing'—state institutions. My private life is interwoven with the general life of the state which demands of me an unchristian activity directly contrary to the law of Christ. Now with universal military service and the liability of all to serve on a jury this dilemma is sharply presented to us all in a very striking manner. Every man must take the weapons of murder—a sword and a bayonet—and must either kill, or at least load the rifle and sharpen the sword, that is, prepare to kill. Every citizen must appear at the law-courts and participate in trial and punishment, that is to say, must repudiate Christ's law about not resisting him that is evil, and must do it not merely in words but in deeds.

The grenadier's question—The Gospel or the military code? The law of God or man's law?—now presents itself to humanity as it did in the days of Samuel. It presented itself to Christ himself, and to his disciples. It stands before those who now wish to be Christians in deed, and it stood before me.

The law of Christ, and his teachings of love, humility, and self-repudiation had previously always touched my heart and attracted me. But from all sides, both in history and around me at the present day and in my own life, I saw a contrary law, repugnant to my heart and conscience and reason, but harmonizing with my animal instincts. I felt if I accepted the law of Christ I should be isolated and it would go ill with me, I should be one of the persecuted and suffering, as Christ predicted. While if I accepted man's law everyone would approve of it, and I should be at peace, secure, and have at my service all manner of theological subtleties to set my conscience at rest. I should laugh and be merry as Christ said. I felt this, and therefore did not penetrate into the meaning of Christ's law, but tried to understand it so that it should not prevent my living my accustomed animal life. But to understand it so was impossible, and therefore I did not understand it at all.

In this non-comprehension I reached a state of perplexity which now astonishes me, and as an example of that perplexity I will give my former understanding of the words, 'Judge not, that ye be not judged' (Matt. vii. 1), 'Judge not and ye shall not be judged: condemn not, and ye shall not be condemned' (Luke vi. 37). The institution of law-courts in which I took part and which defended the safety of my property, appeared to me so indubitably sacred and accordant with the law of God that it never occurred to me that these sayings could mean anything but that one must not speak ill of one's neighbour. It never entered my head that in those words Christ could have spoken of the law-courts, of the Zémstvo, of the Criminal Court, of the District Courts and magistrates, and of all the Senates and departments. Only when I understood in the direct sense the words about not resisting him that is evil, only then did the question occur to me of Christ's attitude to all those courts and departments. And seeing that he must have disapproved of them, I asked myself: Does it not mean that one must not merely refrain from condemning one's neighbour verbally, but must not judge him in the courts—must not condemn one's neighbour by means of our law-courts?

In Luke vi. 37-49, these words are spoken immediately after the teaching of non-resistance to evil and of returning good for evil. Following the words, 'Be merciful as your Father in heaven is merciful', come the words, 'Judge not, and ye shall not be judged: condemn not, and ye shall not be condemned'. Does not this mean that besides not blaming one's neighbour one must not set up law-courts, nor judge one's neighbour in them? said I. And I only had to formulate that question, and my heart and my common sense at once replied affirmatively.

I know how this understanding of the words startles one at first. It startled me too. To show how far I was from such an understanding of the words I will confess to a shameful stupidity. When I had already become a believer and read the Gospels as a divine book, I used as a joke to say to my friends, on meeting any of them who were public prosecutors or judges: 'And you go on judging, though it is written, "Judge not that ye be not judged".' So sure was I that those words could mean nothing more than a prohibition of evil-speaking, that I did not understand the terrible mockery of holy things my words contained. I had gone so far that, being convinced that these plain words did not mean what they do mean, I used them jokingly in their true sense.

I will recount in detail how all my doubts—whether these words could be understood except as meaning that Christ totally forbids the human institution of any law-court, and that he could mean nothing else by those words—were destroyed.

The first thing that struck me when I understood the law of non-resistance to the evil man in its direct meaning, was that man's courts of law are not in accord with it, but are directly opposed to it and to the meaning of the whole teaching, and that Christ therefore, if he thought of the law-courts, must have condemned them.

Christ says: 'Resist not him that is evil.' The purpose of the courts is to resist the evil man. Christ tells us to return good for evil. The courts repay evil for evil.[1] Christ tells us not to distinguish good people from bad. The courts are entirely concerned in making the distinction. Christ says, forgive all men. Forgive not once, not seven times, but

---

[1] It certainly deserves serious consideration whether it may not benefit a man to be forcibly restrained from pursuing an evil course. Confusion arises from a simultaneous discussion of the actual words attributed to Jesus and of the general question of what really is true and sensible about man's relation to his fellow men. Tolstóy argued, in another place, that Christ's words should only be accepted as authoritative because they are true and reasonable, it therefore will not do to assume that they are true and reasonable because they are attributed to Christ.—A.M.

endlessly. Love your enemies and do good to them that hate you. The courts do not forgive, but punish. They deal out not good but evil to those they call the enemies of society. So it appeared evident that Christ must have condemned the courts. But, thought I, perhaps Christ had nothing to do with the law-courts and was not thinking of them. But I saw that this could not be: from the day of his birth and until his death Christ came in conflict with the courts of Herod, of the Sanhedrin, and of the high priests. And I noticed that Christ often spoke directly of the courts as of an evil. He warned his disciples that they would be judged, and he told them how to bear themselves in the courts. Of himself he said that he would be condemned; and he himself set an example of how one should treat man's courts of law. Therefore Christ did think of these human courts, which condemned him and his disciples and which have condemned and are condemning millions of people. Christ saw this evil and plainly indicated it. At the execution of the sentence of the court on the woman taken in adultery he plainly repudiated the court and showed that man must not judge because he is himself guilty. And he expressed that same thought several times, saying that with dirt in one's own eye one cannot see the dirt in another's eye and that the blind must not lead the blind. He even explains what results from such a blunder. The pupil becomes like his master.

But perhaps having said this about the judgement on the woman taken in adultery and having put forth parables about the foundations of the house, referring to the general weakness of mankind, he nevertheless does not forbid appeals to human courts of law for the purpose of obtaining protection from evil men. But I saw that this is quite inadmissible.

In the Sermon on the Mount, addressing every-body, he says: 'And if any man will sue thee at law and take away thy coat, let him have thy cloak also.' Therefore he forbids anyone to go to law. But perhaps Christ speaks only of each man's personal relation to the courts and does not condemn the process of law itself, but allows people to judge others provided they do so in the institutions estab-lished for that purpose? But neither can this be supposed. Christ, in the prayer he gave, bids all men without exception forgive others, that they may be forgiven their own sins. And he repeats the thought often. Therefore every man when he prays and before bringing his gift to the altar should for-give everyone. How can a man, who by the faith he professes must always forgive all men, judge and condemn anyone in the law-courts? It follows that, according to Christ's teaching, there can be no such things as Christian courts which inflict punishment.

But perhaps the context shows that in this passage Christ, when he says, 'Judge not, that ye be not judged', was not thinking of human courts of justice? But this again is not so; on the contrary, it is clear from the context that when he said, 'Judge not', Christ was speaking precisely of the institution of law-courts. In Matthew and Luke, before saying, 'Judge not', he says: Resist not him that is evil, endure evil, do good to all men. And before that, in Matthew, he repeats the words of the Hebrew criminal code, 'An eye for an eye, and a tooth for a tooth'. And after this reference to the criminal law, he says: But ye shall not do so; resist not him that is evil; and then he adds, 'Judge not'. Therefore Christ speaks precisely of human criminal law, and repudiates it by the words, 'Judge not'.

Moreover, in Luke, he not only says, 'Judge not',

but 'Judge not . . . and condemn not'. That word
'condemn', which has so similar a meaning, was
not added for nothing. The addition can have had
only one aim—to elucidate the sense in which the
word 'judge' is used.

If he had meant to say, do not judge *your neighbour*, he would have added that word 'neighbour',
but he adds the word which is translated 'do not
condemn', and then adds, 'that ye be not condemned; forgive all men and you will be forgiven'.

But perhaps, all the same, Christ was not thinking
of the law-courts when he said this and I may be
attributing my own thought to his words which had
a different meaning.

So I asked myself how Christ's first disciples, the
Apostles, regarded man's law-courts. Did they
acknowledge them or approve of them?

In chap. iv. 11, the Apostle James says: 'Speak
not evil one of another, brethren. He that speaketh
evil of his brother, and judgeth his brother, speaketh evil of the law, and judgeth the law: but if
thou judge the law, thou art not a doer of the law,
but a judge. There is one lawgiver who is able
to save or to destroy: who art thou that judgest
another?'

The word translated 'speak evil of' is κατα λαλέω.
Without referring to the dictionary one can see that
this word must mean indict. And so it does, as anyone may convince himself by a reference to the
dictionary. It is translated, 'Who speaks evil of his
brother, speaks evil of the law'. One involuntarily
asks, Why? However much I may speak evil of my
brother, I do not speak evil of the law; but if I indict
and bring my brother before the court of law, I
evidently thereby condemn the law of Christ: that
is to say, I consider the law of Christ insufficient and
indict and condemn his law. Then it is clear that I

do not fulfil his law but constitute myself its judge. The judge, says Christ, is he who can save. But how shall I, who am not able to save, be a judge and inflict punishments?

The whole passage speaks of human law-courts and repudiates them. The whole of the Epistle is full of that thought. In the Epistle of James (ii. 1–13) it is said: (1) 'My brethren, let the faith of our Lord Jesus Christ be held without respect of persons. (2) For if there come unto your assembly a man with a gold ring, in fine clothing, and there come in also a poor man in vile clothing; (3) And ye have regard to him that weareth the fine clothing, and say unto him, Sit thou here in a good place; and say to the poor, Stand thou there, or sit here under my footstool: (4) Are ye not then partial in yourselves, and are become judges of evil thoughts? (5) Hearken, my beloved brethren, Hath not God chosen the poor of this world rich in faith, and heirs of the kingdom which he hath promised to them that love him? (6) But ye have despised the poor. Do not rich men oppress you, and themselves drag you before the judgement seats? Do not they blaspheme that worthy name by the which ye are called? (8) If ye fulfil the royal law according to the scripture, Thou shalt love thy neighbour as thyself (Lev. xix. 18), ye do well. (9) But if ye have respect to persons, ye commit sin, and are convicted by the law as transgressors. (10) For whosoever shall keep the whole law, and yet offend in one point, he is guilty of all. (11) For he who said, Do not commit adultery, said also, Do not kill. Now if thou commit no adultery, yet if thou kill, thou art become a transgressor of the law (Deut. xxii. 22; Lev. xviii. 17–25). (12) So speak ye, and so do, as they that shall be judged by the law of liberty. (13) For he shall have judgement without mercy that hath showed no mercy; and mercy rejoiceth against judgement.' The last words have often been translated: 'Mercy is proclaimed in the courts', and were so translated to imply that there may be Christian courts of law, but that they must be merciful.

James exhorts the brethren not to make distinctions between people. If you make distinctions, you διεκρίθητε, are divided in your minds, like the judges with evil intentions in the courts. You have judged the poor to be worse. But on the contrary it is the rich man who is worse. He both oppresses you and drags you before the courts. If you live according to the law of love of your neighbour, according to the law of charity (which, in distinction from the other law, James calls the 'law of the Lord'), you do well. But if you regard persons, and make distinctions between man and man, you are offenders against the law of mercy. And, having probably in mind the example of the woman taken in adultery whom they brought before Christ that she might be stoned, or the sin of adultery in general, James says that he who executes the adulterers will be guilty of murder and will infringe the external law. For the same external law forbids both adultery and murder. He says: '*Behave like men who are judged by the law of liberty.* For there is no mercy for him who has no mercy, and *therefore mercy destroys the courts.*'

How could that be said more clearly and definitely? All discrimination between people is forbidden, every judgement that this man is good and that man evil directly indicates that the human courts are undoubtedly bad, and proves that the court itself is criminal, as it executes people for offences and therefore itself infringes God's law of charity.

I read the Epistles of St. Paul, who himself suffered

from the courts, and in the very first chapter of the Epistle to the Romans I found a reprimand which he addresses to the Romans for their various sins and errors, and among the rest for their courts (v. 32): 'Who knowing the judgement of God, that they which commit such things are worthy of death, not only do the same, but have pleasure in them that do them.' Chap. ii. 1: '*Therefore thou art without excuse, O man, whosoever thou art, who judgest; for wherein thou judgest another, thou condemnest thyself; for thou that judgest dost practise the same things.* (2) And we are sure that the judgement of God is according to truth against them which commit such things. (3) And thinkest thou this, O man, that judgest them which do such things, and doest the same, that thou shalt escape the judgement of God? (4) Or despisest thou the riches of his goodness and forbearance and long-suffering; not knowing that the goodness of God leadeth thee to repentance?'

The Apostle Paul says that they, knowing the righteous law of God, themselves do wrong and teach others to do the same, and therefore the man who judges cannot be justified.

Such is the attitude to the law-courts which I found in the Epistles of the Apostles, and in their lives, as we all know, man's courts appeared an evil and a temptation which had to be endured with firmness, and with submission to the will of God.

By reconstructing in one's imagination the position of the first Christians among the heathen, one can easily understand that the Christians, who were persecuted in man's law-courts, could not prohibit law-courts. Only incidentally could they allude to that evil, condemning its foundations, as they did.

I consulted the Fathers of the Church of the first centuries, and saw that they always define the difference between their teaching and that of all others by the fact that they never put compulsion on anyone in any way and never went to law with anyone (see Athenagoras and Origen), did not execute, but only endured the torments to which they were condemned by man's courts. All the martyrs, by their deeds, made the same profession. I saw that all the Christians till the time of Constantine regarded the law-courts not otherwise than as an evil which had to be patiently endured, and that the thought could never enter the head of any Christian of those days that Christians could take part in prosecutions. I saw that the words of Christ, '*Judge not that ye be not judged*', were understood by his first disciples as I now understand them in their direct meaning: 'Do not prosecute in the courts, and do not participate in them.'

Everything indubitably confirmed my conviction that the words 'Judge not and condemn not' mean, do not judge in the courts; yet the explanation that it means do not malign your neighbour is so generally accepted, and so boldly and confidently do the courts flourish in all Christian countries, supported even by the Church, that I long doubted the correctness of my interpretation. If everybody could explain the matter in this way and organize Christian courts, then probably they had some ground for so doing and there is something I do not understand, said I to myself. There must be grounds on which the words are understood to mean 'to malign', and there must be grounds for instituting Christian courts.

And I examined the explanations of the ecclesiastical theologians. In all these interpretations, from the fifth century onward, I found that the words were taken in the sense of condemnation of one's neighbour, that is, maligning. And as the words are taken only to mean condemning one's neighbour in words, the question arises—how can one refrain from condemning? Evil must be condemned! Therefore all the interpretations revolve round the question, what one may and what one may not condemn. It is said (St. Chrysostom and Theophilus) that for the servants of the Church it must not be understood as a prohibition to judge, for the Apostles themselves judged. It is said that probably Christ referred to the Jews who condemned their neighbours for small sins and themselves committed great ones.

But nowhere is a word said of the institution of courts of law and of the relation in which the courts stand to this condemnation of judging. Does Christ forbid them or allow them?

To that particular question no reply is given, as though it were quite obvious that as soon as a Christian occupied a judge's seat, he might not merely condemn his neighbour, but have him executed.

I consulted the Greek, the Catholic, and the Protestant writers, and the writers of the Tübingen School and of the historical school. All of them, even the most free-thinking, understood those words as a condemnation of evil-speaking. But why, contrary to the whole teaching of Christ, the words are understood so narrowly that the courts are not included in the prohibition of judging; why it is supposed that Christ, forbidding as an evil deed a condemnation of one's neighbour that involuntarily slips from one's tongue, does not consider as evil and does not forbid a similar condemnation uttered deliberately and associated with the infliction of violence on the person condemned, is not explained, nor is there the slightest hint that it is possible for 'condemnation' to mean the judging which takes place in the law-court and from which millions of people suffer. More than that, in dealing with these words, 'Judge not and condemn not', reference to that most cruel habit of legal condemnation is carefully avoided, and even fenced off. The theologian-interpreters remark that Christian law-courts must exist and do not conflict with the law of Christ.

Noticing this, I began to doubt the good faith of these interpretations and referred to the translation of the words 'judge' and 'condemn'—the very matter with which I ought to have begun.

In the original these words are κρίνω and καταδικάζω. The incorrect translation of the word καταδικάζω in the Epistle of James, where it is translated by the words 'speak evil of', confirmed my suspicion of the incorrectness of the translations.

I looked how the words κρίνω and καταδικάζω are translated in the Gospels in different languages, and I saw that the word which in the Vulgate is translated *condemnare*, is translated in a similar way in French, while in Slavonic it is 'condemn', and Luther translates it *Verdammen*, to curse.

The contrast of these translations strengthened my doubts, and I asked myself: What does and what can the Greek word κρίνω, employed in both the Gospels, mean, and also the word καταδικάζω, used by Luke the Evangelist, who, in the opinion of the experts, wrote rather good Greek? How would a man translate those words who knew nothing of the Gospel teaching and the existing interpretations of it, but had before him merely that saying?

I consulted the general dictionary and found that the word κρίνω has many different meanings, and among them very commonly the meaning of sentencing in the law-court, even executing, but that it never has the meaning of evil-speaking. I consulted the New Testament dictionary and found that the word is often used in the New Testament in the sense of to sentence in court. It is sometimes used in the sense of differentiation, but never in the sense of evil-speaking. And so I see that the word κρίνω may be translated variously, but that a translation which makes it mean 'speak evil' is the most far-fetched and unexpected of all.

Then I inquired about the word καταδικάζω coupled to κρίνω, the word of many meanings—evidently on purpose to define the sense in which the writer was using that word. In the general dictionary I found that *the word never has any other meaning than to condemn in court to punishment or execution*. I looked in the New Testament dictionary, and found that the word is used in the Epistle of James v. 6, 'Ye have condemned and killed the just'; the word 'condemned' is this same word καταδικάζω, used in reference to Christ, who was condemned. *And in no other way is this word ever used in the whole of the New Testament, or in any Greek dialect.*

What does this all mean? What absurdity have I arrived at? I, and everyone in our society, if we have ever considered the fate of mankind, have been horrified at the sufferings and the evil introduced into man's life by man's criminal law—an evil both for the judged and for those who judge—from the executions of Genghiz Khan to the executions of the French Revolution and those of our day.

No one with a heart can have escaped an impression of horror and doubt in goodness at even hearing of, not to say seeing, the execution[1] of men by other men: the floggings to death with rods,[2] the guillotines, and the scaffolds.

---

[1] See *Confession*, p. 12.

[2] A method of punishment frequently practised in the army under Nicholas I. The sentence was so many thousand strokes, and the prisoner had to run the gauntlet between ranks of soldiers, the result often being death from collapse.—A.M.

In the Gospels, each word of which we consider holy, it is directly and clearly said: You have had a criminal law—'An eye for an eye'—but I give you a new law: 'Resist not him that is evil.' Obey this law, all of you: do not inflict evil for evil, but do good always and to all men, forgive all men.

Further, it is clearly said: '*Do not go to law.*' And that doubt about the meaning of the words may be impossible, it is added, '*Do not condemn to punishment in the courts*'.

My heart says clearly and distinctly: do not execute. Science says, do not execute; the more you execute the more evil will there be. Reason says, do not execute, evil cannot be cut off by evil. The word of God, in which I believe, says the same. And I, reading the whole teaching and reading the words: '*Judge not that ye be not judged, condemn not that ye be not condemned, forgive and ye shall be forgiven*', admit that this is the word of God, say that it means that I must not go about talking scandal and maligning people, and continue to consider the law-court to be a Christian institution and to consider myself both a judge[1] and a Christian. And I was horrified at the grossness of the deception in which I was involved.

IV

MISUNDERSTANDING OF CHRIST'S TEACHING

I NOW understand what Christ meant when he uttered the words: 'It was said to you: an eye for an eye, and a tooth for a tooth. But I say unto you: resist not him that is evil, but bear with him.'

[1] Tolstóy was an Arbiter of the Peace for about a year in 1862 after the emancipation of the serfs, his duties being to adjust differences between the landed proprietors and the newly emancipated serfs.—A.M.

Christ said: It has been instilled into you and you are accustomed to think that it is good and reasonable to resist evil by force and to tear out an eye for an eye, to institute criminal courts, police, an army, and to defend yourselves from foes; but I say, Do not use violence, do not take part in violence, do no harm to anyone,[1] not even to those whom you call 'enemies'.

I now understand that Christ, in the position he takes up of non-resistance to the evil man, is speaking not only of what will result directly for each man from non-resistance to him that is evil but, in contradiction to the principle under which mankind lived in his time under the law of Moses and under the Roman law, and now lives under various legal codes, he sets up the principle of non-resistance to the evil man, which principle according to his teaching should be the basis of man's social life and should free mankind from an evil they inflict on themselves. He says: 'You think that your laws correct evil—they only increase it. There is but one way to end evil—by rendering good for evil to all men without distinction. For thousands of years you have tried your principle; now try my contrary one.'

I have recently spoken to people of most divergent opinions about this law of Christ's—non-resistance to the evil man. It did occur, though rarely, that I met some who agreed with me. But,

---

[1] Tolstóy intended no sophistry, but there is unconscious sophistry in the suggestion that the purpose of the Criminal Courts is to injure certain people. He leaves unnoticed the benefit those Courts confer by making it plain what we are not permitted to do. One of the greatest benefits conferred by law is that it supplies a degree of definiteness to human relations which renders co-operation possible even among people whose opinions differ. It diminishes the amount of strife and friction that would otherwise exist.—A.M.

strange to say, two kinds of people never, even in principle, tolerated a straightforward understanding of the law, but always warmly defended the justice of resistance to the evil-doer. These are people who belong to the two extreme poles: patriotic Conservative Christians, who consider their Church to be the only true one, and Revolutionary Atheists. Neither these nor those wish to abandon the right to resist by violence what they consider evil. And the wisest and most learned of them are quite unwilling to see the simple and obvious truth that if one admits that one man may use violence to oppose what he considers evil, another may do the same to resist what he, in turn, considers evil.

A correspondence lately passed through my hands between an Orthodox Slavophil and a Christian-Revolutionary, which was instructive in this respect. The one advocated the violence of war on behalf of our oppressed brother-Slavs; the other, a revolutionary violence on behalf of our oppressed brethren, the Russian peasants. Both demanded violence, and both relied on the teaching of Christ.

People in general understand Christ's teaching in very various ways, but not in the direct, simple meaning which inevitably flows from his words.

We have arranged our whole life on the very foundations he denies. We do not wish to understand his teaching in its simple, direct meaning, and we assure ourselves and others either that we do not acknowledge his teaching or that it is unsuited to us. The so-called believers believe that Christ is God, the Second Person of the Trinity who descended to earth to show us how to live, and they arrange most elaborate ceremonies necessary for the administration of the sacraments, for erecting churches, for sending out missionaries, for ordaining priests, for the direction of their flocks, for amending the creeds, but one little thing they forget—namely, to do what he told us to do. The unbelievers try to arrange their lives in all sorts of ways, only not according to the law of Christ, having decided in advance that that law will not do. But no one wishes to try doing as Christ bids us. Moreover, before even trying to do it, both the believers and the non-believers decide in advance that it is impossible.

He says simply and clearly: the law of resistance by violence to him that is evil which you have made the basis of your lives, is false and unnatural; and he gives another basis—non-resistance—which in his opinion can alone deliver mankind from evil. He says: You think your laws of violence correct evil; they only increase it. You have tried for thousands of years to destroy evil by evil, but instead of destroying it you have increased it. Do what I do, and you will know whether it is true.

He not only says this but in his whole life, and by his death, he carries out his teaching of non-resistance to the evil man.

Believers hear all this, they read it in their churches, they say the words are divine and that he who spoke them was God, but they say: It is all very well, but it is impossible with our arrangement of life—it would upset the whole way of life to which we are accustomed and which we like. Therefore we believe all this only as being an ideal towards which humanity must strive—an ideal to be attained by prayer and by faith in the sacraments and the redemption and in the resurrection from the dead. Others, the unbelievers, the free-thinking investigators of Christ's teaching—Strauss, Renan, and others—who follow the historic method, having thoroughly imbibed the Church's explanation that Christ's teaching has no direct reference to life but is a visionary doctrine consoling to feeble-minded people, say most seriously that Christ's teaching was only fit to be preached to the savage inhabitants of the wilds of Galilee, but that for us, with our culture, it appears merely a sweet dream—'du charmant docteur', as Renan says. In their opinion Christ could not rise high enough to understand all the wisdom of our civilization and culture. Had he stood on the height of education on which these learned people stand he would not have talked such charming rubbish about the birds of the air, about turning one's cheek, and about not being troubled for to-morrow. These learned historians judge of Christianity by the Christianity they see in our society. The Christianity of our society and day regards our present life as true and sacred, with its organizations, prisons, solitary confinements, *Ciros*,[1] factories, newspapers, brothels, and parliaments, and from the teaching of Christ it selects only what does not infringe that life.[2] But as Christ's teaching is the negation of all that life, nothing is accepted of it except mere words. The learned historians see this, and, as they are under no necessity to hide it as it is hidden by the pseudo-believers, this version of Christ's teaching deprived of all substance is subjected to profound criticism and very rightly re-

[1] The translator finds himself in a difficulty when he has to devise an equivalent for the most improper type of Moscow restaurant.

[2] This passage is an excellent example of Tolstóy's power of sarcasm. The scorn he pours both on those who wish Christianity to be a mere epicurean consolation, and on those who, while criticizing Christianity, see it through the eyes of the others, is effective; but one should note how, urged by his moral and intellectual indignation against these people, he slips in a juxtaposition of brothels and parliaments, which is the first word of an argument he pushed later to far-reaching and questionable conclusions.—A.M.

pudiated. The deduction is clear that there never was anything in Christianity except dreamy ideals.

It would seem as though before judging Christ's teaching one should understand what it consists of, and to decide whether his teaching is reasonable or not one should first of all admit that he said what he said; but that is just what is not done either by the Church or by the free-thinking expositors. And we know very well why they do not do it.

We know very well that Christ's teaching always included and includes the denial of all those human illusions, those 'vain things', empty idols, which we, by calling them Church, State, culture, science, art, and civilization, think we can separate from the ranks of delusions. But it is just against them that Christ speaks, without excluding any 'empty idols'.

Not Christ only, but all the Hebrew prophets, John the Baptist, and all the world's true sages, have spoken of that same State, culture, and civilization, as an evil, ruinous to mankind.

Suppose a builder says to a man, 'Your house is bad, it must be entirely rebuilt', and then gives details as to what beams should be cut, and how it should be done and where they should be placed. The man does not listen to the words about the house being bad and being rebuilt, but with a pretence of respect listens to the builder's further instructions and arrangements in the house. Obviously all the advice given by the builder will appear inapplicable, and any disrespectful person will say plainly that his advice is stupid. This is what happens with regard to Christ's teaching.

Not finding a better comparison, I made use of the above. And then I remembered that Christ when preaching his doctrine used that same comparison. He said: I will destroy your temple and in three days will build a new one. For that he was crucified; and it is for that very thing that his teaching is now crucified.

The least one can demand of people who judge any doctrine is that they should judge of it in the sense in which the teacher himself understood it. And he understood his teaching not as a distant ideal for humanity, obedience to which is impossible, nor as a mystical poetic fantasy wherewith he captivated the simple-minded inhabitants of Galilee. He understood his teaching as a real thing, and a thing which would save mankind. And he did not dream on the cross but died for his teaching, and many others are dying and will yet die. Of such a teaching one cannot say that it is a dream!

Every true doctrine is a dream to those in error. We have come to this, that there are many people (of whom I was one) who say that this teaching is visionary because it is not natural to man. It is not in accord, they say, with man's nature to turn the other cheek when one cheek is struck; it is not natural to give what is one's own to another; it is unnatural to work for others instead of for oneself. It is natural to man, they say, to defend his safety and the safety of his family and his property: in other words, it is natural for man to struggle for his own existence. The learned jurists prove scientifically that man's most sacred duty is to defend his rights, that is—to struggle.

But it is sufficient to free oneself for a moment from the thought that the order which exists and has been arranged by men is the best and is sacrosanct, for the objection that Christ's teaching is not accordant with man's nature to turn against the objector. Who will deny that to murder or torture, I will not say a man, but to torture a dog or kill a hen or calf is contrary and distressing to man's nature? (I know people who live by tilling the land,

and who have given up eating meat merely because they had themselves to kill their own animals.) Yet the whole structure of our lives is such that each man's personal advantage is obtained by inflicting suffering on others, which is contrary to human nature. The whole order of our life and the whole complex mechanism of our institutions designed for the infliction of violence, witness to the extent to which violence is contrary to human nature. Not a single judge would decide to strangle with a rope the man he condemns to death from the bench. Not a single magistrate would make up his mind himself to take a peasant from his weeping family and shut him up in prison. None of our generals or soldiers, were it not for discipline, oaths of allegiance, and declarations of war, would, I will not say kill hundreds of Turks and Germans and destroy their villages, but would even decide to wound a single man. All this is only done thanks to a very complex state and social machinery the purpose of which is so to distribute the responsibility for the evil deeds that are done that no one should feel the unnaturalness of those deeds. Some men write the laws; others apply them; a third set drill men and habituate them to discipline, that is to say, to senseless and implicit obedience; a fourth set—the people who are disciplined—commit all sorts of deeds of violence, even killing people, without knowing why or wherefore. But a man need only, even for a moment, free himself mentally from this net of worldly organization in which he is involved to understand what is really unnatural to him.

As soon as we cease to affirm that the customary evil we employ is an immutable divine truth, it becomes obvious which of the two is natural and accordant to man: violence, or the law of Christ. Is it to know that my tranquillity and safety and

that of my family, and all my pleasures, are purchased by the destitution, corruption, and misery of
millions, by hangings every year, by hundreds of
thousands of suffering prisoners, by millions torn
from their homes and stupefied by discipline—
soldiers, policemen, and gendarmes who, armed
with pistols against hungry people, safeguard my
amusements—to purchase every sweet morsel I put
into my mouth or into the mouths of my children,
by the sufferings of humanity that are unavoidable
for the procuring of these morsels? Or to know that,
be the morsel what it may, it is mine only when no
one else needs it and when no one has to suffer on
account of it?[1]

It is only necessary once to understand that this
is so, and that every pleasure of mine, every moment of tranquillity under our organization of life,
is purchased by the deprivations and sufferings of
thousands who are restrained by violence; one need
but once understand that fact, to understand what
is natural to man's entire nature—that is to say, not
merely to his animal nature, but to his reasonable
nature as well. One need only understand the law
of Christ in its full meaning, with all its consequences, in order to understand that Christ's teaching is not contrary to man's nature, but that it really
consists in rejecting what is contrary to man's nature,
namely, the visionary human doctrine of resistance
to evil which now makes life unhappy.

[1] This passage, which occurs here incidentally, forms the
keynote of some of Tolstóy's later economic treatises. He says,
and means, that no one has a right to keep anything anyone
else wishes to take. A man who wishes to get needful work
efficiently done and requires accustomed tools for the purpose,
may hardly find himself able to agree with the thesis. One
consideration clashes with another, and in the experience of
life we have to deal with comparative values more often than
with absolute and abstract principles.—A.M.

Christ's doctrine of non-resistance to him that is evil is a dream! But that the life of men in whose souls pity and love for one another is implanted, has been passed, and is now being passed, by some in organizing executions at the stake, knouts, and breakings on the wheel, lashes, the splitting of nostrils, tortures, handcuffs, penal servitude, gallows, shootings, solitary confinements, prisons for women and children, in arranging the slaughter of tens of thousands in wars, in organizing periodic revolutions and Pugachëv[1] revolts, and the life of others in carrying out all these horrors, and the life of a third set in evading these sufferings and avenging themselves for them—is this not a dreadful dream?

One has but to understand Christ's teaching to understand that the world, not that which God gave for man's delight but the world men have devised for their own destruction, is a dream, and a very wild and terrible dream—the raving of a maniac from which one need but awake in order never to return to that terrible nightmare.

God descended to earth; the Son of God—one of the Persons of the Trinity—became flesh and redeemed Adam's sin; this God, we were taught to think, must have said something secret, mystical, difficult to understand, and only to be understood by the aid of faith and the sacraments; and suddenly it appears that the word of God is so simple, so clear, so reasonable. God says simply: Do not do evil to one another—and there will be no evil. Is it possible that God's revelation is so simple? Can it be that God only said that? It seems to us that we all knew that: it is so simple.

Elijah the prophet, fleeing from men, hid in a

---

[1] Pugachëv was the Cossack leader of a very serious peasant revolt in the time of Catherine II.—A.M.

cave, and it was revealed to him that God would appear to him at the entrance to the cave. A storm arose that broke the trees. Elijah thought this was God, and looked; but God was not there. Then came thunder; the thunder and lightning were terrible. Elijah went out to look whether God was not there; but God was not there either. Then there came an earthquake; fire arose from the earth, the rocks were rent, and the mountains quaked. Elijah looked, but God was still not there. Then a light, quiet breeze arose, bringing the refreshing scent of the fields. Elijah looked—and God was there! Such, too, are these simple words of God: 'Resist not him that is evil.'

They are very simple, but in them is expressed the law of God and man, one and eternal. The law is to such an extent eternal that if there is in history a movement forward towards the elimination of evil, it is thanks only to those men who have so understood Christ's teaching and have endured evil and not resisted it by violence. Progress towards the welfare of mankind is made not by the persecutors but by the persecuted. As fire does not extinguish fire, so evil cannot extinguish evil. Only goodness, meeting evil and not infected by it, conquers evil. That this is so is in man's spiritual world an immutable law comparable to the law of Galileo, but even *more immutable*, clearer and more complete. People may deviate from it and hide it from others, but nevertheless the progress of humanity towards what is good can only be accomplished by that path. Every step forward is made solely in the path of non-resistance to evil. And in the face of all possible temptations and threats the disciples of Christ may, with more assurance than Galileo, declare: 'And yet, not by violence, but by goodness alone can you destroy evil.' If that advance is slow, this is thanks solely to the fact that the clearness, simplicity, reasonableness, inevitability, and necessity of Christ's teaching is hidden from the majority of men in the most cunning and dangerous way, hidden under a different doctrine falsely called his.

V

JESUS AND THE MOSAIC LAW

EVERYTHING confirmed the fact that the meaning of Christ's teaching that had disclosed itself to me was true. But it was long before I could accustom myself to the strange idea that after Christ's law had been professed by millions of people for 1800 years, and after thousands of men had devoted their lives to the study of that law, it had now been my fate to rediscover it as a novelty. But, strange as it might be, such was the case; Christ's teaching of non-resistance to evil arose before me as a total novelty of which I had not had the slightest conception. And I asked myself: How could this come about? I must have had some false conception of the meaning of the teaching to cause me so to misunderstand it. And such a false conception really existed.

When approaching the Gospel doctrine I was not in the position of one who never having heard anything of Christ's teaching suddenly hears it for the first time, but I already possessed a whole ready-made theory of how I ought to understand it. Christ did not appear to me as a prophet who was revealing a divine law, but as one who completed and explained a divine law already known to me and indubitable. I already possessed a complete, definite, and very complex teaching about God, the creation of the world and of man, and about His commandments given to man through Moses.

In the Gospels I encountered the words, 'Ye have heard that it was said, An eye for an eye, and a tooth for a tooth; but I say unto you, Resist not him that is evil'. The words, 'an eye for an eye and a tooth for a tooth', were the law of Moses. The words, 'Resist not evil, or him that is evil', were the new law which repealed the first.

Had I approached Christ's teaching without that theological theory imbibed with my mother's milk, I should have understood the simple meaning of his words. I should have understood that Christ denies the old law and gives a new law of his own. But it had been instilled into me that Christ did not deny the law of Moses, but on the contrary confirmed it all to the last jot and tittle and completed it. Verses 17 and 18 of Matt. v, in which this is affirmed, had always, when I read the Gospels, struck me as obscure and had evoked doubts. From what I then knew of the Old Testament, especially the last books of Moses in which such minute, meaningless, and often cruel, rules are laid down, each preceded by the words: 'And the Lord said unto Moses', it seemed to me strange that Christ could confirm the whole of that law, and incomprehensible why he did so. But I then left the question undecided: I accepted unverified the interpretation instilled into me from childhood that both these laws are productions of the Holy Ghost, that they agree, and that Christ confirms the law of Moses, supplements it, and completes it.

How that completion was effected, how the contradictions are solved which strike one's eye in the Gospels themselves, both in these verses and in the words, 'But I say unto you', I never clearly explained to myself. But now, having recognized the simple and direct meaning of Christ's teaching, I understood that these two laws are contradictory and that there can be no talk of their agreement or of completing the one by the other, but that we must accept one or the other, and that the common explanation of verses 17 and 18 in Matt. v. (which had formerly struck me by their obscurity) must be incorrect.

And on re-reading those verses (the ones which had always seemed to me so obscure) I was amazed by the simple and clear meaning in them which suddenly revealed itself to me.

That meaning revealed itself to me not because I devised or transposed anything, but simply because I rejected the artificial interpretation which has been attached to that passage.

Christ says (Matt. v. 17–19): 'Think not that I came to destroy the law or the teaching of the prophets; I came not to destroy, but to fulfil. For verily I say unto you, Till heaven and earth pass away, one jot or one tittle shall in no wise pass away from the law till all things be accomplished.'

And verse 20 adds: 'Except your righteousness shall exceed the righteousness of the scribes and Pharisees, ye shall in no wise enter into the kingdom of heaven.'

Christ says: I have not come to destroy the eternal law, for the fulfilment of which your Scriptures and prophecies were written, but I have come to teach you to fulfil the eternal law; and I speak not of that law of yours which your scribes and Pharisees call the Law of God, but of that eternal law which is less changeable than the heavens and the earth.

I express the thought in fresh words merely to tear the meaning away from the customary false interpretation. Were it not for that false interpretation it would be impossible to express this thought better or more exactly than it is expressed in those verses.

The interpretation that Christ does not deny the law is based on the fact that to the word 'law' in this passage—thanks to the comparison made with the iota (jot) of the written law—is attributed the meaning of the 'written law' instead of the 'eternal law'—though this is quite gratuitous and in contradiction to the meaning of the words. But Christ is not speaking of the written law. If he had spoken of the written law he would have used the customary expression, the law *and* the prophets, as he always does when speaking of the written law. But he employs a different expression: the law *or* the prophets. If he were speaking of the written law he would also in the next verse, which supplies a continuation of the thought, have used the words 'the law *and* the prophets', and not the word 'the law' without addition, as actually stands in that verse. More than that however, Christ uses the same expression in the Gospel of Luke in a connexion which makes its meaning indubitable. In Luke xvi. 15, 16 Christ says to the Pharisees who assumed righteousness in the written law: 'Ye are they that justify yourselves in the sight of men; but God knoweth your hearts: for that which is exalted among men is an abomination in the sight of God. *The law and the prophets* were until John: from that time the Gospel of the Kingdom of God is preached, and everyone entereth into it [by his own efforts].'[1]

And then in the following verse, 17, he says: 'But it is easier for heaven and earth to pass away, than for one tittle of the law to fail.' By the words, '*the law and the prophets* were until John', Christ repeals the written law. By the words, 'It is easier for heaven and earth to pass away than for one tittle

---

[1] Where Tolstóy's translation diverges in meaning from our Revised and Authorized Versions, his words are enclosed in square brackets.—A.M.

of the law to fail', he confirms the eternal law. In the first words he says, 'the law and the prophets'— that is to say the written law; in the second he says simply *'the law'*, therefore the law eternal. Consequently it is clear that here the eternal law is contrasted with the written law,[1] and that just the same contrast is made in the context in Matthew, where the eternal law is defined by the words, *the law or the prophets*.

The history of verses 17 and 18 in their variations is remarkable. In most of the texts there is only the word 'law' without the addition of 'prophets'. In these versions there can be no suggestion that it means the written law. In other copies, in Tischendorf's and in the canonical version, there is the addition of 'prophets', not with the conjunction 'and', but with the conjunction 'or'—*the law or the prophets*—which also excludes the meaning of the written law and gives the meaning of the eternal law.

In some of the texts not accepted by the Church the addition of 'prophets' with the conjunction 'and', and not 'or', finds place—and in these same versions when the word 'law' is repeated 'and the prophets' is also repeated. So that the meaning of the whole utterance in these versions is given as though Christ spoke only of the written law.

These variations supply the history of the interpretation of that passage. The only clear rendering

---

[1] More than that, as though to prevent any possible doubt as to which law he is speaking of, he immediately, in this connexion, gives an example—a very striking example—of a contradiction of the law of Moses with the eternal law of which no atom can fail; giving the sharpest contradiction to the Mosaic law that occurs in the Gospels, he says (Luke xvi. 18): 'Everyone that putteth away his wife and marrieth another, committeth adultery.' That is to say that, whereas in the written law divorce is allowed, in the eternal law it is a sin.— L.T.

of the passage is that Christ here, as in Luke, is speaking of the eternal law. But among the copyists of the Gospel manuscripts were some who wished to assert the obligatoriness of the written law of Moses, and these scribes added to the word 'law' the additional words 'and the prophets' and changed the meaning.

Other Christians, who did not acknowledge the books of Moses, either excluded the addition or changed the word 'and', καί, to the word 'or', ἤ. And with this word 'or' the passage entered into the canonical version. But despite the clearness and certainty of the meaning of the text in that form in which it had entered the canon, the canonical interpreters continued to interpret it in the spirit that had prompted the alternative which had not been accepted in the text. The passage was submitted to innumerable explanations which were the further removed from its plain meaning in proportion as the interpreter agreed less with the real, direct, simple meaning of Christ's teaching; and most of the interpreters retain the apocryphal sense—the very one rejected by the text.

Fully to convince oneself that in these verses Christ is speaking only of the eternal law, it is worth while to examine the meaning of the word which served the pseudo-interpreters as an excuse. In Russian the word *zakon* (law), in Greek νόμος, and in Hebrew *torah*, all have two main meanings: one is the law itself (that which is right) without reference to its expression; the other conception is that of the written expression of what certain people consider to be the law. These two different meanings exist in all languages.

In Greek, in the Epistles of Paul, this distinction is sometimes marked by the use of the article. Without an article, Paul uses this word chiefly in the meaning of the 'written law', but with the article in the meaning of the 'eternal law of God'.

Among the ancient Hebrews, in the prophets, as Isaiah, the word 'law', *torah*, is always used in the meaning of the one eternal revelation and teaching of God independent of verbal expression. And this same word 'law', *torah*, in Ezra for the first time, and in the latest period in Talmudic times, began to be used to mean the five written books of Moses, over which the general title of *Torah* was inscribed as we use the word Bible, but with this difference, that we have a word to distinguish the conception of the Bible from that of the law of God, while in Hebrew one and the same word was used for both conceptions.

And therefore Christ using the word 'law', *torah*, employs it now to confirm it when he uses it in the meaning given it by Isaiah and the other prophets, of the law of God which is eternal, and now to reject it when he means by it the five books of the law. But for the sake of distinction when (rejecting it) he uses this word in the meaning of the written law he always adds the words 'and the prophets', or prefixes the word 'your' to the word 'law'. When he says, 'Whatsoever ye would that men should do unto you, even so do ye also unto them, for this is the law and the prophets', he is speaking of the written law. He says that the whole of the written law can be compressed into this one expression of the eternal law and by these words he annuls the written law.

When he says (Luke xvi. 16), 'The law and the prophets were until John', he is speaking of the written law and by these words denies its authority.

When he says (John vii. 19), '*Did not Moses give you the law*, and yet none of you doeth the law?' or (John viii. 17), 'In *your* law it is written', or (John

xv. 25), 'The word that is written in *their* law', he is speaking of the written law: the law he denied, the law which condemned him to death. (John xix. 7) 'The Jews answered Pilate, We have a law, *and by that law he ought to die*'. Evidently that law of the Jews, on the basis of which they executed him, is not the law Christ taught. But when Christ says, 'I came not to destroy the law but to teach you to fulfil it, for nothing can change in the law, but all must be fulfilled', he is speaking not of the written law but of the divine eternal law, and is confirming it.

But let us suppose that all these are merely formal proofs; let us suppose that I have carefully selected contexts and variations and have carefully hidden everything opposed to my interpretation; let us suppose that the Church's interpretation is very clear and convincing and that Christ really did not infringe the law of Moses but left it in full strength. Suppose that to be so. But then what did Christ teach?

According to the Church's explanations he taught that he, the Second Person of the Trinity, the Son of God the Father, came to the earth and by his death redeemed Adam's sin. But everyone who has read the Gospels knows that in them Christ says nothing, or speaks very vaguely, about that. And even assuming that we do not know how to read and that the above assertions really are made there, at any rate Christ's indication that he is the Second Person of the Trinity and redeems the sins of humanity occupies the smallest and most obscure portion of the Gospels. What then does all the rest of Christ's teaching consist of? It is impossible to deny, and Christians have always acknowledged, that the chief content of Christ's message is the teaching of life: how men should live with one another.

Having admitted that Christ taught a new way of life, one has to picture to oneself some definite kind of people among whom he taught.

Let us imagine to ourselves Russians, or Englishmen, or Chinese, or Indians, or even savages on an island, and we shall see that every nation always has its rules of life, its law of life, and that therefore if a teacher teaches a new law of life he thereby destroys the former law: without destroying it he cannot teach. So it would be in England, in China, and among ourselves. The teacher will inevitably destroy our laws, which we consider precious and almost holy; but among us it might occur that the preacher teaching us a new way of life will only destroy our civil law, our State law, or our customs, but will not touch the laws we consider divine— though it is hard to imagine this. But among the Jewish people who then had only one code of law —entirely divine and embracing the whole of life to its minutest details—among such a people what could a preacher teach who declared in advance that the whole law of the people among whom he was preaching was valid? But let us say that this, too, is not a proof. Let those who interpret the words of Christ to mean that he confirmed the whole law of Moses explain this to themselves: Who was it that, throughout his active career, Christ exposed? Against whom did he revolt, calling them Pharisees, lawyers, and scribes? Who was it that rejected Christ's teaching? Whose High Priest had him crucified? If Christ acknowledged the law of Moses, where were those true adherents of that law who approved of him for doing so? Can it be that there was not one such?

The Pharisees, we are told, were a sect. The Jews do not say so! They say: The Pharisees were the faithful adherents of the law. But let us grant that they were a sect. The Sadducees were also a sect. Where, then, were the people who were not a sect, but true believers?

In the Gospel of John they all—Christ's enemies —are called simply the Jews. And they did not agree with Christ's teaching and were opposed to him simply because they were Jews. But in the Gospels not only the Pharisees and Sadducees are represented as Christ's enemies: among his enemies the lawyers are also mentioned, the very men who conserved the law of Moses; the Scribes, the very men who read the law; the Elders, the very ones who were always considered the representatives of national wisdom.

Christ said: 'I came not to call the righteous, but sinners to repentance'—to a change of life, μετανοία. Where and who, then, were these righteous? Was Nicodemus the only one? But even Nicodemus is represented to us as a kindly but erring man. We are so accustomed to the very strange explanation that the Pharisees and some wicked Jews crucified Christ, that the simple question never enters our heads: Where were those who were not Pharisees and not wicked, but real Jews who kept the law? One has only to put that question and it all becomes plain. Christ—whether he was God or man —brought his teaching into the world among a people who kept a law which regulated the whole of their lives and was called the law of God. What relation could Christ have to that law?

Every prophet—every teacher of a faith revealing the law of God to men—inevitably encounters among men something people believe to be the law of God, and so he cannot avoid making use of the word law in a double sense; for it means what people falsely consider to be the law of God, 'your law', and it also means the true, eternal law of God.

But besides being unable to avoid a double use of
that word, the preacher usually does not wish to
avoid it, but intentionally unites the two meanings:
indicating that the law, which taken in its entirety
is false and which is professed by those whom he
is addressing, does contain certain eternal truths.
And every preacher will take those laws which are
fundamentally true as the basis of his sermon. That
is what Christ did among the Jews, among whom
both laws were called by the one word *torah*. Christ,
in reference to the law of Moses—and to a yet
greater extent in reference to the prophets, especially Isaiah whose words he constantly quoted—
acknowledged that in the Hebrew law and prophets
there are eternal and divine truths coincident with
the eternal law, and these—such as the saying,
'Love God and thy neighbour'—he takes as the
basis of his teaching. Christ often expresses this
thought. (Luke x. 26) He says, 'What is written in
the law? how readest thou?' In the law also there
are eternal truths to be found, if you only know
how to read it. And he points out more than once
that the commandment in their law relating to the
love of God and of one's neighbour is a commandment of the eternal law. In Matt. xiii. 52, Christ,
after all the parables by which he explained to his
Apostles the meaning of his teaching, finally, as referring to all that had preceded, said: 'Therefore
every scribe [that is every literate person who has
learned the truth] is like unto a householder, which
bringeth forth out of his treasure [indiscriminately,
both together] things new and old.'

St. Irenaeus, and following him the whole Church,
understood these words in that way; but quite
arbitrarily, and to the infringement of the meaning
of the whole speech, attached to them also the
implication that all that was old was sacred. The

plain meaning is that he who seeks what is good takes not only what is new but what is old, and that it must not be rejected simply because it is old. By these words Christ says that he does not deny those things in the old law which are eternal. But when he is spoken to of the whole law or its forms, he says that one must not pour new wine into old bottles. Christ could not confirm the whole law, but neither could he reject the whole law and the prophets—that law in which is said, 'Love thy neighbour as thyself', and those prophets whose words he often used to express his own thoughts. And lo and behold, instead of this simple, clear understanding of these words, which as they were spoken and in the way they confirm the whole of Christ's teaching are very simple, a misty explanation is substituted introducing a contradiction where none existed and thereby destroying the meaning of the teaching and reducing it to verbiage, and practically re-establishing the teaching of Moses in all its savage cruelty.

According to all the Church's interpretations, especially since the fifth century, Christ did not infringe the written law but confirmed it. But how did he confirm it? How can the law of Christ be united with the law of Moses? To that no reply is given. In the interpretations a play of words is made use of, and it is said that Christ fulfilled *the law of Moses* in that in him the prophecies were fulfilled, and that Christ *through us*, by man's faith in him, fulfils the law. The only question essential to every believer (as to how to unite two contradictory laws governing human life) is left without even an attempt to meet it. And the contradiction between the verse in which it is said that Christ does not destroy the law and the verses which say, 'Ye have heard that it was said . . . but I say unto you . . .', and again between the whole spirit of the teaching of Moses and that of Christ, remains in full force.

Anyone interested in this question should look at the Church's interpretations of this passage, from St. John Chrysostom to our times. Only by reading these long dissertations will he be clearly convinced that here no solution of the contradiction is offered, but that a contradiction is artificially introduced where none existed.

The impossible attempts to unite the un-uniteable clearly indicated that this union is not the result of a mistake but has a clear and definite aim —it was needed. And it is even obvious why it was needed.

This is what St. John Chrysostom says, replying to those who rejected the Mosaic law (*Homilies on the Gospel of Matthew.* Part I. Homily xvi. Pusey's Library of the Fathers, pp. 236–7):

'In the next place, they criticize the Law in the Old Covenant, which bids us put out *an eye for an eye, and a tooth for a tooth*, and straightway they insult and say: "Why, how can he be good who speaks so?" What then do we say in answer to this? That it is the highest kind of philanthropy. For He made this law, not that we might strike out one another's eyes, but that fear of suffering by others might restrain us from doing any such thing to them. As therefore He threatened the Ninevites with over-throw, not that He might destroy them (for had that been His will He ought to have been silent), but that He might by fear make them better and so quiet His wrath: so also hath He appointed a punishment for those who wantonly assail the eyes of others, that if good principles dispose them not to refrain from such cruelty, fear may restrain them from injuring their neighbour's sight.

'And if this be cruelty, it is cruelty also for the

murderer to be restrained, and the adulterer checked. But these are the sayings of senseless men and of those that are mad to the extreme of madness. For I, so far from saying that this comes of cruelty, should say that the contrary to this would be unlawful, according to men's reckoning. And whereas thou sayest, "Because He commanded to pluck out *an eye for an eye*, therefore He is cruel"; I say that if He had not given this commandment then He would have seemed, in the judgement of most men, to be that which thou sayest He is.'

St. John Chrysostom definitely accepts the law of a tooth for a tooth as divine, and *what opposes the taking of a tooth for a tooth* (that is to say, Christ's teaching of non-resistance) as unlawful (pp. 237–8). 'For let us suppose that this law has been done away', says St. John Chrysostom, 'and that no one feared the punishment ensuing thereupon, but that licence had been given to all the wicked to follow their own dispositions in all security, to adulterers, and to murderers, to perjured persons and to parricides; would not all things have been turned upside down? Would not cities, market-places and houses, sea and land, and the whole world, have been filled with unnumbered pollutions and murders? Everyone sees it. For when there are laws, and fear, and threats, our evil dispositions are hardly checked; were even this security taken away, what is there to prevent men's choosing vice? and what degree of mischief would not then come revelling upon the whole of human life? The rather, since cruelty lies not only in allowing the bad to do what they will, but in another thing too quite as much; to overlook, and leave uncared for, him who hath done no wrong, but who is without cause or reason suffering ill. For tell me: were anyone to gather together wicked men from all quarters, and arm them with swords, and bid them go about the whole city and massacre all that came in their way, could there be anything more like a wild beast than he? And what if some other should bind, and confine with the utmost strictness, those whom that man had armed, and should snatch from out those lawless hands them who were on the point of being butchered, could anything be greater humanity than this?'

St. John Chrysostom does not say by what standard one would be guided in determining who are evil. What if he were himself evil and imprisoned the good?[1]

'Now then, I bid thee transfer these examples to the Law likewise, for He that commands to pluck out *an eye for an eye*, hath laid the fear as a kind of strong chain upon the souls of the bad, and so resembles him who detains those assassins in prison; whereas he who appoints no punishment for them, doth all but arm them by such security, and acts the part of that other who was putting the swords in their hands and letting them loose over the whole city.'

If St. John Chrysostom acknowledged the law of Christ, he should explain who will pluck out the eyes and the teeth and cast others into prison. If he who forbids us to do so, that is to say if God Himself, plucked them out, there would be no contradiction, but it is men who have to do it; and these men the Son of God has commanded that it should not be done. God said, pluck out teeth, and His Son said, do not pluck them out. One or

[1] Here Tolstóy introduces an argument which occurs repeatedly in his works. He diverts the argument as to whether a man of good will who desires to preserve the peace is morally justified in forcibly restraining a murderer, by a reference to the difficulty of judging the facts of each case rightly. The moral issue is perplexed by the introduction of a simultaneous consideration of the fact that man is intellectually fallible.—A.M.

the other has to be acknowledged; and St. John Chrysostom, and following him the Church in general, acknowledges the command of God the Father, that is to say of Moses, and rejects the command of the Son, that is of Christ, whose teaching he is supposed to profess. Christ rejects the law of Moses and gives his own. For a man believing in Christ there is no contradiction. Disregarding the law of Moses he believes in the law of Christ and fulfils it. For one believing in the law of Moses there is also no contradiction. The Jews consider the words of Christ vain, and believe in the law of Moses. There is a contradiction only for those who wish to live by the law of Moses but assure themselves and others that they believe the law of Christ —for those whom Christ calls hypocrites, the offspring of vipers.

Instead of acknowledging one of the two, the law of Moses or of Christ, they acknowledge both to be divinely true.

But when the question touches life itself, the law of Christ is simply denied and the law of Moses acknowledged.

In this false interpretation, if one examines its meaning, lies a terrible drama of the struggle of evil and darkness with goodness and light.

Among the Jewish people, confused by innumerable external rules laid on them by the Levites as divine laws and each stamped with the words 'The Lord said unto Moses', Christ appeared. He found not only the relations of man to God, his sacrifices, holidays, and fasts, but all the relations of man to man—the national, civil, and family relations—and all the details of private life—circumcisions, the washings of man's person, and of his cups and his dress—all defined to the last detail and all acknowledged as the command of God, the law of God. What can, I will not say Christ—God—but a prophet or an ordinary teacher, teach to such a people without infringing this law, which defines everything down to the smallest details? Christ, like all the prophets, selects from among the things the people considered to be the law of God that which was really the law of God. He takes the foundations and rejects all the rest, and unites his own revelation of the eternal law with these foundations. There is no need to destroy everything, but inevitably the law, which was considered equally obligatory in all its parts, is broken. Christ does this; and he is accused of breaking what was considered to be the law of God, and for this he is executed. But his teaching remains among his disciples and passes into another circle and into other centuries. But in this other circle and these other centuries the new teaching is again overgrown by similar accretions, interpretations, and explanations—again mean human inventions replace the divine revelation. Instead of 'And the Lord said unto Moses', we are told:[1] 'It seemed good to the Holy Ghost and to us', and again the letter hides the spirit. And, most surprising of all, the teaching of Christ becomes involved with all that *torah* (in the meaning of the written law) which he could not but reject. That *torah* is acknowledged to be the production of the revelation of his Spirit of truth, of the Holy Ghost, and he is himself caught in the meshes of his own revelation and his whole teaching is reduced to nothing.

So that is why, after 1800 years, so strange a thing befell me as to have to discover the meaning of Christ's teaching as though it were something new.

[1] By the Councils of the Church. The expression first occurs in Acts xv. 28.—A.M.

I did not have to discover it, but I had to do what has been done and is being done by all who seek God and His law: to disentangle the eternal law of God from among all the other things people have called by that name.

VI

THE FIVE COMMANDMENTS

AND so when I understood Christ's law to be the law of Christ and not the law of Moses and Christ, and understood the statement of that law which directly disavows the law of Moses, the Gospels as a whole, instead of their former obscurity, disunion, and contradictoriness, disclosed themselves as one indivisible whole, and amid them the essence of the whole teaching became clear, expressed in the five simple, clear commandments of Christ, accessible to everyone (Matt. v. 21–48), but about which I had till then known nothing. Throughout the Gospels Christ's commandments and their fulfilment are spoken of.

All the theologians speak of Christ's commandments, but what those commandments were I formerly did not know. It seemed to me that the commands of Christ consisted in this: to love God, and my neighbour as myself. But I did not see that this could not be Christ's commandment, because it is a commandment of 'them of old time' (Deut. and Lev.). The words (Matt. v. 19) 'Whosoever shall break one of these least *commandments*, and shall teach men so, shall be called least in the kingdom of heaven', I attributed to the laws of Moses. And the fact that the new commandments of Christ are clearly and definitely expressed in verses 21–48 of Matt. v never entered my head. I did not see that where Christ says, 'It was said to you; but I say unto

you', new and definite commands of Christ are
given, namely, according to the number of references to the ancient law (and counting two references to adultery as one), five new, clear, and
definite commandments of Christ.

About the Beatitudes and their number I had
heard and had met with enumerations and explanations in Scripture lessons, but of Christ's commands
I had never heard anything. To my surprise I had
to discover them.

This is how I did so. In Matt. v. 21–6, it is said:
'Ye have heard that it was said by them of old time,
Thou shalt not kill [Exod. xx. 13], and whosoever
shall kill shall be in danger of the judgement. But
I say unto you, that whosoever is angry with his
brother without a cause shall be in danger of the
judgement: and whosoever shall say to his brother,
Raca, shall be in danger of the council; and whosoever shall say, Thou fool, shall be in danger of hell
fire. If therefore thou art offering thy gift at the
altar, and there rememberest that thy brother hath
aught against thee; leave there thy gift before the
altar and go thy way, first be reconciled to thy
brother, and then come and offer thy gift. Agree
with thine adversary quickly, whiles thou art in the
way with him; lest haply the adversary deliver thee
to the judge and the judge deliver thee to the officer,
and thou be cast into prison. Verily I say unto thee,
Thou shalt by no means come out thence, till thou
hast paid the uttermost farthing.'

When I understood the commandment of non-
resistance to him that is evil it seemed to me that
these verses about anger ought to have as clear a
meaning, and one as applicable to life, as the commandment about resisting him that is evil. The
meaning I had formerly attributed to those words
was that everyone should always avoid anger against

others and should never use words of abuse, but should live at peace with all men without exception; but there were words in the text which excluded that meaning. It was said: Do not be angry 'without a cause', so that no unconditional injunction to be peaceable is found in the words. Those words 'without a cause' perplexed me: and to solve my doubts I consulted the interpretations of the theologians, and to my amazement I found that the interpretations of the Fathers of the Church are chiefly directed to explaining when anger is excusable and when it is not excusable. All the Church interpretations lay particular stress on the meaning of the words *without a cause*, and explain the passage in the sense that one must not insult innocent people and one must not employ words of abuse, but that anger is not always unjustifiable; in confirmation of which view they quote the anger of saints and Apostles.

I could not but admit that, though it contradicts the whole sense of the Gospels, this explanation that anger, as they say, is not forbidden by the word of God, follows from and finds support in the words *without a cause*—which occur in verse 22. These words change the meaning of the whole utterance.

Be not angry *without a cause*. Christ bids us forgive all, forgive endlessly. He himself forgives, and forbids Peter to be angry with Malchus when Peter, not without cause it would seem, defended his Master who was being led to crucifixion. And this same Christ, for the instruction of all men, says: Do not be angry *without a cause*, and thereby sanctions anger with a cause—anger which is deserved. Christ preaches peace to all the plain folk and suddenly, as though explaining that this does not refer to all cases but that there are cases when one may be angry with one's brother, he inserts the words *without a cause.* In the interpretations it is explained that there is timely anger. But who, asked I, is to be judge of when anger is timely? I have never seen angry people who considered their anger untimely. They all consider their anger just and useful. Those words destroy the whole meaning of the verse. But the words stood in Holy Writ and I could not cancel them. Yet those words were as though to the saying, *Love thy neighbour* were added, *Love thy good neighbour*, or, *Love the neighbour whom thou approvest of*.

The whole meaning of the passage was destroyed for me by the words *without a cause*. The verses that said that before praying one must be reconciled to those who are angry with one, which without the words 'without a cause' would have had a plain and obligatory meaning, also acquired this conditional meaning.

It seemed to me that Christ should have forbidden all anger, all ill will, and for its elimination bidden everyone, before he brings his sacrifice—that is to say, before entering into communion with God —to remember whether there is not someone who is angry with him. And if there is anyone who rightfully or wrongfully is angry with you, you must first go and be reconciled, and only then bring your offering or your prayer. So it seemed to me; but according to the commentaries the passage must be understood conditionally.

In all the commentaries it is explained that one must try to be at peace with all, but if that is impossible owing to the depravity of those who are at strife with you, you must be at peace in your soul, in your thoughts, and then the enmity of the others against you need not prevent your praying. Besides this, the words that declare that whoso says 'Raca' and 'Thou fool' is terribly guilty always seemed to me strange and obscure. If one is forbidden to scold, why are such weak almost unabusive words selected as examples? And also why is so terrible a threat directed against him who lets fall such a weak word of abuse as 'Raca', which means 'a nobody'? This too is obscure.

I felt that there was a misunderstanding similar to that which occurred with reference to the words, 'judge not'. I felt that as in that interpretation so in this, what is simple, important, definite, and practicable is all changed into what is obscure and indefinite. I felt that Christ could not understand the words, 'Go, be reconciled to thine adversary', in the way they are explained to us, as meaning, 'Be reconciled in your thoughts'. What does being reconciled in one's thoughts mean? It seemed to me that Christ was demanding what he elsewhere expressed in the words of the prophets: 'I will have mercy and not sacrifice'—that is to say, love to man. And therefore if you wish to please God, before praying at morning and evening, at matins and evensong, remember whether anyone is angry with you and go and arrange matters so that he may not be angry with you, and after that pray if you please. And then we are told that this is only 'in thought'. I felt that the whole interpretation which destroyed for me the direct and clear meaning of the passage was based on the words 'without a cause'. If they were struck out the meaning would be clear; but against my interpretation all the expositors were ranged, as well as the canonical Gospel with the words, 'without a cause'. If I yield on this point I may as well yield on others at my fancy, and other people may do the same. The whole matter lay in those words. If they were not there all would be clear. And I tried to find some philological explanation of the words which would not infringe the whole meaning. I looked up the Greek word interpreted 'without a cause' in the dictionaries; and I saw that this word, in Greek εἰκῆ, means 'without purpose', 'inconsiderately'. I tried to give it a meaning which would not infringe the sense of the passage, but evidently the addition of that word has the meaning which is given it. I consulted other dictionaries, but the meaning given of the word was the same. I consulted the context and found that the word is employed only once in the Gospel, namely, in this passage. In the Epistles it is employed several times. In the First Epistle to the Corinthians, xv. 2, it is used just in this sense. Therefore it is impossible to explain it otherwise, and one has to admit that Christ said: *Do not be angry unnecessarily!* I must confess that for me to admit that Christ could in this passage use such obscure words, which can be understood so that nothing remains of their meaning, was tantamount to rejecting the whole Gospel. There remained one last hope: Is the word found in all the manuscripts? I looked up the manuscripts. I referred to Griesbach, who shows all the variations—that is to say, he shows in what manuscripts and by what Fathers of the Church an expression is used. I looked, and was at once thrown into an ecstasy by observing that to this passage there are remarks—there are variations. I went on and found that the variations all refer to the word εἰκῆ, 'without a cause'. Most of the manuscripts of the Gospel and the quotations of the passage in the Fathers of the Church do not contain the word at all! Therefore most of them understood the matter as I do. I then referred to Tischendorf—to the oldest text—and the word was not there at all! I looked at Luther's translations, where I might have got at the matter most quickly, and the word was not there either.

The very word which infringes the whole meaning of Christ's teaching was added to the Gospels in the fifth century and is not to be found in the best manuscripts.

Someone inserted the word, and there were others who approved of it and wrote commentaries upon it.

Christ could not and did not utter that dreadful word; and the first, simple, direct meaning of the whole passage, which occurred to me and occurs to everyone, is the true meaning.

But more than this, I had only to understand that Christ's words always forbid all anger against anyone whatever, for the injunction not to say to anyone, 'Raca', or 'Thou fool', which had formerly perplexed me, to receive another meaning than that Christ forbids the use of abusive words. The strange, untranslated Hebrew word, *Raca*, supplied me with the clue. *Raca* means trampled on, destroyed, non-existing; and the word *rak*, a very usual word, has the sense of exclusion, *only not*. *Raca* means a man who should not be accounted a man. In the plural the word *rekim* is used in the Book of Judges (ix. 4) where it means 'lost persons'. And that is the word Christ bids us not to use of any man. As he bids us not use another word, *fool*, so also he bids us not use *raca*, which professes to free us from our human obligations to our neighbour. We get angry and do evil to men, and to justify ourselves we say that he with whom we are angry is a lost or insane man. And just those two words Christ bids us not to use of men or to men. Christ bids us not be angry with anyone and not justify our anger by declaring a man to be lost or insane.

And so instead of a cloudy, indefinite expression admitting of arbitrary interpretation, in Matt. v. 21–8, I found Christ's first clear and definite commandment: Live at peace with all men and never consider your anger against any man justified. Do not consider anyone, or call anyone, lost or a fool (v. 22). And not only must you not consider your anger against another justifiable, but you must not consider another's anger against yourself causeless; and therefore if anyone is angry with you, though he be in the wrong, yet before saying your prayers go and remove his hostile feeling (v. 23, 24). Try in advance to destroy any enmity between yourself and others that it may not flame up and destroy you (v. 25, 26).

After the first commandment the second revealed itself to me with equal clearness. It also begins with a reference to the ancient law. In Matt. v. 27–30 it is said: 'You have heard that it was said by them of old time, Thou shalt not commit adultery [Exod. xx. 14]. But I say unto you, that whosoever looketh on a woman to lust after her hath committed adultery with her already in his heart. And if thy right eye causeth thee to stumble, pluck it out, and cast it from thee;[1] for it is profitable for thee that one of thy members should perish, and not thy whole body be cast into hell. But if thy right hand causeth thee to stumble, cut it off and cast it from thee: for it is profitable for thee that one of thy members should perish, and not thy whole body go into hell.'

Matt. v. 31–2: 'It was said also, Whosoever shall put away his wife, let him give her a writing of divorcement [Deut. xxiv. 1]. But I say unto you, everyone that putteth away his wife [besides the sin of adultery, gives her cause to commit adultery],

---

[1] Tolstóy sometimes carries his adherence to the letter of Christ's saying to an extreme, but in the case of this text it will be noticed that he does not agree with those Russian sectarians who rely on the surgical operation of castration as a desirable corrective of sexual desire.—A.M.

and whosoever shall marry her that is put away committeth adultery.'[1]

The meaning of these words appeared to me to be this: a man should not admit even the thought that he can have connexion with any woman but the one with whom he first has sexual relations,[2] and must never change her for another as was permitted by the Mosaic law.

As in the First Commandment against anger we are advised to extinguish anger at its commencement, advice that is illustrated by the comparison with a man brought before a court of justice, so here Christ says that adultery arises from the fact that women and men regard each other as objects of desire. That this may not be so it is necessary to remove all that might arouse lust. One must avoid all that evokes lust, and having once united oneself with a woman must under no circumstances abandon her, for the abandonment of wives causes depravity. The abandoned wives tempt other men and spread depravity abroad in the world.

The wisdom of this commandment impressed me. It removes all the evil that flows from sexual relations. Men and women, knowing indulgence in sexual relations to lead to strife, should avoid all that evokes desire; and, knowing it to be the law of man's nature to live in couples, should unite with one another in couples and never under any circumstances infringe these alliances; so that the

[1] It will be noticed that Tolstóy's translation of this passage, in the words inserted in square brackets, differs from our Authorized or Revised Versions and helps to make sense of the passage.—A.M.

[2] Note that this view was alluded to in *Anna Karénina* (vol. i, chap. xxiv), where the incident was borrowed from the actual life of Tolstóy's brother, Dmítry, who took a woman he had found in a brothel to live with him, and regarded her as a wife to whom he was bound for life.—A.M.

whole evil of strife caused by sexual relations is removed by the fact that there are no solitary men or women left deprived of married life.[1]

But the words which had always surprised me when reading the Sermon on the Mount, *except for the sin of adultery*, understood in the sense that a man may divorce his wife if she has committed adultery, now struck me yet more forcibly.

In addition to the fact that there is something undignified in the way of expressing this thought, putting this strange exception to the general rule (which is introduced like a note to a paragraph of a code of laws) beside profoundly important truths, the exception itself contradicts the fundamental thought.

I turned to the commentators, and they all (St. John Chrysostom and the others), and even the learned theological critics such as Reuss, admitted that these words meant that Christ sanctions divorce in case of a wife's adultery, and that in Matt. xix in Christ's remarks forbidding divorce, the words 'except for fornication' mean the same thing. I read and re-read chapter v. 32, and it seemed to me that it could not mean an approval of divorce. To verify this I referred to the contexts, and found in the Gospels of Matt. xix, Mark x, and Luke xvi, and

[1] Tolstóy delighted in absolute laws and was eager to attribute perfection and finality to those he formulated. But this law, of which he fully approved when he wrote this book in 1884, no longer satisfied him when in 1889 he wrote the *Kreutzer Sonata* and in the *Afterword* thereto expressed the opinion that man can best serve God and man by remaining celibate. The explanation of his change of view lay in the fact that his wife disagreed with his wish to renounce his property, and he found that his union with her, and even their affection for one another made it hard for him to adhere to his principles. Marriage was therefore an obstacle to right life, and as such, it seemed to him, should be shunned by a Christian.—A.M.

in the First Epistle of Paul to the Corinthians, an explanation of the teaching of marriage inviolability without any exceptions.[1]

In Luke xvi. 18 it is said: 'Every one that putteth away his wife, and marrieth another, committeth adultery: and he that marrieth one that is put away from a husband committeth adultery.'

In Mark x. 5–12 it is also said, without any exception: 'For your hardness of heart Moses wrote this commandment. But from the beginning of the creation, male and female made he them. For this cause shall a man leave his father and mother, and cleave unto his wife; and the twain shall become one flesh: so that they are no more twain, but one flesh. What therefore God hath joined together let no man put asunder. And in the house his disciples asked him again of this matter. And he said unto them, Whosoever shall put away his wife, and marry another, committeth adultery against her. And if she herself shall put away her husband, and be married to another, she committeth adultery.' The same is repeated in Matt. xix. 4–9.

In the First Epistle of Paul to the Corinthians, vii. 1–12, the idea of forestalling depravity by each husband and wife, when once they have united, not abandoning one another, but satisfying one another in sexual relations is developed. It is also plainly said that neither of them must on any account desert the other to have relations with someone else.

By Mark, Luke, and Paul's Epistle divorce is not sanctioned. The sense of the explanation that a husband and a wife are one flesh, united by God—

---

[1] At a time when Parliament has to deal with the marriage laws, it is in place to remember that Tolstóy wrote solely of what he considered to be Christian duty, entirely apart from legal enactment or Church ceremony of any kind. He disapproved of legal interference with the right of man or woman to form or rescind unions with one another.—A.M.

an explanation repeated in two of the Gospels—does not sanction divorce. By Christ's whole teaching which bids us forgive all and makes no exception in the case of an unfaithful wife, divorce is not sanctioned. The meaning of the whole passage, which explains that the dismissal of a wife is the cause of depravity, gives it no sanction.

On what is the interpretation based which sanctions divorce from an adulterous wife? Only on the words in Matt. v. 32, which seemed to me so strange. They are interpreted by everyone to mean that Christ sanctions divorce if a wife commits adultery, and these same words are repeated in many of the copies of the Gospels and by many Fathers of the Church instead of the words *except for fornication* (Matt. xix. 5–9).

Again I began to consider these words, but it was long before I could understand them. I saw that there must be a mistake in translation and interpretation, but where the mistake lay I was long unable to discover. The mistake was evident. Contrasting his commandment with the law of Moses under which any man, as is there said, who hates his wife, can dismiss her and give her a writing of divorcement, Christ says: '*But I say unto you, that everyone that putteth away his wife, saving for the cause of fornication* [or, *besides the cause of fornication*], *causeth her to commit adultery.*' These words present no antithesis to the Mosaic law, nor even any decision as to whether one may, or may not, divorce. It is only said that putting away a wife gives her occasion to commit adultery.

And then suddenly an exception is made in the case of a wife guilty of adultery. This exception concerning a wife guilty of adultery when the matter in hand related to the husband, would in any case be strange and unexpected, and occurring

where it does it is simply stupid, for it destroys even
such doubtful meaning as the verse otherwise had.
It is said that putting away a wife occasions her to
commit adultery, and it then allows you to put away
a wife guilty of adultery; as though a wife guilty of
adultery will then no longer commit adultery.

But, more than that, when I examined this
passage more carefully I noticed that it does not
even make sense grammatically. It is said that
*everyone that putteth away his wife, saving for the cause of
fornication, causeth her to commit adultery*, and the
sentence ends! It refers to a man, and says that
if he puts away his wife he gives her occasion to
commit adultery. Why is it said, *saving for the cause
of the wife's adultery*? If it were said that a man
divorcing his wife for any cause except her com-
mission of adultery, commits adultery, then the
sentence would be correct. As it is, to the grammatical subject *everyone that putteth away*, there is no
predicate except *causeth*. How can that predicate
relate to the words *saving for the cause of fornication*?
It is impossible to 'cause, saving for the wife's
fornication'! Even if with the words 'saving for the
cause of fornication' were included the words 'the
wife's', or 'her' (which is not done), even then those
words could not relate to the predicate 'causeth'.
These words in the accepted interpretation are
related to the predicate, *putteth away*, but *putteth
away* is not the chief predicate: the chief predicate is
causeth. Why is 'except for the cause of fornication'
wanted? With adultery or without it a husband
who puts away his wife equally *causeth*. The expression reads as though someone were to say:
'Whoso depriveth his son of food, except for [or
besides] the sin of cruelty, causeth him to be cruel.'
Such an expression evidently cannot imply that the
father may deprive his son of food if the son is cruel.

If it has any meaning it can only be that the father who deprives his son of food, besides the sin of being cruel himself, causes the son too to be cruel. So the Gospel expression would have a meaning if, instead of the words *the sin of fornication*, it read 'the sin of voluptuousness, dissoluteness,[1] or anything of that kind, expressing not an action but a quality.

And I asked myself: Is it not simply said that he who puts away his wife, besides being himself guilty of dissoluteness (since people divorce one wife in order to take another), causes his wife also to commit adultery? If the word 'fornication' in the text is expressed by a word that may also mean dissoluteness, the meaning is clear.

What has so often happened in such cases occurred again this time. The text confirmed my supposition so that no further doubt about it was possible.

The first thing that caught my eye on looking at the Greek text was that the word πορνεία is

[1] Tolstóy's indictment of the received translation of various passages in the Gospels has had considerable circulation, and by many readers is accepted as authoritative. As yet, so far as the present translator knows, no prominent Churchman has either admitted any of the alleged errors or produced any reasoned rejoinder to Tolstóy's assertions. A pronouncement on these matters from some recognized and impartial authority of admitted competence would therefore be valuable as a help towards clearing up questions which are as important as they are doubtful.

The only contribution the present translator can make to the matter is to record the fact that, some fifteen years after *What I Believe* was written, he asked Tolstóy whether he still held to the interpretations he had advanced when dealing with the Gospels. Tolstóy replied that he had ceased to attach special importance to precise words attributed to Jesus, and admitted that in his anxiety to counteract the bias he detected in the 'Orthodox' translation, he had sometimes overstrained the sense too much in a contrary direction, as one engaged on demagnetizing a watch may sometimes expose it to too strong an opposite influence; but he thought his Greek reliable.—A.M.

translated by the same word 'fornication' that is used to translate the word μοιχᾶσθαι, which is quite a different word. But perhaps these words are synonymous, or are used in the Gospels alternatively? I looked up all the dictionaries, both the general dictionary and the Gospel dictionary, and I saw that the word πορνεία, which corresponds to the Hebrew *zono*, and to the Latin *fornicatio*, the German *Hurerei*, French *libertinage*, and the English 'incontinence', has a most definite meaning, and never in any dictionary has meant or can mean the act of fornication, *adultère*, *Ehebruch*, as it is translated. It means a sinful condition or quality, and never an action, and should not be translated by 'fornication'. Moreover, I see that the word 'adultery', and 'to commit adultery', is everywhere in the Gospels, and even in these verses, represented by the word μοιχάω. And I only had to correct this evidently intentional error in translation for the meaning given by the commentators on this passage and on the passage in chap. xix to become quite impossible, and for it to become indubitable that πορνεία relates to the husband.

The translation anyone knowing Greek would make is this: παρεκτός—besides, λόγου—the guilt, πορνείας—of dissoluteness, ποιεῖ—causes, αὐτήν—her, μοιχᾶσθαι—to commit adultery; and the result is, word for word: 'he who puts away his wife, besides the sin of dissoluteness, causes her to commit adultery.'

The same sense is found in ch. xix. One need but correct the erroneous translation of the word πορνεία, and replace the word 'fornication' by the word 'dissoluteness', for it to become plain that the words: εἰ μὴ ἐπὶ πορνείᾳ cannot refer to the wife. And as the words παρεκτὸς λόγου πορνείας can only mean 'besides the husband's sin of dissoluteness', so the words εἰ μὴ ἐπὶ πορνείᾳ in ch. xix can only refer to the husband's dissoluteness. The words are—εἰ μὴ ἐπὶ πορνείᾳ, word for word: 'if not from dissoluteness.' And this meaning appears: that Christ, replying in this passage to the belief of the Pharisees, who supposed that if a man left his wife, not to live dissolutely but in order to marry another woman, he was not committing adultery—Christ says that the leaving of one's wife, i.e. the cessation of marital relations with her, even if not occasioned by dissoluteness, but done for the sake of marriage-union with another, is also adultery. And a plain meaning results which accords with the whole teaching, with the context, with the grammar, and with logic.

And this clear and simple meaning, flowing from the words themselves and from the whole teaching, I had to discover with the greatest difficulty. Indeed, read the verse in German or in French, where it is plainly said *pour cause d'infidélité*, and, *à moins que cela ne soit pour cause d'infidélité*, and can you guess that it means something quite different? The word παρεκτός, which in all the dictionaries means *excepté, ausgenommen, besides*, is translated by a whole sentence—*à moins que cela ne soit*; the word πορνείας is translated *infidélité, Ehebruch*, fornication. And on this intentional perversion of the text rests an interpretation which infringes the moral, religious, grammatical, and logical sense of Christ's words.

Again I was confirmed in the terrible but joyful truth that the meaning of Christ's teaching is plain and simple and its statements are important, but that interpretations of it, based on a wish to justify existing evil, have so obscured it that it has to be rediscovered with difficulty. It became plain to me that if the Gospels had been discovered half burnt or obliterated it would have been easier to recover their meaning than it is now, when dishonest interpretations have been applied to them with the direct purpose of perverting and hiding the meaning of the teaching. In this case it was still plainer than in the former that some private aim of justifying the divorce of some Iván the Terrible had been the reason for obscuring the whole doctrine of marriage.

As soon as one rejects the commentaries, in place of what was obscure and indefinite the definite and clear second commandment of Christ reveals itself.

Do not make the desire for sexual relations into an amusement; let every man, if he is not a eunuch —that is, if he needs sexual relations—have a wife, and each wife a husband, and let the husband have only *one* wife and the wife only *one* husband, and under no pretext infringe the sexual union of one with the other.

Immediately after the second commandment comes again a reference to the ancient law, and the third commandment is set forth (Matt. v. 33–7): 'Again, ye have heard that it hath been said by them of old time, Thou shalt not forswear thyself, but shalt perform unto the Lord thine oaths [Lev. xix. 12; Deut. xxiii. 21]: but I say unto you, Swear not at all; neither by heaven, for it is God's throne: nor by the earth; for it is his footstool: neither by Jerusalem; for it is the city of the great King. Neither shalt thou swear by thy head, because thou canst not make one hair white or black. But your speech shall be, Yea, yea; Nay, nay: for whatsoever is more than these is of the evil one.'

This passage when I had read it before had always perplexed me. It did so, not by its obscurity (as did the passage about divorce), nor by contradicting other passages (as did the sanction of anger with a cause), nor by the difficulty of fulfilling it (as with the passage about offering the other cheek); on the contrary, it perplexed me by its clearness, simplicity, and ease. Side by side with rules the profundity and importance of which terrified and touched me, one suddenly found such an unnecessary, empty, easy rule, which was of no consequence to me or to others. As it was, I swore neither by Jerusalem, nor by God, nor by anything else, and it cost me no effort to abstain: besides which it seemed to me that whether I swore or not could have no importance to anyone. And wishing to find an explanation of this rule which perplexed me by its ease, I turned to the interpreters; and this time the interpreters really helped me.

They all see in these words a confirmation of the third commandment of Moses—not to swear by the name of God. They explain these words to mean that Christ, like Moses, forbids us to pronounce God's name in vain. But besides this the interpreters also explain that this law of Christ's—not to swear—is not always obligatory and does not relate at all to an oath of loyalty which each citizen gives to those who hold authority;[1] and texts are selected from Holy Writ not to confirm the direct meaning of Christ's injunction, but to prove that it may and should be disobeyed.

It is said that Christ himself confirmed an oath in a court of law when in reply to the High Priest's words, 'I adjure thee by the living God', he replied, 'Thou hast said'. It is said that the apostle Paul called God to witness the truth of his words, which is evidently the same as an oath; it is said that oaths were enjoined by the law of Moses and that

[1] A reason Tolstóy ignores for forbidding oaths is, that as the belief (common in primitive times) that men can stake their lives or possessions on the veracity of their assertions and that the deity will enforce the penalties should the oath be a false one, fades away, the use of such oaths becomes incompatible with intellectual integrity, and therefore fails to accomplish its object and even conflicts with it.—A.M.

God did not abolish these oaths; it is said that it is only vain, pharisaical, hypocritical oaths that are abolished.

And on understanding the meaning and aim of these explanations I understood that Christ's injunction concerning oaths is not at all so insignificant, easy, and unimportant as it had seemed to me when, among the oaths prohibited by Christ, I had not included oaths demanded by the State.

And I asked myself: Is it not said here that the oath is also forbidden for which the Church commentators are so anxious to make an exception? Is not the oath here forbidden, that very oath without which the separation of men into nations is impossible and without which a military class is impossible? Soldiers are those who do all the violence, and they call themselves 'the sworn'.[1] Were I to ask the Grenadier how he solves the contradiction between the Gospels and the military code he would tell me that he has been sworn in: that is to say, has taken an oath on the Gospels. Such replies have always been given me by military men. So necessary is an oath for the organization of the terrible evil which is produced by violence and war, that in France, where Christianity is officially rejected, the oath is nevertheless retained. Indeed if Christ had not said 'Swear not at all', he ought to have said it. He came to destroy evil, and had he not abolished the oath this enormous evil would have remained in the world. Perhaps it will be said that in the time of Christ that evil was not noticeable. But this is untrue: Epictetus and Seneca spoke about not taking an oath to anyone; in the laws of Manu

---

[1] In Russian literally 'the oath'. The equivalent English expressions, 'volunteers' or 'conscripts', do not carry the same significance, though in England they also take an oath of allegiance.—A.M.

that rule is found. Why should I say that Christ did not see this evil? And especially when he said this so directly, clearly, and even minutely.

He said: *Swear not at all.* That expression is as simple, clear, and indubitable as the words 'Judge not and condemn not' and as little susceptible of misinterpretation, especially as it is added in conclusion, that anything demanded of you beyond *yes* and *no* comes from the source of evil.

Really, if Christ's teaching is that one should always obey the will of God, how can a man swear to obey the will of man? The will of God may not coincide with the will of man. Indeed, in this very passage Christ says that very thing. He says, Swear not by thy head, for not only thy head but every hair of it, is in God's power. The same is said in the Epistle of James.

At the end of his Epistle, in conclusion, the Apostle James says (ch. v. 12): *But above all things, my brethren, swear not, neither by the heaven, nor by the earth, nor by any other oath: but let your yea be yea, and your nay, nay; that ye fall not under judgement.* The Apostle says plainly why one should not swear: the oath by itself appears innocent, but from it people fall under judgement, and therefore *swear not at all.* How could what is said both by Christ and by the Apostle be said more plainly?

But I had been so entangled that I long asked myself in astonishment: Can it be that it means what it does mean? How is it that we are all made to swear on the Gospels? It is impossible!

But I had already read the commentators and had seen how this impossibility was accomplished.

As with the explanations of the words, Judge not, do not be angry with anybody, do not break the bond of husband and wife, so also here. We have established our ways of life, we like them and wish to consider them sacred. Then comes Christ, whom we consider to be God, but we do not wish to abandon our ways of life. What are we to do? Where possible, slip in the words *without a cause*, and reduce the rule against anger to nothing; where possible, like the most unscrupulous of unjust judges, interpret the meaning of the articles of the law so as to make it mean the very reverse, and that instead of a command never to divorce one's wife it should mean that one may divorce her. And where, as in the case of the words *Judge not, and condemn not, and swear not at all*, it is quite impossible to misinterpret, act boldly and directly contrary to the teaching, affirming that we are obeying it. Indeed the chief obstacle to understanding that the Gospels forbid every vow, and especially every oath of allegiance, is that pseudo-Christian teachers with extraordinary effrontery oblige men, on the Gospels themselves, to swear by the Gospels—that is to say, oblige them to do what is contrary to the Gospels.

How can it occur to a man who is obliged to swear on a cross, or on the Gospels, that the cross is sacred because on it he was crucified who forbade us to swear, and that when taking an oath one perhaps kisses, as what is sacred, the very place[1] in the book where it clearly and definitely says: *Swear not at all*.

But this effrontery no longer disconcerted me. I saw clearly that in Matt. v, verses 33 to 37, a definite and practicable third commandment is clearly expressed: Never take an oath to anyone, anywhere, about anything. Every oath is extorted for evil ends. Following this third commandment comes a fourth reference and a fourth commandment (Matt. v. 38–42; Luke vi. 29, 30): 'Ye have

[1] In Russian Courts the oath was administered on the open Gospels.—A.M.

heard that it was said, An eye for an eye, and a tooth for a tooth: but I say unto you, Resist not him that is evil: but whosoever smiteth thee on thy right cheek, turn to him the other also. And if any man would go to law with thee, and take away thy coat, let him have thy cloak also. And whosoever shall compel thee to go one mile, go with him twain.[1] Give to him that asketh thee, and from him that would borrow of thee turn not thou away.'

I have already spoken of the direct and definite meaning of these words and of the fact that we have no right to give them an allegorical interpretation. The commentaries on these words, from St. John Chrysostom's till to-day, are truly amazing. These words please everybody, and in references to them they make all kinds of profound conjectures, excepting one only, namely, that the words have their plain meaning. The Church commentators, not at all embarrassed by the authority of him whom they call God, most calmly restrict the meaning of his words. They say: 'It is, of course, understood that all these commandments about enduring wrongs, about renouncing revenge, are in fact directed against the Jewish spirit of relentlessness, and do not prohibit either public measures for restricting evil and *punishing evil-doers*, or the private, personal exertions and efforts of each individual to maintain the inviolability of his rights, to correct wrong-doers, and to deprive ill-intentioned men of the possibility of harming others; for otherwise the

[1] If Christ wished to lay down that it is wrong ever to use physical force to prevent any man from doing what he wishes to do (and that is the rule Tolstóy deduces) it is curious that he gives here an illustration of going two miles with a man who demands that you accompany him one; for, with regard to the second mile, there is clearly no reference to the use of physical force, any more than in the following example of lending to him who asks.—A.M.

spiritual laws of the Saviour would themselves in the Jewish way become mere words, and might serve to promote the success of evil and the suppression of virtue. A Christian's love should be like God's love; but the divine love refrains from limiting and punishing evil only so long as it remains within limits more or less innocuous to God's glory and to the safety of one's neighbours; in the contrary case evil should be limited and punished, a duty which is specially incumbent on the Government.' (The *Annotated Gospel* of the Archimandrite Michael, which is all based on the commentaries of the Fathers of the Church.) The learned and free-thinking Christians are also not embarrassed by the meaning of Christ's words and correct him. They say that this is a very lofty saying, but one lacking in any possible application to life; for an application to life of the law of non-resistance to evil destroys the whole order of life which we have so admirably arranged: so say Renan, Strauss, and all the free-thinking commentators.

But one need only take the words of Christ as we take those of the first man we meet and who speaks to us—that is to say, assume that he means what he says—to do away with the necessity for any profound conjectures. Christ says: I consider that your method of securing your life is stupid and bad. I propose to you quite another method, as follows. And he speaks the words given in Matt. v. 38-42. It would seem that before correcting those words one should understand them. But that is just what no one wishes to do, having decided in advance that the order of our life which is infringed by those words is a sacred law of humanity.

I did not consider our life either good or sacred, and therefore understood that commandment sooner than other people. And when I had understood the words as they are spoken, I was amazed by their truth, exactitude and clarity. Christ says: 'You wish to destroy evil by evil. That is unreasonable. That there should be no evil, do none.' And then he enumerates the cases in which we are accustomed to do evil, and says that in these cases it should not be done.

This fourth commandment of Christ was the first I understood, and it was the one which disclosed to me the meaning of all the others. This fourth, simple, clear, practicable commandment says: Never resist the evil-doer by force, do not meet violence with violence. If they beat you, endure it; if they take your possessions, yield them up; if they compel you to work, work; and if they wish to take from you what you consider to be yours, give it up.

And following that fourth commandment comes a fifth reference to the old law, and the fifth commandment (Matt. v. 43–8): 'Ye have heard that it was said, Thou shalt love thy neighbour, and hate thine enemy [Lev. xix. 17, 18]: but I say unto you, Love your enemies, bless them that curse you, do good to them that hate you, and pray for them which despitefully use you, and persecute you; that ye may be sons of your Father which is in heaven: for he maketh his sun to rise on the evil and the good, and sendeth rain on the just and the unjust. For if ye love them that love you, what reward have ye? do not even the publicans the same? And if ye salute your brethren only, what do ye more than others? do not even the *Gentiles* the same? Ye therefore shall be perfect, as your heavenly Father is perfect.'

Those verses formerly seemed to me to be an explanation, completion, and enforcement—I would even say an exaggeration—of the precept about not resisting the evil-doer. But having found a simple, applicable, and definite meaning in each passage that began with a reference to the ancient law, I anticipated that the same would be the case here. After each quotation a law was announced, and each verse of the commandment had a meaning and could not be omitted, and so it should be here also. The concluding words, repeated by Luke, that God does not make distinctions between people but sends His blessings upon all, and that you therefore should be like God, not making distinctions between people, and should not do as the Gentiles do, but should love all men and do good to all alike— those words were clear, and they appeared to me to be like a confirmation and explanation of some definite rule; but what that rule was it was long before I could discern.

To love one's enemies. That seemed impossible. It was one of those beautiful phrases which can only be regarded as indications of an unattainable moral ideal. It was either too much, or nothing at all. One could abstain from injuring an enemy, but to love him was impossible. Christ could not prescribe an impossibility. Besides that, the very first words, the reference to the ancient law, 'Ye have heard that it was said: *Thou shalt hate thine enemy*', were questionable. In previous passages Christ quotes the actual, precise words of the Mosaic law, but here he uses words which had never been uttered. He appears to misrepresent the law.

As in the case of my former perplexities, the commentaries on the Gospels explained nothing to me. They all admit that the words, 'Thou shalt hate thine enemy', do not occur in the Mosaic law, but no explanation of this incorrect citation is given. They speak of the difficulty of loving enemies and bad people; and in most cases they correct Christ's words and say it is impossible to love one's enemies, but possible not to wish them evil or to do them harm; incidentally it is suggested that one may and should expose, that is to say oppose, one's enemies; mention is made of various degrees of attainability of this virtue, so that the ultimate deduction to be made from the Church commentaries is that Christ, for some unknown reason, made an incorrect citation of the Mosaic law and uttered many beautiful, but really empty and inapplicable, words.

It seemed to me that this was unsatisfactory. There should be some clear and definite meaning here, as in the first four commandments. And to understand this meaning I first of all tried to understand the meaning of the incorrect citation from the law: *hate your enemies*. It is not for nothing that Christ, before each of his injunctions, quoted the words of the law: 'Thou shalt not kill, shalt not commit adultery', &c., and contrasted those words with his own doctrine. Without understanding what was alluded to in the words he cites from the old law one cannot understand what he enjoined. In the commentaries it is plainly said, what cannot but be admitted, that he cites words which are not found in the law; but it is not explained why he did so, nor what this incorrect citation means. It seemed to me that one had first to explain what Christ may have meant when he cited those words which do not occur in the law. And I asked myself: What can the words mean which Christ has incorrectly quoted from the Mosaic law? In all his former citations of the law only one precept of the ancient law is quoted, as: 'Thou shalt not kill; Thou shalt not commit adultery; Thou shalt not forswear thyself; A tooth for a tooth.' And in connexion with that single precept Christ's corresponding doctrine is announced. Here, however, two precepts are cited and contrasted one with the other; 'Ye have heard that it was said, Thou shalt love thy neighbour, and hate thine enemy', so that evidently the basis of the new law should deal with the difference between the two injunctions of the ancient law in reference to neighbours and enemies. And to understand more clearly wherein that difference lay, I asked myself: What do the words 'neighbour' and 'enemy' mean in Gospel language? And, on consulting the dictionaries and concordances of the Bible, I convinced myself that 'neighbour', when used by a Jew, always meant, and only meant, a Jew. That meaning of 'neighbour' is found also in the Gospel parable of the Good Samaritan. According to the view of the Jewish lawyer who asked 'Who is my neighbour?' a Samaritan could not be a neighbour. A similar definition of 'neighbour' is given in Acts vii. 27. 'Neighbour', in the language of the Gospels, means fellow-countryman, a man of one's own people. Therefore, surmising that the contrast Christ is setting up in this passage by citing the words of the law, 'Ye have heard that it was said, Thou shalt love thy neighbour and hate thine enemy', lies in the contrast of fellow-countrymen with foreigners, I asked myself what was an 'enemy' in the Jewish conception, and I found confirmation of my conjecture. The word 'enemy' is used in the Gospels almost always in the sense not of a personal foe but of a public, national enemy (Luke i. 71–4; Matt. xxii. 44; Mark xii. 36; Luke xx. 43, &c.). The singular number used for the word 'enemy' in these verses, in the phrase 'hate thine enemy', indicated to me that the national enemy is referred to. The singular number refers to the collective whole of the enemy people. In the Old Testament the conception of a hostile people is always expressed in the singular.

And as soon as I understood this the difficulty was immediately removed as to why and how

Christ, after previously always quoting the precise words of the law, could here cite words which had never been uttered. I had only to understand the word 'enemy' in the sense of national enemy, and 'neighbour' in the sense of compatriot, for that difficulty to disappear. Christ speaks of how, in the Mosaic law, the Jews were told to treat their national enemy. All those passages, scattered through different books of the Bible, in which they are bidden to oppress, slay, and exterminate other tribes, Christ sums up in the one expression, to 'hate' —to harm—the enemy. And he says: Ye have heard that it was said that you should love your own people and hate your nation's enemy, but I say to you that you should love all men without discrimination of the race to which they belong. And as soon as I understood the words in this way the other and chief difficulty was disposed of, as to how one should understand the words, 'love your enemies'. It is impossible to love one's personal enemies. But one can love a hostile people in the same way that one does one's own. And it became plain to me that Christ is speaking of the fact that everyone is taught to consider the people of his own race as his 'neighbours' and to consider other nations as 'enemies', but that he bids us not to do so. He says: The law of Moses makes a distinction between Jews and Gentiles, the national enemy, but I say unto you, that you should not make that distinction. And in fact both in Matthew and Luke, following this commandment, he says that before God all men are equal; the sun rises and the rain falls for them all. God does not distinguish between the peoples, but does good to all alike; so should men also do to all without distinction of nationality, and not as the Gentiles who divide themselves into different nations.

So that, once again, from different sides a plain, important, clear, and applicable meaning of Christ's words confirmed itself for me. Again, instead of misty expressions of vague philosophy, a clear, definite, important, and practicable rule discloses itself: not to make distinctions between one's own and other nations and not to do all the things that flow from making such distinctions; not to bear enmity to foreign nations; not to make war or to take part in warfare; not to arm oneself for war, but to behave to all men, of whatever race they may be, as we behave to our own people.

This was all so clear and simple that I was astonished I had not understood it immediately.

The cause of my not having understood it was the same as the cause of my not having promptly understood the prohibition of law-courts and of oaths. It was very difficult to understand that those courts—which are opened with a religious cere- mony and blessed by those who consider them- selves the guardians of Christ's teaching—that those same courts are incompatible with a confession of Christ, being directly opposed to him. Yet more difficult was it to guess that the very oath ad- ministered to all men by the guardians of the law of Christ is directly prohibited by that law; but to guess that what in our life are considered not merely necessary and natural but most excellent and brave —the love of one's fatherland, its defence, its exaltation, resistance to its enemies, and so forth— are not merely offences against the law of Christ but a plain repudiation of it—to guess that this is so, was very difficult. Our life has so diverged from the teaching of Christ that that very divergence has become the chief hindrance to our understanding his teaching. We have so disregarded and for- gotten all he said about our way of life—his injunction not merely not to kill, but not even to hate any man; not to defend ourselves but to turn the other cheek and to love our enemies—that now, being accustomed to call people who devote their lives to killing, 'the Christ-loving army',[1] being accustomed to hear prayers addressed to Christ for victory over our enemies, to pride ourselves on slaying, and having made of the sword a holy symbol of murder (until a man without a sword, without a dagger, is a man to be held in contempt) —it now seems to us that Christ did not forbid war and that if he had forbidden it he would have said so more explicitly

We forget that Christ could not imagine people believing in his teaching of humility, love, and universal brotherhood, quietly and deliberately organizing the murder of their fellow men.

Christ could not imagine that, and therefore did not forbid Christians to go to war, any more than a father when giving his son instructions to live honestly, to wrong no one, and to give to others, would bid him abstain from highway robbery. No one of the apostles or disciples of Christ during the first centuries of Christianity could imagine that it was necessary to forbid Christians to commit the murders that are called war. This, for instance, is what Origen says in his reply to Celsus (*The Writings of Origen: Origen contra Celsum*, Lib. viii. c. 73. Ante-Nicene Christian Library, vol. xviii.)

He says: 'And in the next place Celsus urges us to help the King with all our might, and to labour with him in the maintenance of justice, to fight for him; and if he requires it to fight under him, or lead an army along with him. To this our answer is, that we do when occasion requires, give help to Kings,

[1] Or, if that Russian expression sounds strange to English ears, we might call it 'the Christian army'.—A.M.

and that, so to say, a divine help, "putting on the whole armour of God". And this we do in obedience to the injunction of the Apostle, "I exhort, therefore, that first of all, supplications, prayers, intercessions, giving of thanks, be made for all men; for Kings and all that are in authority", and the more any one excels in piety, the more effective help does he render to Kings, even more than is given by soldiers who go forth to fight and slay as many of the enemy as they can. And to those enemies of our faith who require us to bear arms for the commonwealth, and to slay men, we reply: "Do not those who are priests at certain shrines, and those who attend on certain gods, as you account them, keep their hands free from blood that they may with hands unstained and free from human blood offer the appointed sacrifices to your gods?" '

And, finishing this chapter with an explanation that Christians are of more use by their peaceful life than are soldiers, Origen says: 'And none fight better for the King than we do. *We do not indeed fight under him, although he require it.*'

Such was the attitude of the Christians of the first centuries towards war, and so did their teachers speak when addressing those who ruled the world; and they spoke so when hundreds and thousands of martyrs were perishing for professing the Christian faith.

And now? Now no question is asked as to whether a Christian can take part in war. All young men, educated in the teaching of the Church which is called Christian, when the time comes each autumn present themselves at the Army Office and, with the assistance of Church pastors, violate the law of Christ. Only recently one peasant turned up who on Gospel grounds refused military service. The teachers of the Church expounded to him his error;

but, as the peasant believed not them but Christ, he was put into prison and kept there till he renounced Christ. And all this is done 1800 years after a quite clear and definite commandment was announced to Christians by our God: Do not consider the people of other nations to be enemies, but account all men as brothers and treat them as you treat people of your own nation: and therefore, not only do not kill those whom you call your enemies, but love them and do good to them.

And having so understood these very simple, definite commands of Christ, not subjected to any interpretation, I asked myself: How would it be if the Christian world believed in these commandments not in the sense that they must be sung or read for the propitiation of God, but that they must be obeyed for the welfare of man? How would it be if people believed in the duty of keeping these commandments as firmly as they believe, for instance, that one must say one's prayers every day, go to Church every Sunday, avoid flesh food on Fridays, and fast every Lent? How would it be if people believed these commandments even as much as they believe in the demands made by the Church? And I pictured to myself the whole of Christendom living and educating the young according to these commandments. I pictured to myself that it was inculcated on us all and on our children from childhood upwards, by word and by example—not as now, that a man must maintain his dignity and preserve his rights against others (which can only be done by humiliating and offending others), but that it was taught that no man has any rights or can be superior or inferior to another, and that he only is inferior to all and most ignoble who desires to set himself above others; that there is no more humiliating condition for a man than that of being angry with another; and that my conviction that someone is insignificant or mad cannot justify my anger against him or my strife with him. Instead of all the arrangements of our life, from the shop-windows to the theatres, novels, and women's dresses, which excite sexual desire, I imagined to myself that it was suggested to us and to our children by word and deed, that to amuse oneself with voluptuous books, theatres, and balls, is the basest kind of amusement, and that every act which has for its aim to *adorn or show off* the body is the very basest and most shameful of acts. Instead of the organization of our life, in which it is considered necessary and good that a young man should be dissolute until he marries, and instead of a way of life that separates married couples being considered most natural; instead of the legalization of a class of women set apart for the service of depravity; instead of the admission of and the sanctification of divorce—instead of all this, I imagined to myself that it was instilled into us by word and deed that the condition of a man who has reached the age for sexual relations and has not renounced them but yet remains single and unmarried, is an abnormity and a shame, and that a man's desertion of her with whom he has come together and the exchanging of her for another, is not only an unnatural action, like incest, but is a cruel, inhuman action. Instead of our whole life being founded on violence, instead of each of us being punished or punishing from childhood to advanced old age, I imagined to myself that it was instilled into us all by word and deed that revenge is a most degrading animal feeling, and that violence is not merely a shameful thing but one which deprives a man of true happiness, and that the only happiness of life is such as need not be defended by violence and that the highest respect is deserved, not by him who takes or retains what is his from others, but by him who gives up the most and serves others most. Instead of it being considered admirable and right that each man should be sworn in and should surrender all that he holds most valuable—that is to say, his whole life—to the will of he knows not whom, I imagined that it was instilled into all that man's reasonable will is that highest sanctuary which he may yield to no one else, and that to bind oneself by oath to anyone, and about anything, is a repudiation of one's rational being and a defilement of that highest sanctuary. I pictured to myself that instead of these national enmities which are instilled into us under the guise of love of one's country, and instead of those applauded slaughters called war, which from childhood are represented to us as the most heroic deeds—I imagined that we were imbued with horror at and contempt for all those activities, political, diplomatic, and military, which promote the separation of peoples; and that it was suggested to us that the recognition of any kingdoms, exclusive laws, frontiers, or territories is an indication of most savage ignorance; and that to go to war—that is to say, to kill people, people personally unknown to us, without any grounds—is the most horrible villainy, to which only a lost and perverted man, degraded to the level of a beast, can descend. I pictured to myself that all men believed this, and I asked: What would be the result?

Formerly I had asked myself what would result from putting Christ's teaching, as I then understood it, into practice, and had involuntarily replied: Nothing. We shall all pray, receive the blessings of the sacraments, believe in the redemption and in salvation for ourselves and for the whole world through Christ, and nevertheless that salvation will come about not from what we do, but because the end of the world will arrive. Christ will come in his own time, in glory, to judge the living and the dead and establish the kingdom of God, independently of our life. Now Christ's teaching as it had revealed itself to me had another meaning, and the establishment of the kingdom of God on earth depended on us also. The fulfilment of Christ's teaching expressed in the five commandments, would establish the kingdom of God. The kingdom of God on earth is the peace of all men one with another. Peace among men is the highest blessing attainable by man on earth. So did the kingdom of God present itself to all the Hebrew prophets. And so has it presented itself, and does present itself, to the heart of every man. All the prophecies promise peace to mankind.

The whole of Christ's teaching consists in giving the kingdom of God, that is peace, to man. In the Sermon on the Mount, in the talk with Nicodemus, in his charge to his disciples, and in all his sermons, Christ speaks only of the things that divide men and hinder them from being at peace and entering the kingdom of God. All the parables are but a description of what the kingdom of God is and an explanation that only by loving one's brother-men and being at peace with them can one enter it. John the Baptist, Christ's forerunner, said that the kingdom of God was drawing near and that Jesus Christ would give it to the world.

Christ says that he brought peace on earth (John xiv. 27): 'Peace I leave with you; my peace I give unto you: not as the world giveth, give I unto you. Let not your heart be troubled, neither let it be fearful.'

And those five commandments of his really give man this peace. All five commandments have but that one aim—peace among men. Men need only trust Christ's teaching and obey it and there will be peace on earth; and not such a peace as men devise, temporary, accidental, and partial, but a general peace, inviolable and eternal.

The first commandment says: Be at peace with all men; do not allow yourself to consider any man insignificant or senseless (Matt. v. 22). If peace be infringed, employ all your strength to restore it. The service of God is the abolition of enmity (Matt. v. 23, 24). Be reconciled after the least difference, in order not to lose the true life. In this commandment everything is said; but Christ foresees the snares of the world which disturb peace among men, and he gives the second commandment, against the snare of sexual relations, which disturb peace. Do not regard the beauty of the flesh as an amusement; avoid this snare in advance (verses 28–30); let a man take one wife and a woman one husband and on no account abandon one another (32). Another snare is the oath, which leads men into sin. Know in advance that this is evil, and take no vows (34–7). The third snare is revenge, calling itself human justice. Do not avenge yourself, and do not excuse yourself on the ground that you are wronged; bear with wrongs and do not return evil for evil (38–42). The fourth snare is the difference of nationalities— the enmity of tribes and states. Know that all men are brothers, sons of one God, and do not infringe peace with anyone for the sake of national aims (43–8). If people fail to fulfil any one of those commandments, peace will be disturbed; but if they fulfil them all, the kingdom of peace will have come on earth. These five commandments exclude all evil from the life of man.

With the fulfilment of these commandments the life of men will be such as every human heart seeks

and desires. All men will be brothers, and everyone
will be at peace with others, enjoying all the blessings of the world during the term of life appointed
him by God. Men will beat their swords into
ploughshares, and their spears into pruning-hooks.
Then the kingdom of God will have come: that
kingdom of peace promised by all the prophets,
which drew nigh in the days of John the Baptist and
which Christ foretold and proclaimed in the words
of Isaiah: 'The Spirit of the Lord is upon me, because
he anointed me to preach good tidings to the poor;
he hath sent me to bind up the broken-hearted, to
proclaim liberty to the captives, and recovery of
sight to the blind, to set at liberty them that are
bruised; to proclaim the acceptable year of the
Lord' (Luke iv. 18, 19; Isaiah lxi. 1, 2).

The commandments of peace given by Christ
are simple and clear; they foresee all causes of
strife and by averting it they throw open the kingdom of God on earth. Therefore Christ is actually
the Messiah. He has fulfilled that which was
promised. It is we who do not carry out what all
men have always desired, though it is that for which
we have prayed and still pray.

VII

CHRIST'S TEACHING. FALSE DOCTRINE.
MAN IS A SON OF GOD

WHY do people not act as Christ told them to, and
in the way that would give the greatest bliss attainable by man—such as they have always longed for
and still long for? From all sides I hear one and the
same reply, differently expressed: 'The teaching of
Christ is very good, and it is true that were it ful-

filled the kingdom of God would be established on earth; but it is difficult, and therefore impracticable.'

Christ's teaching of how men should live is divinely true and gives men blessedness; but it is hard for them to obey it. We so often repeat this, and hear it, that the contradiction contained in the words no longer strikes us.

It is accordant with human nature to seek for what is best, and every teaching for the guidance of man's life is a teaching of what is best. If men are shown what is best for them, how can they say that they desire to do what is best but cannot? Man's rational activity, since mankind existed, has been directed to finding out what is best among the contradictions that fill the individual life and the life of humanity in general.

Men fight for land, for things they desire, and then divide everything up and call it property; they consider that though this is difficult to institute, yet it is better so, and they hold on to property; men fight for wives and abandon children, and then conclude that it is better that each man should have his own family; and though it is very difficult to provide for a family, people retain property and family and much else. And as soon as people considered that it was better so, then, however difficult it might be, they did it. What then do we mean when we say, The teaching of Christ is admirable, life according to Christ's teaching is better than the life we live, but we cannot live in the better way because it is difficult?

If one understands difficult to mean that it is difficult to sacrifice the momentary satisfaction of desire for the sake of a great good, then why do we not say that it is difficult to plough in order to obtain grain for bread or to plant apple-trees in order to get apples? That it is necessary to overcome difficulties to gain a great advantage is known to every being endowed with the rudiments of reason. And yet we say that Christ's teaching is admirable, but is impracticable because it is difficult. Difficult because to follow it we must deny ourselves something we had possessed till then. It is as if we had never heard that it is sometimes better to endure and forgo than to suffer nothing and always satisfy our lusts.

Man may be an animal, and no one need reproach him for that; but a man cannot argue that he wishes to be merely an animal. As soon as he argues he acknowledges that he is a rational being, and, admitting that, he cannot but admit the distinction between reasonable and unreasonable. Reason enforces nothing, it only sheds light.

In the dark I hurt my hand and my knee seeking the door. A man enters with a light, and I see the door. When I see the door I need no longer knock myself against the wall, and still less is it reasonably possible to assert that though I see the door and consider it better to pass through the door, it is difficult to do so and I therefore wish to continue to knock my knee against the wall.

There is an obvious misunderstanding in this extraordinary argument that the Christian teaching is desirable for and beneficial to the world, but that men are weak, men are bad, and continue to do worse though they wish to do better, and that therefore they cannot do better.

It is evidently not a mere error in argument, but something else. There must be some false perception here. Only a false opinion that that is which is not, and that that is not which is, could bring people to such a strange denial of the practicability of that which they admit gives them blessedness. The false perception which has led to this is what is called the dogmatic Christian faith—the very thing that all who profess the Christian faith according to the Church learn from childhood in the various Orthodox, Catholic, and Protestant Catechisms.

That faith, as defined by believers, is 'the giving substance to things hoped for' (this is said by Paul, and repeated in all the theological works and catechisms as the best definition of faith). And it is this acknowledgement of the unreal as real that has led people to the strange assertion that though Christ's teaching is good for men, it does not suit men.

The teaching of this faith, in its exact expression, is as follows: A personal God, ever existing, One in Three Persons, suddenly decided to create a world of spirits. The good God created this world of spirits for their good; but it happened that one of the spirits became bad of himself and therefore unhappy. Much time passed and God created another world, a material world, and in it man, also for man's own benefit. God created man blessed, immortal, and sinless. The blessedness of man consisted in his enjoying the good of life without labour; his immortality consisted in that he should always so live; his sinlessness consisted in his not knowing evil.

This man was tempted in paradise by that spirit of the first creation who had become bad, and from that time man fell and bore similar fallen children; and from that time people began to work, bear sickness, suffer, die, and struggle physically and spiritually; that is to say, this imaginary man became real, such as we know him and such as alone as we have any right or reason to imagine him to be. Man's condition, labouring, suffering, choosing good and avoiding evil, and dying—that condition which exists and other than which we cannot imagine—according to the teaching of this faith is not man's real position, but an unnatural, accidental, and temporary position.

Although this condition continued for everybody, as this teaching tells us, from the banishment of Adam from paradise—that is to say, from the commencement of the world—till the birth of Christ, and continues in just the same way for everybody since then, yet believers have to suppose this to be only an accidental, temporary condition. According to this teaching, the Son of God, being himself God, the Second Person of the Trinity, was sent by God to earth in human form to save men from that condition which was for them accidental and temporary, and to free them from all the curses which that same God had put upon them for Adam's sin, and in order to reinstate them in their former natural condition of blessedness—that is to say, in freedom from disease and in immortality, sinlessness, and idleness. According to this teaching, the Second Person of the Trinity, Christ, by the fact that people executed him, redeemed Adam's sin and terminated man's unnatural condition which had lasted since the beginning of the world. And since then a man who believes in Christ has again become such as he was in paradise—that is to say, immortal, free from disease, sinless, and idle.

On that part of the accomplishment of the redemption in consequence of which, since Christ, the earth has everywhere brought forth its fruits without labour, by which sickness has ceased, and children have been born without pain to their mothers—the teaching does not much insist, for, however much they may believe, it is difficult to instil into people who find it hard to toil and painful to suffer a perception that it is not hard to work nor painful to suffer. But that part of the teaching according to which death and sin are annulled is most strongly insisted on.

It is stated that the dead continue to live. And as the dead are quite unable to affirm that they have died or that they are alive (just as a stone cannot affirm that it can or cannot speak) the absence of a denial is accepted as a proof; and it is asserted that those who have died have not died. With yet greater solemnity and confidence is it asserted that since Christ came, man by faith in him is freed from sin—that is to say, that since Christ's time a man need no longer shed the light of reason on his path through life and choose what is best; he need only believe that Christ has redeemed him from sin and then he is always sinless—that is to say, completely good. According to this teaching people should imagine that reason in them is powerless, and that therefore they are sinless—that is to say, cannot make a mistake.

A true believer should imagine that since the time of Christ the earth yields her produce without labour, children are born painlessly, there are no diseases, no death, and no sins—that is to say, no mistakes—in other words, that that which is, is not, and that which is not, is.

That is what is said by strictly logical theological theory.

That teaching taken by itself seems harmless. But divergence from the truth never is harmless, but produces consequences that are the more important, the more important is the subject misrepresented. In this case the subject of the falsehood is the whole life of humanity.

What in this teaching is called true life is personal, blissful, sinless, and eternal—that is to say, life such as no one has ever known and such as does not exist. Life as it exists, the only life we know, the life we live and that all humanity has lived and still lives, according to this teaching is a fallen, bad life, merely a simulacrum of the good life proper to us.

The struggle between the inclination towards an animal life and a rational life, which lies in the soul of each man and forms the essence of each life, is completely set aside by this teaching. That struggle is relegated to an event which happened to Adam in paradise at the time of the creation. And the question whether I should eat or should not eat those apples which tempt me does not exist for us according to this teaching. The question was decided once and for all by Adam in paradise in a negative sense. Adam sinned for me—that is to say, he made a mistake, and all men, all of us, fell irreparably, and all our attempts to live rationally are useless and even irreligious. I am incorrigibly bad, and ought to know it. And my salvation does not depend on the fact that I can enlighten my life by reason and, recognizing good and evil, can choose the better path. No; Adam has once and for all done for me what was bad, and Christ has once and for all corrected that evil done by Adam, and therefore I, as a spectator, should grieve for the fall of Adam and rejoice in the redemption by Christ.

All the love of goodness and truth which lies in the soul of man, all his efforts by reason to shed light on life's phenomena, all man's spiritual life, is not merely unimportant according to this teaching, but is a snare or an arrogance.

Life such as we have on earth, with all its joys and beauties, with all its struggles of reason against darkness—the life of all who have lived before me, and my whole life with its inner strivings and victories of reason, is not a true life, but a fallen, hopelessly perverted one; while the true sinless life is in faith—that is in imagination, that is to say, in insanity.

Let a man, setting aside the habit he has retained from childhood of accepting all this, try to look simply and straight at this teaching; let him transform himself mentally into a new man, educated outside the range of this teaching, and let him imagine what it would appear like. Surely it is utter insanity.[1]

And, strange and terrible as it was to think it, I could not but admit that it is so, for this alone explained to me the amazing, contradictory, senseless objection which I hear from all sides as to the practicability of Christ's teaching: *It is good and would bring happiness to men, but men cannot fulfil it.*

Only the representation as existent of that which does not exist, and as non-existent of that which does exist, could lead to this astonishing contradiction. And such a false representation I found in the pseudo-Christian faith which has been preached for 1500 years.[2]

But the objection to Christ's teaching (that it is good but impracticable) is made not only by believers but also by unbelievers, by people who do not believe, or think they do not believe, in the dogma of the fall and redemption. The objection to Christ's teaching on the score of its impracticability is made also by scientists, philosophers, and in general by people who are educated and consider

[1] Tolstóy had the Russo-Greek Church primarily in mind, and was writing when that Church was particularly subservient to the Civil power. Also opinions were then still current both in the English and in the Eastern Churches to which assent is now rarely demanded. But he certainly addressed both his rejection of the Church dogmas and his insistence on the teaching of Jesus to all Churches alike.—A.M.

[2] Tolstóy counts from the First General Council of Christians at Nicæa, under Constantine, in A.D. 325.—A.M.

themselves quite free from any superstition and who do not believe, or think they do not believe, in anything; and who therefore consider themselves free from the superstitions of the fall and the redemption. And so at first it seemed to me. I too thought that these learned people had other grounds for their denial of the practicability of Christ's teaching. But on penetrating deeper into the reason of their denial I became convinced that the nonbelievers have the same false perception that our life is not what it is, but is what they imagine it to be; and that this conception rests on the same basis as the believers' conception. Those who consider themselves unbelievers do not, it is true, believe in God, nor in Christ, nor in Adam; but in the fundamental, false conception of man's right to a blissful life, on which everything rests, they believe as firmly or even more firmly than the theologians.

However much privileged science and philosophy may boast themselves, asserting that they are the guides and directors of man's mind—they are not the directors but the servants. A ready-made outlook on life is always supplied to science by religion, and science only works along the paths indicated to it by religion. Religion shows man the meaning of life, and science and philosophy apply this meaning to various sides of life. And therefore if religion gives a false meaning to life, science, educated to that religious outlook, will apply that false perception to the various phases of human life. And that is what has happened with our European-Christian science and philosophy.

Church teaching has presented the fundamental meaning of human life as being this, that man has a right to a blissful life and that this bliss is not obtainable by man's exertion but by something outside himself; and this idea underlies all our science and philosophy.

Religion, science, and public opinion, all with one voice declare that the life we lead is bad, but that the teaching which shows how we ourselves can become better and thereby make life better, is impracticable.

The teaching of Christ, aiming at improving human life by man's own reasonable efforts, is impracticable, says religion, because Adam fell and the world is in an evil state.

That teaching is impracticable because man's life is regulated by certain laws which are independent of man's will, says our philosophy. Philosophy and all science only repeat in other words just what religion announces by the dogma of original sin and redemption.

In the doctrine of redemption there are two fundamental propositions on which everything depends: (1) Real human life is a blissful life, but life in the world here is a bad life, irreparable by any effort of man; and (2) Redemption from this life lies in faith.

These two propositions have come to underlie the outlook on life both of believers and of unbelievers in our pseudo-Christian society. From the second proposition arose the Church with her institutions. From the first come our public opinion and our philosophic and political theories.

All the philosophic and political theories that justify the existing order, Hegelianism and its children, are founded on that basis. Pessimism, demanding of life what life cannot give and therefore repudiating life, also arose from it. Materialism, with its wonderful and enthusiastic assertion that man is a process and nothing else, is the lawful child of this doctrine which acknowledges life here to be a fallen life. Spiritualism, with its scientific followers, is the best proof that the scientific and philosophic outlook is not free, but based on the religious doctrine that a blissful eternal life is natural to man.

This perversion of the meaning of life has perverted the whole rational activity of man. The dogma of man's fall and redemption has hidden from men the most important and legitimate realm of human activity and has shut out of the realm of human knowledge the knowledge of what man should do that he may become happier and better. Science and philosophy, imagining that they are counteracting pseudo-Christianity and priding themselves thereon, are only serving it. Science and philosophy deal with anything you please, save only with the question how man can himself become better and lead a better life. What is called ethics—moral teaching—has quite disappeared from our pseudo-Christian society.

Neither believers nor unbelievers ask themselves how they should live and how use the reason that has been given us; but they ask: Why is our human life not such as we have imagined it should be, and when will it become what we desire?

Only as a result of that false teaching absorbed into the flesh and blood of our generation, could such an astonishing thing occur as that man—as though he had spat out the apple of knowledge of good and evil, which tradition says he ate in paradise, and had forgotten that the progress of mankind lies only in solving the contradictions between our rational and our animal natures—should set to work to use his reason in discovering the historic laws of his animal nature and of that alone.

Except the philosophic teaching of our pseudo-Christian world, the religions and philosophic teachings of all the nations known to us—Judaism, Confucianism, Buddhism, Brahminism, and the philosophy of the Greeks—all aim at arranging human life and explaining to people how each one should strive to be better and to lead a better life. All Confucianism consists in personal perfecting of oneself; Judaism, in the personal following of each law of God; Buddhism, in the teaching of how each man can save himself from the evil of life. Socrates taught the personal perfecting of oneself in the name of reason, and the Stoics acknowledged rational freedom as the only basis of a true life.

Man's whole rational activity could not but consist, and has always consisted, in one thing—in illuminating by reason the striving towards what is good. Free-will, says our philosophy, is an illusion; and it prides itself much on the boldness of this assertion. But free-will is not merely an illusion, it is a phrase devoid of meaning. It is a phrase invented by the theologians and criminalists, and to refute that phrase is to tilt at windmills; but reason—that which illumines our life and obliges us to alter our actions—is not an illusion and cannot be denied. To follow wisdom for the attainment of what is good—in that has always consisted the doctrine of the true teachers of humanity and in that lies the whole teaching of Christ, and, being reason, it can in no way be rejected by reason.

The teaching of Christ is the teaching of the son of man that is present in us all—that is to say, it is the teaching of the striving common to all men for what is good, and of the reason, shared by all, which illuminates that striving. (To prove that 'the son of man' means 'son of man' is quite superfluous. To understand by 'son of man' something else instead of what the words mean, one would have to show that Christ to indicate what he meant to say, intentionally used words which have quite another meaning. But even if, as the Church wishes

to make out, 'son of man' means son of God, even
then 'son of man' also essentially means man, for
Christ calls all men the sons of God.)

Christ's teaching of the son of man—son of God—
which forms the basis of all the Gospels, is expressed
most clearly in his talk with Nicodemus. Each man,
says he, besides consciousness of his personal life in
the flesh, which proceeds from a male parent in the
womb of his physical mother, cannot but be conscious of his birth from above (John iii. 5, 6, 7).
That which man is conscious of in himself as free is
that which is born of the eternal—that which we
call God (vv. 11, 14). That which is born of God
(the son of God in man) we should exalt in ourselves in order to attain true life (vv. 14, 17). The
son of man is the son of God 'of a like nature' (not
'only begotten'). He who exalts in himself that son
of God above all else, he who believes that life
dwells only in that, will not be in discord with life.
Discord with life results only because people do not
believe in the light within themselves (vv. 18–21)
(that light of which it is said in John's Gospel that
in it is life, and the life was the light of man).

Christ taught us to exalt the son of man, who is
the son of God and the light of men, above all else.
He says: When you exalt [honour, raise up] the son
of man, you will know that I speak nothing of
myself (John xii. 32, 44, 49). The Jews did not
understand his teaching, and asked: 'Who is this son
of man, that must be lifted up?' (John xii. 34). And
to this question he replies (v. 35): 'Yet a little while
is the light in you.[1] Walk while ye have the light,

[1] In all the Church's translations an intentionally false
rendering is given: instead of the words 'in you', wherever
those words occur the rendering is given 'with you'.—L.T.

The English Authorized Version gives 'with you', but our
Revised Version, published in 1881, gives 'among you', and in
a footnote adds the translation 'in you'; so that the meaning

that darkness overtake you not; he that walketh in the darkness knoweth not whither he goeth.' To the question, what is meant by 'lift up the son of man', Christ replies: Live in the light that is in man.

The son of man, according to Christ's reply, is that light in which men ought to walk while they have light within them.

Luke xi. 35: 'Look therefore whether the light that is in thee be not darkness.'

Matt. vi. 23: 'If the light that is in thee be darkness, how great is the darkness!' says he, teaching the multitude.

Before and after Christ men have said the same thing: that a divine light which has descended from heaven dwells in man, and that that light is *reason*, and that one must serve it only and by its aid seek for what is good. This was said by the teachers among the Brahmins and by the Hebrew prophets, and by Confucius, and Socrates, and Marcus Aurelius, and Epictetus, and by all the true sages— not the compilers of philosophic theories but those who sought truth for their own welfare and for that of all men.[1]

Tolstóy considers correct is not entirely inaccessible to English readers of the Gospel.—A.M.

[1] Marcus Aurelius says: 'Honour that which is more powerful than anything on earth, which rules and guides all men. Honour also that which is most powerful within thyself. The latter is like the former, because it uses what is within thee to guide thy life.'

Epictetus says: 'God sowed His seed not only in my father and grandfather, but in all that live on the earth, especially in those that reason, for they alone enter into relation with God, through the reason by which they are united with Him.'

In the book of Confucius it is said: 'The law of great science consists in developing and establishing the principle of the light of reason, which we have received from heaven.' That proposition is repeated several times, and serves as the basis of Confucius's teaching.—L.T.

But suddenly, according to the dogma of redemption, we admit that it is quite unnecessary to speak or think about this light within us. We must think, say the believers, about the nature of each separate person of the Trinity; what sacraments must or must not be performed; because the salvation of man comes not from our efforts, but from the Trinity and the correct observance of the sacraments. We must think, say the non-believers, of the laws which regulate the movements of infinitely small atoms of matter in infinite space and infinite time; but of what man's reason demands for his good there is no need to think, because the betterment of man's condition does not depend on him, but on general laws which we discover.

I am convinced that a few centuries hence the so-called 'scientific' activity of our belauded recent centuries of European humanity will furnish an inextinguishable fund of mirth and pity to future generations. For some centuries the learned men of a small western part of the great continent were in a condition of epidemic madness, imagining that eternal blissful life belonged to them, and they occupied themselves with every kind of investigation as to how, and according to what laws, this life would come to them; but they themselves did nothing and never thought of doing anything to make their life better. And what will seem yet more pathetic to the future historian is that he will find that these people had had a teacher who clearly and definitely indicated to them what they should do to live more happily, and that the words of this teacher were explained by some to mean that he would come on the clouds to arrange everything, and by others that this teacher's words were excellent but impracticable, because man's life was not such as they wished it to be and therefore it was not worth while to concern themselves with it, but man's reason had to be directed to the investigation of the laws of life without regard to what is good for man.

The Church says: Christ's teaching is impracticable because life here is but an imitation of true life; it cannot be good, it is all evil. The best way to live such a life is to despise it and live by faith— that is, by imagining a future, blissful, eternal life, and to live here as one is living, and to pray.

Philosophy, science, and public opinion say: Christ's teaching is impracticable because man's life depends not on that light of reason by which he can himself illuminate this life, but on general laws; and therefore it is not necessary to illuminate this life by reason and to live in accord therewith, but one must live as one is living, firmly believing that according to historical, sociological, and other laws of progress, after we have lived badly a very long time our life will of itself become very good.

People come to a farm and there find everything necessary for their life: a house with all needful utensils, barns full of corn, cellars, vaults containing all kinds of supplies; in the yard are agricultural implements, tools, harness, horses, cows, sheep, and a complete inventory—all that is needful for a well-supplied life. People from various parts come to this farm and begin to make use of all they find there, each only for himself, not thinking of leaving anything either for those who are there with him in the house or for those who will come later. Each wishes to have everything for himself. Each hastens to make use of what he can seize, and the destruction of everything begins—strife and a struggle for possession. A milch cow, unshorn sheep and sheep bearing young, are killed for meat; fires are fed with benches and carts and people fight for milk and grain, and spill, scatter, and destroy more than they use. No one eats a morsel quietly, he eats and snarls; a stronger than he comes and takes the piece away, and another takes it from him. Having tormented themselves, these people, beaten and hungry, leave the place. Again the master arranges everything in the place so that people could live quietly in it. Again in the farm there is abundance, and again passers-by come in; but again there is a scrimmage and a fight; all is wasted in vain; and again, tormented and embittered, people go away, scolding, angry with their comrades and also with their host for having prepared the place badly and insufficiently. Again the good host rearranges the place so that people could live in it; and again the same thing occurs, and again, and again, and again. Then in one of the fresh parties a teacher is found who says to the others, 'Brothers, we are not acting rightly. See how many goods there are in the place and how well it is all arranged! There is enough for us all and there will be a surplus for those who come after us, only let us live reasonably. We will not snatch from one another, but will help one another. Let us sow, and plough, and tend the cattle, and all will be able to live well.' And it happened that some people understood what the teacher said, and those who understood began to do as he bade them; they ceased fighting and snatching from one another and began to work. But the rest, who had either not heard the words of the teacher or had heard but did not believe him, did not follow his advice, but fought as before and spoilt their host's goods and went away. Others came and the same thing occurred. Those who attended to the teacher ever repeated the same thing: 'Do not fight, do not destroy the host's goods, and it will be better for you all. Do as the teacher says.'

But there were still many who had not heard or did not believe, and matters long went on in the old way. This was all comprehensible, and things might happen so as long as people did not believe what the teacher said. But at last, it is told, a time came when all in the place had heard the teacher's words, all understood them, and not only understood them but acknowledged that it was God Himself who spoke through the teacher and that the teacher was himself God, and all believed every word the teacher spoke to be sacred. And it is told that after this, instead of all living as the teacher advised, no one any longer refrained from the brawls, and they started thrashing one another and all began to say that we know now for certain that it should be so and that nothing else is possible!

What does it all mean? Even cattle manage to eat their fodder so that it should not be wasted uselessly, but men, having learnt how they might live better and believing that God Himself ordered them to do so, live even worse, because they say it is impossible to live otherwise. These people have imagined something that is not true. Well, what could these people at the farm have imagined, which let them, having believed the teacher's words, continue to live as before, snatching from one another, fighting, and ruining the goods and themselves? The teacher had told them: 'Your life at this farm is bad; live better and your life will become good'; but they imagined that the teacher had condemned any kind of life at that farm, and had promised them another, a good life, not at that farm but somewhere else. And they decided that this farm was a temporary inn, and that it was not worth while arranging to live well in it, but that it was only necessary to be on the alert not to miss the good life promised in another place. Only so can the strange conduct of these people at the farm be explained who believed the teacher to be God, and of those others who considered him a wise man and his words to be true, but continued to live as before in contradiction to his advice.

Men have heard all and understood all; but have let slip past their ears that the teacher said that men must create their own happiness here, at this farm at which they have met; and have imagined that this farm was an inn and that the real one will be somewhere else. And from this has come their amazing argument that the words of the teacher were very admirable, and were even the words of God Himself, but that it was now difficult to obey them.

If only people would cease from destroying themselves and expecting someone to come and help them—Christ on the clouds with the sound of trumpets, or an historic law, or a law of the differentiation and integration of forces! No one will help them unless they help themselves. Nor do they need help. They only need, instead of expecting anything from heaven or from earth, to cease to destroy themselves.

VIII

THE PATH OF LIFE

BUT granting that Christ's teaching is beneficial to the world—granting that it is rational and that one has no reasonable right to reject it—still, what can one man do in a world of those who do not act on Christ's law? If all men suddenly agreed to fulfil Christ's teaching its observance would be possible; but one man cannot go against the whole world.

'If', it is generally said, 'I alone, in a world of those

people who do not fulfil Christ's law, fulfil it: give away what I have, turn my cheek to the smiter without defending myself, do not even put in an appearance to take the appointed oaths or when summoned to war, and submit to be plundered; I shall, if I do not die of hunger, get beaten to death, or if not beaten, imprisoned or shot. So I shall have sacrificed all my happiness in vain and ruined my whole life.'

This reply is based upon the same misunderstanding as the reply about the impracticability of Christ's teaching.

It is what one usually hears said, and I myself agreed with it until I had quite emancipated myself from Church teaching and so became able to understand the full meaning of Christ's doctrine about life.

Christ offers his teaching of life to redeem us from the ruinous life people live who do not follow his teaching; and suddenly we declare that we should be glad to follow his teaching were we not sorry to ruin our life. Christ teaches us how to escape from our ruinous life, and we grudge the sacrifice of that same life. It follows that we are far from considering our life ruinous, but consider it something in our possession, real and valuable. In that acknowledgement of our present worldly life as a real thing and something that is our own, lies the mistake which hinders a comprehension of Christ's teaching. Christ was aware of this mistake which causes people to consider this worldly life of theirs as something real that belongs to them, and by a whole series of discourses and parables he showed them that they have no right to life, and possess no life till they obtain true life by rejecting the shadow they now call their 'life'.

In order to understand Christ's doctrine of saving

one's life, one must first understand what was said
by all the prophets, what was said by Solomon, by
Buddha, and by all the sages of the world concerning man's personal life. One may, as Pascal expresses it, disregard the matter and carry a shield
before one to hide the abyss of death towards which
we are all running; but one need only consider what
man's isolated personal life is, to convince oneself
that this whole life, if it be only a personal life, has
for each separate person no sense or meaning, but is
a malicious mockery of one's heart and reason and
of all that is good in man. Therefore to understand
Christ's teaching one has first of all to bethink
oneself and to consider. It is necessary that in us
μετάνοια should take place: that is what Christ's
forerunner, John the Baptist, when preaching, said
to people who were ensnared like ourselves. He said:
'First of all, repent—that is, bethink yourselves.
Even now is the axe laid to the root of the trees to
cut them down. Death and destruction are here
beside each one of you. Do not forget it: bethink
yourselves.' And Christ, beginning his teaching,
says the same thing: 'Repent, or you will all
perish.'

In Luke xiii. 1–5, Christ spoke of the destruction
of the Galilæans slain by Pilate, and he said: 'Think
ye that these Galilæans were sinners above all the
Galilæans because they have suffered these things?
I tell you, Nay: but, except ye repent, ye shall all in
like manner perish. Or those eighteen, upon whom
the tower in Siloam fell, and killed them, think ye
that they were offenders above all the men that
dwell in Jerusalem? I tell you, Nay: but, except ye
repent, ye shall all likewise perish.'

Had he lived in our day in Russia he would have
said: Think ye that those who were burnt in the
circus at Berdíchev, or those who perished at the

Kukúevsky embankment[1] were worse than others?
You also will all perish unless you bethink yourselves and find in your life that which does not
perish. The death of those crushed by the tower or
burnt in the circus, horrifies you; but your death,
just as terrible and as unavoidable, awaits you, and
in vain do you try to forget it. If it comes unexpectedly it will be all the more terrible.

He says (Luke xii. 54–7): 'When ye see a cloud
rising in the west, straightway ye say, There cometh
a shower; and so it cometh to pass. And when ye
see a south wind blowing, ye say, There will be a
scorching heat; and it cometh to pass. Ye hypocrites, ye know how to interpret the face of the earth
and the heaven; but how is it that ye know not how
to interpret this time? And why even concerning
yourselves judge ye not what is right?'

You can forecast the weather by its indications;
how is it you perceive not what will befall yourselves? Avoid danger, safeguard your life as much
as you please, and all the same, if Pilate does not
kill you a tower will fall on you, or if neither Pilate
nor the tower destroys you, you will die in your bed
with yet greater suffering.

Make a simple calculation, as worldly people do
when they undertake anything: either to build a
tower, or to go to war, or to erect a factory. They
plan and toil at an undertaking that may have a
reasonable end.

Luke xiv. 28–31: 'For which of you, desiring to
build a tower, doth not first sit down and count the
cost, whether he have wherewith to complete it?
Lest haply, when he hath laid a foundation, and is
not able to finish, all that behold begin to mock
him, saying, This man began to build and was not

[1] The reference is to two disasters that occurred in Russia
at the time Tolstóy was writing this book.—A.M.

able to finish. Or what king, as he goeth to encounter another king in war, will not sit down first and take counsel whether he is able with ten thousand to meet him that cometh against him with twenty thousand?'

Is it not really senseless to work at something which, however much you may try, will never be accomplished? Death will always come sooner than the completion of the tower of your worldly happiness. And if you know in advance that however you may strive against death, not you, but he, will conquer, is it not better to refrain from struggling against it, and not to devote your life to what will certainly perish, but rather seek some undertaking which will not be destroyed by inevitable death?

Luke xii. 22–7: 'And he said unto his disciples, Therefore I say unto you, Take no thought for your life, what ye shall eat; nor yet for your body, what ye shall put on. For the life is more than the food, and the body than the raiment. Consider the ravens, that they sow not, neither reap; which have no store-chamber, nor barn; and God feedeth them: of how much more value are ye than the birds! And which of you by being anxious can add a cubit unto his stature? If then ye are not able to do even that which is least, why are ye anxious concerning the rest? Consider the lilies, how they grow: they toil not, neither do they spin; yet I say unto you, Even Solomon in all his glory was not arrayed like one of these.'

However much you may concern yourself about your body and your clothes, no one can add a single hour to his life.[1] Is it not senseless then to concern yourself about something you cannot do?

[1] The word ἡλικία—age, time of life, is incorrectly translated 'stature'. So the whole expression means: can add an hour to his life.—L.T.

You know very well that your life will end with death, and you exert yourself to safeguard your life by property. Life cannot be safeguarded by property. Understand that this is an absurd deception with which you delude yourself.

The meaning of life cannot consist, Christ says, in what we possess and what we acquire—what is not ourselves—it must consist in something else.

He says (Luke xii. 15–21): 'A man's life consisteth not in the abundance of the things which he possesseth. The grounds of a certain rich man', he says, 'brought forth plentifully: and he reasoned within himself, saying, What shall I do, because I have not where to bestow my fruits? And he said, This will I do: I will pull down my barns, and build greater; and there will I bestow all my corn and my goods. And I will say to my soul, Soul, thou hast much goods laid up for many years; take thine ease, eat, drink, be merry. But God said unto him, Thou foolish one, this night is thy soul required of thee; and the things which thou hast prepared, whose shall they be? So is he that layeth up treasure for himself, and is not rich toward God.'

Death always, every instant, stands over you. And therefore (Luke xii. 35, 36, 38, 39, 40): 'Let your loins be girded about, and your lamps burning; and be ye yourselves like unto men looking for their lord, when he shall return from the marriage feast; that, when he cometh and knocketh, they may straightway open unto him. And if he shall come in the second watch, and if in the third, and find them so, blessed are those servants. But this ye know, that if the master of the house had known in what hour the thief was coming, he would have watched, and not have left his house to be broken through. Be ye also ready: for in an hour that ye think not the Son of man cometh.'

The parable of the virgins awaiting the bridegroom, and of the end of the age and the day of judgement—all these passages, in the opinion of all the commentators, besides relating to the end of the world also relate to death, which stands always before us every hour.

Death, death, death awaits you every second. Your life passes in the presence of death. If you labour personally for your own future, you yourself know that the one thing awaiting you is—death. And that death ruins all you work for. Consequently life for oneself can have no meaning. If there is a reasonable life it must be found elsewhere; it must be a life the aim of which does not lie in preparing further life for oneself. To live rationally one must live so that death cannot destroy life.

Luke x. 41: 'Martha, Martha, thou art anxious and troubled about many things: but one thing is needful.'

All the innumerable things we do for our own future are unnecessary: it is all deception with which we delude ourselves. Only one thing is needful.

From the day of man's birth, his position is such that inevitable destruction awaits him—that is to say, a meaningless life and a meaningless death, unless he finds that one thing necessary for true life. It is that one thing which Christ shows to men. He does not invent it or promise to give it by his divine power, he only shows people that, together with that personal life which is certainly a deception, there must be something that is true and not a deception.

In the parable of the husbandmen (Matt. xxi. 33–42) Christ explains the source of the error which hides that truth from men and causes them to mistake the phantom of life (their own personal life) for true life.

Men living in the cultivated garden of a house-holder took it into their heads that they owned that garden. And from this false conception flowed a series of insensate and cruel actions performed by them which ended in their expulsion, in their being ejected from that life. In just such a way have we imagined that the life of each of us is his own personal possession and that we have a right to it and can do with it as we please, bound by no obligation to anyone. And for us, having imagined this, a similar series of insensate and cruel actions and misfortunes is inevitable, resulting in a similar expulsion from life. And as the husbandmen thought that the more cruel they were the better would they secure themselves (for instance, by killing the messengers and the householder's son), so we also imagine that the more cruel we are the better we shall be safeguarded.

As the inevitable end of the husbandmen who would not yield the fruit of the garden to anyone was that the householder expelled them, so also will be the end of those who imagine personal life to be real life. Death drives them from life, replacing them by others; and this not as a punishment but merely because they have not understood life. As the dwellers in the garden had either forgotten or wished to ignore the fact that the garden was handed to them ready cultivated, hedged, and supplied with a well, and that someone had laboured there before and therefore expected them to work; so people living a personal life have forgotten, or wish to forget, all that was done for them before their birth and is being done all the time they are alive, and that something is therefore expected of them: they wish to forget that all the good things of life which they use have been given and are being given, and should therefore be passed on and returned.

This correction of the understanding of life, this μετάνοια is the corner-stone of Christ's teaching, as he said at the end of that parable. According to Christ's teaching, as the husbandmen in the garden they had not planted should have understood and realized that they owed more to the householder than they could repay, so we also should understand and feel that, from the day of our birth to our death, we are overwhelmingly in debt to others, to those who lived before us, those now living, and those who will live, and to that which was, is, and will be —the source of all things. They should understand that each hour of their life, while they retain it, they admit that obligation, and that therefore a man living for himself, who denies that obligation uniting him with life and with the source of life, deprives himself of life, and must understand that by living so he destroys his life—while wishing to save it, as was repeatedly said by Christ.

That only is true life which carries on the life of the past, promotes the welfare of the present, and prepares the welfare of the future.

To participate in that life a man must forgo his own will and do the will of the Father of life who has given life to the Son of man.

In John viii. 35, Christ, again expressing the same thought, says that a slave who follows his own will and not the will of the master abideth not in the house for ever: only the son, who fulfilleth the will of the Father, abideth for ever.

The will of the Father of life is not the life of an individual man, but of the only son of man dwelling within men, and therefore a man preserves his life only when he takes his life as a loan, a talent entrusted to him by the Father for the service of the life of all, and lives not for himself but for the son of man.

Matt. xxv. 14–46: A master gave part of his property to each of his bondsmen and, without giving them any instructions, left them alone. Some of the bondsmen, though they had received no orders from their master as to the use of his property, understood that it was not theirs but the master's, and that it should increase; and they worked for their master. And those who worked for their master became partakers in the master's life, but those who did not work were deprived of what had been given them.

The life of the son of man is given to all men and they are not told why it is entrusted to them. Some understand that life is not their own, but is received as a gift, and that they should serve the life of the son of man, and they live accordingly. Others, on the pretext of not understanding the aim of life, do not serve life. And those who serve life merge with the source of life, while those who do not serve life are deprived of it. And (in verses 31 to 46) Christ tells us wherein the service of the son of man consists, and what the reward of that service is. The son of man, as Christ expressed it, will say like a king: 'Come, ye blessed of my Father, inherit the kingdom, for ye gave me meat and drink, clothed me, took me in and comforted me, for I am ever one and the same, in you and in these little ones whom you have pitied and to whom you have done good. You have not lived the personal life, but the life of the son of man; therefore you have eternal life.'

Only of eternal life of that kind does Christ teach in all the Gospels, and, strange as it may sound to say it of Christ, who personally rose and promised resurrection to all, never did Christ by a single word assert a personal resurrection and personal immortality beyond the grave; and to the restoration of the dead in the kingdom of the Messiah, which the Pharisees taught, he gave a meaning which excluded the conception of personal resurrection.

The Sadducees denied the restoration of the dead. The Pharisees acknowledged it and it is now acknowledged by orthodox Jews.

The restoration of the dead (and not the resurrection, as the word is incorrectly translated), according to the belief of the Jews will be accomplished at the coming of the time of the Messiah and the establishment of the kingdom of God on earth. And Christ, encountering this belief in a temporary, local, and corporeal resurrection, denies it and puts in place of it his teaching of eternal life in God.

When the Sadducees, who did not acknowledge the restoration of the dead, asked Christ, whom they supposed to share the view of the Pharisees, 'To whom will the wife of the seven brothers belong?' he replies clearly and definitely on both points.

He says (Matt. xxii. 29–32; Mark xii. 24–7; Luke xx. 34–8): 'Ye do err, not knowing the Scriptures, nor the power of God.' And rejecting the Pharisees' view, he says: The restoration of the dead is neither corporeal nor personal. Those who attain to a restoration from the dead become sons of God and live like the angels (the powers of God) in heaven (i.e. with God); and personal questions—such as whose wife a woman will be—cannot exist for them, for they, united with God, cease to be personalities. 'As touching the restoration of the dead', says he, replying to the Sadducees who only acknowledged earthly life, 'have ye not read that which was spoken unto you by God?' In the book of Moses it is said that God from the bush spake unto Moses, saying, 'I am the God of Abraham, and the God of Isaac, and the God of Jacob.' If God said to Moses that he is the God of Jacob, then Jacob is not dead for God, since God is the God of the living only and not of the dead. *For God, all are alive.* And therefore if there is a living God, that man also lives who has entered into communion with the ever-living God.

Against the Pharisees Christ says that the restoration of life cannot be corporeal and personal. Against the Sadducees he says that besides a personal and temporary life there is also a life in communion with God.

Christ denies the personal, the corporeal resurrection,[1] but acknowledges a restoration of life in a man who merges his life into God's. Christ teaches salvation from personal life and places that salvation in the exaltation of the son of man and life in God. Uniting this teaching of his with the Jewish doctrine of the coming of a Messiah, he speaks to the Jews of the raising of the son of man from the dead, meaning by this not a corporeal and personal restoration of the dead, but an awakening of life in God. He never spoke of a corporeal, personal resurrection. The best proof that he never preached the resurrection of man is furnished by the two solitary passages quoted by the theologians in proof of his having taught the doctrine of resurrection. These

[1] We are so accustomed to the religious assertion of a physical resurrection and to the supposition that the only alternative to that is the denial (commonly made by materialists) of any life beyond the grave, that many people find it difficult to grasp what Tolstóy is here saying. His argument is that even now, in the present existence, our only real life lies in what results from the workings of our reasonable consciousness, that voice within which makes us 'sons of God', and not in our rapidly changing and perishing physical body, and he looks forward not to a cessation of existence after the final disintegration of our body, as materialists suppose will be the case, but to a continuance of that sonship to God which is even now our only real life.

This perception is more fully and clearly brought out in *On Life*, which will appear in the next volume of this edition. —A.M.

two passages are Matt. xxv. 31–46 and John v. 28, 29. The first of these speaks of the coming, i.e. of the restoration, the exaltation, of the son of man (just as in Matt. x. 23) and therefore the majesty and power of the son of man are compared to a king. In the second passage what is spoken of is the restoration of true life here on earth, as it is expressed in the preceding twenty-four verses.

One need only reflect on the meaning of Christ's teaching of eternal life in God, and recollect the teaching of the Hebrew prophets, to understand that if Christ wished to teach the doctrine of the resurrection of the dead, which was then only beginning to find a place in the Talmud and was a subject of dispute, he would have stated that doctrine clearly and definitely; but on the contrary not only did he not do so, but he rejected it; and not a single place can be found in any one of the Gospels which confirms that doctrine. The two passages referred to above mean something quite different.

Of his own personal resurrection—strange as this may sound to people who have not themselves studied the Gospels—*Christ never spoke at all!* If, as the theologians teach, the basis of Christian faith lies in the resurrection of Christ, one would think that the least one could wish would be that Christ, knowing that he would rise again and that this would constitute the chief dogma of the Christian faith, should at least once say so clearly and definitely. But not only did he not say so definitely and clearly, he never once, not one single time in all the canonical Gospels, even mentioned it! What Christ taught was to exalt the son of man; that is to say, the essential life of man, and to acknowledge oneself a son of God. Christ personified in himself a man acknowledging sonship to God (Matt. xvi. 13–20). He asked the disciples what men said of him—*the son of man?* The disciples replied that some considered him to be John the Baptist miraculously risen from the dead, or a prophet; others, Elijah descended from heaven. 'But who do you say I am?' asked he. And Peter, understanding Christ as he understood himself, replied: 'Thou art the Messiah, the son of the living God.' And Christ replied: 'Not flesh and blood hath revealed this unto thee, but our Father which is in heaven.' That is to say, you have understood this not because you believed human explanations, but because you, recognizing yourself to be a son of God, have understood me. And, explaining to Peter that on this sonship to God the true faith rests, Christ warned the other disciples (v. 20) that they should not in future say that he, Jesus, was the Messiah.

And after this Christ says that notwithstanding the fact that he would be tortured and killed, the son of man, knowing himself to be God's son, would nevertheless be re-established and triumph over all. And it is these words that are interpreted as a prediction of his resurrection!

John ii. 19–22; Matt. xii. 40; Luke xi. 30; Matt. xvi. 4–21; Mark viii. 31; Luke ix. 22; Matt. xvii. 23; Mark ix. 31; Matt. xx. 19; Mark x. 34; Luke xviii. 33; Matt. xxvi. 32; Mark xiv. 28. Those are all the thirteen passages which are understood as being predictions by Christ of his resurrection. In three of them what is spoken of is Jonah in the whale's belly, and in one the reconstruction of the Temple. In the remaining ten passages it is said that the son of man cannot be destroyed, but nowhere is there one word about the resurrection of Jesus Christ.

In none of these passages in the original does the word 'resurrection' even occur. Give a man who does not know the theological interpretation but who knows Greek, these passages to translate, and he will never translate them as they have been translated. In the original, two different words are used in three passages; the one is ἀνίστημι and the other ἐγείρω. One of these words means, 'to up-raise'; the other means 'to awaken', and, in the middle voice, 'to wake up', 'to rouse oneself'. But neither the one nor the other can ever, under any circumstances, mean 'to raise from the dead'. In order fully to convince oneself that these Greek words, and the corresponding Hebrew word *kum*, cannot mean 'to raise from the dead', one need only compare the other passages in the Gospels where these words are used. They are used frequently and never translated by the words 'to raise from the dead' (*auferstehen*, *ressusciter*); such words did not exist in Greek or in Hebrew, nor was there the conception that corresponds to them. To express the conception of resurrection in Greek or in Hebrew, one has to employ a circumlocution and say: 'arose from the dead' or 'awoke from the dead'. So in the Gospels (Matt. xiv. 2) where the matter in hand is that Herod assumed the resurrection of John the Baptist, the words used are 'is risen from the dead'. So also in Luke xvi. 31 it is said, in the parable about Lazarus, that if there were a resurrection the man who returned from the dead would still not be believed, and the expression used is: 'if one rise from the dead'. Where the words 'from the dead' are not added to the words 'to rise', 'to awaken', the words 'rise' and 'awaken' never imply or could imply 'resurrection'. And speaking of himself, Christ did not once, in all the passages quoted as proof of his prediction of his resurrection—not one single time did he employ the words, 'from the dead'.

Our conception of the resurrection is so different from the Jewish conception of life that it is impossible even to imagine how Christ could have

spoken to the Jews about resurrection and an everlasting, personal life belonging to each man. The
conception of a future personal life has come to us
neither from Jewish teaching nor from Christ's
teaching. It entered church doctrine quite from
without. Strange as it may appear, it cannot but be
said that a belief in a future personal life is a very
low and gross conception (based on a confusion of
sleep with death) and one natural to all savage
tribes, and that the Hebrew doctrine, not to speak
of the Christian doctrine, stood immeasurably
above it. We are convinced that this superstition
is something very elevated, and seriously try to
prove the superiority of our teaching to other doctrines by the fact that we hold this superstition,
while others, such as the Chinese and Hindus, do
not hold it. This is argued not only by theologians
but also by the free-thinking, scholarly historians of
religion (Tiele, Max Müller, and others), who,
when classifying religion, reckon those which share
this superstition as superior to those which do not
share it. The free-thinking Schopenhauer plainly
calls the Hebrew religion the vilest (*niederträchtigste*)
of all religions, because it contains no idea (*keine
Idee*) of the immortality of the soul. Actually in the
Hebrew religion neither that conception nor that
word exists. Eternal life, in Hebrew, is *khaye-olam*.
Olam means endless, unchangeable in time. *Olam*
also means the world, the cosmos, life in general,
and especially endless life. *Khaye-olam*, according
to the Hebrew doctrine, is an attribute of the one
God. God is the God of life, the living God. Man
in the Hebrew conception is always mortal; only
God is ever-living. In the Pentateuch the words
'live for ever' are twice employed. Once in
Deuteronomy, xxxii. 39, 40, God says: 'See now
that I, even I, am he, and there is no God but me:

I kill, and I make alive; I have wounded and I heal; and there is none that can deliver out of my hand. For I lift up my hand to heaven, and say, I *live for ever*. . . .' The other time, in Genesis iii. 22, God says: 'Behold, the man has eaten of the fruit of the tree of knowledge of good and evil, and is become as us [one of us]; and now, may he not put forth his hand, and take also of the tree of life, and eat, and *live for ever*?' Except in one chapter of the apocryphal book of Daniel, these are the only two instances of the use of the words 'live for ever' in the Pentateuch or in the whole of the Old Testament, and they clearly define the Jews' conception of life generally and of life eternal. Life itself, in the conception of the Jews, is eternal, and so is life in God; but man is mortal, such is his nature.

Nowhere in the Old Testament is it said, as taught in our Bible-classes, that God breathed into man an *immortal soul*, or that the first man before he sinned was immortal. God created man, as is told in the first story in the book of Genesis (ch. i. 26) just as He created the animals, of the male and female gender: and He ordered them to be fruitful and multiply in just the same way. Just as it is not said of the animals that they are immortal, so it is not said of man. In the following chapters it is plainly said that God drove man out of paradise and warded him off from the way to the tree of life. So that man did not eat of the fruit of the tree of life, and did not obtain *khaye-olam*—that is to say, 'life for ever'—but remained mortal.

According to the Jewish teaching man is man just as we know him—that is to say, he is mortal. Life in him is only life continuing itself in the race from generation to generation. Only the race according to the teaching of the Jews has in itself the possibility of life. When God says: 'You shall live and not die', He speaks to the race. The life breathed by God into man is mortal for each separate man; but this life is continued from generation to generation if men fulfil their covenant with God—that is to say, fulfil the conditions demanded for this by God.

Having set forth all the laws, and said that these laws are not from heaven but are in their hearts, Moses says in Deuteronomy xxx. 15: 'See, I have set before thee life and good, and death and evil; in that I command thee to love God, to walk in his ways, and to keep his commandments, that thou mayest live.' And in verse 19: 'I call heaven and earth to witness against you this day, that I have set before thee *life and death*, the blessing and the curse: therefore choose life, that thou mayest live, thou and thy seed: to love God, to obey his voice, and to cleave unto him; for from him is thy life and the length of thy days.'

The chief distinction between our understanding of human life and that of the Jews consists in this, that according to our understanding our mortal life, transmitted from generation to generation, is not real life but a fallen life, for some reason temporarily spoilt; but in the Jewish conception this life is the most real, it is the highest good, given to man on condition that he fulfils the will of God. From our point of view the transmission of that fallen life from generation to generation is the continuation of a curse. From the point of view of the Jews, it is the highest blessing attainable by man and to be reached only by fulfilling God's will.

It is on that understanding of life that Christ bases his teaching of the true or eternal life, which he contrasts with personal and mortal life. 'Ye search the scriptures', says Christ to the Jews (John v. 39), 'because ye think that in them ye have eternal life.'

A young man asked Christ (Matt. xix. 16) how to
enter into eternal life. Christ, replying to the
question of eternal life, says: 'If thou wouldest enter
into *life* (he does not say eternal life, but simply life),
keep the commandments.' He says the same to the
lawyer (Luke x. 28): 'This do, and thou shalt live',
and here also he said *live* simply, without adding
'live eternally.' Christ in both cases defines what
would be understood by the words 'eternal life';
when he uses them he says to the Jews what had
often been said in their law, namely, that the fulfilment of God's will is eternal life.

Christ, in contradiction to temporal, private,
personal life, teaches that eternal life which, in
Deuteronomy, God promised to Israel, only with
this difference, that according to the Jewish conception eternal life endured only in the chosen
people of Israel and to obtain that life it was
necessary to observe the exceptional laws God had
given to Israel; while by Christ's teaching eternal
life continues in the son of man, and what is needed
to preserve it is the observance of the laws of Christ
which express God's will for the whole of humanity.

Christ contrasts with personal life, not a life beyond the grave but common life bound up with the
past, present, and future, the life of the whole of
humanity, the life of the son of man.

The salvation of personal life from death, according to the teaching of the Jews, lay in the fulfilment
of the will of God expressed in the law of Moses by
His commandments. Only on that condition did
life as the Jews understood it not perish but pass on
from generation to generation among God's chosen
people. The salvation of personal life from death,
according to Christ's teaching, lies in a similar fulfilment of the will of God expressed in Christ's
commandments. Only on that condition according

to Christ's teaching does personal life not perish but become ever secure in the son of man. The difference is only in this, that Moses' service of God is a service of the God of one people, while Christ's service of God is a service of the God of all mankind. The survival of life in the generations of one race was doubtful, for that people itself might disappear, and also because that survival depended on corporeal descendants. The survival of life by Christ's teaching is indubitable, because life according to his teaching is transferred to the son of man who lives by the will of the Father.

But even supposing the words of Christ about a day of judgement, the end of the age, and other sayings in John's Gospel, have a meaning referring to a life beyond the grave for the souls of those who have died, nevertheless it is unquestionable that his teaching about the light of life and the kingdom of God also has the meaning, comprehensible to his hearers and comprehensible to us, that the only true life is the life of the son of man according to the will of the Father. It is easier to admit this, since the doctrine of true life according to the will of the Father of life can include the conception of immortality and of life beyond the grave.

It may be more correct to suppose that after this worldly life lived for the fulfilment of his personal will, an everlasting personal life still awaits a man in paradise with all possible delights: perhaps that is more correct; but to think that it is so and to try to believe that for good deeds I shall be rewarded with everlasting bliss and for bad deeds with everlasting torments, does not conduce to an understanding of Christ's teaching. On the contrary, to think so deprives Christ's teaching of its chief basis.

The whole teaching of Christ is that his disciples, having understood the illusory nature of personal life, should renounce it and transfer it into the life of the whole of humanity; the life of the son of man. The teaching of the immortality of the personal soul, on the other hand, does not call for the renunciation of one's personal life, but rivets that personality for ever.

According to the conception of the Jews, the Chinese, the Hindus, and all the people of the world who do not believe the dogma of the fall of man and his redemption, life is life as we know it. A man copulates, has children, brings them up, grows old, and dies. His children grow up and continue his life, which goes on uninterruptedly from generation to generation just as all goes on in the world: stones, earth, metals, plants, animals, stars, and everything in the universe. Life is life and must be used as well as possible. To live for oneself is irrational. Therefore since people existed they have sought an aim of life outside themselves, and live for their child, their family, their tribe, or for humanity, for all that does not die with their personal life.

According to the teaching of our Church, on the contrary, human life, as the greatest good known to us, is represented as being only an atom of the life that is for a time held back from us. Our life according to that view is not life as God wished to give and should have given it us, but is a spoilt, bad, fallen life, a copy of life, a caricature of the real life we for some reason imagine God ought to have given us. The chief aim of our life, according to this view, is not to live this mortal life as the Giver of life desires, nor to make it permanent in the generations of men as the Jews teach, nor does it lie in merging it with the will of the Father as Christ taught, but in convincing oneself that after this life the true life will begin.

Christ does not speak of this imaginary life of ours which God ought to have given, but for some reason did not give, to man. The theory of the fall of Adam and everlasting life in paradise and an immortal soul breathed into Adam by God, was unknown to Christ and he did not refer to it, nor by a single word hint at its existence. Christ speaks of life as it is and always will be. But we speak of a life we have imagined for ourselves—such as never existed; how then can we understand Christ's teaching?

Christ could not imagine such a strange conception among his followers. He assumes that everyone understands that personal life inevitably perishes, and he shows a life that does not perish. He gives welfare to those who are in evil plight; but to those who have persuaded themselves that they have much more than Christ gives, his teaching can offer nothing. I may exhort a man to work, assuring him that for his labour he will receive food and clothing, but suddenly the man becomes convinced that he is a millionaire; evidently he will not listen to my exhortations. The same thing occurs with Christ's teaching. Why should I try to earn, when I can be rich without work? Why should I try to live this life according to the will of God, when I am confident that without that I shall have an everlasting personal life?

We are taught that Christ saved people by the fact that he was the Second Person of the Trinity, that he was God and became incarnate, and having taken on himself the sins of Adam and of all mankind, he redeemed the sins of men before the First Person of the Trinity, and for our salvation established the Church and the sacraments. By believing this we are saved and receive everlasting personal life beyond the grave. But it cannot be denied that he saved and saves people also by the fact that having shown them the inevitable destruction awaiting them, he, by his words, '*I am the way, the truth, and the life*', showed them a true path of life in place of the false path of personal life we previously followed.

There may be people who have doubts about life beyond the grave and salvation based on the redemption, but about the salvation of men, individually and collectively, by showing them the inevitability of the destruction of their personal life and by merging their will with that of the Father, there can be no doubt. Let any rational man ask himself what his life and death is. Can he give to that life and death any other meaning than that which Christ gave?

Any meaning given to a personal life if it be not based on the renunciation of self for the service of man, humanity, the son of man, is a delusion which flies to pieces at the first contact with reason. That my personal life perishes and that the life of the whole world in the will of the Father does not perish, and that only by merging with it can I possibly be saved, of that I can have no doubt. But this is so little in comparison with those exalted religious beliefs in a future life! Though it be little, it is sure.

We are lost in a snow-storm. A man assures us, and he believes, that there are lights and there is a village, but it only seems so to him and to us because we wish it were so. We have walked towards those lights, and there were none. Another man has walked through the snow, he has reached the road and shouts to us: 'You will get nowhere, the lights are in your eyes, you will go astray and perish. But here is the hard road; I am on it, it will keep us right.' That is very little. When we believed in the lights that glittered in our bewildered eyes we seemed close to a village and a warm hut, and to safety and rest, and here we have only a firm road. But if we listen to the first man we shall certainly perish, and if we listen to the second we shall certainly reach our destination.

And so what should I do if I alone have understood Christ's teaching and believed in it—alone among people who do not understand it and do not fulfil it?

What am I to do? Live like everyone else, or live according to Christ's teaching? I have understood Christ's teaching in his commandments, and I see that their fulfilment offers blessedness to me and to all men. I have understood that the execution of these commandments is the will of that Source of all from which my life also has come.

I have understood that whatever I may do I shall inevitably perish in a meaningless life and death, with all who surround me, if I do not fulfil the will of the Father, and that in its fulfilment lies the only possibility of salvation.

Doing as all do I shall certainly counteract the welfare of all, I shall certainly act contrary to the will of the Father of life, I shall certainly deprive myself of the only possibility of bettering my desperate position. Doing what Christ teaches me, I continue what has been done by people who preceded me: I co-operate in the welfare of all men now living as well as of those who will come after me; I do what is desired of me by Him who brought me into existence, and I do what alone can save me.

The circus at Berdíchev is on fire: all push and suffocate one another, pressing against the door which opens inwards. A saviour appears and says: 'Stand back from the door, turn back; the more you push the less chance you have of being saved. Turn

back, and you will find an exit and will be saved.'
Whether many people, or I alone, hear this and
believe it—in any case having heard and believed,
what can I do but stand back and call on all to
listen to the saviour? They may smother, crush,
and kill me; but all the same there is no salvation
for me except by going the only way that makes an
exit possible. And I cannot but go that way. A
saviour should really be a saviour—that is to say,
should really save. Christ's salvation is really
salvation. He came, spoke, and humanity is saved.

The circus has been burning an hour and one
must make haste, and the people may not be in
time to escape. But the world has been burning for
1800 years, since the day when Christ said, 'I have
come to bring fire upon earth; and how am I
straitened till it is kindled'—and that fire will burn
till people save themselves. Is not that why men
exist, and is not that why the fire burns, in order
that people may have the joy of being saved?

And having understood this, I understood and
believed that Jesus is not only the Messiah, the
Christ, but that he is really the Saviour of the
world.

I know that there is no other exit either for me
or for all those who together with me are tormented
in this life. I know that for all, and for me together
with them, there is no way of escape except by fulfilling those commands of Christ which offer to all
humanity the highest welfare of which I can
conceive.

I am not frightened about whether I shall have
more unpleasantness or whether I shall die sooner.
This may be terrible to one who does not see how
senseless and ruinous is his separate, personal life,
and who thinks he will not die. But I know that my
life, aiming at personal, solitary happiness, is the

greatest absurdity, and that at the end of this stupid life there is inevitably nothing but a stupid death. Therefore things cannot be at all terrible for me. I shall die like everyone else, like those who do not fulfil the teaching; but both for me and for all, my life and death will have a meaning. My life and death will serve the salvation and life of all, and that is what Christ taught.

IX

FAITH AND WORKS

WERE all people to fulfil Christ's teaching the kingdom of God would have come on earth; if I alone fulfil it, I do the best that is possible for myself and for all men. Without the fulfilment of the teaching of Christ there is no salvation. 'But how is one to get the faith to fulfil it, always to follow it, and never to be unfaithful to it?' 'Lord, I believe; help Thou my unbelief.'

The disciples asked Christ to confirm their faith; 'I wish to do good, but I do evil', says the Apostle Paul. 'It is hard to be saved', men in general say and think.

A man is sinking and asks to be saved; a rope is thrown him which alone can save him, and the drowning man says: 'Confirm my faith that the rope will save me. I believe', says he, 'that the rope will save me, but help my unbelief.'

What does this mean? If the man does not seize the thing that can save him it only means that he does not understand his position.

How could a Christian, believing in the divinity of Christ and all his teachings (however he understand them), say that he wishes to believe but cannot? God himself, coming to earth, said: You have before you everlasting torment, fire, everlasting infernal darkness—and here is your salvation—in my teaching and in its fulfilment.

It is impossible for such a Christian not to believe in the offered salvation, not to fulfil it, and to say, 'Help thou my unbelief'.

In order that man might say that, he must disbelieve in his own destruction and must believe that he will not perish.

Children jump from a ship into the water. They are still upheld by the current, by their clothes which are not yet soaked, and by their own feeble movements, and they do not understand their peril. From above, from the departing ship, a rope is thrown to them; they are told that they will certainly perish, and are begged by those on the ship to save themselves (the parables of the woman who found a piece of silver, of the shepherd who found a lost sheep, of the supper, and of the prodigal son, speak only of this). But the children do not believe; they disbelieve, not in the rope but in the fact that they are perishing; other frivolous children like themselves have assured them that they will always continue merrily bathing even after the ship has gone. They do not believe that their clothes will soon be soaked, that their little arms will be tired, that they will begin to gasp, will be choked, and will go to the bottom; they do not believe in all this, and solely for that reason do not believe in the rope which would save them.

As the children who have fallen from the ship do not believe that they will perish, and therefore do not catch at the rope, so people who believe in the immortality of the soul have convinced themselves that they are not perishing, and therefore they do not obey the teaching of Christ-God. They do not believe that which it is impossible to disbelieve, and this simply because they believe in that which it is impossible to believe.

And so they call to someone: 'Confirm in us the belief that we are not perishing.'

But this it is impossible to do; in order that they should have faith that they will not perish they must cease to do the things that destroy them and must begin to do the things that save them— they must catch at the rope which would save them; and they do not wish to do this but to assure themselves that they are not perishing, despite the fact that one after another their comrades perish before their eyes. And this desire of theirs to believe in that which is not true, they call faith. It is natural that they always have little faith and want to have more.

Only when I understood the teaching of Christ did I understand also that what these people call faith is not faith, and that this false faith is what the Apostle James rejected in his Epistle. (That Epistle was long not acknowledged by the Church, and when it was accepted it underwent certain perversions, some words were thrown out, and some transposed or arbitrarily translated. I follow the accepted translation, merely correcting the inaccuracies, in accordance with Tischendorf's text.[1])

James ii. 14–22, 24, 26: 'What doth it profit, my brethren', says James, 'if a man say he hath faith, and have not works? can that faith save him? If a brother or sister be naked, and in lack of daily food, and one of you say unto them, Go in peace, be ye warmed and filled; and yet ye give them not the things needful to the body; what doth it profit? Even so faith, if it have not works, is dead in itself. Yea, a man may say, Thou hast faith, and I have

---

[1] The English Revised Version accords with Tolstóy's translation, and has been followed here.—A.M.

works: show me thy faith apart from thy works, and
I by my works will show thee my faith. Thou be-
lievest that God is one; thou doest well: the devils
also believe, and shudder. But wilt thou know, O
vain man, that faith apart from works is barren?
Was not Abraham our father justified by works, in
that he had offered up Isaac his son upon the altar?
Thou seest that faith wrought with his works, and
by works was faith made perfect. . . . Ye see that by
works a man is justified, and not only by faith. For
as the body apart from the spirit is dead, even so
faith apart from works is dead.'

James says that the only signs of faith are the
works which flow from it, and that therefore faith
from which works do not flow is a matter of mere
words, which, as they will not feed anyone, will also
not justify anyone or save him, and therefore faith
from which works do not flow is not faith but only
the desire to believe something: only a mistaken assertion in words that I believe what I do not believe.

Faith, according to this definition, is that which
promotes deeds, and deeds are what faith produces
—that is to say, that which makes faith really faith.
The Jews said to Christ (John vi. 30), 'What then
doest thou for a sign, that we may see, and believe
thee? What workest thou?'

That is what was said to him when he was on the
cross (Mark xv. 32): 'Let the Christ, the King of
Israel, now come down from the cross, that we may
see and believe.' (Matt. xxvii. 42): 'He saved others;
himself he cannot save. He is the King of Israel;
let him now come down from the cross, and we will
believe on him.' And to this demand to increase
their faith, Christ replies that their wish is vain
and that nothing can compel them to believe that
which they do not believe. (Luke xxii. 67) He said,
'If I tell you, ye will not believe'. (John x. 25–6)

'I told you, and ye believe not. But ye believe not, because ye are not of my sheep.'

The Jews demanded what is demanded by Church Christians, some external sign which would compel them to believe in the teaching of Christ, and he replies and explains to them why it is impossible. He says that they cannot believe because they are not of his sheep—that is to say, do not follow that path of life which he has shown to his sheep. He explained (John v. 44) wherein lies the difference between his sheep and others, explaining what some believe and others do not believe, and on what faith rests. 'How can ye believe', says he, 'which receive teaching[1] one of another, and the teaching that cometh from the only God ye seek not?'

To believe, says Christ, you must seek that teaching which flows from the only God. He who speaks from himself seeks his own teaching (δόξαν τήν ἰδιαν), but he who seeks the teaching of him who sent me is true, and there is no untruth in him (John vii. 18). The teaching of life is the basis of faith.

Actions all flow from faith, faith comes from *doxa*, that meaning which we attribute to life. There may be innumerable actions; there are also very many faiths; but there are only two *doxa*, doctrines of life. One of these is denied and the other affirmed by Christ. One teaching, that which is denied by Christ, is that personal life is something really existing and belonging to men. This is the doctrine which was held, and is held, by the majority of men, and from which flow all the various faiths held by worldly men and all their actions. The other doctrine is that which was preached by all the prophets and by Christ: it is that our personal life

[1] δόξα, as in many other passages, is here quite wrongly translated by the word 'glory'; δόξα, from δοκέω, means opinion, judgement, doctrine.—L.T.

gains meaning only by the fulfilment of the will
of God.

If a man has for his *doxa* that the most important
thing is his personality, he will consider that his
personal welfare is the most important and desirable
thing in life, and according to the direction in which
he seeks that welfare—whether in obtaining property, or distinction, or fame, or in the satisfaction
of his desires—he will have a faith corresponding
to that outlook, and all his actions will accord
with it.

If his *doxa* is different, if he understands life in
such a way that its meaning lies only in the fulfilment of the will of God, as it was understood by
Abraham and as Christ taught, then his view of
faith will accord with his perception of the will of
God, and all his actions will conform therewith.

That is why those who believe that our life is
satisfactory cannot believe in the teaching of Christ
and all their efforts to believe it always remain vain.
In order to believe, they would have to alter their
outlook on life; and until they alter that, their actions
will always conform to their belief and not to what
they wish to believe and say they believe.

The desire to believe in the teaching of Christ,
in those who asked a sign of him and in our believers,
does not correspond and cannot correspond with
their life, however they may try to make it. They
may pray to Christ-God, and receive Communion,
and do deeds of charity, and build churches, and
convert others; all this they do, but they cannot do
Christ's deeds, because such deeds flow from faith
based on quite another teaching (*doxa*) than that
which they hold. They cannot offer up in sacrifice
their only son as was done by Abraham, whereas
Abraham could not have hesitated about presenting
or not presenting his son in sacrifice to God, that

God who alone gave meaning and blessedness to his life. And in just the same way Christ and his disciples could not but give up their lives for others, for in that alone lay the meaning and welfare of their life. From this misunderstanding of the essence of faith flows that strange desire people have to believe that it would be better to live according to the teaching of Christ, while with all the strength of their souls, in accordance with their faith in personal life, they seek to live contrary to that teaching.

The basis of faith is the meaning of life, from which flows the valuation of what is important and good and what is unimportant and bad in life. The valuation of all the phenomena of life depends on one's faith. And as now people having faith based on their own teaching, cannot in any way make it accord with the faith which flows from the teaching of Christ, so was it also impossible for his disciples to do so. And this misunderstanding is frequently and clearly expressed in the Gospels. Christ's disciples often asked him to confirm their faith in what he told them (Matt. xix. 23–8 and xx. 20–8; Mark x. 35–45). According to both the Evangelists, after the sayings—terrible to every believer in personal life and to everyone who sees welfare in worldly riches—after the words that the rich will not enter the kingdom of heaven, and the words still more terrible for those who believe only in personal life—that whosoever does not leave all, even life itself, for the sake of Christ's teaching, will not be saved—Peter asks, 'What shall we have who have left all and followed thee?' Afterwards, James and John, themselves according to Mark, but their mother according to Matthew, asked him to grant that they should sit on each side of him when he should be in his glory. They

asked him to confirm their faith by promising a
reward. To Peter's question Jesus replied with the
parable of the labourers hired at different hours
(Matt. xx. 1–16). To James's question he answered:
You know not yourself what you ask—that is to say,
you ask impossibilities, you do not understand the
teaching. The teaching lies in the renunciation of
personal life and you are asking for personal fame,
personal reward. You can drink the same cup (live
the same life) as I, but to sit on my right and left
hand, that is, to be equal with me, is what no one
can do. And here Christ says: Only in worldly life
do the powerful enjoy and delight in the fame and
power of personal life; but you, my disciples, should
know that the meaning of human life does not lie
in personal happiness, but in serving all, in humiliation before all. Man lives not to be served, but
himself to serve and give up his personal life as a
ransom for all. Christ, in reply to his disciples'
demand, which showed him how completely they
failed to understand his teaching, did not tell them
to believe—that is to say, to change that valuation
of the good and evil in life which flowed from their
conception (he knew that this was impossible) but
explained to them the meaning of life on which his
faith rested—that is to say, the true valuation of
what is good and evil, important and unimportant.

To Peter's question (Matt. xix. 27) 'What shall
we have, what reward for our sacrifices?' Christ
replies with the parable of the labourers hired at
different times and receiving identical payment.
Christ explains to Peter his misunderstanding of the
teaching, from which his absence of faith results.
Christ says: Only in personal and meaningless life
is it precious and important that the remuneration
for work should accord with the amount of work
done. The belief in a remuneration for work ac-

cording to the amount of work flows from the doctrine of personal life. That belief rests on the assumption that we have a claim to something; but man has no rights and can have none. He is ever in debt for the welfare given him, and therefore can make no demands on anyone. Even if he gives up his whole life he still cannot repay what has been given him, and therefore his master cannot be unjust to him. If a man asserts rights to his life and keeps account with the Source of all things which has given him life, he thereby only shows that he does not understand the meaning of life.

People who had received happiness demanded something more. These people stood in the market-places idle and unhappy, lacking life. The master took them, and gave them the greatest blessing of life—work. They accepted the kindness of the master, and then remained dissatisfied. They were dissatisfied because they had no clear consciousness of their position; they had come to work holding a false doctrine to the effect that they had rights to their life and to their labour, and that therefore their labour should be rewarded. They did not understand that this labour was the highest blessing, which is freely given to them and for which they should only try to return a similar blessing but could not demand reward. And therefore people having a perverted understanding of life, like these workmen, cannot have a just and true faith.

The parable of the master and the workman who returned from the field, spoken in reply to the disciples' direct request that he would confirm their faith, defines yet more clearly the foundations of the faith Christ teaches.

(Luke xvii. 3–10) Horrified at the difficulty of fulfilling the rule Christ lays down, that one must forgive one's brother not seven times, but unto

seventy times seven, the disciples say: Yes, but . . .
in order to fulfil this, one must have faith; confirm,
increase, our faith. As previously they had asked:
'What shall we get for it?' so now they ask what all
so-called Christians ask to-day: We want to believe,
but cannot; confirm our belief that the rope of
salvation will save us. They say: Do something to
make us believe, just as the Jews had asked of him
a sign. By miracles, or by promising rewards, make
us believe in our salvation.

The disciples said, as we say: It would be well to
arrange so that we, living the personal, self-willed
life we do, could also believe that if we were to
fulfil God's teaching things would be still better for
us. We all make that demand, which is one contrary
to the whole sense of Christ's teaching, and we are
surprised that we are quite unable to believe. And
to this most fundamental misunderstanding, which
existed then as it exists now, he replies with a
parable in which he shows what true faith is. Faith
cannot result from credulous acceptance of what is
said; faith comes only from recognizing one's
position. Faith rests only on reasonable consciousness of what it is best to do being in the position in
which we are. He shows that it is impossible to
arouse this faith in others by promising a reward or
by threats of punishment, and that this could result
only in a weak credulity which would crumble at
the first temptation; that the faith which moves
mountains—that which nothing can disturb—rests
on a consciousness of inevitable impending destruction, and of the only possible means of safety in this
position.

To have faith, no promises of reward are necessary. It is only necessary to understand that salvation from inevitable destruction lies in living a
common life according to the Master's will. Who-

ever understands that, will not seek for confirmation but will save himself without any exhortations.

To the disciples' request for a confirmation of their faith Christ says: When a workman returns from the field, his master does not at once tell him to have dinner, but tells him to stall the cattle and serve him, and only then will the workman sit down to table and have dinner. The workman does all this without considering himself ill-used, and does not boast or demand gratitude or reward, but knows that so it should be and that he is but doing what is needful: that this is a necessary condition both of the service and of the true welfare of his life. So also you, says Christ, when you have done all that is demanded of you, must consider that you have only done your duty. He who understands his relation to the Master will understand that only by submitting to his Master's will can he have life; and he will know wherein his welfare lies and will have a faith to which nothing will be impossible. This is the faith Christ teaches. Faith, according to Christ's teaching, rests on a reasonable consciousness of the meaning of one's life.

The foundation of faith, according to Christ's teaching, is light.

(John i. 9–12) 'That was the true light, which lighteth every man coming into the world. He was in the world, and the world was made through him, and the world knew him not. He came unto his own, and his own received him not. But as many as received him, even to them that believe on his name, gave he the right to become the children of God.' (iii. 19–21) 'And this is the judgement,[1] that the light is come into the world, but men loved the darkness rather than the light: for their works were

---

[1] The judgement (κρίσις) does not mean the *judgement*, but the *division*.—L.T.

evil. For everyone that doeth ill hateth the light, and cometh not to the light, lest his works should be reproved. But he that doeth the truth cometh to the light, that his works may be made manifest, because they have been wrought in God.'

For him who has understood the teaching of Christ there cannot be any question of confirming his faith. Faith, according to Christ's teaching, rests on light, on truth. Christ nowhere demands faith in himself: he demands faith in the truth.

(John viii. 40) He says to the Jews: 'Ye seek to kill me, a man that hath told you the truth, which I heard from God.' (46) 'Which of you convicteth me of sin? If I say truth, why do ye not believe me?' (xviii. 37) He says, 'To this end was I born, and to this end am I come into the world, that I should bear witness unto the truth. Everyone that is of the truth heareth my voice.' (xiv. 6) He says, 'I am the way, and the truth, and the life.' (16) 'The Father', says he to the disciples, 'shall give you another comforter, that he may be with you for ever.' (17) 'That comforter is the spirit of truth, whom the world neither sees nor knows, but whom ye know, for he is with you and shall be in you.'

He says that his whole teaching, and that he himself, is truth.

The teaching of Christ is the teaching of truth. And therefore faith in Christ is not credulously accepting something concerning Jesus, but is knowledge of the truth. The teaching of Christ is not a thing anyone can be induced to believe in, nor is it possible to bribe anyone to fulfil it. He who understands the teaching of Christ will also have faith in it, because that teaching is the truth. And he who knows the truth necessary for his welfare cannot but believe it, as a man who has understood that he is really sinking cannot but catch at the rope of salvation. And the question: What must I do to believe? is a question which merely displays a non-comprehension of Jesus Christ's teaching.

X

'MY YOKE IS EASY'

WE say, 'It is difficult to live in accordance with the teaching of Christ!' And how can it but be difficult when we ourselves, by the arrangement of our whole life, laboriously hide our position from ourselves and laboriously confirm ourselves in a credulous belief that our position is not at all what it is, but is quite different? And having called this credulity 'faith', we make of it something sacred, and by every means—by working on their feelings, by threats, flattery, and deception—we allure men to this false credulity. In this demand for credulous belief in the impossible and unnatural we have reached such a pass that the very irrationality of that for which we demand credulous belief is considered a sign of its validity. A man, 'a Christian', was found who said, *Credo quia absurdum*,[1] and other Christians repeated this with enthusiasm, assuming that absurdity is the very best method of teaching people the truth. Recently I had a conversation with a learned and clever man who told me that Christian teaching, as a moral teaching of life, is unimportant. 'All that', said he to me, 'could be found among the Stoics and the Brahmins and in the Talmud. The essence of the Christian teaching is not in that, but in the theosophic teaching

---

[1] The actual words used by Tertullian were, *Certum quia impossibile*. One might amend the above passage to make it read: 'Others have repeated this, assuming that the assertion of impossibilities is the best method of inculcating truth.'—A.M.

expressed in its dogmas.' In other words, not that is precious in Christian teaching which is eternal and common to all mankind, necessary for life and reasonable, but what is important and precious is what is quite unintelligible and therefore unnecessary, and for the sake of which millions of people have been slaughtered.

We have formed for ourselves a false perception of our life and of the life of the world, based on nothing but our own enmities and personal desires; and we consider belief in this false perception, which is artificially connected with Christ's teaching, to be what is most necessary and important for life. Were it not for this credulous belief in falsehood, which has been maintained among men for centuries, the falsity of our conception of life and the truth of Christ's teaching would long ago have become plain.

It is terrible to say, but it sometimes appears to me that if Christ's teaching, with the Church teaching which has grown out of it, had not existed at all, those who now call themselves Christians would have been nearer to the truth of Christ— that is to say, to a reasonable understanding of what is good in life—than they now are. The moral teaching of the prophets of all humanity would not have been closed to them; they would have had their own small preachers of truth and would have believed in them. But now that the whole truth is open to them, that whole truth has seemed so terrible to those whose deeds are evil, that they have reinterpreted it into falsehood, and people have lost their belief in what is true. In our European civilized society, in reply to Christ's statement that he came into the world to witness to the truth and that therefore everyone who is of the truth hears him—people have long ago answered in the words of Pilate, 'What is truth?' Those words, which so bitterly and profoundly expose the mental condition of one Roman ruler we have accepted seriously and have adopted as our belief. All in our world live, not merely without the truth, not merely without a desire to know it, but with a firm conviction that of all useless occupations the most useless is the search for truth defining human life.

The teaching of life—which among all nations before the age of European society was always considered the most important thing, and of which Christ said that it was the one thing needful—this one thing is excluded from our life and from the whole activity of humanity. With this matter the institution which calls itself the Church is occupied: an institution in which all, including even those who are its members, have long ceased to believe. The solitary window towards the light, to which the eyes of all who think or who suffer are directed, has been boarded up. In reply to the question, 'What am I?' and 'What am I to do? Can I not aid my life by the teaching of that God who, you say, came to save me?' I am told, 'Obey the demands of the powers that be, and believe in the Church'. 'But why is it so hard for me to live in this world?' asks a despairing voice; 'Why is there all this evil? Is it not possible for me in my own life to abstain from participating in this evil? Can it be that it is impossible to lessen this evil?' They reply: 'It is impossible. Your wish to live your life well and to help others to do the same is pride and a snare. The one thing you can do is to save yourself; that is, to save your soul for a future life. If you do not wish to participate in the evil of the world, retire from it; that path is open to everyone', says the teaching of the Church. 'But know that on choosing that path you must not take part in the life of the world,

but must cease to live and slowly kill yourself.'
There are two paths, say our teachers: (1) to believe
and to obey us and the powers that be and participate in the evil we have organized, or (2) to retire
from the world and go into a monastery, not sleep-
ing and not eating, rotting your flesh on the top
of a column,[1] bending and unbending and doing
nothing of any use to men. Either admit the teaching of Christ to be impracticable, and therefore
acquiesce in the lawlessness of life the Church has
sanctified, or renounce life—which is equivalent to
slow suicide.

Astonishing (to anyone who understands Christ's
teaching) as is the delusion which admits Christ's
teaching to be very good for men but impracticable,
still more amazing is that delusion which acknowledges that a man who wishes to carry out the
teaching of Christ not in words only but in deeds,
ought to retire from the world.

The delusion that it is better for men to withdraw from the world is an old delusion, familiar
long ago to the Jews, but quite foreign to the spirit
not only of Christianity but even to that of Judaism.
Against that fallacy, long before the time of Christ,
was written the story of the prophet Jonah of which
Christ was so fond and which he so often quoted.
The thought of that story from beginning to end
is identical. Jonah, the prophet, wishes personally,
by himself alone, to be a just man, and he withdraws from among depraved people, but God shows
him that he is a prophet and that therefore it is
necessary that he should impart his knowledge to
the people who are in error, and so he should not
flee from the erring people, but should live in

[1] Like St. Simeon Stylites and the other Stylites, who are
more highly honoured in the Eastern than in the Western
world.—A.M.

contact with them. Jonah despises the depraved Ninevites and flees from them; but, try as he may to escape from his destiny, God brings him back to the Ninevites by means of the whale, and what God desires is accomplished, namely, the Ninevites receive God's teaching from Jonah, and their life becomes better. But Jonah, far from being glad that he is the instrument of God's will, is discontented, and is jealous of God's favour to the Ninevites, and would like to be reasonable and good alone by himself. He withdraws into the desert, weeps over his fate, and reproaches God: then a gourd grows up in one night over him and shields him from the sun, and in another night a worm eats the gourd, and Jonah reproaches God still more desperately because the gourd he valued has been lost. Then God says to him, 'You regret the gourd you call yours, which grew up in one night; but do I not regret the great people which was perishing, living like beasts unable to distinguish their right hand from their left? Your knowledge of the truth was only of value if it was communicated to those who had it not'.

Christ knew the story and frequently quoted it, and we are also told in the Gospels how Christ himself after visiting John the Baptist, who had withdrawn into the desert, underwent that same temptation before commencing his own preaching, and how he was led away by the devil (by a deception) into the desert to be tempted, and how he conquered that deception and in the strength of his spirit returned into Galilee, and how from that time on, he did not avoid depraved people, but spent his life among publicans, Pharisees, and sinners, teaching them the truth (Luke iv. 1).[1]

---

[1] Christ was led into the wilderness in order there to be tempted (Matt. iv. 3–7). The deception told Christ that he

According to Church teaching, Christ, the God-Man, gave us an example of life. The whole of the life of Christ known to us was led in the very whirlpool of life among publicans and adulterers in Jerusalem, and with the Pharisees. The chief injunctions of Christ were love of one's neighbour and the preaching of the truth to others; the one and the other demand continual intercourse with the world. Suddenly out of this is deduced the conclusion that according to the teaching of Christ one should withdraw from everything, have nothing to do with anyone, and stand on a column. In order to follow the example of Christ it appears that one must do exactly the opposite of what he taught and of what he did. The teaching of Christ, according to Church commentators, is presented both for worldly people and also for the Religious Orders not as a teaching of life—how to make it better for ourselves and for others—but as a teaching of what the worldly people, while living badly, should believe in order to save themselves in the next world; and for the Religious Orders, how to make this life still worse for themselves than it is.

But that is not what Christ taught. Christ taught

was not a Son of God if he could not turn stones into bread. Christ replied: 'I can live without bread; I live by that which was breathed into me by God.' Then the deception said: 'If you live by that which was breathed into you by God, throw yourself down from this high place; you will kill your flesh, but the spirit breathed into you by God will not perish.' Christ replied: 'It is the will of God that I should live in the flesh; to kill my flesh means to act contrary to the will of God—to tempt God' (Matt. iv. 8–11). Then the deception said: 'If that is so, then serve your flesh as all men do, and your flesh will reward you.' Christ replied: 'I am not the owner of my flesh. My life is in the spirit; but I cannot destroy my flesh, because my spirit is in my flesh by the will of God, and therefore only by living in the flesh can I serve my Father, God.' And Christ departed from the wilderness into the world.—L.T.

truth, and if abstract truth is truth it will also be true in practice; and if life in God is the only true life blessed in itself, then it is true and blessed here on earth, amid all the possible accidents of life. If life here did not confirm the teaching of Christ about life, that teaching would be untrue.

Christ does not call us to something worse instead of something better, but on the contrary to something better instead of something worse. He pities people who appear to him like lost sheep perishing without a shepherd, and he promises them a shepherd and good pasture. He says that his disciples will be persecuted for his teaching and will have to suffer and to endure worldly persecution with fortitude, but he does not say that by following his teaching they will suffer more than by following the world's teaching; on the contrary, he says that those who follow the teaching of the world will be unhappy, and those who follow his teaching will be blessed.

Christ does not teach salvation by faith or by asceticism—that is, by a deception of the imagination or by voluntarily tormenting oneself in this life; but he teaches life in which besides salvation from the loss of personal life, there will, here in this world, be less of suffering and more of joy than in a personal life.

Christ, revealing his teaching, says to people that by following it, even among those who do not follow it, they will not be more unhappy than before but on the contrary will be happier than those who reject it. He says that there is true worldly advantage in not taking thought for the worldly life.

'And Peter began to say unto him: Behold we have left all and followed thee; what shall we receive?' Jesus answered him and said, 'Verily, I say unto you, there is not one who has left home, or brother, or sister, or father, or mother, or wife, or child, or lands, for my sake and the Gospel's, who will not receive now, in this time, amid persecutions, a hundred times more houses, and brethren, and sisters, and fathers, and mothers, and children, and lands, and in the age to come life eternal'. (Matt. xix. 27, 29; Mark x. 28–30; Luke xviii. 28–30.)

Christ, it is true, says that those who follow him will be persecuted by those who do not listen to him, but he does not say that the disciples will lose anything thereby; on the contrary, he says that his disciples will have more of joy here in this world than those who do not follow him.

That Christ says and thinks this is shown beyond possibility of doubt by the clearness of his words and the drift of his whole teaching, as well as by his way of life and that of his disciples. But is it true?

Examining the abstract question whether the position of the disciples of Christ or of the disciples of the world is the better, one cannot but see that the position of the disciples of Christ should be better, because they, doing good to all men, would not evoke hatred. The disciples of Christ, doing harm to no one, would only be persecuted by evil men, but the disciples of the world would be persecuted by all, since the law of their life is the law of strife—that is to say, the persecution one of another. The chances of suffering are the same for these as for those, with only this difference, that Christ's disciples will be prepared for the sufferings, but the world's disciples will employ all the powers of their souls to escape them; and that Christ's disciples when suffering will think that the world needs their sufferings, but the world's disciples when suffering will not know why they suffer. Arguing in the abstract, the position of Christ's followers should be better than that of those of the world. But is it so in reality?

To verify this let everyone remember all the painful moments of his life, all the physical and spiritual sufferings he has endured and still endures, and ask himself for what has he borne all these misfortunes, for the sake of the world's teaching or for that of Christ's? Let every sincere man remember well his whole life, and he will see that never, not once, has he suffered from obeying the teaching of Christ, but that most of the misfortunes of his life have come about because contrary to his own inclination he has followed the world's teaching which constrained him.

In my own life, exceptionally fortunate in a worldly sense, I can recall sufferings borne by me in the name of the world's teaching which would be sufficient to supply a good Christian martyr. All the bitterest moments of my life, from the drunkenness and debauchery of student-days, the duels, war, and so on, to that ill-health and those unnatural and trying conditions of life in which I now live—all this was martyrdom in the name of the world's teaching.

And I speak of my own life, which is exceptionally fortunate in a worldly sense. But how many martyrs are there who have endured and are now enduring, for the sake of the world's teaching, sufferings which I cannot even vividly imagine to myself!

We do not see all the difficulty and danger of obeying the world's teaching, merely because we consider that all we endure for it is unavoidable.

We have assured ourselves that all these misfortunes which we inflict on ourselves are necessary conditions of our life, and therefore we are unable to grasp the fact that Christ teaches just how we should free ourselves from these misfortunes and live happily.

To be in a condition to discuss the question which life is happier, we should dismiss that false notion, if only in thought, and look without prejudice within ourselves and around us.

Go among a large crowd of people, especially townsfolk, and notice the wearied, distressed, sickly faces, and then remember your own life and the lives of people about whom you have known; remember all the violent deaths, all the suicides of which you have heard, and ask yourself for whose sake was all this suffering, death, and suicidal despair? And you will see, strange as it at first seems, that nine-tenths of these sufferings are endured for the sake of the world's teaching, that all these sufferings are unnecessary and need not exist, and that the majority of people are martyrs to the world's teaching.

Recently, one rainy autumn Sunday, I went by tram through the Bazaar at the Súkharev Tower. For nearly half a mile the car made its way through a dense crowd of people who immediately closed in again behind it. From morning to night these thousands of people, of whom most are hungry and ragged, swarm here in the dirt, scolding, cheating, and hating one another. The same thing occurs in all the bazaars of Moscow. The evening is passed by these people in the dram-shops and taverns, the night in their corners[1] and hovels. Sunday is the best day in their week. On Monday, in their infected dens, they will again resume the work they detest.

[1] It was common for Moscow workmen to live in a corner of a room or passage, generally not even screened off from the rest of the room in which other people, besides the owner and his family, had other corners.—A.M.

Consider the life of all these people in the positions they left to choose that in which they have placed themselves, and remember the unceasing toil these people voluntarily endure—men and women—and you will see that they are real martyrs.

All these people have left their homes, fields, fathers, brothers, and often their wives and children, and have abandoned everything, even their very lives, and have come to town to acquire that which according to the teaching of the world is considered indispensable for each of them. And they all—not to mention those tens of thousands of unfortunate people who have lost everything and struggle along on garbage and vodka in the doss-houses—they all, from the factory hands, cabmen, seamstresses and prostitutes, to the rich merchants and Ministers of State with their wives, endure the most trying and unnatural manner of life and yet fail to acquire what, according to the teaching of the world, they need.

Search among these people for a man, poor or rich, for whom what he earns secures what he considers necessary according to the world's teaching, and you will not find one in a thousand. Everyone struggles with his whole strength to obtain what he does not need, but what is demanded of him by the teaching of the world and the absence of which therefore makes him unhappy. And as soon as he obtains what is required, something else, and again something else, is demanded of him, and so this work of Sisyphus continues endlessly, ruining the life of men. Take the ladder of wealth of people who spend from £30 to £5,000 a year, and you will rarely find one who is not tormented and worn out with work to obtain £40 when he has £30, and £50 when he has £40, and so on endlessly. And there is not one who having £50 would voluntarily exchange into the way of life of one having £40, or if there are

such cases the exchange is made not to live more
easily, but to save money and hide it away. They
all have to burden their already overladen life more
and more with work and to devote their life and
soul entirely to the service of the world's teaching.
To-day I obtain a coat and goloshes, to-morrow a
watch and chain, after to-morrow a lodging with a
sofa and a lamp, then carpets in the sitting-room
and velvet clothes, then race-horses and pictures in
gilt frames, till finally I fall ill from my excessive
labours and die. Another continues the same
labour and also sacrifices his life to that same
Moloch; he too dies and also does not know why
he did what he did. But perhaps the life itself
during which a man does all this is happy?

Test that life by the measure of what all men have
always described as happiness and you will see that
this life is terribly unhappy. Indeed, what are the
chief conditions of earthly happiness—those which
no one disputes?

One of the first conditions acknowledged by
everyone is that man's union with nature should not
be infringed—that is to say, that he should live
under the open sky, in the light of the sun and in
the fresh air, in contact with the earth, with vegeta-
tion, and with animals. All men have always considered that to be deprived of those things was a
great misfortune. Men confined in prison feel this
deprivation more than anything else. But consider
the life of people who live according to the teaching
of the world: the more they achieve success according to the world's teaching the more are they deprived of this condition of happiness. The higher
they climb in the scale of worldly fortune the less
do they see of the light of the sun, of the fields and
the woods, and of wild or domestic animals. Many
of them, almost all the women, live on to old age

seeing the rising of the sun only once or twice in
their lives, and never seeing the fields and the woods
except from a carriage or a railway train, and not
only without having sown or planted anything, or
fed or reared cows, horses, or hens, but without even
having an idea of how those animals are born, grow,
and live. These people only see textiles, stone, and
wood shaped by human toil, and that not by the
light of the sun but by artificial light. They only
hear the sounds of machines, vehicles, cannons, and
musical instruments; they smell scents and tobacco-
smoke; under their feet and hands they have only
textiles, stone, and wood; for the most part, on
account of their weak digestions, they eat highly-
spiced food that is not fresh. Their movements
from place to place do not save them from these
deprivations. They move about in closed boxes.
In the country and abroad, wherever they go, they
have the same textiles and wood under their feet,
the same curtains hiding the light of the sun from
them, the same footmen, coachmen and porters
depriving them of contact with the earth, with
plants, and with animals. Wherever they may be
they are deprived, like prisoners, of this condition
of happiness. As prisoners console themselves with
a tuft of grass that grows in the prison yard, with a
spider or a mouse, so these people sometimes console themselves with puny indoor plants, a parrot,
or a monkey, and even these they do not themselves
rear.

Another undoubted condition of happiness is
work; in the first place voluntary work which one is
fond of, and secondly physical work which gives one
an appetite and sound, restful sleep. Again the more
good fortune people have secured according to the
world's teaching, the more are they deprived of this
second condition of happiness. All the fortunate

ones of the world, the men in important places and the rich, either live like prisoners, quite deprived of work and vainly struggling with diseases that arise from the absence of physical labour, and still more vainly with the ennui which overcomes them (I say vainly, because work is only joyous when it is undoubtedly needful—and they need nothing), or they do work they hate, as bankers, public prosecutors, governors, or ministers, while their wives arrange drawing-rooms, china, and costumes for themselves and their children. (I say hateful because I have never yet met one of them who praised his occupation, or did it with even as much pleasure as that with which a porter clears away the snow from before the house.) All these fortunate people are either deprived of work or are burdaned with work they dislike—that is to say, they find themselves in the position in which prisoners are placed.

The third indubitable condition of happiness is a family. And again, the further people have advanced in worldly success the less is that happiness accessible to them. Most of them are adulterers, and consciously renounce the happiness of a family, submitting only to its inconveniences. If they are not adulterers, still their children are not a joy to them but a burden, and they deprive themselves of them, trying in every way—often by most tormenting means—to make their marital unions barren. Or if they have children they are deprived of the joy of intercourse with them. By their rules they have to hand them over to strangers, for the most part quite alien people; first to foreigners,[1] and then to the Government instructors;[2] so that their

---

[1] This is a reference to the common Russian practice of having a foreign nurse, governess, or tutor for young children, that they may learn a foreign language in the nursery.—A.M.

[2] The Russian schools are State institutions.—A.M.

family only causes them grief, their children from infancy becoming as unhappy as their parents and having only one feeling towards their parents—a desire for their death in order to inherit their property.[1] They are not shut up in prison, but the consequences of their life in regard to their family, are more tormenting than the deprivation of family life to which prisoners are exposed.

The fourth condition of happiness is free, amicable intercourse with all the different people in the world. And again, the higher the rank attained by men of the world the more are they deprived of this chief condition of happiness: the higher, the narrower and the more restricted is the group of people with whom it is possible for them to associate and the lower in mental and moral development are the few people who form the enchanted circle from which there is no escape. For a peasant and his wife intercourse is open with the whole world of mankind, and if one million people do not wish to have intercourse with him he still has eighty millions of people such as himself, labouring people with whom, from Archangel to Astrakhan, without waiting for visits or introductions, he can at once enter into the closest brotherly relations. For an official with his wife there are hundreds of people on the same level as himself, but those above him

---

[1] The defence of such a life that one often hears from parents is amazing. 'I want nothing', say the parents; 'this kind of life is hard for me, but as I love my children I bear it for their sakes.' That is to say, I know by undoubted experience that our life is unhappy, and therefore . . . I educate my children so that they shall be as unhappy as I am. And therefore, out of my love for them, I place them in the full physical and moral contagion of a town; I hand them over to strangers who have only a mercenary aim in educating them; and so physically, morally, and mentally I take pains to injure my children. And this contention has to serve as justification for the irrational life the parents themselves lead!—L.T.

do not receive him and those below him are all separated from him. For a rich man of the world and his wife a few dozen worldly families are accessible, all the rest are cut off from him. For a Minister of State, or a millionaire, and his family, there are a single dozen similarly important or wealthy people. For Emperors and Kings the circle is yet more restricted. Is not this a form of imprisonment in which the prisoner can only have intercourse with two or three warders?

Finally, a fifth condition of happiness is a healthy and painless death. And again, the higher people stand on the social ladder the more are they deprived of this condition of happiness. Take for example a moderately rich man and his wife and an average peasant and his wife: notwithstanding all the hunger and excessive toil which, not by his fault but by the cruelty of man, a peasant has to bear, you will see that the lower the healthier and the higher the sicklier are men and women.

Count over in your memory the rich men and their wives you have known or now know, and you will notice that most of them are ill. Among them a healthy man, who is not undergoing treatment continually or periodically summer after summer, is as much an exception as is a sick man among the peasantry. All these fortunate people without exception, begin with onanism (which has become in their class a natural condition of development), they all have bad teeth, are all grey or bald at an age when a workman is just reaching his full strength. They are nearly all subject to nervous, digestive, and sexual illnesses from gluttony, drunkenness, debauchery, and doctoring, and those who do not die young spend half their life in being doctored and taking injections of morphia, or are shrivelled cripples unfitted to live by their own exertions and capable of existing only like parasites or like those ants who are fed by slave-ants. Consider their deaths: this one shot himself; that one rotted with syphilis; another old man died from the effects of a stimulant, while another died young from a flogging to which he submitted in his desire for sex-stimulation; one was eaten alive by lice, another by worms; one drank himself to death, another died of over-eating; one from morphia, and another as the result of an abortion. They perish one after another for the sake of the world's teaching. And the crowd throngs after them and seeks, like martyrs, for suffering and destruction.

One life after another is flung under the chariot-wheels of that god: the chariot passes on tearing them to pieces, and more and more victims, with groans, cries, and curses, fall beneath it!

To fulfil the teaching of Christ is hard! Christ says: 'Let him that would follow me leave house, and fields, and brothers, and follow me in God's way, and he shall receive in this world a hundred times more houses, fields, and brothers, and shall also gain eternal life.' And no one follows him. But the teaching of the world says: 'Abandon house, and fields, and brothers, and go from the village to the rotten town. Live all your life as a naked bath-attendant soaping other people's backs amid the steam, or serve in a money-changer's basement-office all your life counting other people's pence; or live as a public prosecutor, spending your whole life in the courts over law-papers and devoting yourself to making miserable people's fate yet worse; or as a Minister of State, signing unnecessary papers in a hurry all your life; or as a colonel, killing people all your life—live such a monstrous life as this, always ending in a painful death, and you will neither gain anything in this world nor will you

receive life eternal.' And everyone follows this
course. Christ said: 'Take up your cross and follow
me'—that is to say, endure submissively the fate
that has befallen you and obey me, God; and no
one follows him. But the first abandoned man wearing epaulets and fit for nothing but murder, into
whose head it enters, says: 'Take, not a cross but
a knapsack and rifle, and follow me to all kinds of
torment and to certain death'—and all follow him.

Having abandoned their families, parents, wives,
and children, and having been dressed up like fools
and submitted themselves to the authority of the
first man of higher rank that they happened to meet:
cold, hungry, and exhausted by forced marches,
they go like a herd of bullocks to the slaughter; yet
they are not bullocks but human beings. They
cannot but know that they are being driven to
slaughter with the question unanswered—Why?
And with despair in their hearts they go: and die of
cold, hunger, and infectious diseases, till they are
placed under a shower of bullets and cannon-balls
and ordered to kill people who are unknown to
them. They slay and are slain. And no one of the
slayers knows why or wherefore. The Turks roast
them alive on the fire, skin them, and tear out their
entrails. And again to-morrow someone will whistle,
and again all will follow to horrible sufferings, to
death, and to obvious evil. And no one considers
this hard! Neither those who endure the sufferings,
nor their fathers and mothers, consider this difficult.
The parents even themselves advise their children
to go. It seems to them that not only is this necessary
and unavoidable, but that it is also good and moral.

It would be possible to believe that the fulfilment of Christ's teaching is difficult and terrible
and tormenting, if the fulfilment of the world's
teaching were easy, safe, and pleasant. But in fact

the fulfilment of the world's teaching is much more dangerous and tormenting than the fulfilment of Christ's teaching.

There used, it is said, to be Christian martyrs, but they were the exception; they have been reckoned at 380,000—voluntary and involuntary, in 1800 years. But count the worldly martyrs, and for each Christian martyr you will find a thousand worldly martyrs whose sufferings are a hundred times more terrible. Those slain in war, during the present century, are reckoned at thirty millions.[1]

Now these were all martyrs to the world's teaching, who needed not even to follow the teaching of Christ but simply to abstain from following the teaching of the world, in order to have escaped from suffering and death.

A man need only do what he wishes to do— refuse to go to war—he will be set to dig trenches, but will not be tormented in Sevastopol or Plevna. A man need but disbelieve the world's teaching that he must wear over-shoes[2] and a watch-chain and have a drawing-room he does not need, and that he must do all the stupid things demanded of him by the world's teaching, and he will not be exposed to excessive toil and suffering, never-ending cares, and work without rest or aim; he will not be deprived of intercourse with nature, will not be deprived of congenial work, of family, and of health, and will not perish by a senseless and tormenting death.

It is not necessary to be a martyr in Christ's name —that is not what he teaches. He only bids us cease

---

[1] This book was written in 1884; and the figures relate to the nineteenth century.—A.M.

[2] The wearing of over-shoes or goloshes to keep one's feet dry and warm and to be able on entering a house to kick them off and have clean shoes, is here instanced as a sign of distinction from the peasant, who usually wore nothing over his high boots.—A.M.

to torment ourselves in the name of the world's false teaching.

Christ's teaching has a profound metaphysical meaning, it has an all-human meaning, and it has the simplest, clearest, and most practical meaning for the life of every single man. That last meaning can be expressed thus: Christ teaches men not to commit stupidities. Therein lies the simplest meaning of Christ's teaching, accessible to all.

Christ says: Do not be angry, do not consider anyone your inferior—to do so is stupid. If you get angry and insult people it will be the worse for you. Christ also says: Do not run after women, but unite with one woman and live with her—it will be better for you so. He also says: Do not promise anything to people,[1] or else they will oblige you to do stupid and evil actions. He also says: Do not return evil for evil, or the evil will return to you yet more bitterly than before: like the heavy log suspended over the store of honey, which kills the bear.[2] He also says: Do not consider men foreign to you merely because they live in another country and speak another language. If you consider them as enemies and they consider you such, it will be worse for you. So do not commit all these stupidities, and it will be better for you.

'Yes', people reply, 'but the world is so arranged

---

[1] We have here a very sweeping conclusion, a serious objection to which is that it is desirable to be able to co-operate with one's fellows, and co-operation is practically impossible if those engaged on an undertaking do not know what they may expect of their fellow workers.—A.M.

[2] The reference is to the practice of hanging a heavy block, or log, over a deposit of honey. When a bear tries to take the honey he knocks himself against the log, which swings back and hits him. The bear then strikes more fiercely at the log, which rebounding, strikes him still more heavily, and so on, until, it is said, the bear is sometimes killed by the blows he receives.—A.M.

that to resist its arrangements is more painful than to live in accord with them. If a man refuses military service he will be sent to a fortress and perhaps shot. If a man does not safeguard his life by acquiring the property he and his family need, he and they will die of hunger.' So people say, trying to defend the world's arrangement, but they do not think so themselves. They only speak so because they cannot deny the justice of the teaching of Christ in whom they are supposed to believe, and they must justify themselves in some way for not fulfilling that teaching. They not only do not think this, but they have never even thought about the matter at all. They believe the world's teaching and merely employ the excuse the Church has taught them, to the effect that if one fulfils Christ's teaching one must endure great suffering; and therefore they have never even tried to fulfil it. We see the innumerable sufferings people endure for the sake of the world's teaching, but in our time we never see sufferings for the sake of Christ's teaching at all. Thirty millions have perished for the world's teaching in warfare; thousands of millions have pined in a tormenting life for the sake of the world's teaching, while I know not only no millions, but not even thousands or dozens, or even one single man, who has perished by death or by a painful life of hunger and cold for the sake of Christ's teaching. It is only a ridiculous excuse, showing to what a degree Christ's teaching is unknown to us. Not only do we not share it, we have never even seriously considered it. The Church has been at pains to explain Christ's teaching so that it has appeared to us not as a teaching of life but as a bugbear.

Christ calls men to a spring of water which is there beside them. Men are tormented by thirst, eat dirt, and drink one another's blood, but their teachers tell them that they will perish if they go to the spring to which Christ directs them. And people believe this; they suffer and die of thirst at two steps from the water, not daring to go to it. But it is only necessary to believe Christ, that he has brought blessing on earth and that he gives us who thirst a spring of living water, and to come to him, to see how insidious is the Church's deception and how insensate are our sufferings when salvation is so near at hand. It is only necessary to accept Christ's teaching simply and plainly for the terrible deception in which we all and each are living to become clear.

Generation after generation we labour to secure life by means of violence and by safeguarding our property. Our happiness seems to us to lie in obtaining the maximum of power and the maximum of property. We are so accustomed to this that Christ's teaching, that a man's happiness cannot depend on his power or his estate and that a rich man cannot be happy, seems to us like a demand to make a sacrifice for the sake of future bliss. But Christ did not think of calling us to sacrifice; on the contrary, he teaches us not to do what is worse but to do what is better for us here in this life. Christ, loving men, teaches them to refrain from securing themselves by violence and by property, just as others who love men teach them to refrain from brawling and drunkenness. He says that men, if they live without resisting others and without property, will be happier; and by the example of his own life he confirms this. He says that a man living in accord with his teaching must be prepared to die at any moment by the violence of others, by cold or hunger, and cannot be sure of a single hour's life. And we imagine this to be a terrible demand of sacrifice; but it is only a declaration of the conditions in which every man always and inevitably lives. Christ's disciple must be prepared at any moment for suffering and death. But is not a disciple of the world in the same position? We are so accustomed to our pretence that all we do for the imaginary security of our life—our armies, fortifications, stores, clothes, and doctoring, our property and our money—seems to us something that really and seriously secures our life. We forget, though it is obvious to everyone, what happened to the man who planned to build barns in order to be safe for many years. He died that same night. Indeed all we do to safeguard our life is just what an ostrich does, standing still and hiding its head in order not to see how it is being killed. We do worse than the ostrich: doubtfully to safeguard our doubtful life in a doubtful future, we certainly destroy our certain life in the certain present.

The deception consists in the false conviction that our life can be secured by strife against others. We are so accustomed to this deception—an imaginary safeguarding of our life and property—that we do not notice all we lose by it. And we lose all—our whole life. Our whole life is so absorbed in cares for this safeguarding of life, this preparation for life, that no life at all is left us.

We need only discard our habits for a moment and regard our life from outside, to see that all we do for the supposed safeguarding of our life we really do not at all to safeguard our life, but only to forget, by busying ourselves with these things, that life is never secure. But not only do we deceive ourselves and spoil our real life for the sake of an imaginary one; we generally by this effort to make ourselves safe, ruin the very thing we wish to secure. The French armed themselves to secure their life in 1870, and in consequence of this safeguarding hundreds of thousands of Frenchmen perished. The same is done by all nations that arm themselves. The rich man secures his life by having money, and that very money attracts a robber who kills him. A nervous man safeguards his life by undergoing a cure, and the cure itself slowly kills him, or if it does not kill him certainly deprives him of life, like that sick man who deprived himself of life for thirty-eight years, by waiting for the angel at the pool (John v. 2–8).

Christ's teaching that life cannot be made safe, but that one must always, at each moment, be ready to die, is certainly better than the world's teaching that one must secure one's life: it is better because the inevitability of death and the insecurity of life remain the same whether one adopts the world's teaching or that of Christ; and in Christ's teaching life itself is not entirely absorbed in the useless occupation of pseudo-safeguarding one's life, but becomes free and can be devoted to its one natural aim, the welfare of oneself and one's fellows. A disciple of Christ will be poor. Yes; that is to say, he will always make use of all those blessings which God has given him. He will not ruin his life. We have called poverty,[1] which is a happiness, by a word that indicates misfortune, but the reality of the matter is not altered thereby. To be poor means that a man[2] will not live in a town but in a village, and will not sit at home but will work in the woods or fields; will see the light of the sun, the earth, the sky, and animals; will not consider what he can eat to arouse his appetite and how to get his bowels to move, but will be hungry

[1] Poverty, in Russian, is *bédnost*, from the same root as *bedá*, a misfortune.—A.M.

[2] Tolstóy has in mind a Russian country peasant, whom he contrasts with a rich townsman, and the description relates to things as they were under the Tsars in the pre-Revolutionary days.—A.M.

three times a day; will not toss about on soft
cushions wondering how he is to escape from sleep-
lessness, but will sleep; he will have children and
will live with them; will have free intercourse with
all men, and above all will not do things he does not
wish to do, and will not be afraid of what will
happen to him. He will sicken, suffer, and die, as
everyone does (though, to judge by the way poor
men sicken and die, it will be better for him than it
is for the rich) but he will certainly live more
happily. To be poor, to be indigent and a vagrant
(πτωχός means vagrant) is what Christ taught; that
without which it is impossible to enter the kingdom
of God, without which it is impossible to be happy
here on earth.

'But no one will feed you and you will die of
hunger', is said in reply to this. To the objection
that a man living according to Christ's teaching will
die of hunger Christ replied by one brief sentence
(the one which is interpreted as a justification for
the sloth of the clergy, Matt. x. 10; Luke x. 7).

He said: 'Take no wallet for your journey, neither
two coats, nor shoes, nor staff: for the labourer is
worthy of his food.' 'In that same house remain,
eating and drinking such things as they give, for
the labourer is worthy of his hire.'

The labourer is worthy, ἄξιός ἐστιν literally
means: can and should have his subsistence. It is
a very short saying; but for anyone who understands it as Christ did, there can be no idea of
arguing that a man who has no property will die of
hunger. To understand these words in their real
meaning one must first of all quite renounce the
supposition (which has become so common among
us as a consequence of the dogma of the redemption)
that man's welfare consists in idleness. One must
return to the conception natural to all unperverted

people, that the necessary condition of happiness
for man is not idleness, but work; that a man cannot
reject work; that not to work is dull, wearisome, and
hard, as it is dull and hard for an ant, a horse, or
any other animal not to work. One must forget our
savage superstition that the position of a man with an
inexhaustible purse—that is to say, with a Government post, the ownership of land, or of bonds bearing interest, which make it possible for him to do
nothing—is a naturally happy condition. One must
restore in one's imagination that view of work which
all unperverted people have, and which Christ had
when he said that the labourer was worthy of his
subsistence. Christ could not imagine people who
would regard work as a curse, and therefore could
not imagine a man who did not work or did not
wish to work. He always supposes that his disciples
work. And therefore he says: 'If a man works, then
his work will feed him.' If another man takes the
produce of this man's labour, then the other man
will feed the worker just because he reaps the advantage of his labour. And so the worker will receive his subsistence. He will not have property,
but there can be no doubt about his subsistence.

The difference between Christ's teaching about
work and the teaching of our world lies in this, that
according to the world's teaching work is man's
peculiar merit for which he keeps account with
others and considers that he has a right to the more
subsistence the more he works; while according to
Christ's teaching work is a necessary condition of
man's life and subsistence is the inevitable consequence of work. Work produces food, food produces work, that is the unending circle: the one is
the consequence and the cause of the other. However evil a master may be, he will feed his workman
as he will feed the horse that works for him; and will

feed him so that the workman may produce as much as possible, in other words, can co-operate in that which provides the welfare of man.

'The son of man came not to be ministered unto, but to minister, and to give his life a ransom for many.' According to the teaching of Christ each individual man, independently of what the world may be like, will have the best kind of life if he understands that his vocation is not to demand work from others but to devote his own life to working for others, and to give his life a ransom for many. A man who acts so, says Christ, is worthy of his subsistence—that is to say, cannot but receive it. In a word, man does not live that others should work for him, but that he should work for others. Christ sets up the basis which undoubtedly ensures man's material existence, and by the words 'The labourer is worthy of his subsistence', he sets aside that very common objection to the possibility of fulfilling his teaching which says that a man carrying out Christ's teaching among people who do not carry it out will perish of hunger and cold. Christ shows us that a man ensures his subsistence not by taking it from others, but by doing what is useful and necessary for others. The more necessary he is to others the more safe will be his existence.

Under the existing arrangements of the world people who do not fulfil Christ's law but who work for their neighbours and have no property, do not die of hunger. How then can one make it an objection to Christ's teaching that those who obey it—that is to say, those who work for their neighbours—will die of hunger? A man cannot die of hunger while the rich have bread. In Russia, at any given moment, there are always millions of people living without any property, simply by their labour.

Among the heathen a Christian will be provided for as among Christians. He works for others, consequently they need him, and therefore he will be fed. Even a dog that is wanted is fed and cared for, how then should a man not be fed and cared for who is of use to everyone?

But a sick man, one with a family and children, is not wanted and cannot work—so people will cease to feed him, say those who are bent on making out a case for a bestial life. They will and do say this, and do not notice that they themselves, who say so and would like to act so, cannot do it, but behave quite otherwise. Those very people who do not acknowledge the practicability of Christ's teaching, follow it! They do not cease to feed a sheep, a bull, or a dog which falls ill. They do not even kill an old horse, but give it such work as it can do; they feed their family, as well as lambs, little pigs, and puppies, expecting them to be of use. So how should they not feed a useful man when he is ill, and how should they fail to find work within their strength for the old and the young, or cease to rear those who will one day work for them?

They not only will do this, but they are doing this very thing. Nine-tenths of the people—the common labourers—are fed like working cattle by the one-tenth who are not common people but are rich and powerful. And however gross the delusion in which that one-tenth live, however much they may despise the other nine-tenths, this one-tenth of powerful people never deprive the nine-tenths of necessary subsistence, though they have the power to do so. In order that they may have offspring who should labour for them, they do not deprive the common people of what is necessary for them. Latterly this one-tenth have consciously endeavoured to arrange for the nine-tenths to be properly fed, that as large an output of work may be got from them as possible, and that fresh workmen may be produced and reared. Even the ants breed and rear their own milch-cows, so how should men not do as much and breed those who will work for them? Workers are needed. And those who make use of their work will always be much concerned to see that the workers do not die out.

The objection to the practicability of Christ's teaching, which says that if I do not acquire for myself, and do not retain what I have acquired, no one will feed my family, is correct, but only in relation to idle, useless, and therefore harmful, people such as the majority of our wealthy class. No one except stupid parents will bring up idle people, because idle people are of no use to anyone, not even to themselves; but even the worst men will feed and rear workers. Calves are reared, and man as a working animal is more valuable than a bull, as the prices in the slave-markets have always proved. That is why children will never be left without care.

Man does not live that others should serve him, but that he should himself serve others. He who labours will be fed. That is a truth confirmed by the life of the whole world.

Till the present time, always and everywhere, where man has worked he has obtained sustenance, as every horse receives his feed. And such sustenance was received by the workers involuntarily, against the grain, for they only desired to free themselves from toil, to get as much as possible, and to seat themselves on the neck of those who were sitting on their necks. Such an involuntary, unwilling worker, envious and angry, was not left without sustenance, and was even more fortunate than the man who did not work but lived on the labour of others. How much more fortunate still will he be who works according to Christ's law, and whose aim is to work as much as he can and to take as little as possible! And how much more happy will his position be when around him there are at least some, and perhaps even many, men like himself, who will serve him!

Christ's teaching of work and its fruits is expressed in the story of the feeding of the five and the four thousand with five loaves and two fishes. Humanity will reach the highest happiness possible for it on earth when people do not try to swallow and consume everything themselves, but when they do as Christ taught them by the sea-shore.

Some thousands of people had to be fed. A disciple told Christ that he had seen a lad who had some fishes, the disciple also had some loaves. Jesus understood that some of the people coming from a distance would have brought food, but that others would not. (That some had supplies with them is shown by the fact that in all four Gospels it is mentioned that when the meal was ended remnants were collected in twelve baskets. If no one but the lad had brought anything, there would not have been those twelve baskets in the field.) If Christ had not done what he did, namely, performed the miracle of feeding the thousands of people with five loaves, what happens in our world would have happened there. Those who had supplies would have eaten what they had. They would have eaten it all, and even over-eaten themselves so as not to leave anything over. The mean ones, perhaps, would have carried home their surplus. Those who had nothing would have remained hungry, watching the eaters with angry envy, and perhaps some of them would have snatched from those who saved and there would have been quarrels and fights, and some would have gone home satiated, others hungry and angry. It would have been as it is in our life.

But Christ knew what he wanted to do (as is said in the Gospels). He bade them all sit round, and he told his disciples to offer to others what they themselves had, and to bid others do the same. And then it appeared that, when all who had supplies had done like Christ's disciples—that is to say, had offered what they had to others—all ate moderately, and, after going round the circle, there was food enough left for those who had at first not eaten. And all were satisfied and much food remained over, so much that they gathered up twelve baskets full.

Christ taught men that they should deliberately behave in this way in life, because such is the law of man and of all humanity. Work is a necessary condition of man's life. Work also gives welfare to man. And therefore the withholding from others of the fruits of one's labour or of other people's labour, hinders the welfare of man. Giving one's labour to others promotes man's happiness.

'If people do not take away property from one another they will die of hunger', we say. It would seem that we should rather say the contrary: if people take by force from one another there will be some who will die of hunger—and this actually occurs.

Really every man, however he lives—whether according to Christ's teaching or to the world's—is alive only thanks to the work of other people. Others have protected him and given him drink and fed him, and still protect him and feed him and give him drink. But by the world's teaching man, by violence and threats, obliges others to continue to feed him and his family. By Christ's teaching man is equally protected, nourished, and supplied with drink by others; but in order that others should continue to guard, to feed, and to give him drink, he does not bring force to bear on anyone, but tries himself to serve others and to be useful to all men as he can, and thereby he becomes necessary to all. Worldly people will always wish to cease to feed one who is unnecessary to them and who compels them by force to feed him, and at the first opportunity they not only cease to feed him, but kill him as unnecessary. But all men, always, evil as they may be, will carefully feed and safeguard one who works for them.

In which way then is it safer, more reasonable, and more joyous to live: according to the world's teaching or according to Christ's?

XI

THE DEAD CHURCH

THE teaching of Christ establishes the kingdom of God on earth. It is not true that the fulfilment of this teaching is difficult; it is not only not difficult, but it is inevitable for a man who has comprehended it. This teaching supplies the only possible salvation from the inevitably impending destruction of personal life. Finally, not only does the fulfilment of this teaching not call us to sufferings and deprivations in this life, but it releases us from nine-tenths of the sufferings we endure for the sake of the world's teaching.

And having understood this I asked myself; why, till now, have I not fulfilled this teaching which offers me welfare, salvation, and happiness, but have followed quite a different teaching—that which has made me unhappy? And the only answer that could be given was: I did not know the truth, it was hidden from me.

When the meaning of Christ's teaching revealed itself to me for the first time I had no idea that the elucidation of that meaning would cause me to repudiate the teaching of the Church; it merely seemed to me that the Church had not reached the conclusion which flows from Christ's teaching, but I did not suspect that the new meaning of Christ's teaching which had revealed itself to me, and the deductions which followed therefrom, would separate me from the teaching of the Church. I was afraid of that, and therefore during my researches, far from seeking for mistakes in the Church's teaching I on the contrary intentionally shut my eyes to such propositions as seemed to me obscure and strange, but which did not contradict what I considered to be the essence of the Christian teaching.

But the further I travelled in the study of the Gospels and the more clearly the meaning of Christ's teaching revealed itself to me, the more inevitable became the choice between the teaching of Christ—reasonable, clear, accordant with my conscience and giving me salvation—and the directly opposite teaching, disagreeing with my reason and conscience and giving me nothing except a consciousness of destruction for myself and others, and I could not help rejecting the Church's propositions one after another. I did this unwillingly, with a struggle, and with a desire as far as possible to soften my disagreement with the Church, not to separate from it and not to deprive myself of that most joyous support to one's faith—community with many people. But when I had finished my work I saw that, try as I might to retain at least something of the Church's teaching, nothing remained. Not only did nothing remain, but I was convinced that nothing could remain.

During the conclusion of my work the following incident occurred. My young son told me that two quite uneducated and scarcely literate people, who were our servants, had had a dispute about a passage in a religious book in which it was said that it is not a sin to kill criminals or kill people in war. I did not believe that this could have been printed, and I asked to have the book shown to me. The booklet which had provoked the dispute was called *An Explanatory Prayer-book* (3rd edition, 80th thousand, Moscow, 1879). On page 163 of that booklet is said:

'What is the sixth of God's commandments? Thou shalt not kill. What does God forbid in this commandment? He forbids us to kill—that is to say, to deprive men of life. Is it a sin legally to punish a criminal with death, or to kill one's enemies in war? It is not a sin. A criminal is deprived of life in order to stop the great evil which he commits; enemies are killed in war because in war one fights for one's ruler and country.' And to those words is limited the explanation of why the commandment of God is repealed. I did not believe my eyes.

The disputants asked my opinion about their difference. I told the one who considered that what the book said was right that the explanation was incorrect.

'How is it that people print what is wrong and contrary to the law?' said he. I had no reply to give him. I kept the book and looked it all through. The book contains (1) thirty-one prayers, with instructions about genuflections and how to hold one's fingers when crossing oneself; (2) an explanation of the Creed; (3) a quite unexplained extract from the fifth chapter of St. Matthew, which for some reason is called, 'Commands for obtaining bliss'; (4) the

Ten Commandments of Moses with explanations, which for the most part annul them; (5) hymns for Church Festivals.

As I have said, I not only tried to avoid condemning the faith of the Church, but I tried to see it in the best light and therefore did not seek for its weaknesses, and though well acquainted with its academic I was quite unacquainted with its pedagogic literature. The circulation in 1879 of such an enormous number of copies of a prayer-book which evoked the doubts of the simplest people amazed me. I could not believe that the plainly pagan contents of the prayer-book (having nothing in common with Christianity) were the teaching the Church deliberately disseminated among the people. To verify this, I bought all the books published by the Synod or with its blessing and containing brief statements of the Church's faith for children and the common people; and I read them through.

Their contents were for me almost new. When I had Scripture lessons, such matter did not exist. There were then, so far as I can remember, no 'Commands for obtaining Bliss', nor was there the teaching that to kill is *not a sin*. It is not found in any of the old Russian catechisms. It is not in the catechisms of Peter Mogíla, nor in the catechism of Platón, nor in the catechism of Balyákov, nor in the short Catholic Catechisms. This novelty was introduced by Filarét, who also drew up a catechism for the use of the Army. The *Explanatory Prayer-book* is drawn up in accord with that catechism. The fundamental book is the 'Long *Christian* Catechism of the Orthodox Church, for the use of *all* Orthodox *Christians*, published by order of His Imperial Majesty'.

That book is divided into three parts: On Faith, On Hope, and On Love. In the first part is an

analysis of the Nicene Creed. In the second part
an analysis of the Lord's Prayer, and the eight verses
of the fifth chapter of Matthew forming an introduction to the Sermon on the Mount, and for some
reason called 'Commands for obtaining bliss'.
(Both these parts treat of Church dogmas, of
prayers and sacraments, but give no teaching at all
about life.) In the third part the duties of a
Christian are set forth. In this part, called 'On
Love', are set out, not the commandments of
Christ, but the Ten Commandments of Moses, and
these are set out as though only to teach people not
to fulfil them but to act in opposition to them; as,
after each commandment, there is a reservation
which cancels it. With reference to the first commandment, which orders us to honour one God,
the catechism teaches us to honour angels and
saints, besides, of course, the Mother of God and the
three Persons of the Trinity (*Long Catechism*, pp. 107,
108). With reference to the second commandment,
not to make to oneself idols, the catechism teaches
the obeisance before icons (p. 108). With reference
to the third commandment, not to take oaths in
vain, the catechism teaches people to swear on any
demand of the *legal* authorities (p. 111). With
reference to the fourth commandment, to observe
Saturday, the catechism teaches us to keep not
Saturday but Sunday, and thirteen great holidays
and a multitude of smaller ones, and to observe all
the Fasts, including Wednesdays and Fridays (pp.
112–15). With reference to the fifth commandment,
to honour one's father and mother, the catechism
teaches us to honour the Tsar and the Fatherland,
one's spiritual pastors '*and those in various positions of
authority*' (sic) and on honouring those in authority
there are three pages with an enumeration of all
kinds of authorities: '*Those in authority in schools, the*

civil authorities, the judges, the military authorities, one's masters (sic). *This last injunction refers to those who serve them and whom they command'* (sic—pp. 116–19).

I am quoting from the 1864 edition of the Catechism. Twenty years have passed since the abolition of serfdom and no one has taken the trouble even to strike out the sentences which, with reference to the commandment of God to honour one's parents, were included in the Catechism for the maintenance and justification of slavery. With reference to the sixth commandment, 'Thou shalt not kill', from the first lines one is taught to kill.

Q. What is forbidden in the sixth commandment?

A. Murder, or the taking of life from one's neighbour in any manner.

Q. Is every taking of life a sinful murder?

A. It is not sinful murder when life is taken *in the fulfilment of one's duties*, for instance: (i) When a criminal is *punished* with death by legal sentence. (ii) When enemies are killed *in war* for ruler and country. (The italics are in the original.) And further:

Q. What occasions can be regarded as criminal murder?

A. . . . When anyone *hides or releases* a murderer.

And this is printed in hundreds of thousands of copies and is instilled forcibly, with threats and under fear of punishment, into all Russian people under the guise of Christian doctrine. This is what the whole of the Russian people are taught; this is what all the innocent angel children are taught— those children whom Christ wished not to have driven away from him because 'theirs is the kingdom of God';—those children whom we must resemble in order to enter the kingdom of God (resemble by not knowing such teaching); those children, in defence of whom Christ said, 'Woe unto him that causeth one of these little ones to stumble'. And it is these children to whom this is forcibly taught and who are told that this is the only and the sacred law of God.

This is not a proclamation circulated secretly under fear of imprisonment, but a proclamation disagreement with which is punished by imprisonment. I now write this and I am frightened that I even allow myself to say that one cannot repeal God's chief law, written in all the codes and in all our hearts, by words which explain nothing, 'in the fulfilment of one's duties to King and country', and that people should not be taught so.

Yes, that has come about which Christ foretold (Luke xi. 35, 36; Matt. vi. 23): 'Look therefore whether the light that is in thee be not darkness. If the light that is in thee be darkness, how great is the darkness!'

The light that is within us is become darkness, and the darkness in which we live has become terrible.

'Woe unto you', says Christ, 'woe unto you, scribes and Pharisees, hypocrites! because ye shut the kingdom of heaven against men: for ye enter not in yourselves, neither suffer ye them that are entering in to enter. Woe unto you, scribes and Pharisees, hypocrites! for ye devour widow's houses, even while for a pretence ye make long prayers: therefore ye shall receive greater condemnation. Woe unto you, scribes and Pharisees, hypocrites! for ye compass sea and land to make one proselyte; and when he is become so, ye make him worse than before. Woe unto you, ye blind guides!

'Woe unto you, scribes and Pharisees, hypocrites! for ye build the sepulchres of the prophets, and garnish the tombs of the righteous, and say, If we

had been in those days when the prophets were
tortured, we should not have been partakers in their
blood. Ye are witnesses against yourselves, that ye
are sons of them that slew the prophets. Fill ye up
then the measure begun by those who were like
yourselves. I will send unto you prophets and wise
men; some of them ye will kill and crucify; and
some of them ye will scourge in your assemblies, and
expel from city to city; that upon you may come all
the righteous blood shed on the earth since Abel.'
'Every blasphemy [libel] will be forgiven to men,
but the libel against the Holy Spirit cannot be forgiven.' All this reads as though it had been written
yesterday against those who now no longer compass
the sea and the land, libelling the Holy Spirit and
leading people to a belief which makes them worse,
but directly, by violence, oblige them to accept that
belief, and persecute and destroy all those prophets
and wise men who attempt to expose their fraud.

And I became convinced that the Church's
teaching, although it calls itself Christian, is that
very darkness against which Christ strove and
ordered his disciples to strive.

Christ's teaching, like every religious teaching,
has two sides: (i) The teaching of conduct—of how
we should live, each separately and all together—
the ethical teaching; and (ii) the explanation of
why people should live in that way and not otherwise—the metaphysical teaching. The one is the
result and at the same time the cause of the other.
Man should live so, because such is his destiny:
or the destiny of man is such, and therefore he should
live so—these two sides of Christ's teaching are to
be found in all the religions of the world. Such is the
religion of the Brahmins, of Confucius, Buddha, and
Moses, and such is the religion of Christ. He teaches
life, how to live, and he gives the explanation

why that is how one should live. But as it was
with all other teachings—Brahmanism, Judaism,
Buddhism—so was it with the teaching of Christ.
People lapse from the teaching of life, and among
them some are found who undertake to justify that
lapse. These people seating themselves, to use
Christ's expression, in the seat of Moses, explain the
metaphysical side of the teaching in such a way
that the ethical demands cease to be obligatory and
are replaced by an external service of God—by
ritual. This phenomenon is common to all religions, but never, I think, has it been displayed so
sharply as in Christianity. It has been displayed
with such exceptional sharpness because the teaching of Christ is the highest teaching; and it is the
highest because the metaphysics and ethics of
Christ's teaching are so inseparably united and are
so defined by one another that to separate them is
impossible without depriving the whole teaching
of its meaning, and also because Christ's teaching is
in itself a Protestantism—that is to say, a denial not
merely of the ritual observances of Judaism but of
every external worship of God. And therefore of
necessity in Christianity this tearing asunder completely perverts the teaching and deprives it of any
meaning. And so it was. The sundering of the
teaching of life from the explanation of life began
with the preaching of Paul, who did not know the
ethical teaching expressed in the Gospel of Matthew
and who preached a metaphysical-cabalistic theory
foreign to Christ; and this separation was finally
completed at the time of Constantine, when it was
found possible to clothe the whole heathen order of
life in a Christian dress and therefore to accept it as
Christianity without altering it.

From the time of Constantine—a heathen of the
heathen whom the Church for all his crimes and

vices numbers with the company of the saints—begin the Ecclesiastical Councils, and the centre of gravity of Christianity is transferred completely to the metaphysical side of the teaching. And that metaphysical teaching with the ceremonies that accompany it, diverging even more and more from its fundamental meaning, reaches its present stage —a teaching which explains the most incomprehensible mysteries of life in heaven and gives a most complex ritual of divine service, but supplies *no* religious teaching concerning our life on earth.

All religions except Church Christianity demand from their adherents, besides ceremonies, the performance of certain good actions and abstention from certain bad ones. Judaism demands circumcision, the keeping of the Sabbath, the giving of alms, the observance of the Jubilee year, and much else. Mohammedanism demands circumcision, prayer five times a day, tithes for the poor, worship at the prophet's tomb, and much else. And so with all the other religions. Whether these demands are good or bad, at any rate they demand certain actions. Only pseudo-Christianity demands nothing. There is nothing that it is definitely obligatory for a Christian to do or from which he must definitely abstain, if one does not count fasts and prayers which the Church itself admits to be non-obligatory. All that is necessary for the pseudo-Christian are the sacraments. But the sacrament is not done by the believer himself, it is performed over him by others. A pseudo-Christian is not bound to do anything, and is not bound to abstain from anything, in order to be saved, but all that is necessary is performed over him by the Church: he is baptized, and anointed, and communion is given him, as well as extreme unction, and absolution is even granted on an inarticulate confession, and he is prayed for—and saved! The Christian Church since the time of Constantine has not demanded any actions from its members. It has not even put forward any demands of abstinence from anything. The Christian Church recognized and sanctified everything that existed in the heathen world: it recognized and sanctified divorce, and slavery, and courts of justice, and all the state authorities that existed, and wars and executions, and it only demanded, at baptism, a verbal renunciation of evil, and that only at first; afterwards, with the introduction of infant baptism, it ceased even to demand that.

The Church, acknowledging Christ's teaching in words, directly rejected it in life.

Instead of guiding the life of the world, the Church, to make itself agreeable to the world, interpreted Christ's metaphysical teaching in such a way that no demands relating to life resulted from it, so that it did not prevent people from living as they had done before. The Church yielded to the world and, having done so once, it followed the world's way. The world did whatever it liked, allowing the Church to shape its explanations of the meaning of life accordingly as best it could. The world in everything arranged its life contrary to Christ's teaching, and the Church devised allegories to show that people while living contrary to Christ's law live in accord with it. And finally the life of the world became worse than heathen life had been, and the Church not merely justified that life but asserted that it was in agreement with Christ's teaching.

But a time came when the light of Christ's true teaching which was in the Gospels, despite the fact that the Church feeling its own falsity tried to hide it by forbidding translations of the Bible—a time came when this light (through those who were called sectarians and even through worldly free-thinkers) made its way among the people and the falsity of the Church's teaching became evident to men and they began to alter their way of life (which the Church had justified) to life on the basis of Christ's teaching which had made its way to them independently of the Church.

So people themselves, apart from the Church, abolished slavery (which the Church had justified) and religious executions,[1] and abolished the power (sanctified by the Church) of the Emperors and Popes, and have now begun the task which presents itself next in turn: the abolition of property and of the State.[2] And the Church did not defend and cannot defend any of these things, because the abolition of these wrongs in life took place, and is now taking place, on the basis of that same Christian teaching which was preached and is preached by the Church however it tries to pervert it.

The guidance of the life of man has emancipated itself from the Church and established itself independently of the Church.

The Church retains an explanation, but an explanation of what? The metaphysical explanation of a teaching has significance when the teaching of life which it explains exists. But the Church has no teaching of life left. It had only an explanation of a life it instituted once upon a time and which no longer exists. If the Church still retains an

---

[1] Such as the *autos-da-fé* of the Inquisition, or the decapitations and burnings of the Raskóluiki.

[2] This sentence is remarkable as showing that Tolstóy had then already reached the conclusion that all force-using Government should be condemned. Things have altered much in Russia both in Church and State since this book was written. The use of violence has certainly not diminished, but the present Dictatorship realizes that, while relying on the G.P.U. for support, it cannot tolerate the teaching of Jesus.—A.M.

explanation of that life which used to exist (like the explanation in the Catechism that officials ought to kill) no one any longer believes it. And the Church has nothing left but cathedrals, icons, brocaded vestments, and words.[1]

The Church carried the light of Christian teaching of life through eighteen centuries, and wishing to hide it under its garments has itself been burnt up by that flame. The world, with its arrangements sanctified by the Church, has repudiated the Church in the name of those very principles of Christianity which the Church has reluctantly borne; and the world now lives without the Church. That fact is accomplished and to hide it is impossible. All that is really alive—and does not linger on in angry dejection not really living but merely hindering others from doing so—all that really lives in our European world has rejected the Church, and all churches, and lives its own life independently of the Church. And let it not be said that this is so in 'rotten western Europe';[2] our Russia, with its millions of rationalist Christians, educated and uneducated, who have rejected Church teaching, proves beyond dispute that Russia, in regard to the repudiation of the Church, is, thank God, far more 'rotten' than the rest of Europe.

All that is alive is independent of the Church.

The power of Government rests on tradition, on science, on popular election, on brute force, and on what you will, only not on the Church.

[1] Before the generation had passed away to whom Tolstóy first issued this book, the Church in Russia had been disendowed and disestablished and the words 'Religion is the people's opium' were painted in large letters on the walls of the churches by order of the authorities.—A.M.

[2] A favourite phrase of the Slavophils, ardent patriots, who regarded Russia and her institutions as far superior to anything existing in the democratic West.—A.M.

Wars and the relations of the Powers are arranged on the principle of race, balance of power, or what you will, but not on Church principles.

The State institutions plainly ignore the Church. The idea that the Church could in our times be the foundation of the law or of property is merely ridiculous.

Science not only does not co-operate with the Church teaching, but inadvertently, involuntarily, in the course of its development is always hostile to the Church.

Art, which formerly served the Church exclusively, has now quite departed from it.

It is not merely that life has completely emancipated itself from the Church, life has no relation to the Church; it merely feels contempt for her so long as she does not meddle in the affairs of life and nothing but hatred as soon as she tries to remind it of her former rights. If the form which we call the Church still exists, it is only because people fear to smash a vessel which once held precious contents; only so is it possible to explain the existence in our century of the Catholic, the Orthodox, and the various Protestant Churches.

All the Churches—the Catholic, Orthodox, and Protestant—stand like sentinels laboriously on guard over a prisoner who has long since escaped and is now walking about among the sentinels and even fighting them. Everything that now really animates the world—Socialism, Communism, theories of political economy, utilitarianism, the freedom and equality of individuals, of classes, and of women, all man's moral conceptions, the sanctity of labour, the sanctity of reason, of science and of art, all that moves the world and that the Church regards as inimical, all are parts of that teaching which the Church herself has unwittingly handed on together with the teaching of Christ which she sought to conceal.

In our time the life of the world goes its own way quite independently of the Church's teaching. That teaching has lagged so far behind that the men of the world no longer hear the voices of church teachers. Nor is there anything to hear, for the Church only offers explanations of an arrangement of life which the world has already outgrown and which has already ceased to exist or is now being irresistibly destroyed.

People went rowing in a boat, and a helmsman steered them. The people came to believe in their helmsman, and he guided them well; but the time came when the good helmsman was replaced by another who did not steer. Yet the boat glided on quickly and easily. At first it was not noticed that the new helmsman was not steering and the people were only pleased that the boat moved quickly. But afterwards, having realized that the new helmsman was useless, they began to laugh at him, and dismissed him.

This would not have mattered, but the trouble was that people, moved by their annoyance with the useless helmsman, forgot that without a helmsman one does not know which way one is going. That is what has happened in our Christian society. The Church does not direct, and it is easy to drift, and we have gone far; and all the successes of science that our nineteenth century is so proud of are but the mileage we have gone without a rudder. We advance, but know not whither. We live and get through our life, and positively do not know why. But it does not do to drift and row not knowing one's direction, and one must not live and pass through life not knowing why.

If men did nothing themselves but were placed by

some external force in the position they occupy, they might in reply to the question, 'Why are you in this position?' quite reasonably reply, We do not know, but we find ourselves placed as we are. But people make their position for themselves, for others, and in particular for their children, and therefore they must reply to the questions: Why do you enroll others, and have been yourselves enrolled, into armies of millions with which you kill and mutilate one another? Why have you spent, and why are you spending, tremendous human energies, expressed in milliards, on the building of towns unnecessary and harmful to you? Why do you arrange your absurd law-courts and send people you consider criminals from France to Cayenne, from Russia to Siberia, and from England to Australia,[1] knowing yourselves that this is unreasonable? Why do you abandon the field-work you love, for work in factories and workshops which you yourselves dislike? Why do you educate your children so that they should continue this life of which you do not approve? Why do you do all this?

These questions cannot be left unanswered. Even had all these things been pleasant things you like doing, you should be able to give a reason for them. But as they are terribly difficult things and you do them only with effort and with murmurs, it is impossible for you not to consider why you do them all. It is necessary either to cease to do all this or else to explain why we do it. Without a reply to that question people never have lived and never can live. And such a reply people have never been without.

[1] As a matter of fact, banishment to Australia had ceased some twenty years before Tolstóy wrote this, but the memory of legal barbarities committed in distant countries lingers long in men's minds, as is illustrated by frequent references in England to the knout, the use of which was abolished generations ago.—A.M.

The Jews lived as they did—that is to say, fought, executed people, built the temple, and arranged their whole life in one way and not in another, because this was all prescribed by their law which according to their conviction had come down to them from God Himself. So it is with a Hindu or a Chinaman, and so it was with a Roman, and is with a Mohammedan; and the same was the case with a Christian till a hundred years ago; and so it is now for the masses of ignorant Christians. To those questions these ignorant Christians now reply that army-service, wars, law-courts, and executions, all exist by God's law, given to us by the Church. This world is a fallen world. All the evil that exists, exists by the will of God as a punishment for the sins of the world, and we therefore cannot remedy this evil.[1] We can only save our souls by faith, sacraments, prayers, and by submission to the will of God, as taught us by the Church. The Church teaches us that every Christian should submit absolutely to the Tsar, the anointed of God, and to all officials appointed by him, and should defend by violence his own and other people's property, and should fight, execute, and endure execution, at the will of those God-appointed authorities.

Whether such explanations be good or bad, they explained for a believing Christian—as was the case for a Jew, a Buddhist, or a Mohammedan—all the peculiarities of life; and a man did not renounce his reason when living according to the law he accepted as divine. But now a time has come when only the

---

[1] The amazing submission shown by the Russian people to the misrule they suffered under the Tsars for centuries, and, stranger still, to the greater oppression they have endured since the Bolsheviks seized power and organized a Dictatorship supported by the Cheká and the G.P.U., may be partly explained by the habit of submission deeply engrained in them, to which Tolstóy alludes.—A.M.

most ignorant people believe in these explanations, and the number of such people diminishes every day and every hour. It is quite impossible to arrest this movement. All men irresistibly follow those who go in advance, and all will reach the place where the advanced people now stand. But the advanced people are standing at the brink of a precipice. Those in front are in a terrible position, they are shaping life for themselves and preparing life for all who follow them and are completely ignorant of why they do what they do. Not one civilized and progressive man is now in a position to reply to the plain question, Why do you live the life you are living? Why are you doing all that you are doing? I have tried to ask about this and have questioned hundreds of people, and have never received a direct reply. Always, instead of a direct reply to the personal question, Why do you live so and do so? I have received an answer not to my question but to one I had not put.

A believing Catholic, Protestant, or Orthodox Churchman, in reply to the question why he lives as he is living—that is to say, in contradiction to that teaching of the Christ-God which he professes, always, instead of a straight answer, begins to speak of the woeful extent of incredulity in the present generation; about the bad people who promote infidelity, and of the significance and the future of the true Church. But why he himself does not do what his faith bids him do he does not say. Instead of replying about himself he speaks about the general condition of humanity and about the Church, just as though his own life was of no importance to him at all and he was concerned only with the salvation of the whole of humanity and with what he calls the Church.

A philosopher, of whatever denomination—

idealist, spiritualist, pessimist, or positivist—in reply to the question why he lives as he does, that is to say, not in accord with his philosophical teaching, will always, instead of replying to that question, speak of the progress of humanity and the historic law of that progress which he has discovered and in accord with which mankind strives towards its welfare. But he never replies directly to the question why he himself in his own life, does not do what he considers reasonable. The philosopher, like the believer, seems as though he were not concerned with his own life, but only with observing the general laws of humanity.

An average man, one of the immense majority of semi-believing, semi-sceptical civilized people, those who always without exception complain of their life and of the organization of our life and anticipate the ruin of everything, this average man in reply to the question why he himself lives this life he condemns and does nothing to improve it, will always, instead of a direct reply, begin to speak not of himself but on some general question: the law, trade, the State, or civilization. If he is a policeman or a public prosecutor he will say: 'But how will law and order get on if I, to improve my life, cease to take part in them?' 'And how about trade?' says he, if he is a commercial man. 'And how about civilization if I, to improve my own life, do not co-operate in it?' He always speaks as though the aim of his life were not to secure the good for which he always yearns, but to serve the State, or trade, or civilization. The average man replies exactly like the believer and the philosopher. For the personal question he substitutes a general question, and, like the believer and the philosopher, the average man makes this substitution because he has no reply to the question concerning his personal life, since he possesses no real philosophy of life. And he feels ashamed.

He is ashamed because he feels himself to be in the humiliating position of one who has no philosophy of life; whereas man never has lived, and cannot live, without a philosophy of life. Only in our Christian world instead of a philosophy of life and an explanation why life should be such and not other—that is to say, instead of a religion—we have merely an explanation of why life should be what it once used to be, and something is called religion which is of no sort of use to anybody and life itself has become emancipated from any sort of teaching —that is to say, it lacks any definition.

Nor is that all: as always occurs, science has accepted this accidental, monstrous position our society is in as a law for all humanity. Tiele, Herbert Spencer, and others treat of religion quite seriously, understanding by it a metaphysical teaching concerning the origin of all things, and without suspecting that they are talking not of the whole of religion but of only a part of it.

From this has arisen the amazing phenomenon that in our age we see wise and learned people most naïvely convinced that they are free from all religion merely because they do not acknowledge the metaphysical explanations of the origin of things which at some period and for some people served as an explanation of life. It does not enter their heads that they have got to live somehow and do live somehow, and that whatever it is that induces them to live so and not otherwise is their religion. These people imagine that they have very elevated convictions but no faith. But whatever they may say, they have a faith if they perform any reasonable actions. For reasonable actions are always defined by one's faith. And the actions of these people are

defined solely by the faith that one must always do
what one is ordered to do. The religion of these
people who do not acknowledge religion is the
religion of submission to all that is done by the
powerful majority, or, more briefly, it is the religion
of submission to the existing authorities.

One may live according to the world's teaching—
that is to say, live an animal life not acknowledging
anything higher and more obligatory than the
decrees of the powers that be. But he who lives so
cannot assert that he is living rationally. Before
asserting that we live rationally, we must answer the
question, What teaching about life do we consider
rational? And we unfortunates not merely have no
such teaching but have even lost the consciousness
that any reasonable teaching about life is necessary.

Ask men of our day, believers or sceptics, what
teaching they follow in their lives. They will have
to confess that they follow only one teaching, the
laws which are written by officials in the Judicial
Department or in the Legislative Assemblies and
which are enforced by the police. That is the only
teaching our European people acknowledge. They
know that that teaching has not come down from
heaven, nor from the prophets, nor from sages; they
constantly condemn the regulations made by those
officials or Legislative Assemblies, but all the same
they acknowledge that teaching and submit to its
executors—the police; and they implicitly obey its
most terrible demands. If the officials or the
Assemblies have written that every young man
must be ready to be abused, to be killed, and to
murder others—all the fathers and mothers who
have reared sons submit to this law written yesterday by a venal official and capable of being altered
to-morrow.

The conception of law indubitably rational and

may be persecuted, however much they may be slandered, they are the only people who do not unmurmuringly submit to all that is decreed, and therefore they are the only people in our world who are living not an animal but a rational life—they are the only believers.

The thread connecting the world with the Church that used to give the world a meaning has become ever weaker and weaker as the essence, the sap of life, has more and more flowed over to the world. And now, when the sap has all flowed over, the connecting cord has become a mere hindrance.

That is the mysterious process of birth which is being performed before our eyes. At one and the same time the last bond with the Church is being dissolved and the independent process of life is being established.

Church teaching (with its dogmas, councils, and hierarchy) is undoubtedly connected with Christ's teaching. That connexion is as evident as the connexion of a new-born babe with its mother's womb. But if the navel-cord and the afterbirth become unnecessary bits of flesh, which from respect for what they have preserved must be carefully buried in the earth, so also the Church has become an unnecessary, obsolete organ, which, merely from respect for what it once was, should now be hidden away somewhere far off. Directly the breathing and the circulation of the blood has been established, the bond which was formerly the source of nourishment becomes a hindrance. And

propaganda among the people. Passages relating to social questions were underlined in it and I often pointed these out to Tolstóy.' It is to the Socialist propaganda on behalf of the poor that Tolstóy refers in this passage. (See the *Life* of *Tolstóy*, vol. ii, pp. 14, 15 in this edition.)—A.M.

efforts to maintain that connexion and compel the babe that has now come into the world to nourish itself through the navel-cord, and not to live by means of its own mouth and lungs, are irrational.

But the babe's emancipation from its mother's womb is not yet life. The life of the child depends on the setting up of a new connexion with its mother for the supply of nutriment. And the same must be accomplished for our Christian world. Christ's teaching has borne our world and brought it to life. The Church—one of the organs of Christ's teaching —has done its part and has become unnecessary and a hindrance. The world cannot be guided by the Church, but the emancipation of the world from the Church is not yet life. Its life will come when it realizes its impotence and feels the necessity of fresh nourishment. And this must occur with our Christian world: it must cry out with consciousness of its impotence. Only consciousness of its impotence, consciousness of the impossibility of receiving nourishment as heretofore and of the impossibility of obtaining any other nourishment than that of its mother's milk (Christ's teaching) will bring it to its mother's breasts, swollen as they are with milk.

In our European world, superficially self-confident, bold and resolute, but in the depth of its consciousness frightened and perplexed, the same thing is occurring as happens with a new-born babe: it flings itself about, fidgets, cries, pushes as though it were angry, and it does not understand what it has to do. It feels that its former source of nourishment has dried up, but it does not know where to seek fresh nourishment.

A new-born lambkin moves his eyes and his ears, shakes his tail, jumps, and kicks. To judge by his assurance it seems as though he knew everything, but he, poor little thing, knows nothing. All this confidence and energy is the result of his mother's juices, the transfer of which has now ceased and cannot be renewed. He is in a happy but at the same time a desperate condition. He is full of freshness and strength; but he is lost unless he takes to his mother's teats.

The same is occurring with our European world. See what a complex, seemingly reasonable, energetic life is seething in the world. It is as if all these people knew what they were doing and why they were doing it all. See how resolutely, confidently, and briskly the men of our world undertake all that they do. Art, science, industry, social and state activities—all is full of life. But it lives only because it has been till recently nourished by its mother's juices through its navel-cord. There used to be a Church which transmitted Christ's reasonable teaching to the life of the world. All the energies of the world were nourished by it and grew and developed. But the Church has played its part and dried up. All the organs of the world are alive, the source of their former nourishment is exhausted and they have not yet found a fresh one. They seek it everywhere except from the mother from whom they have been released. They, like the lambkin, still live by the former nourishment and have not yet come to understand that only from their mother can food be had, but that it must be got in a different way than formerly.

The business that now awaits the world consists in understanding that the former process of unconscious feeding is done with and that a new, conscious process is necessary.

That new process consists in conscious acceptance of those truths of the Christian teaching which were formerly unconsciously imbibed by humanity through the instrumentality of the Church, and by which humanity still lives. Men must raise once more that light by which they lived but which was hidden from them, and they must lift it high before themselves and before others, and must consciously live by that light.

The teaching of Christ, as a religion defining life and explaining the life of man, stands now, as it stood 1800 years ago, before the world. But formerly the world had the Church's explanations, which though they hid the teaching nevertheless seemed to suffice for the world's former life; now however a time has come when the Church has been outlived and the world lacks explanation of its new life and cannot but feel its impotence and therefore can no longer avoid accepting Christ's teaching.

Christ teaches, first of all, that men should believe in the light while the light is yet in them. Christ teaches that men should set that light of reason above all else and should live in accord with it, not doing things they themselves consider irrational. If you consider it irrational to go to kill Turks or Germans—do not go;[1] if you consider it unreasonable forcibly to take the labour of the poor in order to wear a silk hat or to tie yourself up in a corset, or to arrange a drawing-room that will incommode you—do not do it; if you consider it unreasonable to put men corrupted by idleness and bad company into prison, that is, into the very worst company and the completest idleness—do not do it; if you consider it irrational to live in an infected town atmosphere

---

[1] When any great evil, such as slavery or war, begins to fall into disrepute and the time for its abolition is approaching, there is sure to be a be a long transition period during which those who are on the side of its abolition may do, or may seem to do, more harm than good by the action they take, as in the case of conscientious objectors to a just war. But Tolstóy felt no doubt on the matter.—A.M.

when it is possible to live in pure air; or if you consider it unreasonable to teach your children dead languages first of all and most of all, do not do it. Only do not do what is done now by the whole of our European world, namely, live a life you consider unreasonable, act while considering your actions unreasonable, disbelieve in your reason and live in discord with it.

Christ's teaching is light. The light shines and the darkness comprehendeth it not. One cannot refuse to accept the light when it shines. One cannot dispute with it, it is impossible to dispute with it. With Christ's teaching one cannot dispute, because it envelops all the errors in which people live and does not collide with them, but like the ether about which the physicists talk it permeates them all. The teaching of Christ is equally unavoidable for everyone in our world whatever his circumstances may be. Christ's teaching cannot but be accepted by men, not because it is impossible to deny the metaphysical explanation of life it gives (it is possible to deny it), but because it alone supplies those rules of life without which humanity has not lived and cannot live, and without which no man has lived or can live if he wishes to live as a man—that is to say, to live a reasonable life.

The strength of Christ's teaching lies not in its explanation of the meaning of life, but in what flows therefrom—the teaching of life. Christ's metaphysical teaching is not new. It is still the same teaching of humanity which is written in the hearts of men and which has been taught by all the true sages of the world. But the strength of Christ's teaching lies in the application of that metaphysical teaching of life.

The metaphysical basis of the ancient teaching of the Jews and of Christ is one and the same: love of God and of one's neighbour. But for the application of that teaching of life according to Moses, as the Jews understood it, the fulfilment of 613 commandments was necessary, many of them senseless and cruel and all resting on the authority of the Scriptures. According to Christ's law the teaching of life which flows from that same metaphysical basis is expressed in five commandments, which are reasonable, beneficent, carry in themselves their meaning and justification, and embrace the whole life of man.

Christ's teaching cannot but be accepted by those believing Jews, Buddhists, Mohammedans, and others who have begun to doubt the validity of their own law. Still less can it be rejected by those of our Christian world who now lack any moral law whatever.

Christ's teaching does not dispute with the men of our world about their conception of the world; it agrees with it in advance and, including this in itself, gives them what they lack, what is indispensable to them, and what they are searching for; it gives them a way of life, and one not novel to them but long familiar and akin to them all.

You are a believing Christian of whatever sect or confession. You believe in the creation of the world, in the Trinity, in the fall and redemption of man, in the sacraments, in prayers, and in the Church. Christ's teaching not only does not argue with you, but fully agrees with your outlook on the world; it merely adds something you have not got. Retaining your present belief you feel that the life of the world and your own life is filled with evil and you do not know how to avoid it. Christ's teaching (obligatory for you because it is the teaching of your God) gives you simple, practicable rules of life which will free you and other people from the evil that torments you. Believe in the resurrection, in heaven and hell, in the Church, in sacraments, in the redemption, and pray as your faith demands, fast and sing psalms—all this does not prevent you from fulfilling what Christ has revealed to be necessary for your welfare: do not be angry; do not commit adultery; do not bind yourself by oaths; do not defend yourself by violence; and do not go to war.

Perhaps you will fail to keep some one of these rules and will be tempted to infringe one of them as now in moments of temptation you infringe the rules of your faith, the rules of the civil law, or the laws of politeness. Similarly in moments of temptation you may perhaps infringe the laws of Christ; but in your quiet moments do not do what you do now—do not arrange your life so that it should be difficult not to be angry, not to commit adultery, not to take oaths, not to defend yourself, and not to fight; but in such a way that it should be hard to do these things. You cannot but acknowledge this, for God commands it of you.

You are an unbelieving philosopher no matter of what denomination. You say everything comes about in the world according to a law you have discovered. Christ's teaching does not dispute with you, and fully admits the law you have discovered. But then, besides that law of yours by which thousands of years hence that welfare will come to pass which you desire and have prepared for mankind, there is also your own life which you can live either in accord with reason or in contradiction to reason; and for that same life of yours you have now no rules except those which are written by men you do not respect and are put in execution by the police. Christ's teaching gives you rules that will certainly accord with your law, for your law of altruism or the common will is nothing else than a paraphrase of Christ's teaching.

You are an average man, half a believer half a sceptic, who has no time to immerse himself in the meaning of human life, and you have no definite outlook on life, you do what everybody else does. Christ's teaching does not dispute with you. It says: 'Very well, you are unable to argue and to verify the truths of the doctrine taught you; it is easier for you to act as everybody else does. But however modest you may be you yet are conscious in yourself of that inward judge who sometimes approves your action that accords with everybody's, and sometimes does not approve of it. However humble your lot may be it yet occurs to you to ponder and to ask yourself: Shall I do this thing as they all do it, or in my own way? And just in these cases—that is to say, just when you have occasion to decide that question—the laws of Christ will present themselves to you in all their strength. And they will certainly furnish a reply to your question for they embrace the whole of your life, and they will reply in accord with your reason and your conscience. If you are nearer to belief than to unbelief, then, acting in this way, you will be acting in accord with the will of God. If you are nearer to free-thought, then, acting in this way, you will act in accord with the most reasonable rules that exist in the world, of which you can convince yourself, for Christ's rules bear in themselves their own reason and justification.

Christ said (John xii. 31): '*Now is the judgement of this world:* now shall the prince of this world be cast out.' He also said (John xvi. 33): 'These things have I spoken unto you, that in me ye may have peace. In the world ye have tribulation: but be of good cheer; *I have overcome the world.*'

And really the world—that is, the evil of the world, is conquered.

If there still exists a world of evil it only exists inertly; it no longer possesses the roots of life. It does not exist for one who believes in the laws of Christ. It has been conquered in the reasonable consciousness of the son of man. The runaway train still moves forward, but all the rational work on it has long since been directed the contrary way.

'For whatsoever is begotten of God overcometh the world: and *this is the victory that hath overcome the world, even our faith*' (1 Epistle of John v. 4).

The faith that overcomes the world is faith in the teaching of Christ.

XII

WHAT IS FAITH?

I BELIEVE Christ's teaching; and this is what I believe.

I believe that my welfare in the world will only be possible when all men fulfil Christ's teaching.

I believe that the fulfilment of that teaching is possible, easy, and joyful.

I believe that before that teaching is universally followed, even were I alone in fulfilling it, there is still nothing for me to do to save my life from inevitable ruin but to fulfil that teaching, just as there is no alternative way of escape from a burning house for a man who has found the door leading to safety.

I believe that the life I lived in accord with the world's teaching was tormenting, and that only life in accord with Christ's teaching gives me in this world the welfare the Father of life intended for me.

I believe that this teaching confers blessedness on

all humanity, saves me from inevitable destruction, and gives me here the greatest possible welfare. Therefore I cannot but accept it.

'The law was given by Moses; grace and truth came by Jesus Christ' (John i. 17). Christ's teaching is welfare and truth. Formerly, not knowing the truth, I did not know welfare. Mistaking evil for good I fell into evil and doubted the rightness of my strivings after goodness. Now I have understood and believed that the goodness towards which I strove is the will of the Father and the most legitimate essence of my life.

Christ has said to me: Live for goodness, but do not trust those snares (σκάνδαλα) which, tempting you with a simulacrum of what is good, deprive you of goodness and trap you into evil. Your welfare lies in your unity with all men; evil is the infringement of that unity of the son of man. Do not deprive yourself of that welfare which is given you.

Christ has shown me that the unity of the son of man, the love of men among themselves, is not, as it formerly seemed to me, an aim towards which people should strive, but that this unity, this love of men among one another, is their natural condition, in which children are born according to Christ's words and in which all men live until this condition is infringed by fraud, error, or temptation.

But Christ not only showed me that; he clearly, beyond possibility of error, enumerated for me in his commandments all the temptations which had deprived me of that natural condition of unity, love, and blessedness and had drawn me into evil. The commands of Christ give me the means of salvation from the temptations which have deprived me of my welfare, and therefore I cannot but believe in those commandments.

I was given the blessing of life, and I myself

ruined it. Christ by his commandments showed me the temptations through which I ruin my happiness and therefore I cannot continue to do what ruins it. In that and in that alone is my whole belief.

Christ showed me that the first temptation which destroys the good of life is enmity, anger against other men. I cannot but believe this, and therefore can no longer deliberately bear ill-will to others; I cannot, as I used to do formerly, take pleasure in my anger, be proud of it, inflame it, and justify it by considering myself important and wise and other people insignificant, *lost*, and senseless. I can now no longer, at the first indication that I am giving way to anger, fail to acknowledge that I alone am guilty and to seek reconciliation with those who strive against me.

But that is not enough. If I now know that my anger is an unnatural condition, harmful for me, I also know what temptation brings me to it. That temptation consists in the fact that I have separated myself from other people, considering only some of them to be my equals and all the rest to be mere ciphers, not real men (ῥακά) or stupid and un-educated (irrational). I now see that this separation of myself from others and this estimation of others, as *raca* and senseless, was the chief cause of my enmity against men. Remembering my former life I now see that I never allowed my hostile feeling to flame up against those I considered to be my superiors and never insulted them, but that the smallest action that was unpleasant to me from a man I considered beneath me provoked my anger and caused me to insult him, and the more I thought myself above such a man the more ready was I to insult him; sometimes the mere imagination of the inferiority of a man's position caused me to insult him. Now I remember that that man alone is superior to others who humbles himself before others and is the servant of all. I now understand why that which is exalted among men is an abomination before God, and why woe befalls the rich and famous and the poor and humble are blessed.

Only now do I understand this and believe it, and this belief has changed my whole appreciation of what is good and lofty and what is bad and mean in life. All that formerly appeared to me good and lofty—honours, fame, education, riches, the complexity and refinement of life and of its surroundings, food, dress, and outward manners—all this has become for me bad and mean; while peasant life, obscurity, poverty, roughness, simplicity of surroundings, food, dress, and manners, has all become for me good and noble. And therefore if, knowing all this, I still in moments of forgetfulness yield to anger and insult my brother-man, yet when calm I can no longer yield to that temptation of placing myself above my fellows which deprives me of my true welfare, unity, and love, just as a man cannot reset for himself a trap into which he has formerly fallen and which nearly destroyed him. Now I cannot participate in anything that would outwardly place me above others, separating me from them; I cannot as formerly recognize, either for myself or for others, any titles, ranks, or distinctions, beyond claiming to be a man; I cannot seek for fame or praise; I cannot seek such knowledge as would separate me from others, and cannot but seek to free myself from my wealth which separated me from others, and I cannot in my life and its surroundings, in food, clothing, and external manners, fail to seek for all that will not divide me from, but unite me with, the majority of men.

Christ has shown me that another snare ruining

my welfare is lustfulness—that is to say, desire for another woman and not for her with whom I have united. I cannot but believe this, and therefore cannot, as I used to, consider adulterous lust a natural and noble quality in a man. I cannot justify it to myself by my love of beauty, by being enamoured, or by defects in my wife. I cannot but recognize, at the first intimation that I am yielding to adulterous desire, that I am in an unhealthy and unnatural state, or fail to seek for all the means which can free me from that evil.

But knowing now that adulterous lust harms me, I also know the temptation which formerly led me into it, and therefore I cannot serve it; I now know that the chief cause of temptation is not that people cannot refrain from fornication, but that most men and women have been deserted by those with whom they first came together. I now know that every desertion of a man or woman by him or her with whom they first had connexion is that very divorce which Christ forbids; because the husbands and wives abandoned by their first mates cause all the depravity in the world. Remembering what it was that led me into lechery, I now see that, besides the barbarous education by which the lust of fornication in me was physically and mentally inflamed and was excused by all sorts of subtleties, the chief snare that entangled me arose from my having abandoned the first woman with whom I had connexion, and the condition of women who had been abandoned and who surrounded me. I now see that the chief strength of the temptation was not in my lust, but in the fact that my lust and that of the women who had been deserted and who surrounded me was unsatisfied. I now understand the words of Christ: God at first created man, male and female, so that the two were one, and therefore man may not and should not divide that which God hath joined. I now understand that monogamy is the natural law of humanity which must not be infringed. I now fully understand the saying that whoso divorceth his wife (i.e. the woman with whom he has first come together) for another, causes her to become dissolute and brings fresh evil into the world to his own detriment. I believe this, and that belief alters my whole former valuation of what is good and lofty and what is bad and mean in life. What formerly seemed to me the best—a refined, elegant life, with passionate and poetic love, extolled by all the poets and artists—all this has come to appear to me bad and repulsive. On the contrary, what seems to me good is a laborious, frugal, rough life which moderates the lusts. High and important seems to me, not so much the human institution of marriage affixing the external seal of legality on a certain union of a man and woman, as the union itself of any man and woman, which once it has been accomplished cannot be infringed without infringing the will of God. If I may even now in a moment of forgetfulness yield to adulterous desire, I can at any rate no longer (knowing the temptation which led me into that evil) serve it as I did formerly. I cannot desire and seek for physical idleness and a life of repletion which inflamed in me excessive desire; I cannot seek those amusements which inflame amatory lust—novels, verses, music, theatres, and balls, which formerly seemed to me not merely harmless but very noble amusements. I cannot leave my wife, knowing that leaving her is the first snare for me, for her, and for others; I cannot take part in the idle life of repletion led by others, I cannot take part in or promote those lustful amusements, novels,[1] theatres, operas, balls, &c.—

[1] This book appeared when de Voguë was writing his work

which serve as a snare for me and for others. I cannot
encourage unmarried life for people who are ripe
for marriage; I cannot be a party to the separation
of husbands and wives; I cannot make distinctions
between unions called marriages and those not so
called; I cannot but consider holy and obligatory
only the first marital union which a man has
formed.

Christ has shown me that a third temptation
ruining my welfare is the temptation of the oath. I
cannot but believe this, and therefore cannot now,
as I did formerly, myself take an oath to anyone or
about anything, and I cannot now, as I did formerly, justify myself for taking an oath by saying
that it does no one any harm, that everybody does
it, that it is necessary for the State, or that it will be
worse for me and for others if I refuse this demand.
I now know that it is an evil for me and for others,
and I cannot do it.

But not only do I know this, I now also know the
temptation which led me into that evil, and I cannot serve it. I know that the deception consists in
this, that people promise in advance to obey what
some man or some men order; whereas man must
never obey anyone but God. I now know that the
most terrible evils in the world by their results, are
murders in war, imprisonments, executions, and
tortures, which are performed thanks only to this
temptation whereby responsibility is lifted from

Le roman russe, and not having before him Tolstóy's subsequent
pronouncements on Art, nor of course the stories, novels, and
plays he wrote later, he relied too much on these few one-sided
words, and by his comments misled a whole string of French,
English, and American critics, who, since then—overlooking
what Tolstóy said later in a series of essays deliberately dealing
with the problem—have again and again repeated the silly
parrot-cry that from the time he began to concern himself with
religion Tolstóy 'abandoned art'.—A.M.

those who commit the evil. Remembering many and many evils which made me blame and dislike people, I now see that they were all caused by the oath—the acknowledgement of an obligation to submit oneself to the will of others. I now understand the meaning of the words: Whatever is more than a simple assertion or denial, 'Yes' or 'No', all that is beyond that, every promise given in advance, is evil. Understanding this, I believe that the oath ruins my welfare and that of others, and this belief changes my valuation of what is good and evil, lofty and mean. All that formerly seemed to be good and lofty, the duty of loyalty to the Government confirmed by an oath of allegiance, the extortion of such oaths from others, and all actions contrary to conscience performed under the influence of such oaths—all this now appears to me both bad and mean. And therefore I cannot now any longer depart from Christ's command which forbids the oath. I cannot any longer swear to anyone, or compel others to swear, or take part in making other people either themselves swear or compel others to swear, and I cannot look upon the oath as either valuable or necessary, or even innocuous as many suppose it to be.

Christ has shown me that a fourth temptation depriving me of welfare is that of resisting evil by means of violence applied to other people. I cannot but believe that this is an evil to me and to others and therefore I cannot consciously employ it, and cannot, as I used to, justify this evil on the ground that it is necessary for my defence and for that of others; nor can I now, at the first reminder that I am committing violence, do other than refrain from it and stop it.

But not only do I know this, I now also know the snare which led me into this evil. I now know that

that temptation consists in the delusion that my life can be secured by defending myself and my property from other people.

I now know that a large part of the ills of mankind proceeds from the fact that instead of doing work for one another, men not only do not do so, but they deprive themselves of work and seize by violence the work of others. Remembering now all the evil I have done to myself and to others and all the evil that the others did, I see that a large part of that evil proceeded from the fact that we considered it possible to secure and improve our lives by defending them. I also now understand the words: Man is born not that others may work for him, but that he should work for others; and also the meaning of the words: the labourer is worthy of his subsistence. I now believe that my welfare and that of other people is only possible when each one labours not for himself but for others, and not only ceases to withhold his work from others but gives it to anyone who needs it. This belief has changed my valuation of what is good and evil and mean. All that formerly seemed to me good and lofty—riches, property of all kinds, honours, consciousness of one's own dignity and rights, has all become evil and mean; while all that seemed to me evil and mean—work done for others, poverty, humiliation, renunciation of all property and all rights—has become good and lofty in my eyes. If now I may, in moments of forgetfulness, be tempted to use violence to defend myself and others, or my own or other people's property, I can at any rate no longer calmly and consciously serve this temptation which ruins me and others, and cannot acquire property. I cannot employ any kind of physical force against anyone except a child, and then only in order to save it from immediately impending danger. I cannot take part in any Governmental activity that has for its aim the defence of people and their property by violence; I cannot be a judge or take part in trials, or be an official, or serve in any Government office;[1] nor can I help others to take part in law-courts and Government offices.

Christ showed me that the fifth temptation which deprives me of welfare is the separation we make of our own from other nations. I cannot but believe this, and therefore if in a moment of forgetfulness feelings of enmity towards a man of another nation may arise within me, yet in my calm moments I can no longer fail to acknowledge that feeling to be a false one, and I cannot justify myself, as I used to do, by claiming the superiority of my own people to others, basing this on the errors, cruelties, and barbarities of another nation, nor can I, at the first reminder of this, fail to try to be more friendly to a foreigner than to a compatriot.

But not only do I now know that my separation from other nations is an evil ruining my welfare, but I also know the temptation that led me into that evil, and I can no longer, as I did formerly, consciously and quietly serve it. I know that that temptation lies in the delusion that my welfare is bound up only with that of the people of my own nation, and not with that of all the peoples of the earth. I now know that my union with other people cannot be severed by a line of frontier and by Government decrees about my belonging to this or that nation. I now know that all men everywhere are equals and brothers. Remembering now all the

[1] This is a logical and quite inevitable conclusion from the non-resistant position—that the use of physical force to prevent men doing what they please is immoral. It is therefore very necessary that that position should be examined and carefully tested, as I have tried to do in my *Life of Tolstóy*. —A.M.

evil I have done, suffered, and seen, resulting from the enmity of nations,[1] it is clear to me that the cause of it all lay in the gross fraud called patriotism and love of one's country. Remembering my education I now see that a feeling of hostility to other nations, a feeling of separation from them, was never really natural to me but that all these evil feelings were artificially inoculated into me by an insane education. I now understand the meaning of the words: Do good to your enemies; behave to them as to your own people. You are all children of one Father; so be like your Father, i.e. do not make distinctions between your own people and other peoples; be the same with them all. I now understand that my welfare is only possible if I acknowledge my unity with all the people of the world without exception. I believe this. And that belief has changed my whole valuation of what is good and evil, lofty and mean. What seemed to me good and lofty—love of fatherland, of one's own people, of one's State, and service of it to the detriment of the welfare of other peoples, the military achievements of men, all this now appears to me repulsive and pitiable. What seemed to me bad and shameful—rejection of fatherland, and cosmopolitanism—now appears to me, on the contrary, good and noble. If now, in a moment of forgetfulness, I can co-operate with a Russian rather than with a foreigner and can desire the success of the Russian State or nation, I can no longer in calm moments serve that temptation which ruins me and other people. I cannot acknowledge any States or nations, cannot take part in the quarrels between

[1] Some of Tolstóy's most vivid recollections, as readers of *Tales of Army Life* will know, related to the Crimean War fought against the French and the English and of which he wrote a remarkable account in *Sevastopol*.—A.M.

nations and States either by writings or (even less) by serving any Government. I cannot take part in all those affairs which are based on the diversity of nations, not in custom-houses and the collection of taxes, nor in the preparation of military stores and ammunition, nor in any activity for creating armaments, nor in military service, nor (still less) in war itself against other nations—and I cannot help other people to do so.

I have now understood wherein my welfare lies; I believe in this and therefore cannot do what undoubtedly deprives me of welfare.

But not only do I believe that I ought to live thus; I also believe that if I live so my life will receive for me the only possible, reasonable, and joyful meaning indestructible by death.

I believe my rational life, my light, was only given me in order to shine before men, not by words but by good works, that men may praise the Father (Matt. v. 16). I believe that my life and knowledge of truth is a talent given me to use, and this talent is a fire which is only a fire when it burns. I believe that I am Nineveh in relation to other Jonahs from whom I have learnt and am still learning the truth, but that I too am a Jonah in relation to other Ninevites to whom I must convey the truth. I believe that the sole meaning of my life lies in living by that light which is within me, and in not hiding it under a bushel but holding it high before men that they may see it. And this belief gives me fresh strength to fulfil Christ's teaching, and destroys those hindrances which formerly blocked my path.

The very thing which formerly militated against the truth and practicability of Christ's teaching and drove me away from it—the possibility of privations, sufferings, and death, inflicted by those who do not know his teaching—that very thing now confirms for me the truth of the teaching and attracts me to it.

Christ said, 'When you exalt the son of man you will all be drawn to me', and I felt that I was irresistibly drawn to him. He also said, 'The truth will make you free', and I felt myself completely free.

'If a hostile army or wicked people attack me', thought I formerly, 'and I do not defend myself, they will despoil me, shame me, and torment and kill me and my neighbours', and this seemed to me terrible. But now all that formerly disturbed me seems to me joyful and confirms the truth. I now know that I and the enemy and the so-called criminals and robbers are all men, all just sons of man as myself, who love good and hate evil as I do, and who also live on the eve of death as I do, seeking salvation and with no possibility of finding it except in Christ's teaching. All evil that they do me will be evil for themselves, and therefore they should do me good. If the truth is unknown to them and they do evil considering it good, I know the truth only in order to show it to those who do not know it. But I cannot show it them except by renouncing participation in evil and acknowledging the truth by my actions.

'Enemies will come: Germans, Turks, savages, and if you do not fight they will slaughter you!' That is not true. If there were a society of Christians doing no harm to anyone and giving the whole surplus of their work to others, no enemies—neither Germans, nor Turks, nor savages—would kill and torture such people. They would take for themselves all that those people (for whom no distinction existed between Russians, Germans, Turks, or savages) were in any case giving away. If Christians are living in a non-Christian society which defends itself by war, and the Christians are called on to take part in the war, then an opportunity occurs for those Christians to help those who do not know the truth. Christians only know the truth in order to testify to it before those who know it not. And they can only testify by action. That action is the repudiation of war and the doing of good to people, without distinguishing between so-called enemies and one's own people.

'But if the foreign enemy does not attack the Christian family, then his own wicked neighbours will, and will pillage, torture, and kill him and those dear to him if they do not defend themselves.' This again is not true. If all the members of the family are Christians and therefore devote their lives to serving others, no man will be found so senseless as to deprive of food or to kill those who serve him. Miklúkha-Makláy[1] settled among the most bestial savages, so it is said, and they not only did not kill him, but grew fond of him and submitted to him, merely because he was not afraid of them, demanded nothing of them, and did them good. If a Christian lives with an un-Christian family and relations who defend themselves and their property by violence and the Christian is called on to take part in that defence, this demand is for him a call to the fulfilment of his duty in life. A Christian knows the truth only to show it to others, and most of all to those near him and bound to him by ties of relationship and friendship, and a Christian can show the truth by not falling into the error others have fallen into, by not ranging himself either on the side of the attackers or on the side of the defenders, but by giving all to others and showing by his life that he

---

[1] N. N. Miklúkha-Makláy was a distinguished Russian explorer (1846–88) who investigated the manners and customs of the inhabitants of New Guinea and Micronesia.—A.M.

wants nothing except to fulfil the will of God, and that he fears nothing except to depart from that will.

'But the Government cannot allow members of society to refuse to acknowledge the foundations of the State organization and to evade the performance of the duties of every citizen. The Government demands from Christians oaths, participation in legal proceedings and military service, and for a refusal of these things subjects them to punishment, banishment, imprisonment, or even execution.' And again this demand made by Government will only serve for a Christian as a call to fulfil the business of his life. For a Christian the Government's demand is the demand of people who do not know the truth. And therefore a Christian who knows it cannot but bear witness to it before those who know it not. Violence, imprisonment, or execution, to which a Christian is subjected in consequence of this, affords him the possibility of witnessing not in words but in deeds. Every violence by war, robbery, or execution, is not a result of the irrational forces of nature, but is perpetrated by erring people, deprived of knowledge of the truth. And therefore the greater the evil these people do to a Christian, the further they are from the truth, the more unfortunate are they and the more do they need a knowledge of the truth. But a Christian cannot impart that knowledge to men otherwise than by refraining from the error in which those dwell who do him evil, and by returning good for evil. And that alone is the whole business of a Christian's life, and its whole meaning, which death cannot destroy.

People bound together by a delusion form, as it were, a collective cohesive mass. The cohesion of that mass is the world's evil. All the reasonable activity of humanity is directed towards the destruction of this cohesion.

All revolutions are attempts to break up that mass by violence. It seems to people that if they break up that mass it will cease to be a mass, and therefore they strike at it; but by trying to break it they only forge it closer. The cohesion of the particles is not destroyed until the inner force passes from the mass to the particles and obliges them to separate from it.

The strength of that cohesion of people lies in a falsehood, a fraud. The force freeing each particle of the human cohesive mass is truth. Man can hand on the truth only by deeds of truth.

Only deeds of truth bringing light into man's consciousness, destroy the cohesion of deception and separate men one after another from the mass bound together by the cohesion of deception.

And this work has been going on already for 1800 years. From the time the commandments of Christ were laid before humanity that work began, and it will not end until all has been accomplished, as Christ said (Matt. v. 18).

The Church formed of those who thought to unite people into one by asserting of themselves with oaths that they possessed the truth, has long since died. But the Church formed of men joined in union not by promises nor by anointings but by deeds of truth and goodness, this Church has always lived and will live. This Church, now as heretofore, is formed not of those who say, Lord, Lord! yet work iniquity (Matt. vii. 21, 23), but of those who hear Christ's words and do them. The members of this Church know that it is only necessary for them not to infringe the unity of the son of man, for their life to be a blessing, and that this blessedness is only infringed by the non-fulfilment of the commandments of Christ. And therefore members of the Church cannot but fulfil those commandments and teach others to fulfil them.

Whether there are now few or many such people, that is the Church which nothing can overcome and to which all men will be united.

'Fear not, little flock, for it is your Father's good pleasure to give you the kingdom' (Luke xii. 32).

Moscow,
  22 *January* 1884.

PRINTED IN GREAT BRITAIN
AT THE UNIVERSITY PRESS, OXFORD
BY VIVIAN RIDLER
PRINTER TO THE UNIVERSITY